Creating Knowledge Based Organizations

Jatinder N. D. Gupta
University of Alabama in Huntsville, USA

Sushil K. Sharma
Ball State University, USA

IDEA GROUP PUBLISHING
Hershey • London • Melbourne • Singapore

Acquisitions Editor:	Mehdi Khosrow-Pour
Senior Managing Editor:	Jan Travers
Managing Editor:	Amanda Appicello
Development Editor:	Michele Rossi
Copy Editor:	Bernard J. Kieklak, Jr.
Typesetter:	Jennifer Wetzel
Cover Design:	Michelle Waters
Printed at:	Integrated Book Technology

Published in the United States of America by
    Idea Group Publishing (an imprint of Idea Group Inc.)
    701 E. Chocolate Avenue, Suite 200
    Hershey PA 17033
    Tel: 717-533-8845
    Fax: 717-533-8661
    E-mail: cust@idea-group.com
    Web site: http://www.idea-group.com

and in the United Kingdom by
    Idea Group Publishing (an imprint of Idea Group Inc.)
    3 Henrietta Street
    Covent Garden
    London WC2E 8LU
    Tel: 44 20 7240 0856
    Fax: 44 20 7379 3313
    Web site: http://www.eurospan.co.uk

Library of Congress Cataloging-in-Publication Data

Creating knowledge based organizations / Jatinder Gupta, editor.
    p. cm.
  ISBN 1-59140-162-3 (cloth) -- ISBN 1-59140-163-1 (ebook) -- ISBN 1-59140-219-0 (pbk.)
  1. Intellectual capital. 2. Knowledge management. 3. Organizational learning. 4. Organizational change--Management. I. Gupta, Jatinder N. D.
  HD53.C72 2004
  658.4'038--dc22
             2003014944

British Cataloguing in Publication Data
A Cataloguing in Publication record for this book is available from the British Library.

All work contributed to this book is new, previously-unpublished material. The views expressed in this book are those of the authors, but not necessarily of the publisher.

Creating Knowledge Based Organizations

Table of Contents

Preface vi

Section I: Knowledge Based Organizations

Chapter I.
An Overview of Knowledge Management 1
Jatinder N. D. Gupta, University of Alabama in Huntsville, USA
Sushil K. Sharma, Ball State University, USA
Jeffrey Hsu, Fairleigh Dickinson University, USA

Chapter II.
Information Technology Assessment for Knowledge Management 29
Sushil K. Sharma, Ball State University, USA
Jatinder N. D. Gupta, University of Alabama in Huntsville, USA
Nilmini Wickramasinghe, Cleveland State University, USA

Section II: Evolving Electronic Markets

Chapter III.
Intelligent Enterprise Integration: eMarketplace Model 46
Hamada H. Ghenniwa, University of Western Ontario, Canada
Michael N. Huhns, University of South Carolina, USA

Chapter IV.
Financial Markets in the Internet Age **80**
    Ross A. Lumley, George Washington University, USA

Chapter V.
Ability of the Actor Network Theory (ANT) to Model and Interpret
an Electronic Market **109**
    Murat Baygeldi, London School of Economics, UK
    Steve Smithson, London School of Economics, UK

Chapter VI.
An Explanatory Approach to the ASP Industry Evolution Where IT
Services Move from P-service to E-service **127**
    Dohoon Kim, Kyung Hee University, Korea

Section III: Knowledge Management

Chapter VII.
Management of Knowledge in New Product Development in
Portuguese Higher Education **149**
    Maria Manuel Mendes, Deloitte and Touche - Quality Firm,
        Portugal
    Jorge F. S. Gomes, Instituto Superior de Psicologia Aplicada (ISPA),
        Portugal
    Bernardo Bátiz-Lazo, Open University Business School, UK

Chapter VIII.
An Interactive System for the Collection and Utilization of Both
Tacit and Explicit Knowledge **169**
    Karen Neville, University College Cork, Ireland
    Philip Powell, University of Bath, UK

Chapter IX.
Inducing Enterprise Knowledge Flows **185**
    Mark Nissen, Naval Postgraduate School, USA

Chapter X.
Developing and Maintaining Knowledge Management Systems for
Dynamic, Complex Domains **203**
    Lisa J. Burnell, Texas Christian University, USA
    John W. Priest, University of Texas, USA
    John R. Durrett, Texas Tech University, USA

Chapter XI.
Virtual Communities as Role Models for Organizational Knowledge
Management 230
    Bonnie Rubenstein Montano, Georgetown University, USA

Section IV: Learning Organizations

Chapter XII.
Learning Maturity: Incorporating Technological Influences in
Individual and Organizational Learning Theory 248
    Gary F. Templeton, Mississippi State University, USA

Chapter XIII.
An Investigation to an Enabling Role of Knowledge Management
Between Learning Organization and Organizational Learning 278
    Juin-Cherng Lu, Ming Chuan University, Taiwan
    Chia-Wen Tsai, Ming Chuan University, Taiwan

Section V: Future Organizations

Chapter XIV.
21ˢᵗ Century Organizations and the Basis for Achieving Optimal
Cross-Functional Integration in New Product Development 299
    J. Daniel Sherman, University of Alabama in Huntsville, USA

Chapter XV.
Fractal Approach to Managing Intelligent Enterprises 312
    Kwangyeol Ryu, Pohang University of Science and Technology,
        Korea
    Mooyoung Jung, Pohang University of Science and Technology,
        Korea

About the Authors 349

Index 357

Preface

In the 21st century, successful organizations are competitive, fast-paced, first-to-market, and global in nature. Creating strategic advantage requires a new type of organization that has the capability to create knowledge to maximize organizational competitiveness and strategic success. Knowledge is viewed as a resource that is critical to an organization's survival and success in the global market. Therefore, organizations need mechanisms to create and manage knowledge as an asset. However, the bulk of organizations have still not approached knowledge management (KM) activity formally or deliberately. The cause of this inattention could be that most organizations are struggling to comprehend the KM concept. KM is still defining itself because the body of theoretical literature and research in this area is small, but growing. According to IDC, the worldwide spending on knowledge management services will grow from US$776 million in 1998 to more than $12.7 billion in 2005. As the industry moves into the so-called "second-generation" phase, managers are being challenged to have more of an in-depth understanding of the issues and the need to demonstrate business performance and learning gains from investing in knowledge-based projects and initiatives.

The New Wealth of Organizations is total quality management, re-engineering, and intellectual capital. The companies that will succeed in the 21st century are those that master the knowledge agenda. While most business leaders appreciate the strategic value of knowledge and the need to manage their knowledge assets, many of them seem unable to derive real benefits from their efforts.

In recent years, an increasing amount of global business school research and literature has focused on concepts such as the "knowledge based economy," "organizational learning," "knowledge workers," "intellectual capital," "virtual teams," and the like. Yet, much of the organizational understanding of these concepts is not based on empirical research; rather, the order of the day does seem to be anecdotal evidence of seemingly successful stories, hearsay, and theory unrelated to actual practice and implementation issues, challenges, successes and failures. Creating knowledge-based organizations will not be an easy exercise because organizations have to overcome tremendous hurdles in bringing disparate enterprise data sources into a cohesive data warehouse or knowledge management system.

The purpose of this book is to bring together some high quality concepts that are closely related to "organizational learning," "knowledge workers," "intellectual capital," and "virtual teams." It includes the methodologies, systems, and approaches needed to create and manage knowledge-based organizations of the 21st century.

The presentations in the book are divided into five sections. The first section, *Knowledge Based Organizations*, presents the evolution and review of knowledge management and information technology available to create and manage knowledge in organizations. This section consists of two chapters.

In Chapter 1, Jatinder Gupta, Sushil Sharma and Jeffrey Hsu take a broad view of the topic of knowledge management and provide a comprehensive overview of the concepts and future challenges related to knowledge management. The authors argue that the categorization and organization of knowledge will become a core competency of every organization and will necessitate strategic thinking about what knowledge is important. Development of a knowledge vocabulary, search tools and navigation aids, and knowledge editors that add context and transform information into knowledge will be needed to be successful in creating and managing knowledge-based organizations.

Chapter 2 describes a technology assessment model for knowledge management. In this chapter, Sushil Sharma, Jatinder Gupta and Nilmini Wickramasinghe highlight the importance of addressing both the subjective and objective perspectives of knowledge management and describe the type of computer and communication systems needed to implement sound knowledge management approaches in organizations.

The second section of the book is titled *Evolving Electronic Markets*. As the title indicates, this section presents the concepts, models, and tools related to the electronic markets. The four chapters in this section cover such topics as: the models for e-marketplace, financial markets in the Internet age, the modeling and interpretations of electronic markets and the evolution of the Application Service Provider (ASP) industry that provides essential infrastructure for the Internet-based e-business transactions.

In Chapter 3, Hamada Ghenniwa and Michael Huhns describe a business-centric and knowledge-oriented architecture for *eMarketplaces* that integrates the interests of an autonomous enterprise into a single open-market environment. The proposed *eMarketplace* architecture exists as a collection of economically motivated software agents. It enables and supports common economic services, such as brokering, pricing, and negotiation, and the cross-enterprise integration and cooperation in an electronic supply-chain.

In Chapter 4, Ross Lumley provides a review of the effect of new technologies on the financial markets. He shows that, time and again, technological advances have impacted the very workflow of the financial market processes including the available financial instruments. An overview of multi-agent systems is provided followed by several examples of multi-agent systems supporting investors in financial markets.

In Chapter 5, Murat Baygeldi and Steve Smithson use the Actor Network Theory (ANT) to describe the actors, intermediaries, framing and power that are the most important components of an electronic market. They highlight the uses and limitations of ANT to define various components involved within an electronic market, especially in modeling computer-trading systems.

In the last chapter of the second section, Dohoon Kim discusses the evolution of the Application Service Provider (ASP) industry that provides essential infrastructure for the Internet-based e-business transactions. Thus, in Chapter 6, the emerging ASP business models are classified and analyzed in order to assess their positions in the competitive landscape based on the economies of scale. This chapter also identifies the prerequisites for the ASP business models to develop themselves into XSPs (eXtended Service Providers). It also develops a scenario for that evolutionary path.

The third section of the book, *Knowledge Management*, presents the state-of-the art developments in knowledge management that are useful to enhance the efficiency and effectiveness of the intelligent enterprises for the 21st century.

In Chapter 7, Maria Manuel Mendes, Jorge Gomes and Bernardo Bátiz-Lazo describe the use of the knowledge process as a means to examine issues relating to knowledge identification, creation, storage, dissemination, and application in new product development. Results from their case study suggest that while the knowledge process may be valuable in assessing the structural elements of knowledge management, it may fail to provide a more comprehensive explanation of the dynamics and complexities involved. The authors suggest that more elaborate models may be needed to explain how knowledge is created, shared and used in knowledge-intensive processes.

Chapter 8 by Karen Neville and Philip Powell outlines the development of a "knowledge base support system" for a university that allows every end user the opportunity to interactively extract from and add to the system. The proposed system can test a student's problem-solving skills with "real world" simulations and cases providing feedback to both lecturers and students.

The importance and development of a model to help induce enterprise knowledge flows are discussed in Chapter 9 by Mark Nissen. Because of the time-critical nature of most knowledge work in modern enterprises, this chapter focuses in particular on knowledge dynamics to help the enterprise become more knowledge-based. Using a global manufacturing firm as an example to illustrate how the knowledge-flow model provides practical guidance, Mark Nissen identifies knowledge elements that are critical to effective performance in an unpredictable and dynamic business environment. The chapter also illustrates how the multi-dimensional model can be augmented to depict the relative flow times associated with various knowledge elements to provide a roadmap for requisite knowledge flows for the knowledge-based organization.

In Chapter 10, Lisa Burnell, John Priest and John Durrett describe appropriate tools, methods, architectural issues and development processes for knowledge management systems (KMS), including the application of organizational theory, knowledge-representation methods, and agent architectures. Details for systems development of KMS are provided and illustrated with a case study from the domain of university advising.

In Chapter 11, Bonnie Rubenstein Montano focuses on those organizations that have not been as successful at knowledge management as they originally planned. She argues that organizations can look to virtual communities as role models for successful knowledge management because many of the features that have been identified in the literature as important for successful knowledge management are present in virtual communities.

The impact of technology and knowledge management in creating and sustaining *Learning Organizations* is the topic of presentations in the next section of the book. The two chapters in this section explore the issues of the development of a theory of learning and intelligence in organizations and explore the relationship between a learning organization and organizational learning.

Chapter 12 by Gary Templeton suggests that the learning theory has not adequately addressed the technology variable in its framework, models, or propositions. The body of theory derived here centers around "learning maturity," the capacity of an actor to effectively exhibit intelligent behavior in a wide range of situated actions. The proposed theory is significant because it uniquely includes technology as a meaningful element in learning and intelligence.

The relationship and interaction between the learning organization and organizational learning is discussed in Chapter 13 by Juin-Cherng Lu and Chia-Wen Tsai. The authors argue that the dynamic process between the learning organization and organizational learning is an important issue in knowledge management and practice. Therefore, the authors explore the relationship and interaction between the learning organization and organizational learning in terms of knowledge management processes in business.

The fifth and final section of the book, termed *Future Organizations*, takes a look at the use of knowledge management in defining the coming of the future organizations. It consists of two chapters.

In Chapter 14, J. Daniel Sherman develops the theoretical basis for achieving optimal levels of cross-functional integration in new product development.

He discusses the structural modes of integration and presents a theoretical framework based on degree of integration required, progressive combined information processing capacity, and cost.

In the final chapter of the book, Kwangyeol Ryu and Mooyoung Jung introduce a fractal-based approach to managing intelligent enterprises. Faced with intense competition in the growing global market, fundamental changes are mandatory in business models, management approaches, and technology resources. In this chapter, therefore, several strategic issues for managing intelligent enterprises are discussed in a comprehensive manner, including: (1) fractal models of an intelligent enterprise with new hierarchies and structures for future organizations, (2) strategic supply chain models of e-biz companies based on fractal architectures, and (3) fractal manufacturing system (FrMS) as a type of a future manufacturing system. The authors hope that understanding the proposed methodologies and approaches based on the fractal concept will facilitate the realization of fractal-based systems and give the readers an insight into the requirements of future organizations.

We believe that the book will be a comprehensive compilation of the thoughts and vision required to create knowledge-based organizations. There is thorough discussion of a variety of information technologies required for knowledge creation and management. The presentations illustrate the concepts with a variety of public, private, societal, and organizational applications. They offer practical guidelines for designing, developing, and implementing knowledge creating and management systems. Thus, the book should benefit undergraduate and graduate students taking knowledge management and related courses and practitioners seeking to better support and improve their decision-making. Hopefully, the book will also stimulate new research about knowledge-creating organizations by academicians and practitioners.

Acknowledgements

This book would not have been possible without the cooperation and assistance of many people: the authors, reviewers, our colleagues, and the staff at Idea Group Publishing. We would like to thank Mehdi Khosrow-Pour for inviting us to produce this book, Jan Travers for managing this project, and our development editor, Michele Rossi, for answering our questions and keeping us on schedule.

We are appreciative of the contributions of many reviewers of the chapters without whose help we could not have maintained the quality of the book. We also acknowledge our respective universities for affording us the time to work on this project and our colleagues and students for many stimulating discussions. Finally, we wish to acknowledge our families for providing time and support for this project.

Jatinder N. D. Gupta, University of Alabama in Huntsville, USA
Sushil K. Sharma, Ball State University, USA

SECTION I:

KNOWLEDGE BASED ORGANIZATIONS

Chapter I

An Overview of Knowledge Management

Jatinder N. D. Gupta
University of Alabama in Huntsville, USA

Sushil K. Sharma
Ball State University, USA

Jeffrey Hsu
Fairleigh Dickinson University, USA

ABSTRACT

One of the key factors that distinguishes the intelligent business enterprise of the 21st century is the emphasis on knowledge and information. Unlike businesses of the past, the fast, high-tech, and global emphasis of businesses today requires the ability to capture, manage, and utilize knowledge and information in order to improve efficiency, better serve customers, manage the competition, and keep pace with never-ending changes. Knowledge management is an important means by which organizations can better manage information and, more importantly, knowledge. Unlike other techniques, knowledge management is not always easy to define because it encompasses a range of concepts, management tasks, technologies, and practices, all of which come under the umbrella of the management of knowledge. This chapter takes a broad view of the topic of knowledge management and aims to provide a comprehensive overview of knowledge management — the technologies, processes, and concepts involved, and the challenges and future of this important area.

INTRODUCTION

Rapid changes in both personal computer technology and electronic communications during the past decade have given us the ability to create, gather, manipulate, store, and transmit much more data and information than ever before. It is now a fact that large amounts of information are transmitted via the Internet and other means on a daily basis (Chase, 1998; Sistla & Todd, 1998). In addition, the enhanced speed and capacity of communication has enabled the existence of a global market for many industries and business sectors (Chase, 1998). Moreover, the pressures of competition within the 24-hour global marketplace have greatly increased demands for better quality, less costly production, more accountability to both customers and shareholders, and improved information about materials, processes, customers and competitors (Chase, 1998; Drucker, 1993). This highly competitive, global environment has fostered the growth of management trends like total quality management, customer satisfaction, benchmarking, re-engineering, restructuring, downsizing and outsourcing, strategic planning, organizational learning and, of course, knowledge management (Skyrme, 2001). Many emerging models of knowledge exchanges represent harbingers of extra-organizational collaborations that will be needed for the execution of an organization's knowledge work. In the 21st century, successful organizations have to be competitive, fast paced, first-to-market, and global in nature. Creating strategic advantage requires a new type of organization that has the capability to create knowledge to maximize organizational competitiveness and strategic success. Knowledge, like any other resource, is viewed as a resource that is critical to an organization's survival and success in the global market. Organizations should have mechanisms to create knowledge and manage knowledge as an asset. However, the bulk of organizations still have not approached knowledge management (KM) activity formally or deliberately. The cause of this inattention could be that most organizations are struggling to comprehend the KM concept. KM is still defining itself because the body of theoretical literature and research in this area is small, but growing (Skyrme, 2001). It is estimated that worldwide spending on knowledge management services will grow from US$776 million in 1998 to more than US$8 billion by 2003 and, as the industry moves into the so-called "second generation" phase, managers are being challenged to have in-depth understanding of the issues and need to demonstrate business performance and learning gains from investing in knowledge-based projects and initiatives. The New Wealth of Organizations is total quality management, re-engineering, and intellectual capital, and the companies that will succeed in the 21st century are those that master the knowledge agenda (Skyrme, 1997, 2000). While most business leaders appreciate the strategic value of knowledge and the need to manage their knowledge assets, many of them seem unable to derive real benefits from their efforts. Creating knowledge-based organizations will not be an easy exercise as organizations have to overcome tremendous hurdles in bringing disparate enterprise data sources into a cohesive data warehouse or knowledge management system (Allee, 1997). This chapter describes the overview of knowledge management concepts that may be required for creating knowledge-based organizations. The chapter has four sections. The first section describes the overview of knowledge management. The second section details the evolution of knowledge management. The next few sections describe knowledge representation, creation and generation and sharing. The next two sections describe the concepts of the learning organization and organizational memory that are useful for creating knowledge-based organizations.

OVERVIEW OF KNOWLEDGE MANAGEMENT

The importance of knowledge to the complex, competitive and global business environments which exist in the 21st century cannot be overemphasized, and those businesses that know how to effectively acquire, capture, share, and manage this information will be the leaders in their respective industries. We have moved into a period where competitive advantage is gained not just merely through access to information but, also — more importantly — from new knowledge creation (Drucker, 1994; Davenport & Prusak, 1997). Knowledge management is an emerging, interdisciplinary business model dealing with all aspects of knowledge within the context of the firm, including knowledge creation, codification, sharing, and using these activities to promote learning and innovation. It encompasses both technological tools and organizational routines of which there are a number of components. These include generating new knowledge, acquiring valuable knowledge from outside sources, using this knowledge in decision making, embedding knowledge in processes, products, and/or services, coding information into documents, databases, and software, facilitating knowledge growth, transferring knowledge to other parts of the organization, and measuring the value of knowledge assets and/or the impact of knowledge management. Knowledge management is becoming very important for many reasons. To serve customers well and to remain in business, companies must reduce their cycle times, operate with minimum fixed assets and overhead (people, inventory and facilities), shorten product development time, improve customer service, empower employees, innovate and deliver high quality products, enhance flexibility and adaption, capture information, create and share knowledge. None of these actions are possible without a continual focus on the creation, updating, availability, quality and use of knowledge by all employees and teams at work and in the marketplace (Leonard, 1998). Seven knowledge layers are possible in organizations as described in Table 1 (Skyrme, 1999, 2001).

Table 1: Seven Knowledge Levels

Level	Key Activities
Customer Knowledge	Developing deep, knowledge-sharing relationships. Understanding the needs of your customers' customers. Articulating unmet needs. Identifying new opportunities.
Stakeholder Relationships	Improving knowledge flows between suppliers, employees, shareholders, community, etc., using this knowledge to inform key strategies.
Business Environment Insights	Systematic environmental scanning including political, economic, technology, social and environmental trends. Competitor analysis. Market intelligence systems.
Organizational Memory	Knowledge sharing. Best practice databases. Directories of expertise. Online documents, procedures and discussion forums. Intranets.
Knowledge in Processes	Embedding knowledge into business processes and management. Decision-making.
Knowledge in Products and Services	Knowledge embedded in products. Surround products with knowledge, e.g., in user guides, and enhanced knowledge-intensive services.
Knowledge in People	Knowledge-sharing fairs. Innovation workshops. Expert and learning networks. Communities of knowledge practice.

There are many definitions of knowledge management. At a generic level, it can be defined as the collection of processes that govern the creation, dissemination, and utilization of knowledge. It involves creation of supportive organizational structures, facilitation of organizational members, putting IT instruments with emphasis on teamwork and diffusion of knowledge (e.g., groupware) into place. Knowledge is the full utilization of information and data coupled with the potential of people's skills, competencies, ideas, intuitions, commitments and motivations. A holistic view considers knowledge to be present in ideas, judgments, talents, root causes, relationships, perspectives and concepts. Knowledge is stored in the individual brain or encoded in organizational processes, documents, products, services, facilities and systems. Knowledge is action, focused innovation, pooled expertise, special relationships and alliances. Knowledge is value-added behavior and activities (Pfeffer & Sutton, 2000). Knowledge encompasses both tacit knowledge (in people's heads) and explicit knowledge (codified and expressed as information in databases, documents, etc.). Knowledge is not static; instead, it changes and evolves during the life of an organization (Skyrme, 2000, 2001). What is more, it is possible to change the form of knowledge, i.e., turn existing tacit knowledge into new explicit knowledge and existing explicit knowledge into new tacit knowledge or to turn existing explicit knowledge into new explicit knowledge and existing tacit knowledge into new tacit knowledge. These transformations are depicted in Table 2.

Table 2: Knowledge Transformations

From/To	Tacit Knowledge	Explicit Knowledge
Tacit Knowledge	Socialization (Sympathized Knowledge) Where individuals acquire new knowledge directly from others.	Externalization (Conceptual Knowledge) The articulation of knowledge into tangible form through dialogue.
Explicit Knowledge	Internalization (Operational Knowledge) Such as learning by doing, where individuals internalize knowledge from documents into their own body of experience.	Combination (Systematic Knowledge) Combining different forms of explicit knowledge, such as that in documents or on databases.

The KM architecture and KM process model that could be used for knowledge capture, creation, distribution and sharing is shown in Figures 1 and 2.

Knowledge management draws from a wide range of disciplines and technologies. These include cognitive science, artificial intelligence and expert systems, groupware and collaborative systems, and various other areas and technologies as described in Table 3.

So in summary, we can describe knowledge management as an audit of "intellectual assets." Knowledge management complements and enhances other organizational initiatives such as total quality management (TQM), business process re-engineering (BPR) and organizational learning, providing a new and urgent focus to sustain competitive position. A wide variety of practices and processes are used in knowledge management. Some of the more common ones are shown in Table 4.

Over time, considerable knowledge is also transformed to other manifestations such as books, technology, practices, and traditions within organizations. Knowledge management for the organization consists of activities focused on the organization gaining knowledge from its own experience and from the experience of others and on the judicious application of that knowledge to fulfill the mission of the organization. These activities are executed by marrying technology, organizational structures, and cognitive-based strategies to raise the yield of existing knowledge and to produce new knowledge. Critical in this endeavor is the enhancement of the cognitive system (organization, human, computer, or joint human-computer system) in acquiring, storing and utilizing knowledge for learning, problem solving, and decision-making.

Figure 1: KM Architecture

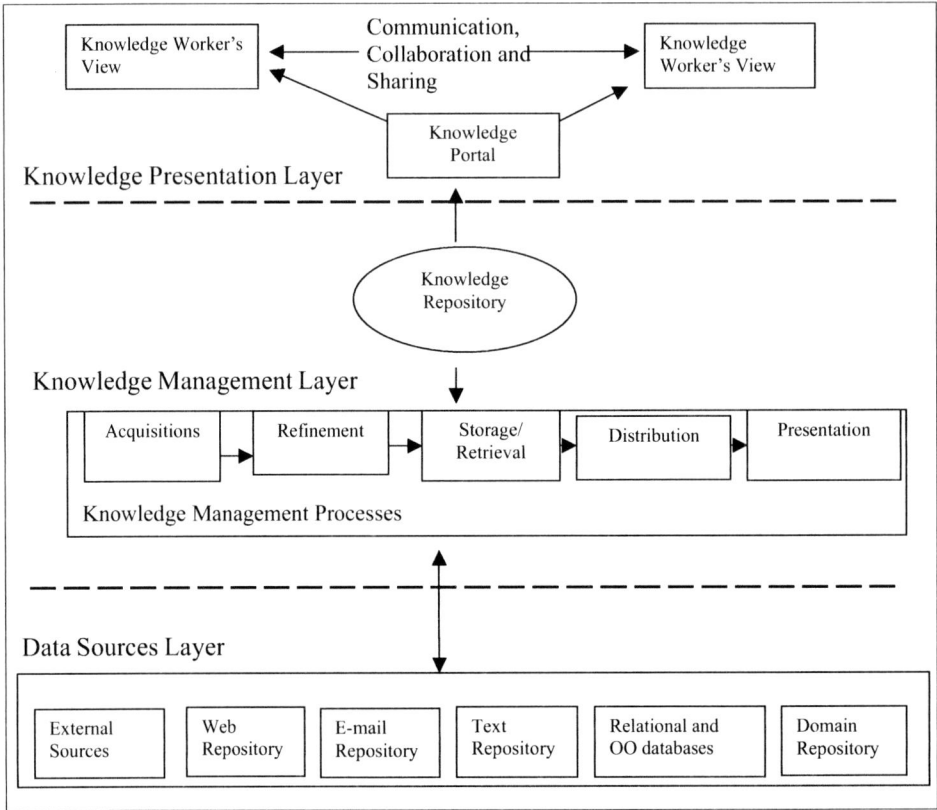

Figure 2: Knowledge Management Process Model

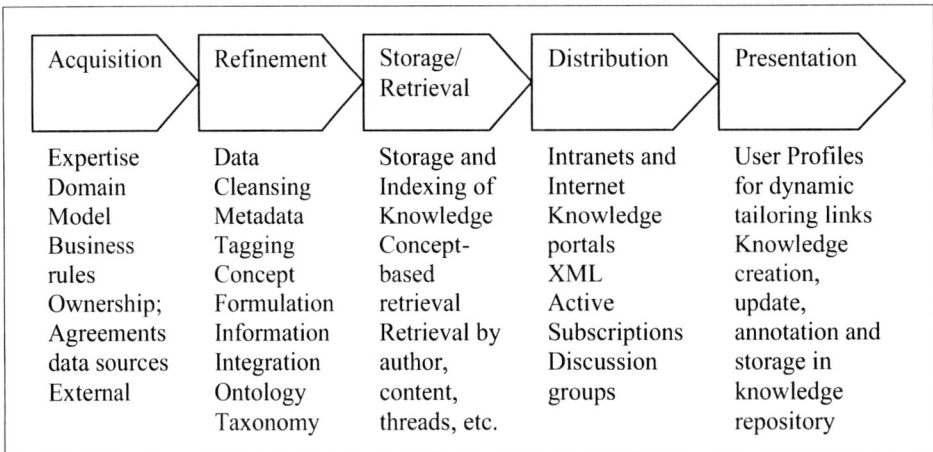

Table 3: Wide Range of Disciplines and Technologies for Knowledge Management

Disciplines and Technologies	Description
Cognitive science	Since knowledge management is related to how we learn and know, the study of cognitive science certainly has a usefulness towards gathering and transferring knowledge.
Expert systems, artificial intelligence and knowledge-based management systems (KBMS)	AI and related technologies are directly applicable to knowledge management. Expert systems, for example, have as its goal the capture of knowledge within a computerized knowledge base.
Computer-supported collaborative work (groupware)	*Knowledge management* is often closely linked with and, in some cases, is almost synonymous with *groupware* and Lotus Notes. Sharing and collaboration are clearly vital to organizational knowledge management -- with or without supporting technology.
Library and information science	The body of research and practice that encompasses libraries, information science, and knowledge organization can be applied to management of knowledge. These include tools for thesaurus construction and controlled vocabularies.
Document management and technical writing	Originally concerned primarily with managing images, document management has moved on to making content more accessible and usable. Early recognition of the need to associate "meta-information" with a document object suggests a connection between document management and knowledge management. Technical writing (often known as *technical communication*) forms a body of theory and practice that is directly relevant to effective representation and transfer of knowledge.
Decision support systems	Decision Support Systems (DSS) have brought together insights from the fields of cognitive sciences, management sciences, computer sciences, and operations research, in key cognitive tasks, including organizational decision-making. The emphasis here is on quantitative analysis, and on tools for managers.
Semantic networks	Semantic networks are formed from ideas and the relationships among them -- sort of "hypertext without the content," but with far more systematic structure according to meaning. Often used for such tasks as textual analysis, semantic nets are now in use in mainstream professional applications, including medicine, to represent domain knowledge in an explicit way that can be shared.
Relational and object databases	Currently, relational databases are used primarily as tools for managing "structured" data, and object-oriented databases for "unstructured" content. Of particular interest are the models on which they are founded, which relate to representing and managing knowledge resources.
Simulation	Knowledge management expert Karl-Erik Sveiby suggests "simulation" as a component technology of knowledge management, referring to "computer simulations, manual simulations as well as role plays and micro arenas for testing out skills."
Organizational science	The science of managing organizations increasingly deals with the need to manage knowledge -- often explicitly. Other technologies include: object-oriented information modeling; electronic publishing technology, hypertext, and the World Wide Web; help-desk technology; full-text search and retrieval; and performance support systems (Barclay & Murray, 1997).

Table 4: KM Practices and Processes

Creating and Discovering	Creativity Techniques Data Mining Text Mining Environmental Scanning Knowledge Elicitation Business Simulation Content Analysis
Sharing and Learning	Communities of Practice Learning Networks Sharing Best Practice After Action Reviews Structured Dialogue Share Fairs Cross Functional Teams Decision Diaries
Organizing and Managing	Knowledge Centers Expertise Profiling Knowledge Mapping Information Audits/Inventory Measuring Intellectual Capital

EVOLUTION OF KNOWLEDGE MANAGEMENT

The history and evolution of knowledge management has not always been that clear or straightforward given that the field has evolved from so many different disciplines and domains. A number of management theorists have contributed to the evolution of knowledge management, among them Peter Drucker, Paul Strassmann and Peter Senge in the United States. Drucker and Strassmann have stressed the growing importance of information and explicit knowledge as organizational resources, and Senge has focused on the "learning organization," a cultural dimension of managing knowledge. Chris Argyris, Christoper Bartlett and Dorothy Leonard-Barton of Harvard Business School have examined various facets of managing knowledge. In fact, Leonard-Barton's well-known case study of Chaparral Steel, a company which has had an effective knowledge management strategy in place since the mid-1970s, inspired the research documented in her book *Wellsprings of Knowledge — Building and Sustaining Sources of Innovation* (Harvard Business School Press, 1995). Everett Rogers' work at Stanford in the diffusion of innovation and Thomas Allen's research at MIT in information and technology transfer, both of which date from the late-1970s, have also contributed to our understanding of how knowledge is produced, used, and diffused within organizations. By the mid-1980s, the importance of knowledge as a competitive asset was apparent even though classical economic theory ignores knowledge as an asset, and most organizations still lack strategies and methods for managing it. Recognition of the growing importance of organizational knowledge was accompanied by a need to deal with exponential increases in the amount of available knowledge and the increased complexity of products and processes. The computer technology that contributed so heavily to this "information overload" started to become part of the solution in a variety of domains. Doug Engelbart's Augment (for "augmenting human intelligence"), which was introduced in 1978, was an early hypertext/groupware application capable of interfacing with other applications and systems. Rob Acksyn's and Don McCracken's knowledge management system (KMS), an open distributed hypermedia tool, is another notable example.

The 1980s also saw the development of systems for managing knowledge that relied on work done in artificial intelligence and expert systems, giving us such concepts as "knowledge acquisition," "knowledge engineering," "knowledge-base systems," and computer-based ontologies. The phrase "knowledge management" finally came into being in the business community during this decade. To provide a technological base for managing knowledge, a consortium of U.S. companies started the Initiative for Managing Knowledge Assets in 1989. Knowledge management-related articles began appearing in journals like *Sloan Management Review*, *Organizational Science*, *Harvard Business Review*, and others, and the first books on organizational learning and knowledge management were published (for example, Senge's *The Fifth Discipline* and Sakaiya's *The Knowledge Value Revolution*). By 1990, a number of management consulting firms had begun in-house knowledge management programs, and several well-known U.S., European, and Japanese firms had instituted focused knowledge management programs. Knowledge management was introduced in the popular press in 1991 when Tom Stewart published "Brainpower" in *Fortune* magazine. Perhaps the most widely read work to date is Ikujiro Nonaka's and Hirotaka Takeuchi's *The Knowledge-Creating Company: How Japanese Companies Create the Dynamics of Innovation* (1995). By the mid-1990s, knowledge management initiatives were flourishing, thanks in part to the Internet. The International Knowledge Management Network (IKMN) that began in Europe in 1989 went online in 1994 and was soon joined by the U.S.-based Knowledge Management Forum and other KM-related groups and publications. The number of knowledge management-based conferences and seminars is growing as organizations focus on managing and leveraging explicit and tacit knowledge resources to achieve competitive advantage. In 1994 the IKMN published the results of a knowledge management survey conducted among European firms, and the European Community began offering funding for KM-related projects through the ESPRIT program in 1995. Knowledge management, which appears to offer a highly desirable alternative to less successful TQM and business process re-engineering initiatives, has become big business for such major international consulting firms as Ernst & Young, Arthur Andersen, and Booz-Allen & Hamilton. In addition, a number of professional organizations interested in such related areas as benchmarking, best practices, risk management, and change management are exploring the relationship of knowledge management to their areas of special expertise (Lipnack & Stamps, 2000).

KNOWLEDGE REPRESENTATION

Knowledge representation — explicit specification of "knowledge objects" and relationships among those objects — takes many forms, with variations in emphasis and major variations in formalisms. Knowledge representation allows computers to reconfigure and reuse information that they store in ways not narrowly pre-specified in advance. *Concept mapping*, *semantic networks*, *hypertext*, *information modeling*, and *conceptual indexing* all exemplify knowledge representation, in somewhat different ways. **Concept mapping** seems to be rooted primarily in educational techniques for improving understanding, retention, and as an aid to writing. A concept map is a picture of the ideas or topics in the information and the ways these ideas or topics are related to each other. It is a visual summary that shows the structure of the material the writer will describe. **Semantic networks** are often closely associated with detailed analysis of texts and networks of ideas. One of the important ways they are distinguished from hypertext systems is their support of semantic typing of links, for example, the relationship between "murder" and "death" might be described as "is a cause of." The inverse relationship might be expressed as "is caused by." Semantic networks are a technique for representing knowledge. As with other networks, they consist of nodes with links between them. The nodes in a semantic network represent concepts. A concept is an abstract class, or set, whose members are things that are grouped together because they share common features or properties. The "things" are called instances of the concept. Links in the network represent relations between concepts. Links are labeled to indicate which relation they represent. Links are paired to represent a relation and its inverse relation. For example, the concept Femur is related to the concept Upper Leg with the relation has-location. The inverse of has-location is the relation location-of, which relates Upper Leg to Femur. Hypertext (an expanded semantic network), known to most people these days by its implementation in the World Wide Web, is sometimes described as a semantic network with content at the nodes. But the content itself, the traditional document model, seems to be the driving organizational force, not the network of links. In most hypertext documents, the links are **not** semantically typed, although they are typed at times according to the medium of the object displayed by traversing the link. **Information modeling** is concerned with precise specification of the meaning in a text and in making relationships of meaning explicit, often with the objective of rapid and accurate development of new software applications for business requirements. Some of the essence of information modeling is expressed in the following definition: "The process of eliciting requirements from domain experts, formulating a complete and precise specification understandable to both domain experts and developers, and refining it using existing (or possible) implementation mechanisms." **Conceptual indexing** is rarely discussed in the same breath as hypertext, conceptual maps, and semantic networks, perhaps because indexers themselves sometimes relish the aura of "black art" surrounding indexing, but the connection is fundamental. Conceptual indexes traditionally map key ideas and objects in a single work. An index is a structured sequence, resulting from a thorough and complete analysis of text, of synthesized access points to all the information contained in the text. The structured arrangement of the index enables users to locate information efficiently. The organization of topics into parent-child, synonym, and "see also" relationships is a critical part of an effective professional index. Good indexes are not flat lists of names and ideas.

Knowledge Sharing/Information Sharing

The terms *knowledge sharing* and *information sharing* are often used in conjunction with discussions of *ontologies* and *knowledge representation*. In the context of the following quote, the primary concern of information sharing is precision of expression and access in order to meet the objective of rapid product development. Information sharing and decision coordination are central problems for large-scale product development. This chapter proposes a framework for supporting a knowledge medium (Stefik, 1986): "a computational environment in which explicitly represented knowledge serves as a communication medium among people and their programs." The framework is designed to support information sharing and coordinated communication among members of a product development organization, particularly for the tasks of design knowledge capture, dynamic notification of design changes, and active management of design dependencies. The proposed technology consists of a shared knowledge representation (language and vocabulary), protocols for foreign data encapsulation and posting to the shared environment, and mechanisms for content-directed routing of posted information to interested parties via subscription and notification services. A range of possible applications can be explored in this framework, depending on the degree of commitment to a shared representation by participating tools. A number of research issues fundamental to building such a knowledge medium are introduced in the chapter.

Metadata/Meta-information/[Document] Profile Information/ [Subject] Classification/Key Words/"Attributes"

Metadata is simply information added to a document (or a smaller unit of information) that makes it easier to access and reuse that content. It's also referred to as simply "data about data." You'll find metadata in many different forms including key words in a software help system, the document profile information attached to documents in a document management system, and the classification information in a library card catalog. There are, of course, distinctions in how these various disciplines and technologies implement metadata, in substance as well as in formalisms. But the value of metadata for critical information is widely accepted as a basic element of knowledge management implementations.

Ontologies [Computer-based]

Computer-based *ontologies*, formal, structured representations of a domain of knowledge, are commonly associated with artificial intelligence technology where they were originally designed to serve as the raw material for computer reasoning and computer-based agents.

ACQUIRING AND GENERATING KNOWLEDGE

Critical to managing knowledge is the generation and dissemination of information, followed by shared interpretation of the processed information into "knowledge." In order for an organization to be able to manage knowledge, it must have knowledge to work with in the first place. There are a number of ways in which to acquire and generate new knowledge for your firm. One of the most obvious ways to acquire new knowledge is either to acquire an organization with the knowledge which you desire, or alternately, to hire people who possess the same knowledge. While, in the case of acquiring a firm, it is not guaranteed that the knowledge (or people who possess it) will necessarily stay with the company, it is possible to retain a significant portion of it. It should also be noted that political and cultural aspects may come into play, affecting how well a new acquisition can be integrated into the parent firm (Nonaka & Takeuchi, 1995).

Another possibility is to "rent" knowledge through the hiring of outside consultants or to help generate new knowledge by supporting (financially or otherwise) the research being conducted at universities and research centers, with the promise of future benefits in terms of developing the technologies for commercial use (Davenport & Prusak, 2000).

Aside from the method of obtaining or generating knowledge externally, it is also possible to do it "in-house." One way is to set up a research center within the auspices of a company with the specific purpose to generate new ideas, technologies and, eventually, commercial products. Notable examples of these include the Xerox PARC (Palo Alto Research Center), which among other things was where the concept of the GUI (graphical user interface), including menus, the mouse, and the use of icons originated. These were later incorporated into various models of the Apple Computer. Firms which have developed their own research centers include IBM, Motorola, and Sharp Electronics (Davenport & Prusak, 2000).

There are a number of other methods by which knowledge can be acquired or brought into an organization. These include data mining, text mining, and knowledge elicitation. Data mining is not a single technique or technology but a group of related methods and methodologies which are directed towards the finding and automatic extraction of patterns, associations, changes, anomalies and significant structures from data (Grossman, 1998). Data mining is emerging as a key technology which enables businesses to select, filter, screen, and correlate data automatically. Data mining evokes the image of patterns and meaning in data, hence the term which suggests the mining of "nuggets" of knowledge and insight from a group of data. The findings from these can then be applied to a variety of applications and purposes including those in marketing, risk analysis and management, fraud detection and management, and customer relationship management (CRM). With the considerable amount of information which is being generated and made available, the effective use of data-mining methods and techniques can help to uncover various trends, patterns, inferences, and other relations from the data which can then be analyzed and further refined. These can then be studied to bring out meaningful information which can be used to come to important conclusions, improve marketing and CRM efforts, and predict future behavior and trends (Han & Kamber, 2001). The possibilities for data mining from textual information are largely untapped, making it a fertile area of future research. Text expresses a vast, rich range of information, but in its original, raw form is difficult to analyze or mine automatically. As such, text data mining (TDM) has relatively fewer research projects and commercial products compared with other data mining areas. As expected, text data mining is a natural extension of traditional data mining (DM) as well as information archeology (Brachman et al., 1993). While most standard data mining applications tend to be automated discovery of trends and patterns across large databases and datasets, in the case of text mining, the goal is to look for patterns and trends like nuggets of data in large amounts of text (Hearst, 1999). Knowledge elicitation is the process of extracting information from an expert source, such as interviewing an expert in a given subject area, so that it can then be coded and otherwise stored in a form which can be accessed by others. Closely related to the term knowledge acquisition in the expert systems field, knowledge elicitation is a difficult process and is often referred to as a "bottleneck" in the acquisition of knowledge. Experts cannot often explain or express their reasoning and thought processes which causes the problem known as the "paradox of expertise."

As discussed above, there are a number of ways in which knowledge can be acquired or brought into an organization. These can include the acquisition of firms and organizations which hold the knowledge which is desired, the hiring of professionals who possess this knowledge, the hiring of outside consultants, or the derivation of new knowledge from such sources as data mining, text mining, and knowledge elicitation. All of these can enhance your firm's capabilities by the introduction of new knowledge into your organization.

CODIFYING KNOWLEDGE

Knowledge which is obtained needs to be captured and stored in a form which would allow it to be accessed by others or to be referenced when needed. This would allow the knowledge to be retained within a firm rather than having it be "carried in the heads" of the company founders or employees, which might result in it being lost if the person was to leave, die, or be otherwise unavailable. A number of different methods and technologies can be used with regards to codifying knowledge, and the specific method used could vary according to the specific type of information which is being coded. According to Davenport and Prusak (2000), the goal of codifying knowledge is to "convert knowledge into accessible and applicable formats." Included within this broad definition are steps and methods such as describing, categorizing, modeling, and mapping knowledge in a "coded" form. Coded knowledge is often put into a computerized form although the word "coded" does not always or necessarily mean coded into a computerized format. The important concepts to keep in mind include the need to decide what business goals the coded information will serve, how a certain set of knowledge will be used to meet these goals, how to select the right knowledge to be coded (form and content) and, finally, what is the medium or method which is to be used to code this information effectively. To start, there are different kinds of knowledge. Knowledge may be as straightforward as a set of rules or definitions (explicit knowledge) or as complex as the skills involved in something like playing a violin or hitting a baseball in the major leagues. This latter form of knowledge, called tacit knowledge, is one of the challenging areas of knowledge management in that it is very difficult to codify this kind of knowledge on paper or in a database. Tacit knowledge can be more formally defined as *"Knowledge that enters into the production of behaviors and/or the constitution of mental states but is not ordinarily accessible to consciousness."* The distinction between tacit knowledge and explicit knowledge has sometimes been expressed in terms of knowing-how and knowing-that, respectively (Ryle, 1949/ 1984, pp. 25-61), or in terms of a corresponding distinction between embodied knowledge and theoretical knowledge. On this account, knowing-how or embod-ied knowledge is characteristic of the expert who acts, makes judgments, and so forth without explicitly reflecting on the principles or rules involved. The expert works without having a theory of his or her work; he or she just performs skillfully without deliberation or focused attention. Knowing-that, by contrast, involves consciously accessible knowledge that can be articulated and is characteristic of the person learning a skill through explicit instruction, recitation of rules, attention to his or her movements, etc. While such declarative knowledge may be needed for the acquisition of skills, the argument goes, it no longer becomes necessary for the practice of those skills once the novice becomes an expert in exercising them and, indeed, it does seem to be the case that, as Polanyi argued, when we acquire a skill, we acquire a corresponding understanding that defies articulation (Polanyi, 1958/1974). Now that the differences between the two main types of knowledge have been explained, attention can be given to a method of codifying knowledge using knowledge maps. A knowledge map is not a collection of the knowledge or information itself but rather is a kind of roadmap or index to the knowledge. This is an important component to have, since a large mass of knowledge may be difficult to understand or manage if there is not some kind of map to guide the user.

TRANSFER OF KNOWLEDGE

The transferability of information and knowledge is a critical determinant of an organization's capacity to confer sustainable competitive advantage. The issue of transferability is paramount in both intra- (such as between functional units and management levels) and inter-organizational settings (such as supply chains, strategic alliances, and joint venture development). Critical to the flow of information and knowledge is the knowing how (tacit knowledge) and the knowing about (explicit knowledge) distinction of knowledge transferability. Knowledge transfer is an important aspect of knowledge management because knowledge, once captured or obtained by an organization, must be able to be shared from and by persons and groups within the organization. There are a number of techniques in which organizations transfer (and related to this, share) information. According to Nancy Dixon (2000), there are five main types of knowledge transfer/sharing. These include serial transfer, near transfer, far transfer, strategic transfer, and expert transfer. Each of these differs according to the purpose, method, and ways in which they are implemented. Serial transfer is a form of knowledge transfer where knowledge (both explicit and tacit) which is gained in one context or setting is then transferred to the next use when it is performed in a different setting. In general, this applies to the same team applying their knowledge from an earlier similar task to a slightly different context at a later date. This involves the management of both explicit and tacit knowledge and usually involves regular meetings, participation by all of the team members, and an emphasis on brief meetings. An example of this might be a team replacing an air conditioning system in an office building and then doing the same task in a different setting, such as an apartment complex. Knowledge gained from the one setting can be used in the new setting (Dixon, 2000). Near transfer differs in that the type of knowledge being transferred is basically explicit in nature, and the specific information which is key to doing a task by one team is then transferred to another team that will be doing a very similar task. This type of transfer is best suited for tasks which are generally routine, frequent, and generally similar when repeated. Often, this information is distributed through electronic means, and the information is both explicit and somewhat brief and concise in nature. For example, one team at the corporate headquarters has perfected a method of doing a certain kind of installation. The methods and steps can be recorded electronically (in e-mail or PDF file or other electronic means) and then distributed to other offices and teams throughout the organization, which can bring about better performance and productivity by the receiving teams. Far transfer focuses on the sharing of tacit knowledge between teams in an organization and often results in the collaboration between the teams, whether face-to-face or using other means. Because the information involved here is tacit, it cannot be easily recorded and transmitted as with the near transfer method. Far transfer of information is best suited to information which is non-routine in nature and for tasks which are likely to be frequently performed. Both teams can collaborate by mutually offering and receiving information. For instance, if a team has been tasked to work on a new and unique project, they may bring another team who has worked on similar projects in the past so that they can share and exchange information and come up with a viable solution to the problem (Dixon, 2000).

Strategic transfer focuses on the transfer of knowledge which can impact the organization as a whole. Involving both explicit and tacit knowledge, it is designed for situations which are neither frequent, nor routine and could involve tasks which are high-level within an organization, such as the knowledge required for corporate mergers and acquisitions. Strategic transfer frequently involves the identification of key knowledge needed by corporate executives and senior-level managers and then the collection and interpretation completed by knowledge specialists. Finally, there is expert transfer, which involves the gaining of explicit knowledge from experts when the scope of a task is outside of the knowledge of a team working on a task. The information in this case, because of its explicit nature, can be transmitted via electronic forums or networks and can be in the form of "bulletin boards," where a question can be posted and various knowledgeable experts who know the answer can then respond with the required knowledge. Having such a network in place can be extremely useful, since problems can occur at any time, and having a network of experts available when problems arise is a valuable resource (Dixon, 2000).

Another useful method of sharing and transferring information is through Communities of Practice (CoPs). A definition of a community of practice is "a group of people who share a concern, a set of problems, or a passion about a topic, and who deepen their knowledge and expertise in an area by interacting on an ongoing basis" (Wenger et al., 2002). Although the term "Community of Practice" is new, CoPs are not. Such groups have been around ever since people in organizations realized they could benefit from sharing their knowledge, insights, and experiences with others who have similar interests or goals. The concept of a community of practice is an extension or a variation of the concept of special interest groups, clubs, medieval guilds, and even regions for certain industries (Silicon Valley for high-tech and Detroit for the automobile industry). One of the best-known examples of a CoP was one formed by the copy machine repair technicians at Xerox Corporation. Through networking and sharing their experiences, particularly the problems they encountered and the solutions they devised, a core group of these technicians proved extremely effective in improving the efficiency and effectiveness of efforts to diagnose and repair Xerox customers' copy machines. The impact on customer satisfaction and the business value to Xerox was invaluable (Wenger, 1999).

TECHNOLOGIES FOR KNOWLEDGE MANAGEMENT

As mentioned previously, knowledge management is an area which is not always easily defined because it is broad and spans various disciplines. The field encompasses the use of management techniques and methods, collaborative concepts and techniques, as well as the use of various computer and related technologies. The purpose of this section is to examine some of the important technologies which are used in the area of knowledge management.

The *computer-supported collaborative work* (CSCW) community has been addressing issues of shared development of knowledge for many years. *Groupware* is sometimes used as a synonym for CSCW, and Lotus Notes often appears to be the defining CSCW application, even though there are other groupware products including Netscape's Collabra Share. Recent developments in corporate *intranets* are likely to dramatically increase the level of interest in CSCW as IP-based technologies replace or complement proprietary products like Notes.

Table 5 is a summary of various tools and technologies available for knowledge management.

Table 5: Summary of Various Tools and Technologies Available for Knowledge Management

Technologies & Tools	Description
Expert systems	An expert system is regarded as the embodiment within a computer of a knowledge-based component from an expert skill in such a form that the system can offer intelligent advice or make an intelligent decision about a processing function. Expert systems are computer-based programs which are designed to record human expertise (knowledge) and then apply this knowledge to applications in a certain domain.
Distributed hypertext systems	*Distributed hypertext systems* have been concerned with the generation and leveraging of organizational knowledge for more than a dozen years. Theodor Holm Nelson coined the term "hypertext" in the 1960s, and his writings about representation, access, and management of knowledge -- embodied in his vision for Project Xanadu, a global "docuverse" that pre-figured the World Wide Web -- are useful for managing information and knowledge.
Document management	*Document management* systems originally were primarily concerned with providing online access to documents stored as bit-mapped images. Document management technology, already in widespread use in large, information-intensive companies, is likely to become an integral part of virtually every "intranet" in one form or another.
Geographic information systems	*Geographic information systems*, a term associated with knowledge management, is used as a graphic tool for *knowledge mapping*. Known by the acronym GIS for short, the technology involves a digitized map, a powerful computer and software that permits the superimposition and manipulation of various kinds of demographic and corporate data on the map.
Help desk technology	*Help desk technology* is primarily concerned with routing requests for help from information seeker to the right technical resolution person within an organization.
Intranets	*Intranets*, intra-corporation networks that use the Internet's IP (Internet Protocol) standard, not only permit sharing of information, but they also view the organization's information (including structured resources like relational databases, as well as unstructured text) through Web browsers like Internet Explorer and Netscape Navigator.
Concept mapping	*Concept mapping* seems to be rooted primarily in educational techniques for improving understanding and retention, and as an aid to writing. A concept map is a picture of the ideas or topics in the information and the ways these ideas or topics are related to each other. It is a visual summary that shows the structure of the material the writer will describe.
Semantic networks	*Semantic networks* are often closely associated with detailed analysis of texts and networks of ideas. One of the important ways they are distinguished from hypertext systems is their support of semantic typing of links. For example, the relationship between "murder" and "death" might be described as "is a cause of." The inverse relationship might be expressed as "is caused by." Semantic networks are a technique for representing knowledge.
Hypertext (an expanded semantic network)	*Hypertext*, known to most people these days by its implementation in the World Wide Web, is sometimes described as a semantic network with content at the nodes. But the content itself, the traditional document model, seems to be the driving organizational force, not the network of links. In most hypertext documents, the links are **not** semantically typed, although they are typed at times according to the medium of the object displayed by traversing the link.

Table 5: Summary of Various Tools and Technologies Available for Knowledge Management (continued)

Technologies & Tools	Description
Information modeling	*Information modeling* is concerned with precise specification of the meaning in a text and in making relationships of meaning explicit, often with the objective of rapid and accurate development of new software applications for business requirements. Some of the essence of information modeling is expressed in the following definition: "The process of eliciting requirements from domain experts, formulating a complete and precise specification understandable to both domain experts and developers, and refining it using existing (or possible) implementation mechanisms."
Conceptual indexes	*Conceptual* (or "back-of-the-book") *indexes* are rarely discussed in the same breath as hypertext, conceptual maps, and semantic networks, perhaps because indexers themselves sometimes relish the aura of "black art" surrounding indexing, but the connection is fundamental. Conceptual indexes traditionally map key ideas and objects in a single work. An index is a structured sequence, resulting from a thorough and complete analysis of text, of synthesized access points to all the information contained in the text. The structured arrangement of the index enables users to locate information efficiently.
Metadata	*Metadata* is simply information added to a document (or a smaller unit of information) that makes it easier to access and re-use that content. It's also referred to as simply "data about data." You'll find metadata in many different forms, including key words in a software help system, the document profile information attached to documents in a document management system, and the classification information in a library card catalog.

LEARNING ORGANIZATION

In recent years, an increasing amount of global business school research and literature has focused on concepts such as the "knowledge-based economy," "organizational learning," "knowledge workers," "intellectual capital," "virtual teams," and the like in order to make sense of this "new discipline" (Gittell & Vidal, 1998). Organizational learning is a fairly recent way to think about learning in organizations. In a time of less organizational change (technological, societal, and economic), it was possible for an organization to develop a strategy for functioning and, assuming the strategy was initially effective, maintain that strategy for several decades. Current organizations, however, must change constantly in order to survive for even one decade. But change in and of itself is not sufficient. The change must be based on appropriate data gathered externally from the environment and internally from lessons learned. Both are a part of organizational learning, and both are critical to effective organizations (Skyrme, 1998, 2000, 2001). Learning organizations or organizational learning are defined in many different ways. A few selected definitions are:

"The essence of organizational learning is the organization's ability to use the amazing mental capacity of all its members to create the kind of processes that will improve its own" (Dixon, 1994);

and

"Organizations where people continually expand their capacity to create the results they truly desire, where new and expansive patterns of thinking are nurtured, where collective aspiration is set free, and where people are continually learning to learn together" (Senge, 1990).

In general, we can define learning organizations as those that have in place systems, mechanisms and processes that are used to continually enhance their capabilities and those who work with it or for it to achieve sustainable objectives, both for themselves and for the communities in which they participate. Companies are seeking to improve existing products and services (continuous improvement) and innovation (breakthrough strategies). This has resulted in a plethora of initiatives such as TQM (Total Quality Management) and BPR (Business Process Re-engineering). But companies are finding that such programs succeed or fail depending on human factors, such as skills, attitudes and organizational culture (Garvin, 2000).

Types of Learning

A learning organization is not about "more training." While training does help develop certain types of skill, a learning organization involves the development of higher levels of knowledge and skill. There could be four different levels of learning. (See Table 6.)

Organizations need to follow different steps to convert themselves into learning organizations.

- **Learning Culture:** An organizational climate that nurtures learning. There is a strong similarity with those characteristics associated with innovation.
- **Management Processes:** Processes that encourage interaction across boundaries. These are infrastructure, development and management processes as opposed to business operational processes (the typical focus of many BPR initiatives).
- **Tools and Techniques:** Methods that aid individual and group learning, such as creativity and problem-solving techniques.
- **Skills and Motivation:** To learn and adapt.

Table 6: Four Different Levels of Learning

Level of Learning	Description
Level 1. **Learning facts, knowledge, processes and procedures**	Applies to known situations where changes are minor.
Level 2. **Learning new job skills that are transferable to other situations**	Applies to new situations where existing responses need to be changed. Bringing in outside expertise is a useful tool here.
Level 3. **Learning to adapt**	Applies to more dynamic situations where the solutions need developing. Experimentation and deriving lessons from success and failure are the mode of learning here.
Level 4. **Learning to learn**	Is about innovation and creativity, designing the future rather than merely adapting to it. This is where assumptions are challenged and knowledge is reframed.

- **Free exchange and flow of information:** Systems are in place to ensure that expertise is available where it is needed and individuals network extensively, crossing organizational boundaries to develop their knowledge and expertise.
- **Commitment to learning, personal development:** Support from top management; people at all levels encouraged to learn regularly; learning is rewarded. Time to think and learn (understanding, exploring, reflecting, developing).
- **Valuing people:** Ideas, creativity and "imaginative capabilities" are stimulated, made use of and developed. Diversity is recognized as a strength. Views can be challenged.
- **Fostering a climate of openness and trust:** Individuals are encouraged to develop ideas, to speak out, to challenge actions.
- **Learning from experience:** Learning from mistakes is often more powerful than learning from success. Failure is tolerated, provided lessons are learned.

Tools and Techniques

Tools and techniques include a wide range of learning and creativity skills in the following groups:

- **Inquiry:** interviewing, seeking information
- **Creativity:** brainstorming, associating ideas
- **Making sense of situations:** organizing information and thoughts
- **Making choices:** deciding courses of action
- **Observing outcomes:** recording, observation
- **Reframing knowledge:** embedding new knowledge into mental models, memorizing

Collective (team and organizational) learning requires skills for sharing information and knowledge, particularly implicit knowledge, assumptions and beliefs that are traditionally "beneath the surface." Key skills here are:
- Communication, especially across organizational boundaries
- Listening and observing
- Mentoring and supporting colleagues
- Taking a holistic perspective — seeing the team and organization as a whole
- Coping with challenge and uncertainty

ORGANIZATIONAL MEMORY

Organizational memory is the record of an organization that is embodied in a set of documents and artifacts. Organizational memory has become a hot topic recently due to the growing recognition that it appears to be so thoroughly lacking in contemporary organizations. The problem is not a scarcity of documents and artifacts for the organizational memory but rather the quality, content, and organization of this material. For example, an effective organizational memory would be able to answer such often-asked questions as, "Why did we do this?" and "How did such and such come to be the case?" Rarely is this possible now (Conklin, 1996).

Basically, the goal of an organization memory is to remember and learn a firm's past. Contemporary organizations seem to have only a weak ability to do this and are thus seeking to gain the capacity for "organizational memory." Networked computers might provide the basis for a "nervous system" that could be used to implement the capacity for organizational memory, but the technology (software and hardware) must provide for easy capture, recall, and learning. Moreover, for an organization to augment its memory, it must shift from the currently pervasive document- and artifact-oriented paradigm (or culture) to one that embraces process as well. This process-oriented paradigm requires the use of a system that integrates three technologies: hypertext, groupware, and a rhetorical method. Groupware allows the organizational record to be built in the course of everyday communication and coordination. Hypertext provides the ability to organize and display this rich informational web. And a rhetorical method, such as IBIS, structures the memory according to content, not chronology. In addition to the computer technology, a shift in organizational culture toward an appreciation of process is required to implement organizational memory (Conklin, 1996).

Organizational memory is perhaps most clearly missing in industries where large numbers of people engage in the design and construction of large, complex systems over long periods of time such as defense, aerospace, utilities, pharmaceuticals, and telecommunications. Engineering organizations in these industries have serious limitations in transferring previous learning to current problems. The design rationale of large, complex systems is thoroughly and systematically lost. Such phrases as "reinventing the wheel," "going in circles," and "having the same discussion over and over," often heard in large engineering organizations, point to a striking phenomenon: while organizations don't seem to learn or remember very well, this limitation was, until recently, regarded as normal and inevitable. It is thus highly desirable to increase the capacity of organizations to remember and to learn. This means capturing more of the "documents and artifacts" of the organization in a way that they can be effectively recalled and reinterpreted. The growth of networked computers for all phases of information work creates the infrastructure – (i.e., the "nervous system") to support this increased capture and reuse of organizational memory (Conklin, 1996).

Three Tools For Organizational Memory

The most immediate barrier to capturing more of the process of work and making it part of organizational memory is that it seems to present an insurmountable and onerous documentation burden on the people doing the work. The key to overcoming this perception is to shift the notion of capturing the process data from being an additional documentation burden to "tapping into" the flow of communication that is already happening in an organization. Not surprisingly, this shift is also a shift from an artifact-oriented to a process-oriented perspective (Conklin, 1996).

The first element of the computer technology is hypertext, because the nature of the process-oriented approach is essentially non-linear, so the representation for capturing and organizing it must also be that rich. Moreover, as time goes by and the organizational record grows more convoluted and complex, the unlimited flexibility of hypertext as a representational medium is essential for ongoing restructuring and summarization.

The second element is groupware, for the same reason that e-mail is a natural first step toward easy capture of organizational process. An MCC/NCR field study showed clearly that it is critical that the technology used to capture rationale be as transparent as possible and that it must closely fit the existing practices and tools of the organization. Groupware by its very nature is not focused on capture, but rather on communication and coordination. The secret to capturing organizational memory then is to "tap into" the existing flow of process interactions between the members of the organization and to crystallize this on an ongoing basis into the key elements of the organizational memory. Groupware can provide the medium for organizational dialogues which, because they occur via the computer, create a computable record of semi-structured documents. The ability then exists to manipulate, distribute or share this information and intelligence throughout the organization or team effectively and on an ongoing basis, creating a memory and learning tool.

The third element of the technology for capturing organizational memory is the use of a rhetorical method, or conversational model, for structuring the conversations occurring with the technology. The reason for this is two-fold. A simple rhetorical method provides a structure for discussing complex problems that can immediately improve the quality of the dialogue process. The IBIS (Issue-Based Information System) method (Kunz & Rittel, 1970) provides this kind of structure and process improvement. IBIS organizes planning and design conversations into issues (stated as questions), positions which offer possible solutions, and arguments which support or object to the positions. Such a model provides a basis for structuring the conversational record which is not simply chronological (as in an e-mail or bulletin board type system). For example, conversations in the IBIS method are structured according to the issues being discussed, providing a content-based index within which the cumulative record of the organizational process is preserved and organized.

Taken together, the technologies of hypertext, groupware, and the IBIS method combine synergistically to form a communication device for teams and teamwork and the ability to create an effective organizational memory for an organization. Thus, the technology for organizational memory must, at a minimum, incorporate hypertext, groupware, and a rhetorical model. But this computer technology alone is not sufficient to create an effective organizational memory. While the technology must be very good and the user interface transparent, the organization must also shift to making capture and use of organizational memory an important and natural practice. This shift towards a process-oriented paradigm and culture requires organizational commitment, and it is the most challenging part of establishing a capacity for memory and learning in an organization.

CONCLUSION

Knowledge management, in an age where there is an overwhelming amount of information and perhaps not sufficient resources or understanding to manage all of it, is a critically important area of concern to 21st century organizations. The basic, yet important, terms and concepts associated with knowledge management and organization memory for learning organizations are discussed in this chapter. Extracting knowledge that already exists in the minds of employees is a difficult process for generating knowledge. Future knowledge extractors will focus on rewards for knowledge, hiring good knowledge creators and providing easy-to-use tools for capture. In the future, categorization and organization of knowledge will be a core competence for every firm. This will require strategic thinking about what knowledge is important, the development of a knowledge vocabulary, prolific creation of indices, search tools and navigation aids, and the constant refinement and pruning of knowledge categories. Knowledge editors will have to combine sources and add context to transform information into knowledge (Prichard et al., 2000).

REFERENCES

Abram, S. (1997). Knowledge management: Is this the answer? Presentation delivered to the Special Libraries Association Toronto Chapter, October 15, 1997.

Allee, V. (1997). *The Knowledge Evolution: Building Organizational Intelligence*. London: Butterworth-Heinemann.

Barclay & Murray (1997). *What is knowledge management?* Retrieved from the World Wide Web: http://www.media-access.com/whatis.html.

Bates, M. E. (1997, Fall). *Information audits: What do we know and when do we know it?* Library Management Briefings.

Blue, A. (1998). Davis drives home the importance of being knowledge based. *Information Outlook*, 2(5), 39.

Broadbent, M. (1998). The phenomenon of knowledge management: What does it mean to the information profession? *Information Outlook*, 2(5), 23-36.

Chase, R. L. (1998). Knowledge navigators. *Information Outlook*, 2(9), 18.

Choo, C. W. (1998a). *Information Management for the Intelligent Organization: The Art of Scanning the Environment*. Medford, NJ: Information Today.

Choo, C. W. (1998b). *The Knowing Organization: How Organizations Use Information to Construct Meaning, Create Knowledge, and Make Decisions*. New York: Oxford University Press.

Conklin, E. J. (1996). *Capturing Organizational Memory in Groupware and Computer-Supported Cooperative Work*. In R. M. Baecker (Ed.). San Mateo, CA: Morgan Kaufmann.

Conklin, E. J. & Burgess Yakemovic, K. C. (1991). A process-oriented approach to design rationale. *Human-Computer Interaction*, 6, 357-391.

Davenport, T. H. (1995). *Some principles of knowledge management*.

Davenport, T. H. & Prusak, L. (1997). *Information Ecology: Mastering the Information and Knowledge Environment.* New York: Oxford University Press.

Davenport, T. H. & Prusak, L. (1998). *Working Knowledge: How Organizations Manage What They Know.* Boston, MA: Harvard Business School Press.

Davenport, T. H., Eccles, R. G. & Prusak, L. (1992). Information politics. *Sloan Management Review,* 34(1), 53-63.

Dixon, N. (1994). *The Organizational Learning Cycle.* New York: McGraw-Hill.

Dixon, N. M. (2000). *Common Knowledge: How Companies Thrive by Sharing What They Know.* Boston, MA: Harvard Business School Press.

Drucker, P. F. (1993). *Post-Capitalist Society.* New York: Harper Collins.

Drucker, P. F. (1994, November). The age of social transformation. *The Atlantic Monthly,* 53-80.

Garvin, D. (2000). *Learning in Action: A Guide to Putting the Learning Organization to Work.* Boston, MA: Harvard Business School Press.

Gittell, R. & Vidal, A. (1998). *Community Organizing: Building Social Capital As Development Strategy.* Thousand Oaks, CA: Sage Publications.

Graham, M. (1991). *Notes on Organizational Memory: Practice and Theory.* Unpublished Xerox PARC working paper.

Krogh, G., Ichijo, K. & Nonaka, I. (2000). *Enabling Knowledge Creation: How to Unlock the Mystery of Tacit Knowledge and Release the Power of Innovation.* New York: Oxford University Press.

Kunz, W. & Rittel, H. (1970). *Issues as elements of information systems.* Working Paper No. 131, Institute of Urban and Regional Development, University of California at Berkeley, Berkeley, California, USA.

Leonard, D. (1998). *Wellsprings of Knowledge: Building and Sustaining the Sources of Innovation.* Boston, MA: Harvard Business School Press.

Liberman, K. (1996). Creating & launching knowledge products. Getting Out of the Box: The Knowledge Management Opportunity. Video package prepared and presented at an SLA Distance Learning Program in October 1996, Washington, D.C., Special Libraries Association.

Lipnack, J. & Stamps, J. (2000). *Virtual Teams: People Working Across Boundaries with Technology,* (2nd ed.). New York: John Wiley & Sons.

Nonaka, I. & Takeuchi, H. (1995). *The Knowledge-Creating Company.* New York: Oxford University Press.

O'Dell, C. et al. (1998). *If Only We Knew What We Know: The Transfer of Internal Knowledge and Best Practice.* New York: Free Press.

Oxbrow, N. (1999). Information audits. *The route to getting value from your intranet.* Retrieved from the World Wide Web: http://www.tfpl.com/

about_TFPL/reports___research/information_audits_article/ information_audits_article.html.

Oxbrow, N. & Abell, A. (1998). *Putting knowledge to work: What skills and competencies are required? Knowledge Management: A New Competitive Asset.* Presented at SLA State-of-the-Art Institute, 25, Washington, D.C.

Pedler, M., Burgoyne, J. & Boydell, T. (1991). *The Learning Company: A Strategy for Sustainable Development.* New York: McGraw-Hill.

Peters, R. F. (1997). Information partnerships: Marketing opportunities for information professionals. *Information Outlook*, 1(3), 14-16.

Pfeffer, J. & Sutton, R, I. (2000). *The Knowing-Doing Gap: How Smart Companies Turn Knowledge into Action.*

Polanyi, M. (1974). *Personal Knowledge: Towards a Post- Critical Philosophy.* Chicago, IL: University of Chicago Press. (Original work published in 1958).

Prichard, C., Hull, R., Chumer, M. & Willmott, H. (eds.). (2000). *Managing Knowledge: Critical Investigations of Work and Learning.* London: Macmillan Business.

Remeikis, L. (1996). Acquiring the new skills and overcoming the barriers. Getting Out of the Box: The Knowledge Management Opportunity. Video package prepared and presented as an SLA Distance Learning Program in October 1996, Washington, D.C., Special Libraries Association.

Rogers, E. (1995). *Diffusion of Innovations.* New York: Free Press.

Ryle, G. (1984). *The Concept of Mind.* Chicago, IL: University of Chicago Press. (Original work published in 1949).

Senge, P. M., Roberts, C., Ross, R. B., Smith, B. J. & Kleiner, N. A. (n.d.). *The Fifth Discipline Fieldbook: Strategies and Tools for Building a Learning Organization.*

Sistla, M. & Todd, J. (1998). Warning: A killer mistake in business — Don't let technology drive your requirements. *Information Outlook*, 2(6), 19-24.

Skyrme, D. J. (1997, September). From Information to Knowledge Management. *Information Age,* 1(20), 16-18.

Skyrme, D. J. (1998, March). Knowledge Management: Solutions: The Role of Technology. *ACM SIGGROUP Bulletin*, Special Issue on Knowledge Management at Work.

Skyrme, D. J. (1999). *Knowledge Networking: Creating the Collaborative Enterprise.* Butterworth-Heinemann.

Skyrme, D. J. (2000). Developing a Knowledge Strategy: From Management to Leadership. In D. Morey, M. Maybury & B. Thuraisingham (Eds.), *Knowledge Management: Classic and Contemporary Works.* Boston, MA: MIT Press.

Skyrme, D. J. (2001). *Capitalizing on Knowledge: From E-business to K-business.* Butterworth-Heinemann.

Skyrme, D. J. & Amidon, D. (1997, September). The Knowledge Agenda. *Journal of Knowledge Management,* 1(1), 27-37.

Skyrme, D. J. & Amidon, D. M. (1999). The Knowledge Agenda. In J. D. Cortada & J. A. Woods (Eds.), *The Knowledge Management Yearbook.* Butterworth-Heinemann.

The Steps to Take for Conducting an Information Audit. (1997). *The Information Advisor,* 9(9), S1-S4.

Wenger, E. (1999). *Communities of Practice: Learning, Meaning, and Identity.*

Zipperer, L. (1998). Librarians in evolving corporate roles. *Information Outlook,* 2(6), 27-30.

Chapter II

Information Technology Assessment for Knowledge Management

Sushil K. Sharma
Ball State University, USA

Jatinder N. D. Gupta
University of Alabama in Huntsville, USA

Nilmini Wickramasinghe
Cleveland State University, USA

ABSTRACT

New technologies, increasingly demanding customers, new aggressive competitors, and innovations in products and value now characterize our current competitive environment. Organizations of the 21st century have no choice but to invest in new technologies, especially knowledge management tools to enhance their services and products in order to meet the demands of today's information-driven, globally competitive marketplace. Knowledge embedded in systems, brains and technology has always been the key to economic development. However, knowledge management is increasingly being viewed as a strategy to leverage a firm's knowledge and best practices to serve customers and to be competitive. Several organizations have already started experimenting with knowledge management initiatives to capture and capitalize on knowledge assets and thereby claim the enormous benefits afforded by such endeavors, including improved profitability and transformation of their businesses into new generation businesses. This chapter develops a technology assessment model for knowledge management indicating what kinds of computing and communication systems any organization needs in order for it to have a sound knowledge management approach.

INTRODUCTION

Any 21st century organization faces a dynamic, new competitive environment consisting of numerous opportunities, possibilities and challenges. As economies are becoming more knowledge-based, consumers' expectations are rising day by day. While new technologies threaten to make present systems and networks obsolete, new competitors threaten to upset existing markets and infrastructures. Global deregulation, allowing new competitors to enter previously guarded national monopolies, and hyper-competition are forcing organizations to offer services and products as a one-stop solution to meet customers' increasingly demanding expectations (Housel & Bell, 2001). To tackle such a global competitive environment, organizations have to invest in new technologies such as knowledge management tools that can contribute to enhance services and products that are offered in information technology-driven marketplaces.

The rules of business are undergoing radical change and these impact the competitive strategies of many businesses. The old laws of production, distribution, and consumption are evolving into new theories of e-businesses. Many organizations have an abundance of data and information but they starve for knowledge (Dean, 2001). Global markets are expanding rapidly, thus capturing new customers and retaining existing ones are becoming daunting tasks for organizations. Organizations are becoming more knowledge intensive in order to learn from past experiences and from others to reshape themselves and to change in order to survive and prosper (Brown & Duguid, 2000). New Web-based technologies have the capabilities to prepare organizations for knowledge management. The recently published report *Knowledge Management Software Market Forecast and Analysis 2000/2004* estimated that the total KM software market would reach $5.4 billion by 2004 (Duffy, 2000). While extensive literature exists to describe the developments in the knowledge management area, little work has been done on the assessment of IT for knowledge management. This chapter endeavors to address this void by developing an IT assessment model for knowledge management. Concisely stated, IT assessment means focusing on the availability and capability of computing and communication resources. Specifically, our model will enable organizations to answer such questions as: What kinds of computing and communication systems does our organization need for knowledge management to be successful? Such questions are critical for organizations as they try to incorporate knowledge management and move to become knowledge-based enterprises.

KNOWLEDGE MANAGEMENT (KM)

Arguably, the most valuable resource available to any organization today is its knowledge that is stored in patents, copyrights, corporate data warehouses, employees' brains, processes and information systems (Duffy, 2001). Knowledge management focuses on how to identify, manage, share, and leverage all information assets, such as databases, policies and procedures, content, and staff and members' expertise and experience to serve the organization (Shepard, 2000). These knowledge assets or repositories are stored in unstructured data formats (i.e., document and content management, groupware, e-mail and other forms of interpersonal communication) and structured data formats (i.e., data warehousing, databases, etc.). KM is the process of creating value from an organization's intangible assets. Organizations are realizing that their human capital (people power) and structural capital (databases, patents, intellectual property and related items) are the distinguishing elements of their organizations (Liebowitz, 2000). KM consists of systems, information and processes that take information and turn it into structured knowledge to support specific and general business purposes. Early attempts at KM included the use of data warehouses and data marts to help to predict future patterns in form of data mining, but now the KM domain is recognized to be much more than mere data warehousing and data mining (Srikantaiah & Koeing, 2000).

KM's major objective is to connect people with people and stimulate collaboration (Lee, 2000). Knowledge management benefits significantly from real-time communication between individuals that encompasses information exchange and provides a shared workspace (e.g., application sharing and videoconferencing). Such communication accommodates shared creation of work products — documents, group decision support, networked virtual meetings, etc. — and provides the ability to link immediately to experts if they are online (Alavi & Leidner, 2001). To support both explicit and tacit knowledge, KM solutions are built with content and collaboration technologies. Data technologies are structured and typically numerically oriented; knowledge technologies deal most often with text. Knowledge technologies need more human interactions than data technologies.

FACILITATING FOR E-COMMERCE AND INTELLIGENT ENTERPRISES

E-business and e-commerce is growing fast and becoming the popular way of doing business. E-business mandates that organizations use new technological tools, have new sharing cultures, incorporate new sets of values and new strategies appropriate for the new knowledge-based economy (Brown & Duguid, 2000). Many experts today believe that e-business is one of the three pillars of the new economy, along with knowledge management and partnering strategies (Moore, 2000). Today, organizations want to know more about their customers, partners and suppliers. Companies are willing to invest in technologies that enable them to track patterns in customers and other partners' transactions (Davenport et al., 2001). Companies are interested in creating an integrated data repository about customers, policies, procedures, suppliers and partners so that the concerned user in one location can learn everything about a customer, procedure or suppliers by accessing information with one click (Davenport et al., 2001).

Knowledge management is becoming a key determinant of value in the marketplace, of an organization's success, and a competitive edge in this e-commerce era. Many organizations leverage the efficient flow and transfer of knowledge across the organization (Silver, 2000) for enhancing markets, revenues and growth opportunities for e-business. Today, many companies compete not only on the basis of product, service and operational superiority, but also through KM assets to drive their competitive edge.

In this e-business era, organizations that offer e-business solutions have a number of automated systems that generate valuable data. But many of these automated systems are disparate systems that do not integrate and relate the stored data, leaving the consolidation and analysis of the data to the end-user (Hammond, 2001). Despite their strength, these systems do not help end-users to make better business decisions. End-users need business intelligence (BI) derived from the systems that provide the in-depth analytical capabilities to analyze the situations and prepare strategies accordingly to compete in a global environment (Hammond, 2001). The growth of Web technologies provides an opportunity to build portal-type applications that integrate a firm's knowledge in the form of KM assets and can be accessed from anywhere through dynamic, end-user-driven querying tools for report distribution and data analysis (McMillin, 2000). Such features of a portal will add value to an enterprise's strategy by improving analysis of interdepartmental data by delivering relevant enterprise data to a greater number of knowledge consumers. Furthermore, such a KM infrastructure would help organizations to improve customer service and partner relationships and to create marketable knowledge products from an enterprise's own internal data (Hammond, 2001). Organizations can allow their customers to view dynamic reports displaying their purchasing habits and identifying areas where they can consolidate purchases from different suppliers to take advantage of volume discounts. Another indirect benefit of implementing a KM solution exists in the capability of an enterprise to package and resell its own internal data to other companies.

Knowledge management is an intelligent process by which raw data is gathered and transformed into information elements. These information elements are assembled and organized into context-relevant structures that represent knowledge (Onge, 2001). It has become necessary for organizations to have their business information stored in databases, file servers, Web pages, e-mails, ERP (enterprise resource planning), and CRM (customer relationship management) systems integrated into a repository which can be accessed by various users. These integrated repositories, which act as knowledge management systems, can cut the time wasted on searching for particular data and allowing better business decisions. Having such knowledge management systems can turn a company into an intelligent enterprise (Hammond, 2001).

A knowledge-based view of the firm identifies knowledge as the organizational asset that enables a sustainable competitive advantage, especially in hyper-competitive environments (Alavi, 1999; Davenport & Prusak, 1998; Kanter, 1999) or in environments experiencing radical discontinuous change (Malhotra, 2000). This is attributed to the fact that barriers exist regarding the transfer and replication of knowledge (Alavi, 1999). Knowledge and knowledge management have strategic significance (Kanter, 1999). Knowledge management addresses the generation, representation, storage, transfer and transformation of knowledge. Therefore, knowledge architecture, designed to capture knowledge and, thereby, enable the knowledge management processes to be efficient and effective (Wickramasinghe & Mills, 2000).

Underlying the knowledge architecture is the recognition of the binary nature of knowledge, namely its objective and subjective components. Knowledge can exist as an object in essentially two forms: explicit or factual knowledge and tacit or "know how" (Polyani, 1958; Polyani, 1966). It is well established that while both types of knowledge are important, tacit knowledge is more difficult to identify and thus manage (Nonaka, 1994). Furthermore, objective knowledge can be located at various levels, e.g., the individual, group or organization (Kanter, 1999). Of equal importance, though perhaps less well defined, knowledge also has a subjective component and can be viewed as an ongoing phenomenon, being shaped by social practices of communities (Boland et al., 1995). The objective elements of knowledge can be thought of as primarily having an impact on process while the subjective elements typically impact innovation. Both effective and efficient processes as well as the functions of supporting and fostering innovation are key concerns of knowledge management.

The knowledge architecture recognizes these two different yet key aspects of knowledge and provides the blueprint for an all-encompassing KMS. Clearly, the knowledge architecture is defining a KMS that supports both objective and subjective attributes of knowledge. Thus, we have an interesting duality in knowledge management that draws upon two distinct philosophical perspectives, namely, the Lockean/Leibnitzian stream and the Heglian/Kantian stream (Wickramasinghe & Mills, 2001). This duality can be best captured in the Yin-Yang of knowledge management (refer to Figure 1) (ibid). The principle of Yin-Yang is at the very roots of Chinese thinking and is centered around the notion of polarity, not to be confused with the ideas of opposition or conflict, thereby making it most apt for describing these two sides of knowledge management because both are necessary in order for knowledge management to truly flourish (ibid).

Models of convergence and compliance that make up one side are grounded in a Lockean/Leibnitzian tradition (Wickramasinghe & Mills, 2001). These models are essential to provide the information processing aspects of knowledge management, most notably by enabling efficiencies of scale and scope and thus supporting the objective view of knowledge management. In contrast, the other side provides agility and flexibility in the tradition of a Hegelian/Kantian perspective (ibid). Such models recognize the importance of divergence of meaning which is essential to support the "sense-making," subjective view of knowledge management. Figure 1 depicts this Yin-Yang view of knowledge management. This figure shows that, given a radical change to an environment or given a highly competitive environment, an organization needs knowledge to survive. From this Yin-Yang depiction of knowledge management we see that knowledge is required for the organization to be effective and efficient, but new knowledge and knowledge renewal is also necessary. The ultimate challenge for KMS is to support both these components of knowledge management. The pivotal function underlined by the knowledge architecture is the flow of knowledge. The flow of knowledge is fundamentally enabled (or not) by the knowledge management tools adopted.

TECHNOLOGY ASSESSMENT MODEL FOR KNOWLEDGE MANAGEMENT

Today's organizations offer e-commerce and conduct business on a 24-hour-seven-day-a-week basis through their own offices as well as with the help of their business partners located geographically in dispersed locations worldwide. Organizations have their databases, people, and technology infrastructure dispersed in many different locations. Organizations need a single database and e-commerce systems of all their activities that allows their customers, staff and

Figure 1: Yin-Yang Model of KM

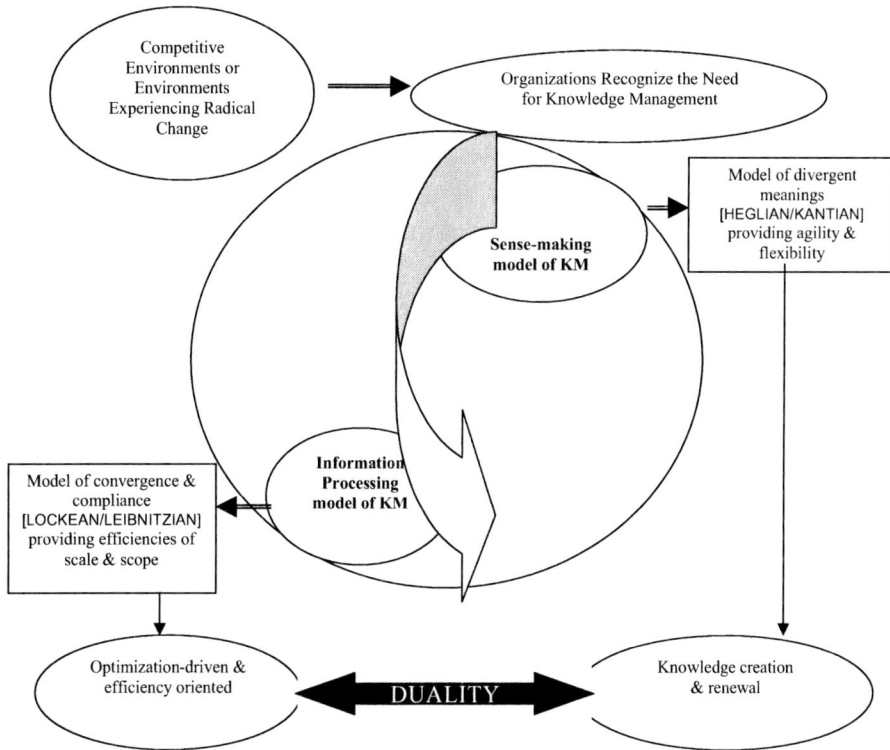

Source: Wickramasinghe and Mills (2001)

business partners to have real-time information for their use (Shepard, 2000). Furthermore, organizations need knowledge by integrating all data stored in these disparate systems. Organizations typically have various systems such as database systems, intranets, groupware, document management, data ware-housing, e-mail and ERP systems. The first step in actualizing the knowledge management systems architecture is concerned with integrating all these systems so that these various formats can be integrated to create a uniform format for users (Nissen et al., 2000).

The first major step needed for embracing KM often includes overcoming hierarchies and building environments in which knowledge sharing and collaboration become a routine way of doing business. This requires a technology infrastructure that encourages collaboration and facilitates knowledge capture and access (Duffy, 2001) as well as changes in business rules, procedures and policies. While organizations generate much data during transactional phases, its systems do not document much of the generated data. The undocumented data potentially could be quite useful for generating business intelligence. Therefore, one of the biggest problems faced by an organization is the need to bring disparate enterprise data sources into a cohesive data warehouse. Data abstraction from databases of enterprises of data storage requires skills to map the actual database fields and tables into the intuitive query tools that end-users will eventually see on their desktops for extracting intelligence or knowledge. This is just one of many instances where a technology assessment model would be beneficial.

The technology assessment model can be divided into five layers (Duffy, 2000) or groups in the typical enterprise systems architecture model. The layers and their purpose are shown in Figures 2, 3 and 4.

Communication Systems Layer

The basic foundation layer for knowledge management is the communication systems layer that represents all the communication systems involved. There are varieties of communication systems such as local area network (LAN) or intranet, extranet and World Wide Web or Internet. The organizations would have connectivity to Internet service providers (ISPs) through various "last-mile technologies" options. The communications systems are used for communicating across or exchanging information through various groupware systems for the

Figure 2: Technology Assessment Model for Knowledge Management

Layers	Domain
End-User Application Layer	Represents the user interface in applications and data used regularly.
Middleware Layer	Integrates the internal knowledge into an easy-to-use interface.
Knowledge Repository Layer	Consists of repositories for unstructured data (i.e., document and content management) and structured data (i.e., data warehousing, generation, and management), groupware for supporting the collaboration needed for knowledge sharing as well as e-mail and other forms of interpersonal communication required for the efficient, time and location-independent exchange of information.
Enterprise Data Source Layer	Consists of databases, file servers, Web pages, e-mails, ERP (enterprise resource planning), and CRM (customer relationship management) systems.
Communication Systems Layer	Made up of local area network, intranet, extranet and Internet systems.

creation of knowledge. Organizations should have their communication systems in place before they opt for knowledge management. It is required that communication systems should support appropriate bandwidths for effective information exchange. It has been experienced that many times organizations have low bandwidth links that restrict effective groupware applications supports.

The next major wave of communication systems would be to deliver the information and experience on demand, in the right form, at the right time and at the right price to fixed or mobile terminals anywhere. Bandwidth, distance and time will ultimately no longer be significant. Service and access will become the dominant features of the changing demands and knowledge-focused society.

Using communication systems would ensure more information and more transparency for customers, suppliers and users. In the world of knowledge management, everybody will know everybody else's business. Advances in communications technology are being driven by the relentless spread of e-commerce. The latest developments in communications technology promise that it will soon be possible to receive up-to-the-second information about the flow of goods from manufacturer to customer with a small and compact handheld device. And in the next two years, developers are promising communications devices that are small and light enough to be worn as jewelry or clothing. Much is riding on the next generation of networks, the so-called "third generation"

Figure 3: Components of Each Layer of KM Solutions

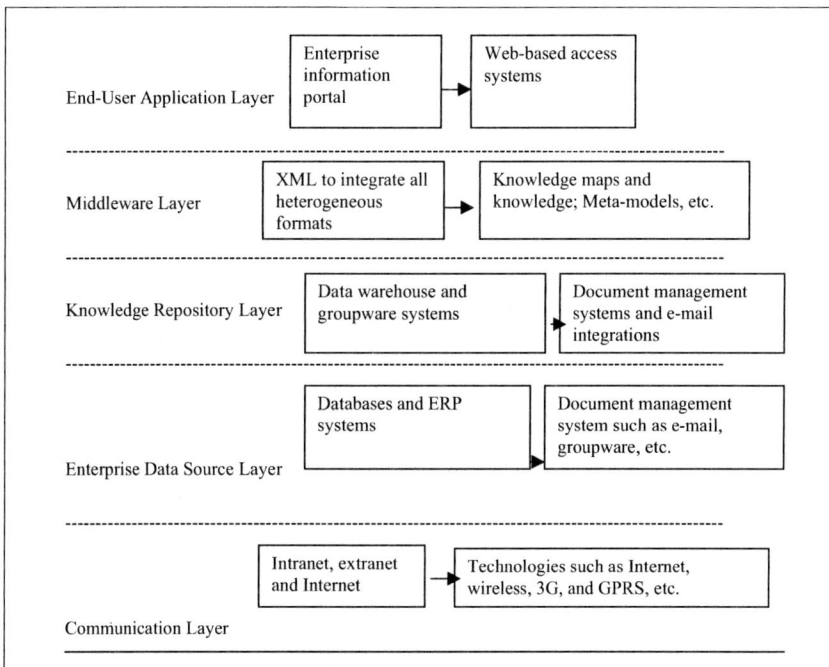

Figure 4: Technologies and Systems of Knowledge Management

Layer	Tools and Technologies
End-User Application Layer	Enterprise information portal (EIP) and Web-based access system.
Middleware Layer	XML technology and various routing and retrieval algorithms.
Knowledge Repository Layer	Data warehouse, data marts, document management systems, groupware applications.
Enterprise Data Source Layer	Databases, ERP, groupware, document management systems, and e-Mail, etc.
Communication Systems Layer	Systems: LAN, intranet, extranet and Internet. Technologies: Internet, 3G, GPRS, Bluetooth, etc.

(3G), which will allow moving pictures and data to be transmitted much more easily to handheld devices.

Network and handset operators are also pinning their hopes on another variant of transmission technology, which allows a mobile device to be continually connected to a network. The technology is known as general packet radio service (GPRS). Today's mobile devices have to dial into a central server and download electronic information and translate it into a voice or digital message. Devices that use GPRS are known as "always on" because they do not need to be switched on and off.

Enterprise Data Source Layer

The enterprise data source layer provides the base or platform upon which KM solutions are built. It consists of repositories for unstructured data (i.e., document and content management) and structured data (i.e., databases, e-mail) and groupware, etc. (Duffy, 2001). Companies use databases and ERP systems for structured data and varieties of document management systems for unstructured data.

This layer acts as a foundation for KM solutions. At this layer data is captured in various databases or document management systems. The technological tools used include relational database management systems, document management systems, messaging technologies (like e-mails systems), groupware, and work flow systems.

The enterprise data source layer represents different types of data (textual data, video, and audio) stored in databases, file servers, Web pages, e-mails, ERP (enterprise resource planning), and CRM (customer relationship management) systems. Enterprise data sources can be fileservers, database servers, groupware servers, document management systems, e-mail servers or web sites. Each repository's structure will depend on the content or knowledge it stores and manages. Although each is a separate physical repository, together they form a single, virtual knowledge repository (Duffy, 2000).

Knowledge Repository Layer

The knowledge repository layer consists of a data warehouse for structured data and document content management and a groupware system for unstructured data. The knowledge repository layer mainly consists of repositories for unstructured data (i.e., document and content management), structured data (i.e., data warehousing, generation, and management), and groupware for supporting the collaboration needed for knowledge (Duffy, 2001).

The knowledge stored may be either created inside an organization or acquired from external sources and then added to the enterprise's knowledge base. There are a variety of tools needed to capture the knowledge at the knowledge repository layer. Traditional tools for capturing knowledge include word processing, spreadsheets, e-mail, and presentation software. Increasingly, newer technologies such as voice recognition, shared workspaces, and video conferencing are also used to support the knowledge-capture process.

This layer is also known as the data abstraction layer and represents the processes through which data is extracted from the enterprise data source layer or operational form of data layer and converted into summarized data. Data abstraction involves suppression of irrelevant data. The relevancy depends on the task and the use of information, thus it changes with the context. There are six main abstraction mechanisms used such as classification, generalization, aggregation, contextualization, materialization and normalization.

Data Warehouse and Data Marts

The data warehouse is the main component of KM infrastructure. Organizations store data in a number of databases. The data warehousing process extracts data captured by multiple business applications and organizes it in a way that is meaningful to the business for any future references in the form of knowledge (Duffy, 2001).

The data warehouse process has two components of data warehousing software to support KM. One component transfers operational data to the warehouse (i.e., data extraction, cleansing, transformation, loading, and administration) and the second component supports warehouse management or utilities for supporting data mining (Shaw et al., 2001).

Collaborative Applications

Collaborative applications' core functions include e-mail, group calendaring and scheduling, shared folders/databases, threaded discussions, and custom application development. Collaborative applications provide the capabilities needed for identifying subject matter experts who can give answers to knowledge seekers (Skyrme, 1999). Collaborative applications systems are the major component of KM systems because it is through these systems that an interaction of experts and users take place.

Content Management

Content management software represents the convergence of full-text retrieval, document management, and publishing applications. It supports the unstructured data management requirements of KM initiatives through a process that involves capture, storage, access, selection, and document publication. Content management tools enable users to organize information at an object level rather than in binary large objects or full documents. The information is broken down by topical area and usually tagged via extensible markup language (XML). Both capabilities dramatically increase the opportunity for re-use.

Middleware Layer

The middleware integrates the applications of the knowledge repository and enterprise information portals. Middleware supports intelligent message routing, business rules that control information flow, security, and system management and administration.

Users like to have information or knowledge without getting into complexities of how knowledge is stored or structured. Thus, there is a need for the middleware layer which can keep the complexities of knowledge repositories hidden from users who want easy access to knowledge. Some authors refer to this layer as the "knowledge about the knowledge" layer (Duffy, 2001) that represents the entire collection of knowledge objects, regardless of category or location, and helps to identify the links between existing islands of information. This layer has two components, i.e., knowledge maps and knowledge meta-model. Thus, the middleware layer is the heart of a knowledge management system. The information about each knowledge object in the repository includes such items as the identity of the person who created the knowledge and the time it was created, the knowledge object's format and media, the knowledge object's purpose, actions and sequences of events surrounding its existence, and linkages with other knowledge objects. The knowledge map (K-map) is the navigational system that enables users to navigate to find the answers they seek (Duffy, 2001). The K-map is the front end of an integrated knowledge management system and helps to create an interactive user interface.

KM uses XML technology as a standard for middleware. Knowledge management technologies have to follow open standards so that they can support a heterogeneous environment on the Internet and foster interoperability among various operating systems and software applications. These standards will promote a common platform that simplifies integration and furthers connectivity between diverse sources of information. XML (extensible markup language) is emerging as a fundamental enabling technology for content management and application integration. XML is a set of rules for defining data structures, thus making it possible for key elements in a document to be categorized according to meaning.

End-User Application Layer

The end-user application layer represents the user interface into the applications and knowledge. Because the Web is used as a medium for interface, it uses Web-based interactive tools to access knowledge from knowledge management systems. In many instances, portals similar to those used to access the Internet (e.g., Yahoo!, Lycos, Excite, or Plumtree) represent the user interface layer (Duffy, 2001). A user interface should be easy to use, interactive and valuable to the users. It should hide all the internal complexities of KM architecture and should respond to users' requests through easy-to-use features.

The end-user application layer has two components, enterprise information portal and Web-based access systems. These two components are supported by varieties of various other tools such as presentation, distribution and Web-mining tools.

Enterprise Information Portals

Enterprise information portals (EIPs) are evolving as a single source of knowledge-based systems (Silver, 2000). They integrate access to knowledge and applications. EIPs provide a single point of entry to all the disparate sources of knowledge and information both within and outside an organization, usually through the Internet or a company intranet (Ruppel & Harrington, 2001). EIPs have to be fully integrated with legacy systems of the organization. Through these EIPs, companies serve their customers, interact with business partners and suppliers, and offer employees access to online tools and the right content and knowledge for decision making. EIP functionality ranges from access to structured data used in classifying and searching unstructured data to supporting collaborative processes. EIPs are poised to integrated access to heterogeneous types of data (Morris, 2000).

Web-Based Access System

The Web has created a noble opportunity for easy access to data from any geographic location. KM supports Web-based access system having thin client architecture for end-user applications. Thin client architecture requires no software installation on the client end.

The KM Web-based access system uses many tools like Text and Web Mining Tools for Query system (Duffy, 2001). Text mining is used to automatically find, extract, filter, categorize and evaluate the desired information and resources. Text mining applies to Web content mining, which is the automatic retrieval of information and resources, filtering and categorization. End-user query and reporting tools are designed specifically to support ad hoc data access and report building by even the most novice users.

Information extraction utility pulls information from texts in heterogeneous formats — such as PDF files, e-mails, and Web pages — and converts it to a single homogeneous form. In functional terms, this converts the Web into a database that end-users can search or organize into taxonomies (Adams, 2001).

CONCLUSION

As we move into the 21st century, the need for rapid access to relevant knowledge has never been greater. The business world is becoming increasingly competitive, and the demand for innovative products and services is growing. Organizations that compete in such an intense competitive environment need to leverage their knowledge assets so that they do not lose markets, revenues and growth opportunities. The importance of KM technology and the role it will play in organizational success cannot be over emphasized. This chapter has discussed a myriad of technologies and tools for knowledge management that are at the disposal of organizations. The importance of addressing both the subjective and objective perspective of KM as well as outlining the significance of the knowledge architecture was highlighted. Necessary technology components that need to be considered by any organization as part of the sound knowledge architecture were discussed. The proposed knowledge assessment model will provide organizations with a useful framework in order for them to successfully embrace KM.

REFERENCES

Adams, K. C. (2001). The Web as a database: New extraction technologies & content management. *Online*, 25(2), 27-32.

Alavi, M. (1999). *Managing organizational knowledge.* Working Paper.

Alavi, M. & Leidner, D. E. (2001). Review: Knowledge management and knowledge management systems: Conceptual foundations and research issues. *MIS Quarterly*, 25(1), 107-136.

Boland, R. & Tenkasi, R. (1995). Perspective Making, Perspective Taking. *Organization Science*, 6, 350-372.

Brown, J. S. & Duguid, P. (2000). KM's future in the e-world. *Information World Review,* 158, 18.

Davenport, T. H. & Prusak, L. (1998). *Working Knowledge.* Harvard Business School.

Davenport, T. H., Harris, J. G. & Kohli, A. K. (2001). How do they know their customers so well? *MIT Sloan Management Review,* 42(2), 63-73.

Dean, J. (2001). Turning data into knowledge. *Government Executive,* 33(4), 76-78.

Duffy, J. (2000). The KM technology infrastructure. *Information Management Journal,* 34(2), 62-66.

Duffy, J. (2001). The tools and technologies needed for knowledge management. *Information Management Journal,* 35(1), 64-67.

Hammond, C. (2001). The intelligent enterprise. *InfoWorld,* 23(6), 45-46.

Housel, T. & Bell, A. H. (2001). *Measuring and Managing Knowledge.* Irwin: McGraw Hill.

James, L., Sr. (2000). Knowledge management: The intellectual revolution. *IIE Solutions,* 32(10), 34-37.

Kanter, J. (1999, Fall). Knowledge management practically speaking. *Information Systems Management,* 7-15.

Liebowitz, J. (2000). *Building Organizational Intelligence – A Knowledge Management Primer.* CRC Press.

Malhotra, Y. (2000). Knowledge management & new organizational forms. In E. Y. Malhotra (Ed.), *Knowledge Management and Virtual Organizations.* Hershey, PA: Idea Group Publishing.

McMillin, K. (2000). Knowledge management lessons aiding e-commerce growth. *Oil & Gas Journal,* 2-3.

Moore, K. (2000). The E-volving organization. *Ivey Business Journal,* 65(2), 25-28.

Nissen, M. E., Kamel, M. N. & Sengupta, K. C. (2000). A framework for integrating knowledge process and system design. *Information Strategy,* 16(4), 17-26.

Nonaka, I. (1994). A dynamic theory of organizational knowledge creation. *Organization Science,* 5, 14-37.

Onge, A. S. (2001). Knowledge management and warehousing. *Modern Materials Handling,* 56(3), 33.

Polyani, M. (1958). *Personal Knowledge: Towards a Post-Critical Philosophy.* Chicago, IL: The University Press Chicago.

Polyani, M. (1966). *The Tacit Dimension.* London: Routledge & Kegan.

Ruppel, C. P. & Harrington, S. J. (2001). Sharing knowledge through intranets: A study of organizational culture and intranet implementation. *IEEE Transactions on Professional Communication,* 44(1), 37-52.

Shaw, M. J., Subramaniam, C., Tan, G. W. & Welge, M. E. (2001). Knowledge management and data mining for marketing. *Decision Support Systems,* 31(1), 127-137.

Shepard, E. (2000). Transforming knowledge into professional power. *Association Management,* 52(13), 16.

Silver, C. A. (2000). Where technology and knowledge meet. *The Journal of Business Strategy,* 21(6), 28-33.

Skyrme, D. J. (1999). *Knowledge Networking — Creating the Collaborative Enterprise.* Butterworth Heinemann.

Srikantaiah, T. K. & Koenig, M. E. D. (2000). ASIS Monograph Series. *Information Today.*

Wickramasinghe, N. & Mills, G. (2001). Integrating e-commerce and knowledge management — What does the Kaiser experience really tell us. Forthcoming article in *International Journal of Accounting Information Systems.*

SECTION II:

EVOLVING ELECTRONIC MARKETS

Chapter III

Intelligent Enterprise Integration: eMarketplace Model

Hamada H. Ghenniwa
University of Western Ontario, Canada

Michael N. Huhns
University of South Carolina, USA

ABSTRACT

This chapter describes an architecture for the eMarketplace *that integrates the interests of autonomous enterprises in a single open-market environment. The environment encompasses several systems and business issues, such as the many-to-many relationships between customers and suppliers, systems, and business-related services. The architecture for this integrated environment is business-centric and knowledge-oriented. In this architecture, the* eMarketplace *exists as a collection of economically motivated software agents. The architecture enables and supports common economic services, such as brokering, pricing, and negotiation, as well as cross-enterprise integration and cooperation in an electronic supply-chain. We demonstrate the* eMarketplace *with two prototype systems.*

INTRODUCTION

It is said that there are only two types of enterprises: those that change and those that disappear. Businesses today must be fast and flexible, responsive to customers, and cost-effective in their operations. They must collaborate more frequently with partners to build virtual organizations and supply-chains that reduce time-to-market and costs. More challenges loom as companies, organizations, and other business entities try to reorient their internal capabilities to exploit electronic business (*eBusiness*) techniques. These are difficult and expensive things to do in a fast-paced world where change drives business. *eBusiness* is the use of the Internet along with other electronic means and technologies to conduct within-business, business-to-consumer, business-to-business, and business-to-government interactions.

Traditional models of *eBusiness*, such as those based on EDI (Electronic Data Interchange), ERP (Enterprise Resource Planning), and enterprise-centric views, are useful for businesses with well-defined trading relationships, but unsuitable for the rapidly growing and changing global marketplace. In these models, point-to-point interfaces are created to support transactions involving replenishment orders for direct production goods of a previously negotiated contract. For example, the sell-side model requires that either a single distributor is responsible for aggregating all the suppliers, or the customer is responsible for comparison-shopping between suppliers. This makes it inefficient and expensive for both customers and suppliers. Another example is the buy-side model, which does not enable dynamic trading and requires the buying organizations to set up and maintain catalogs of their suppliers, and hence is costly and technically demanding.

An electronic marketplace (*eMarketplace*) model appears to be the most promising forum for reshaping *eBusiness* relationships, and will soon affect all businesses in one way or another. In this work, we view *eMarketplace* as a cooperative distributed system that integrates participating business entities, including consumers, suppliers, and other intermediaries. This architecture enables and facilitates common economic services and commerce transactions between the buyers and sellers, such as brokering, pricing, and negotiation, as well as cross-enterprise integration and cooperation in an electronic supply-chain. In this architecture, the *eMarketplace* exists as a collection of economically motivated software agents. We envision that *eMarketplaces* will become viable businesses, and the revenue for these marketplaces could come from several, possibly combined, avenues, including registration fees, advertising fees, commission fees on transactions, and revenue from bid/ask spreads in high volume markets.

The *eMarketplace* will enable one-stop shopping for products by consumers, who depend on a variety of other products and services that can spread across several marketplaces. Likewise, suppliers can reach, discover, and develop new customers across various *eMarketplaces* quickly with low cost. In general, *eMarketplaces* offer businesses the chance to develop and enhance their most important relationships — those with customers and suppliers.

To develop a successful engineering foundation for an open-market *eMarketplace* that supports many-to-many relationships between different business entities, several business and design issues need to be analyzed and addressed. The rest of the chapter is organized as follows. First, it reviews some of the business models related to *eBusiness* applications with a brief analysis of the main architectural design issues for *eMarketplaces*. After that, it briefly describes an architecture for a cooperative distributed system, namely, the Business-Centric Knowledge-Oriented architecture (BCKOA) for *eMarketplace* integration. This is followed by a description of a layered BCKOA implementation for an *eMarketplace*. Then the main components of an agent-oriented BCKOA for an *eMarketplace* are presented, including a supply-chain automation system for integration and management using a group of cooperating software agents. A short description of an ongoing implementation of the proposed model for virtual enterprise *eMarketplace* is described next. Then it discusses some of the related work in both the academic and industrial communities. Finally, it summarizes the main contributions of this chapter.

eBUSINESS MODELS

Surveys of small and large companies have shown that one of the most frequently mentioned barriers to successful *eBusiness* projects is the lack of an appropriate business model. It is certainly one of the most important aspects in *eBusiness* applications. A business model, in simple words, is "an architecture for the product, services, and information flows, including a description of the various business actors and their roles; and a description of the potential benefits for the various business actors; and a description of the sources of revenues" (Timmers, 1999). In an *eBusiness* environment, a business model can be viewed in terms of four principal components (Bartelt & Lamersdorf, 2001): (1) the products and services offered by the business entity, (2) the customer relationships that the business entity creates and maintains in order to generate revenues, (3) the financial aspects of the business, such as cost and revenue structures, and (4) the infrastructure and the network of partners. Possible architectures for business models are constructed by combining interaction patterns with value-chain integration (Timmers, 1999; Dubosson, Osterwalder, & Pigneur, 2002; Bartelt & Lamersdorf, 2001) for the possible creation of marketplaces. These can be fully open, with an arbitrary number of customers and suppliers, or semi-open, with one customer and multiple suppliers or vice-versa. In principle, a large number of architectures can be conceived for *eBusiness* applications. In practice, however, only a limited number can be realized (Timmers, 1999). The following are the most widely realized models (Timmers, 1999).

A basic model of an *eBusiness* is the *eShop* model. It is based on providing a self-service storefront to a customer by displaying the company catalogs and product offers on a web site. The business objective is to lower the sales cost. A major concern in this architecture is the assumption that the customer should be responsible for comparison-shopping between products of different suppliers. While an *eShop* model is based on the selling aspect of the business, an *eProcurement* model focuses on the buying aspect of the business. A typical architecture for *eProcurement* consists of a browser-based self-service front end to the corporate purchasing system or its ERP. The supplier catalogs are presented to end-users through a single unified catalog, thereby facilitating a corporate-wide standard procurement process. In addition, *eProcurement* might support calls for tender through the Web, which might be accompanied by an electronic submission of bids. Nonetheless, an *eProcurement* model does not support dynamic trading. The business objective of this model is cost savings on purchasing operations. Recently, online auction models have received much attention for automating dynamic trading. The prime business objective is to increase efficiency, reduce waste, and minimize overall cost. Other models are based on creating value-chain businesses. One model describes service provisioning of specific functions for the value chain, such as electronic payments or logistics. New approaches are also emerging in production and stock management, where new intermediary service providers are formed to provide specialized expertise to analyze and fine-tune production. The business objective is to generate revenue based on fee or percentage.

Although each of the above models attempts to provide an *eBusiness* solution, none of them addresses the challenge of how to create and leverage services and supply operations in a way that seamlessly integrates business entities (customers, suppliers, partners, and competitors) in a dynamic trading community. A very important and promising business model is the *eMarketplace*. This model supports value-chain integration and provisioning in its structure and services. The objective is to develop an *eBusiness* solution that relieves participating business entities of much of the burden to participate effectively in the *eBusiness* domain. This model combines the advantages of the sell-side, the buy-side, and the value-chain models. The business objective of the *eMarketplace* model can be based on a combination of subscription fees, transaction fees, and service fees.

The feasibility of implementing a business model depends upon the state-of-the-art of the technology, whether for realizing individual functions, for supporting interaction patterns, or for integrating components. The rest of this chapter lays the engineering foundation for developing an architectural framework for *eBusiness,* with special attention on an *eMarketplace* model. The specification of an *eMarketplace* as a cooperative distributed system describes the architecture of an ontology-driven *eBusiness* environment that deals with several technological and business issues.

eMARKETPLACES: REQUIREMENTS ANALYSIS AND DESIGN ISSUES

To develop a successful engineering foundation for an *eMarketplace*, we need a fully realized solution that accommodates the needs of *eBusiness* participants and allows them to extend advanced services to the trading community. As an *eBusiness* grows and becomes viable in the real world, its corresponding *eMarketplaces* must expand to support a broader base of services ranging from baseline interaction and directory services to specialty services, such as dynamic trading, cooperative supply-chain integration, and management. In addition, an *eMarketplace* should enable and facilitate tightening the relationship between suppliers and customers. To this end, a fundamental aspect that an *eMarketplace* architecture supports is the many-to-many relationship between customers and suppliers. This enables both customers and suppliers to leverage economies of scale in their trading relationships and access a more liquid marketplace. This in turn allows the use of dynamic pricing models, such as auctions, which improve the economic efficiency of the market where uncertainty about prices and demand are common. To provide smooth and effective integration at the business level, an *eMarketplace* model accommodates and supports interfaces to the existing business models of the participant entities through cooperative supply-chain integration and management.

Another key factor for the foundation of an *eMarketplace* is the ability to operate in an open environment. This is driven by the fact that in many cases a customer's needs may go beyond the specialist capabilities of any single *eMarketplace*. The ability of *eMarketplaces* to interact extends the idea of liquidity and network effect without sacrificing the ability to be highly specific to the supply-chain node or target the customer groups they serve.

It is also important that the architecture of an *eMarketplace* supports the incorporation and leveraging of the participants' legacy environments with minimum overhead. The support can take place, as is described later, over a cooperative distributed system that is technology-independent and scalable in the sense of supporting a large number of users in a dynamic open environment.

In this new *eMarketplace* environment there are significant interactions between the systems deployed by the participating business units of an enterprise, their customers, and other businesses. Therefore, designing *eMarketplaces* requires embodying greater levels of business knowledge within the *eMarketplace* transactions, activities, and service definitions. Additionally, it requires a greater degree of communication, coordination, and cooperation within and among the business entities and their systems in the *eMarketplace*. In other words, the *eMarketplace* architecture represents an integrated body of people, systems, information, processes, services, and products. Several attempts in business-process re-engineering addressed structural integration by reorganizing enterprises along critical business processes, such as the supply chain and the product life cycle (Hammer & Champy, 1993; Davenport, 1993). However, in this chapter, by integrated we mean the structural, behavioral, and informational integration of the participant business entities. To enable this, we develop an architecture that supports the communication of information and knowledge, the making of decisions, and the coordination of actions. The following subsections address these aspects in more detail in order to set the foundation for the proposed architecture.

Enterprise Model and Ontologies

At the heart of our integration architecture for an *eMarketplace* is a model of the enterprise. An enterprise model is an abstract representation of the structure, activities, processes, information, resources, people, behavior, goals, rules, and constraints of the *eMarketplace*. It can be used to support effective enterprise design, analysis, and operation. From an operational perspective, the enterprise model captures what is planned, what might happen, and what has happened. Therefore, it supplies the information and knowledge necessary to support the operations of an *eMarketplace*.

The information systems of participating business entities are usually built by different people, at different times, to fulfil different business requirements. Consequently, in the absence of an architectural framework for an *eMarketplace* geared toward enterprise integration, there are widely varying viewpoints and assumptions regarding what is essentially the same subject. Therefore, communication among the components supporting a business-to-business application is not possible without at least some translation. This problem, however, is much more than a simple agreement on XML tags or mappings between roughly equivalent sets of tags in related standards. Industry-wide *eBusiness* initiatives and academic studies have shown that complex representation issues can arise. To deal with these issues, an appropriate *eMarketplace* architecture should support enterprise-modeling ontologies. An ontology is a vocabulary along with some specification of the meaning or semantics of the terminology within the vocabulary. Ontologies can vary based on the degree of formality in the specification of meaning. The objective is to provide a shared and common understanding of a domain that can be communicated to people, application systems, and businesses. In an *eMarketplace* model, ontologies are integrated or related to support reasoning among the elements of the model.

Many of the foundation concepts of an ontology have already been established in work on intelligent agents and knowledge sharing, such as the Knowledge Interchange Format (KIF) and Ontolingua languages (Genesereth & Fikes, 1992). With the wide acceptance of XML by the Web and Internet communities, XML gained tremendous potential to be the standard syntax for data interchange on the web. It is also becoming desirable to exchange ontologies using XML. This motivated the development of XML-based ontology languages, such as SHOE (Heflin, Hendler, & Luke, 1999), Ontology Exchange Language (XOL) (Karp, Chaudhri & Thomere, 1999), and the Resource Description Framework Schema (RDFS) (Lassila & Swick, 1999). Other proposals, such as OIL (Ontology Interchange Language) (Fensel, Horrocks, van Harmelen, Decker, Erdmann, & Klein, 2000) and its successors DAML+OIL (Fensel, van Harmelen, & Horrocks, 2002) and more recently OWL (Ontology Web Language), attempt to extend RDF and RDFS for ontology representations.

Other approaches, like ebXML (Eisenberg & Nickull, 2001), attempt to develop an open XML-based infrastructure specification to enable the global use of *eBusiness* information to exchange business messages, conduct trading relationships, communicate data in common terms, and define and register business processes. Simply, ebXML is an attempt to develop and to promote shared ontologies. The W3C Semantic Web (The Semantic Web Community Portal) initiative takes a similar approach. Also, there are various attempts to achieve standardized content descriptions, such as the Common Business Library (CBL) of Commerce Net, Commerce XML (cXML or Commerce eXtensible Markup Language), Dublin core, and RossettaNet.

Market Structure and Economy Model

An important aspect of the *eMarketplace* is the economic model of its structure. A market structure governs the trading process and defines the formal rules for market access, traders' interactions, price determination, and trade generations. Its behavior restricts the set of message sequences that traders may exchange and determines the trading outcome. Therefore, a market institution (McCabe, Rassenti & Smith, 1992) is the specification of the set of admissible messages (i.e., traders' actions, usually price and/or quantity offers), and the final commodity allocation given any combination of messages chosen by the participants and any initial allocation. In classical economic theory there are several market models for specific trading situations and structural behaviors. Here we review some economic models for *eMarketplace* structures, such as a commodity market, auctions, and bargaining, with an objective to realizing them. The focus on realizing different economic models is kept as generic as possible. Special emphasis will be placed on components and heuristics that an *eMarketplace* can support for the participating business entities to establish an appropriate trading approach.

In the commodity market model, various suppliers and consumers partici-pate to trade goods/services (commodity) of the same type. The market price is publicly agreed upon for each commodity independent of a particular supplier. All consumers and suppliers decide whether to buy and how much to buy or sell at each agreed-upon price. The challenge in this market structure is to deploy a pricing methodology that produces price adjustments that bring about market equilibrium (i.e., equalize supply and demand).

In an auction-based market, each participant (consumer and supplier) acts independently and contracts to buy or sell at a price agreed upon privately. An auction-based *eMarketplace* is a form of centralized facility, or clearinghouse, by which costumers and suppliers execute trades in an open and competitive bidding process. All auctions can be classified as open or closed (sealed) auctions. In open auctions, bidders can know the bid value of the others and will have an opportunity to offer competitive bids. In sealed auctions, the partici-pants' bids are not disclosed to others.

The two market structures above are not appropriate for bargaining situations where few participants try to reach an agreement that will leave them at least as well off as they could be if they reached no agreement. Most of these situations cannot be entirely determined by the market forces. In bargaining, both customers and suppliers have their own objective functions and they negotiate with each other as long as their objectives are met. The participants can engage in direct negotiations with each other using their respective bargaining strategies to arrive at a "fair" price for a particular item. This market structure does not support a specific negotiation protocol, rather the participants will use an unrestricted bidding protocol. A major challenge in this structure is how to enable any participant to determine the "fair" price.

Supply-Chain Integration and Management

An *eMarketplace* can be treated as a physically and logically distributed system of interacting autonomous business entities. Yet, there is a need for well-accepted interoperability standards, which must be meshed for supply-chain integration to meet business demands. Conceptually, a supply-chain manages coordinated information and material flows, production operations, and logistics of the *eMarketplace*. It provides the *eMarketplace* with flexibility and agility in responding to customer demand shifts without conflicts in resource utilization. The fundamental objective is to improve coordination within and between various participant business entities in the supply-chain. The increased coordination can lead to reduction in lead times and costs, alignment of interdependent decision-making processes, and improvement in the overall performance of each partici-pant in the chain, as well as the supply chain itself.

In an *eMarketplace* setting, supply-chain management can be viewed as a cooperative, distributed problem-solving activity among a society or group formed by autonomous business entities that work together to solve a common problem (Smirnov & Chandra, 2000). With their collective and collaborative efforts, they sustain the progress of each member as well as the group. The group is responsible for coordination throughout the supply chain, whereas each member provides specialized expert knowledge and product and process technology to the supply chain. The decision-making process is centralized for the group, but decentralized for the local decisions of each member. Therefore, the problem of supply-chain design in an *eMarketplace*, as discussed later, can be solved by the design of a structure and mechanism for coordination in a cooperative, distributed system.

Foundation Architecture for Integration

The architecture of the *eMarketplace* provides the foundation to integrate and leverage the participants' resources, such as applications and databases. Traditionally, the foundation technology that enables enterprises to connect resources together is known as *middleware*. Mainstream middleware solutions focus on integration at the data-level. There are several commercial middleware products and standards, such as OMG CORBA™ (Object Management Group, Inc., 1995), J2EE™ (Java™ 2 Platform, Enterprise Edition), and DCOM (Distributed Component Object Model), that focus on providing infrastructure tools and frameworks of integration. This approach provides a communication framework for the integration of data resources with minor or no support for integration at the business level. Enterprise application integration (EAI) is a trend has recently emerged in designing middleware technology with an objective to ease the burden and lower the costs of application integration. However, different EAI tools are developed to accommodate different levels of integration requirements. Object-level integration provides synchronization of data between different applications or databases. Business process-level integration extends the object-level by supporting multiple, distributed, and heterogeneous applications. Finally, cross-enterprise, process-level integration involves multiple, distributed, heterogeneous business-process applications across different enterprises cooperating in a supply-chain. There are currently very few EAI solutions specifically designed for this type of integration scenario.

While EAI tools focus on technology-centered integration, other complementary approaches focus on integration as an architectural aspect. In this direction, the focus is on the components' ability to perform their functions in a larger system context and not on their precise implementation. One approach is a mediator-based architecture (Wiederhold, 1992), which comprises a layer of "intelligent" middleware services to link data resources and applications, such as integrating data from multiple sources in a way that is effective for the client application. In addition, the mediator architecture partitions system resources and services into two dimensions, horizontal and vertical (Wiederhold &

Genesereth, 1997). The vertical partition includes specific domain services. The horizontal partition includes servers, clients, and mediator layers. Another approach is the facilitator (Genesereth, 1992), in which integration is based on the principle that any system (software or hardware) can inter-operate with any other system without the intervention of human users or their developers. This level of automation depends on supporting ontologies to describe the resources. Facilitators use meta-level information in converting, translating, or routing data and information. Along this direction, several integration tools have been developed for specific application domains. For example, TSIMMIS (Chen, Yerneni, Vassalos, Garcia-Molina, Papakonstantinou, & Ullman, 1998) focused on developing mediator-based tools to access and combine information from heterogeneous data sources. Infomaster (Genesereth, Keller, & Duschka, 1997) is an information integration system that utilizes a facilitator as integration infrastructure and dynamically determines an appropriate way to answer a user's query and harmonizes the heterogeneities among different sources. InfoSleuth (Nodine, Fowler, Ksiezyk, Perry, Taylor, & Unruh, 2000) extends Carnot (Huhns, Jacobs, Ksiezyk, Shen, Singh, & Cannata, 1993) as a mediator-based, agent-oriented infrastructure for semantic integration of information sources in open and dynamic environments. The C3DS project (Shrivastava, Bellissard, & Lacourte, 2001) focused on developing distributed object technologies to create a framework for complex service provisioning.

BUSINESS-CENTRIC KNOWLEDGE-ORIENTED ARCHITECTURE

Now, it is clear that the development of an architecture for an *eMarketplace* requires a new design paradigm, improved integration architectures, and services. The architecture must be semantically rich and describe the organization and the interconnection among the software components, business services, and business ontologies of the *eMarketplace*. These should not be viewed as alternatives to existing technologies, but rather as advanced features that are implemented at a higher level of abstraction. In this architecture, the *eMarketplace* is a cooperative, distributed system composed of economically motivated software agents that interact cooperatively or competitively, find and process information, and disseminate it to humans and to other agents. The architecture also supports common economic services and commercial transactions, such as pricing, negotiation, and automated supply chains, as well as cross-enterprise integration and cooperation. In this work, we deal with both the *fundamental* and the *practical* issues of integration.

Fundamentally, we view integration as an abstraction level at which a distributed system environment can be described as collective, coherent universe of cooperative entities. In a cooperative, distributed system, integration is captured at the foundation architecture that supports all the entities' individual architectures and, therefore, the complete computing environment. Here we describe a business-centric, knowledge-oriented architecture (BCKOA) for cooperative distributed systems. The BCKOA specifications provide the abstraction to support the domain entities and applications independent of any specific technology. The main elements of BCKOA include domain services, integration services, and domain ontology. A key to BCKOA is a service-oriented model in which the overall connectivity of the system supports a "virtual" point-to-point integration mechanism. Therefore, unlike classical tier-oriented architectures, BCKOA supports an abstraction for an *ad hoc* layered architecture without an explicit distinction between application layers, as depicted in Figure 1.

To support heterogeneity and technology-independent properties at the system level, the boundaries between the layers correspond to standardized interfaces (e.g., OMG CORBA). However, industrial standards for interfaces do not support or supply common underlying semantics. To deal with this issue, BCKOA includes a domain ontology. The domain ontology captures and implements the conceptualization of an application domain at the knowledge level. BCKOA provides three families of integration services:

1.   Ontology and semantic integration services support the semantic manipulations needed when integrating and transforming information or knowledge to satisfy a BCKOA task, as well as the capabilities required to reuse components.

2.   Coordination and cooperation services support ad hoc and automated BCKOA configurations. This includes locating and discovering domain and/or BCKOA services that are potentially relevant to a domain or BCKOA service.

3.   Wrapping services make different applications, components, objects, or modules comply with internal or external standards. Such standards may involve the interface to the software system or its behavior.

Figure 1: BCKOA as a Service-Oriented Architecture

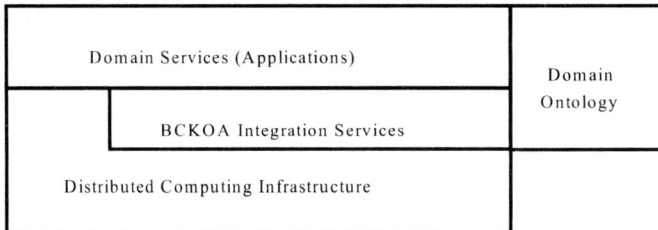

The specifications of BCKOA services are independent of any component framework, but their implementation can be based on the services provided by the target framework, as is described below.

A key challenge in putting BCKOA into a practical context is the transformation or the mapping of its abstract description to the specification of the target component framework. In fact, most distributed computing environments, especially those supporting cross-enterprise integration like *eMarketplaces*, will likely include several different component technologies, such as CORBA, J2EE, and COM+. To deal with this issue, BCKOA requires that the business object implementations, regardless of their component technology, be obligated to conform to the domain ontology. The business object specification itself in the domain ontology becomes the reusable component that can be configured and assembled into multiple solutions (business objects), independent of technology implementation. Therefore, the domain ontology in BCKOA governs the structural and the behavioral semantics of the business objects in a way that is consistent across all implementations, and is accessible from any implementation. The BCKOA framework, shown in Figure 2, provides an integrated execution environment for integrated business object implementations. Mapping a BCKOA description to an implementation framework is driven by three specifications: domain ontology description, maps, and a profile. Technology mapping specifications include a map to specify a transformation from the BCKOA domain ontology and services to the implementation components and

Figure 2: BCKOA Framework

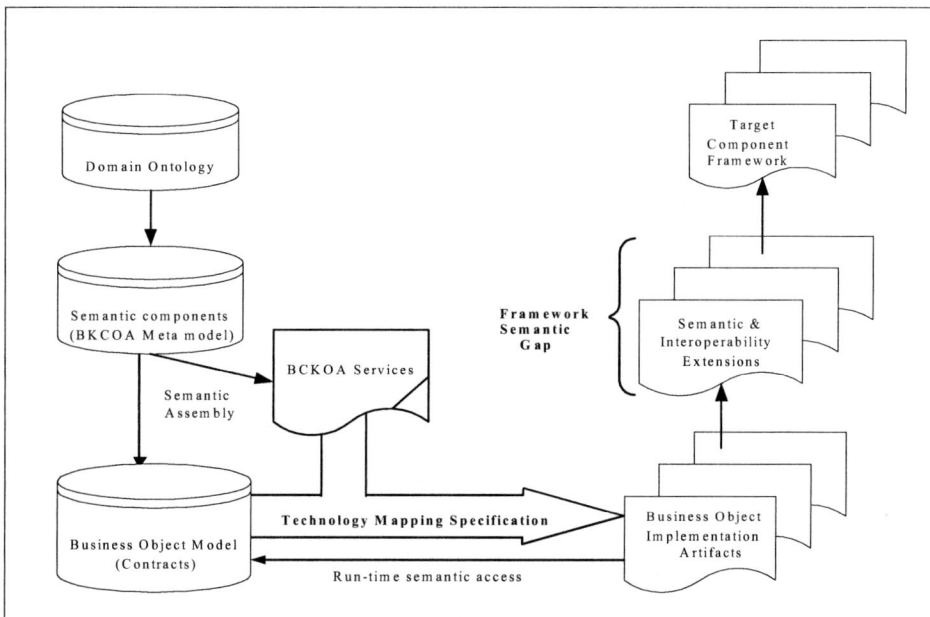

service extensions for the target component framework. The mapping of each business concept representation to its implementation is managed by a *profile*, which is a set of properties that defines the environment for a mapping. This mechanism enables an automated transformation from a relatively stable domain ontology and service description to different component technologies.

BCKOA-BASED eMARKETPLACE

This section describes the use of BCKOA for achieving business integration in an *eMarketplace* with a specific focus on demonstrating its feasibility as a design paradigm for a cooperative, distributed system that is independent of any specific technology. Based on the assumption that an *eMarketplace* is a coherent, service-oriented universe, the BCKOA-based *eMarketplace* is shown in Figure 3(b), which builds upon the abstraction architecture of the *eMarketplace* in Figure 3(a) (Ghenniwa, 2001).

The lower layer of the *eMarketplace* architecture in Figure 3(a) is the infrastructure that might represent one or more physical network-based environments in which *eBusiness* systems can exist. The BCKOA representation, in Figure 3(b), supports the *eMarketplace* infrastructure using two layers: the

Figure 3: Use of BCKOA for the Architecture of an eMarketplace

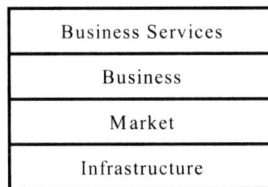

(a) Abstraction layers for *eMarketplace*

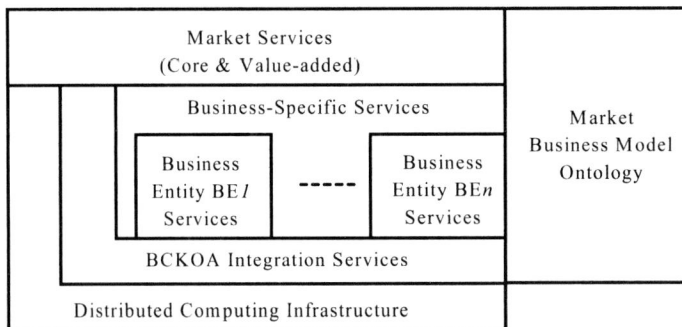

(b) BCKOA-based *eMarketplace*

distributed-computing layer and the integration-services layer. The assumption is that this infrastructure might support various markets for providing or obtaining specific goods and services. Yet, each *eMarketplace* may be independent and may support its own rules, procedures, and protocols as described by the market layer.

The market layer may support several business domains as described in the business layer. BCKOA, in Figure 3(b), provides the integration between the business context of the market, which is described by the market business ontology, and the services provided by the participant entities in the business layer. Note that a business entity may participate in multiple *eMarketplace*s. A bank, for example, could participate in several markets, such as an investment management market, mutual fund management market, and financial advisory market. In this setting, any activities or functions within a specific business entity could participate in an *eMarketplace* dedicated to satisfying its needs as described by the business ontologies of the market.

In BCKOA, the business-service layer is supported by three types of services, depicted in Figure 3(b): (1) business-specific services, (2) business-entity services, which represent the implementation of the business services by the specific business entities, and (3) market services, which are categorized further into core, such as dynamic trading and supply-chain services, and value-added, such as procurement process services. Here we focus on the core services. Ideally, the market services of the *eMarketplace* should be able to offer a wide variety of coordinating and trade mechanisms to fit with multiple business models. Because of the shortcomings of each type of market structure, there is no "one-size-fits-all" structure. Based on the success of applying economic theories in the real world as a sustainable model for exchanging and regulating resources, goods and services, we propose to apply a flexible computational economy framework for the market services layer. Therefore, a BCKOA-based *eMarketplace* incorporates mechanisms for different types of market structures, which are viewed as a set of sessions, as shown in Figure 4, such as commodity and auction markets.

Various suppliers and consumers can register in the commodity market session. Given a system of prices, each participant decides upon a course of action, which may consist of the sale of some commodities and the purchase of others. Thus supply and demand functions for each commodity can be defined as the aggregate behavior of all the participants as described in the following section. These are determined by the set of market prices for the various commodities. Equilibrium for the economy is established when supply is equal to demand (i.e., the excess demand function has a zero value). Practically, it will be sufficient to find approximate equilibrium in the sense of finding a price that makes the values of the excess demands close to zero. One approach is the tâtonnement ("groping") process (Walras, 1874). With tâtonnement, each

Figure 4: BCKOA Market Sessions

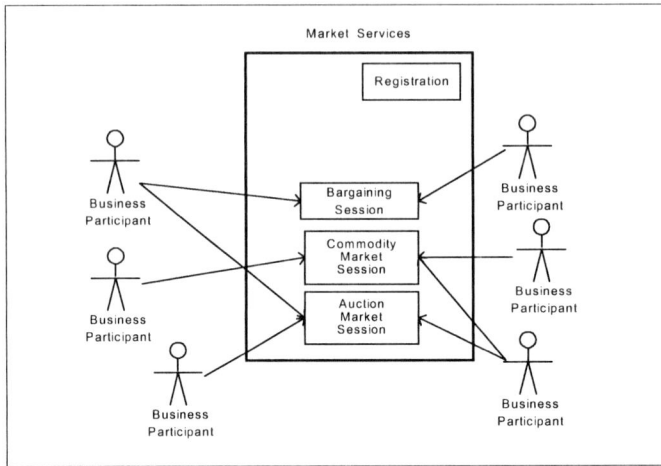

individual price is raised or lowered according to whether that commodity's excess demand is positive or negative. Then, new excess demands are measured, and the process is iterated. The tâtonnement process does bring about convergence to an equilibrium price under the hypothesis of "gross substitutes," i.e., increasing the price of a commodity (say C_j) while holding the others constant will bring about an increase in excess demand in all commodities other than the C_j. In fact, this approach is naturally appealing for automation and direct implementation (Wellman, 1993).

In the auction-based market session, each participant (consumer and supplier) acts independently and contracts to buy or sell at a price agreed upon privately. Here we focus on private-value auctions, such as the Vickrey mechanism (Vickery, 1961), because it provides a market mechanism that is simpler, but more efficient and more stable than open auction mechanisms and classical sealed bid auctions (Varian, 1995). Furthermore, it promotes truthful bidding (or revealing reservation prices as the dominant strategy) among self-interested agents and thus avoids the need for counter speculation. Hence, it combines several advantages. It does not require iterative negotiation strategies, dynamic strategic behavior, or a high degree of security, since truth telling is the dominant strategy and the agents do not need to hide their reservation prices. While it is a simple yet powerful mechanism, the Vickrey mechanism may not be appropriate in all domains. For example, truthful bidding is not necessarily the dominant strategy for domains where an agent's marginal costs (and thus its reservation price) are determined by other agents' valuations, such as the case with *public-value auctions* in the stock market (Sandholm & Lesser, 1995).

In a BCKOA *eMarketplace*, supply-chain integration and management is treated as a coordination methodology that manages information and material flows, production operations, and logistics. The objective is to provide an automated coordination mechanism for the participants in a supply chain. The adopted development framework makes use of the coordination methodologies reported in Van Dyke and Parunak (1996) and Singh (2000). In this work, we particularly extended Singh's application to supply-chain management and B2B interactions (Ivezic, Barbacci, Libes, Potok, & Robert 2000). The methodologies, as described later, promote the interchange of standard business documents and compensate for exceptions that might occur during execution. This methodology requires that the participant business entities in a cooperative supply chain only describe their supply processes using Open Applications Group (OAG) standard business documents and UML interaction diagrams. These are converted automatically into roles and specifications for software agents. These sets of agents then cooperate in automating the resultant supply chain.

A combination of the market services and the business-entity services can be used to generate different business models of an *eMarketplace* as desired by the participating business entities. This structure enables a business entity to integrate and describe the types of business services offered and the information needed to use a particular service offering within the *eMarketplace*. The details of each service type and the required information might vary among business entities, although the definition of the service type is based on some common conventions described for an *eMarketplace*.

BCKOA recognizes the integration services as separate functionalities. Yet, they can be ubiquitously integrated in an *ad hoc* structure to fulfill a complex business service or a market structure. The interaction mechanisms supported by the integration layer describe both the pattern and protocol of exchanging messages between the services.

AGENT-ORIENTED BCKOA FRAMEWORK FOR eMARKETPLACE

All services (business, market, and integration) in a BCKOA-based *eMarketplace* usually involve complex and nondeterministic interactions, often producing results that are ambiguous and incomplete. Auctions and *ad hoc* service integrations are some examples. In addition, the dynamic nature of the environment requires that the components of the system be able to change their configuration to participate in different, often simultaneous roles in *eMarketplaces*. These requirements could not be accomplished using traditional ways of manually configuring software. For this domain, we strongly believe that agent-orientation is a very promising design paradigm for integration. In fact, such a paradigm is essential to model an open environment such as an *eMarketplace*, especially considering the multiple dynamic and simultaneous roles a single business entity may need to participate in given *eMarketplace* sessions (a financial services organization may have representatives acting on its behalf simultaneously within the context of brokering, service provisioning, and marketing).

Software agent technology provides the next step in the evolution of computational modeling, programming methodologies, and software engineering paradigms. The first principle of agenthood is that an agent should be able to operate as a part of a community of cooperative, distributed systems environment, including human users. In our view, an agent can be described as an individual collection of primitive components that provide a focused and cohesive set of capabilities. Figure 5 depicts the Coordinated Intelligent and Rational, Agent (CIR-Agent) model (Ghenniwa & Kamel, 2000). The basic components include a problem solver, interactions, and communication, as shown in Figure 5(b). A particular arrangement or interconnection of the agent's components is required to constitute an agent, as shown in Figure 5(a). This arrangement reflects the pattern of an agent's mental state as related to its reasoning to achieve a goal. However, no specific assumption is made on the detailed design of the agent components. Therefore, the internal structure of the components can be designed and implemented using object-oriented or any other technology, provided that a developer conceptualizes the specified architecture of the agent as described in Figure 5(b).

A CIR-Agent model provides software engineers with features at a higher level of abstraction that are useful for cooperative environments. It supports flexibility at different levels of the design: system architecture, agent architecture, and agent component architecture. These degrees of flexibility allow information systems to adapt to changes with minimum requirements for redesign. Based on this view, an agent within the context of a BCKOA-based *eMarketplace* might play roles as described by the functionality of its problem-solving component and be able to coordinate, cooperatively or competitively, with the other agents, including humans. Therefore, an agent's role can be categorized as user-interface, business-specific service, business-entity service, market service, or integration service.

User interface agents play an important and interesting role in many applications. The main functionality of user interface agents is to support and collaborate with users in the same work environment to achieve the users' goals.

Business-specific service agents are specialists that provide a collection of business services available in the *eMarketplace*. Performing the functionality of a business service is typically the cooperative integration of several agents, including business-entity agents and market service agents. A business-entity service agent may be a representative in the *eMarketplace* for some function-

Figure 5: The CIR-Agent Architecture

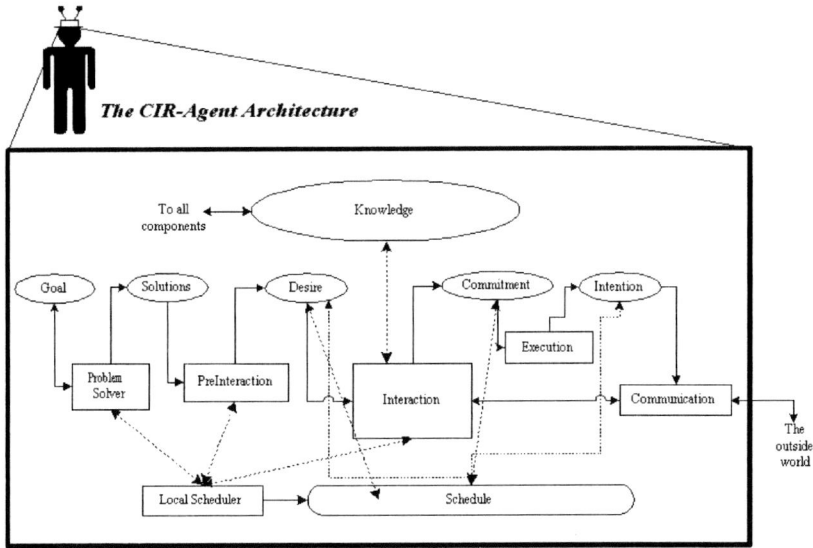

(a) Detailed Architecture of CIR-Agent

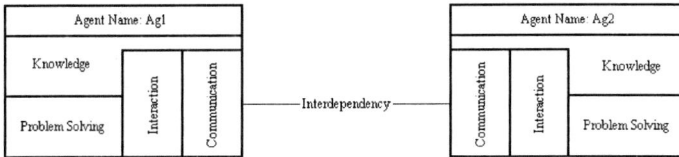

(b) Logical Architecture of CIR-Agent

ality that is based on legacy applications or libraries, such as a product catalogue web site.

Market service agents are specialists that provide a collection of functions for the generic *eBusiness* in the *eMarketplace* environment in which a single entity (usually an agent) can perform its tasks in the *eMarketplace*. Market services, both value-added and core services, are horizontal, i.e., services that are used in several business domains by several business entities. Here the focus is on core services, particularly dynamic trading services, commodity market and Vickery auctions, and supply-chain integration and management.

The commodity market service governs the trading behavior of the participant business entities in the session as described in Figure 6. This service recognizes three types of agents, namely, market-mediators, consumers, and suppliers. Consumers and suppliers are roles assigned to agents or types of a business-entity service or user interface. These roles will be assigned upon registration with the market session. Each market session is assigned to a mediator to coordinate the actions taken by consumers and suppliers in a way that will eventually clear its respective market. There is a one-to-one correspondence between market mediators and commodities. Initially, a mediator agent is assigned to a specific commodity market and broadcasts a randomly chosen initial price vector to all registered participants in its market. Then, each participant computes the demand function for each of its commodities of interest. Each demand function specifies the net quantity demanded of a commodity (which for a net supply is negative) as a function of its price, assuming that the prices for the remaining commodities are constant. The participants then send these demand functions — the *bids* — to the respective mediator for each commodity. Each mediator, upon receiving the bids from all participants, computes the clearing price, for which the aggregate excess demand is zero. The mediator then notifies the participants of the new price. Upon seeing new prices, the consumers and suppliers compute revised demand functions as necessary based on these new prices, and send these updated bids to the mediator. This process continues until the pricing changes are within a specified threshold. Then the process terminates and the mediator reports the final state of the price vector as the equilibrium.

The **auction market session** also recognizes three types of agents representing suppliers, auctioneer, and buyers. However, the trading process mainly involves the auctioneer and buyers (or bidders). Each bidder agent declares its valuation function to the auctioneer. Under the general Vickery mechanism, it is in the interest (the dominant strategy) of the bidder to report its true valuation function. Then, the auctioneer agent:

- Calculates the allocation (x^*_i) that maximizes the sum of the bids subject to the items constraint.
- Calculates the allocation (x^*_{-i}) that maximizes the sum of the bids other than that of bidder agent i such that it excludes all items allocated to agent i.
- Announces the winners and their payment given by $p_i = \sum_{j \neq i} v_j(x^*_{-i}) - \sum_{j \neq i} v_j(x^*)$.

Under the assumption of quasi-linear preferences, each bidder agent calculates its utility. For bidder agent i the utility will be $u_i(x^*) = v_i(x^*) - p_i = v_i(x^*) - \sum_{j \neq i} v_j(x^*_{-i}) - \sum_{j \neq i} v_j(x^*)$.

Agent-based, supply-chain integration and management in an *eMarketplace* is a cooperative, distributed problem-solving activity. Here we briefly describe the methodology and an agent-based system for supply-chain integration. Our methodology is supported by a development environment that automatically generates specifications for the agents in the supply chain. Business participants need only describe their supply processes using OAG standard business documents and UML interaction diagrams. The methodology

Figure 6: Tâtonnement Model of the Commodity Market

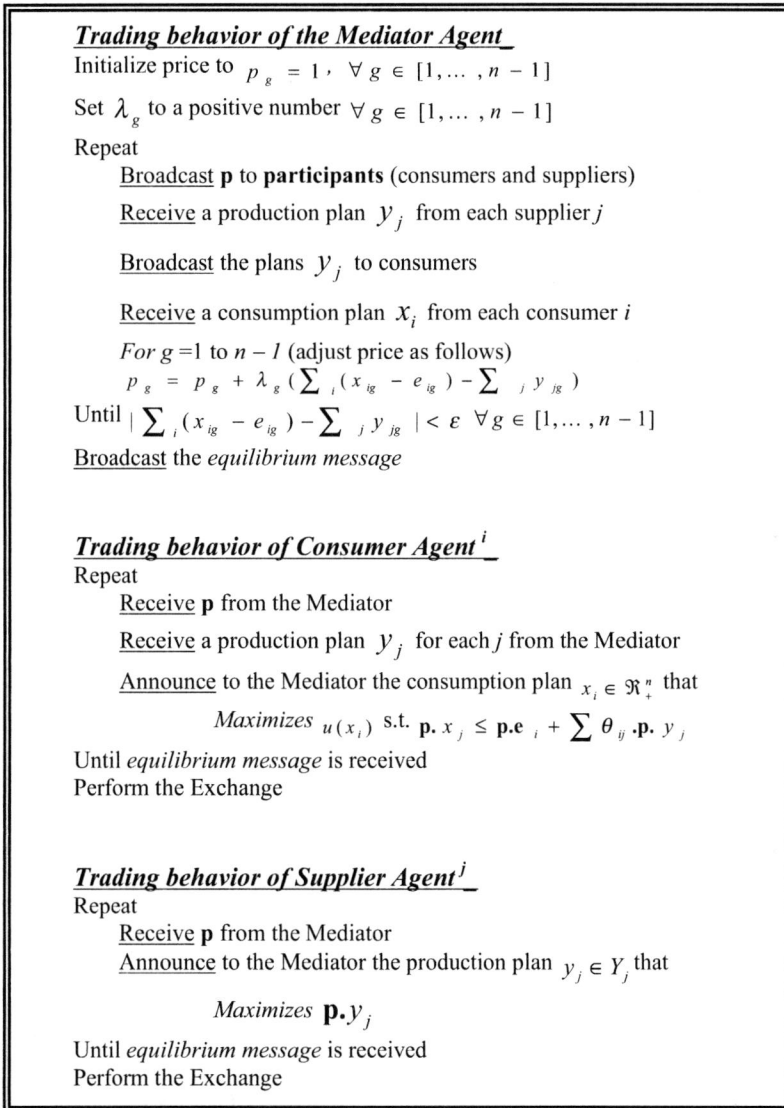

Trading behavior of the Mediator Agent

Initialize price to $p_g = 1$, $\forall g \in [1, \ldots, n-1]$

Set λ_g to a positive number $\forall g \in [1, \ldots, n-1]$

Repeat

    <u>Broadcast</u> **p** to **participants** (consumers and suppliers)

    <u>Receive</u> a production plan y_j from each supplier j

    <u>Broadcast</u> the plans y_j to consumers

    <u>Receive</u> a consumption plan x_i from each consumer i

    For g =1 to n – 1 (adjust price as follows)

$$p_g = p_g + \lambda_g \left(\sum_i (x_{ig} - e_{ig}) - \sum_j y_{jg} \right)$$

Until $\left| \sum_i (x_{ig} - e_{ig}) - \sum_j y_{jg} \right| < \varepsilon \ \forall g \in [1, \ldots, n-1]$

<u>Broadcast</u> the *equilibrium message*

Trading behavior of Consumer Agent ^{i}

Repeat

    <u>Receive</u> **p** from the Mediator

    <u>Receive</u> a production plan y_j for each j from the Mediator

    <u>Announce</u> to the Mediator the consumption plan $x_i \in \Re_+^n$ that

        Maximizes $u(x_i)$ s.t. $\mathbf{p}.x_i \leq \mathbf{p}.e_i + \sum \theta_{ij} .\mathbf{p}. y_j$

Until *equilibrium message* is received

Perform the Exchange

Trading behavior of Supplier Agent ^{j}

Repeat

    <u>Receive</u> **p** from the Mediator

    <u>Announce</u> to the Mediator the production plan $y_j \in Y_j$ that

        Maximizes $\mathbf{p}.y_j$

Until *equilibrium message* is received

Perform the Exchange

---

begins with capturing a supply-chain scenario and its associated UML interaction diagrams, exemplified in Figure 7. The interactions, in Figure 7, consist of the exchange of structured documents, such as the OAG business object documents (BODs).

For B2B interactions, a ProcessPO BOD is a *directive* that carries the composite semantics of *request* and *inform,* in which the sender requests that the recipient evaluate a purchase order and inform the sender of the results. The

Figure 7: Interaction Diagram for the OAG Scenario Involving Ford and Its Suppliers

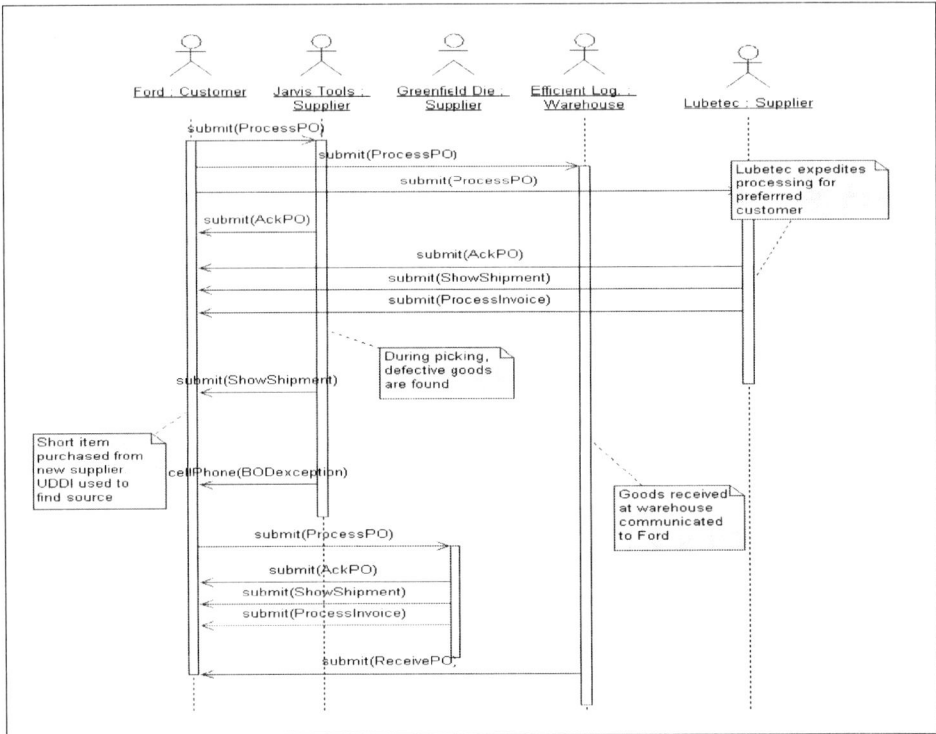

informal semantics is that ProcessPO will be followed by a response from the recipient and that the response will be either an AckPO or a DeclinePO. Using the semantics of each document, the messages in the interaction diagram are converted into a bi-partite conversation graph (not shown here), which delineates each participant's conversations. A bi-partite conversation graph is used to identify the roles of the participants in B2B transactions. This graph is the basis for constructing Dooley graphs, shown in Figure 8, as collaboration diagrams. Note that collaboration participants can fill different roles at different times, and thus can be involved in many conversations simultaneously. Each of the roles identified in the collaboration diagram can be assigned to an agent in the supply chain. Moreover, the diagram for each role is converted directly into a state-machine description for the agent's behavior, enabling automatic agent generation. Agents are then allocated for the corresponding role and business entity, and then collectively they manage the supply-chain process. Figure 9 shows several of the state-machine behavioral descriptions.

The methodology, summarized in Figure 10, uses — and begins to formalize — the BODs that OAG and RosettaNet are standardizing. It provides a basis for

Figure 8: Collaboration Diagram with Participant Roles for Ford Interoperability Scenario

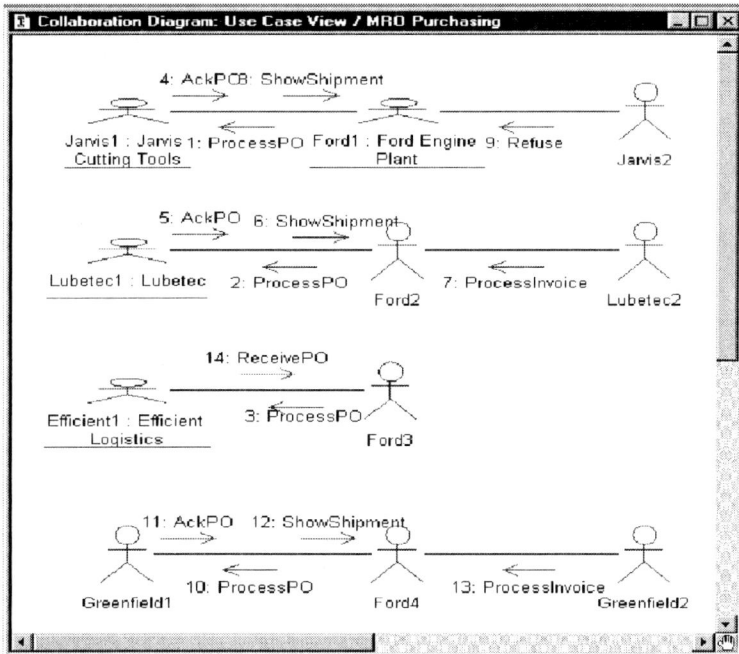

the convergence of multiple standards for supply-chain management, which could become ready-to-use technology for different participant business entities in the *eMarketplace*.

Integration agents are specialists that provide a collection of integration functions for a cooperative distributed system in which a single entity (agent, component, object, etc.) can perform its tasks. Integration services are used by several distributed entities. For example, a brokering agent provides a capability-based integration service in the *eMarketplace*. The brokering agent allows agents (for integration, market, or business services) to describe the properties of a requested service. Then, on behalf of the requester, it establishes interactions with service providers to fulfill the requests. The brokering agent is responsible for identifying and interacting with other integration services, such as resource discovery services and ontology manager services to accomplish its tasks. Another type of integration agent provides view integration, which is a service to merge and map the description of business objects (e.g., source schemas) in the *eMarketplace* supported by the business ontology into an integrated view or schema. For instance, a catalogue service might require information provided by several business entities supporting different product schema. A view-integration service provides the integration into a common

Figure 9: State-Machine Diagrams for Enacting Agents that Implement Supply-Chain Processes

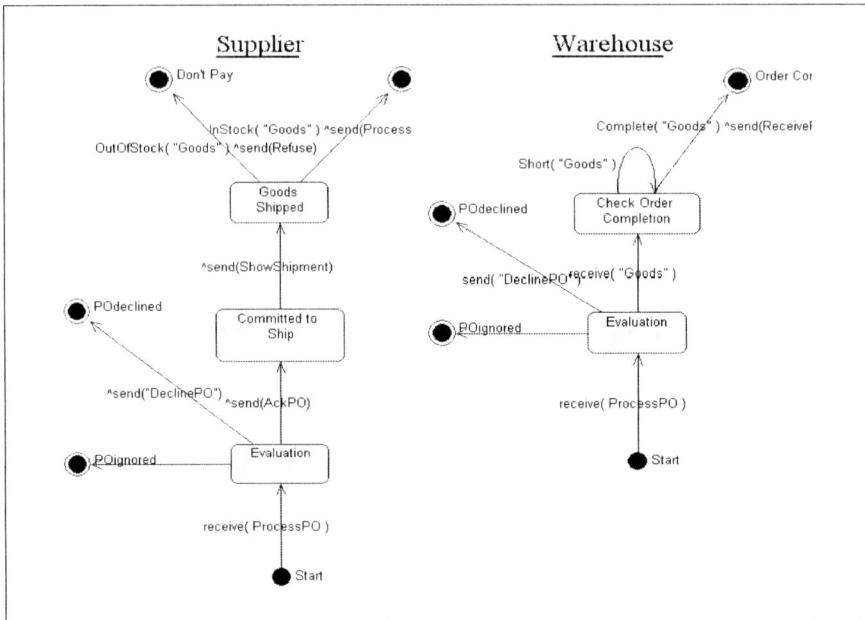

definition language (e.g., XML-based), which is in turn mapped into a target representation language by a specialized language mapping service. View integration is responsible for identifying and interacting with several services to fulfill its functionality, including brokering, source-schema, ontology, and language-mapping services.

PROTOTYPE IMPLEMENTATION OF BCKOA

To validate and experiment with our theoretical analysis and foundations described in the previous sections, we have developed a prototype of an agent-oriented BCKOA for an *eMarketplace,* as shown in Figure 11. *ABC* Corp and *XYZ,* Inc. are virtual business entities registered with the *eMarketplace* for both purchasing and sales services. Both organizations use a BCKOA-based computation environment. As illustrated in Figure 11, individual customers or business-entity personnel in the *eMarketplace* can participate in the market through their user interface agent. Similarly, each business-entity service is represented by an agent in the *eMarketplace.* These agents provide thin, intelligent, highly autonomous interfaces for the business-entity services that might be based on

Figure 10: Agent-Based Coordination Methodology for B2B Automation

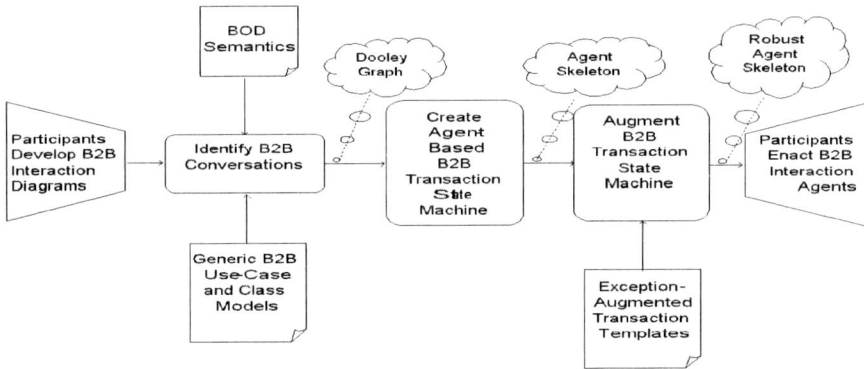

legacy applications. For example, in Figure 11, the ABC purchasing-service agent represents the implementation of the business-specific purchases by ABC in the *eMarketplace*. Each user interface and business-entity service agent is registered in the *eMarketplace*. Thus, a user interface agent can benefit from the market, business-specific, and business-entity services by interacting with their representative agents. Each business-entity service must also be registered with a registry agent for the corresponding business-specific service. Each layer, and its registry services, are intended to provide some aspect of information

Figure 11: Prototype of BCKOA-Based eMarketplace Using JADE

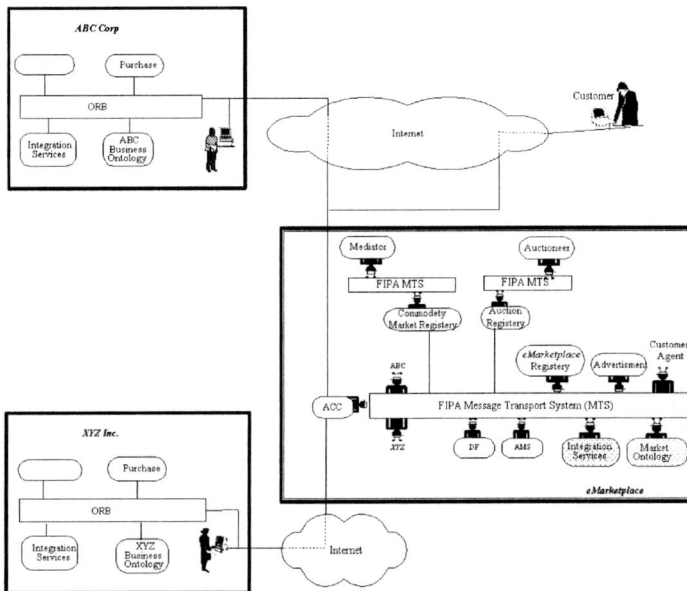

Figure 12: Logical Design of (a) Commodity Market and (b) Auction Market Sessions

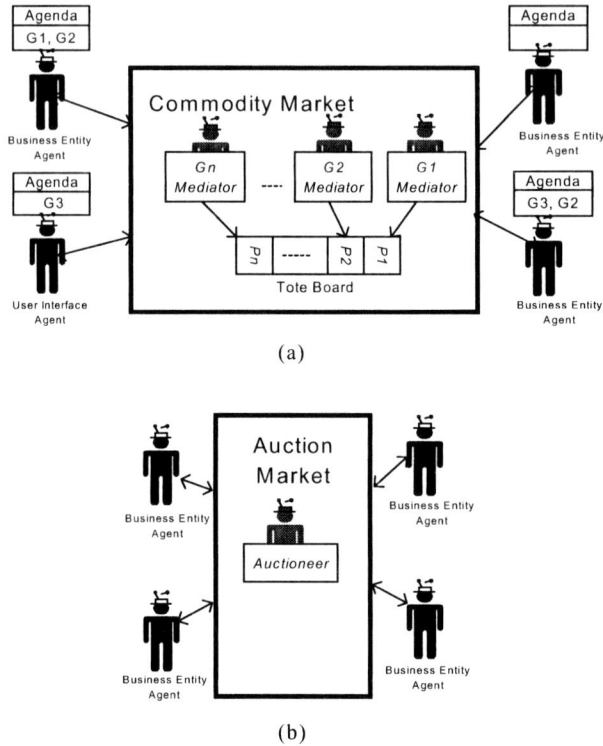

(a)

(b)

about the *eBusiness* environment and enable an interested party to obtain information to potentially use offered services, or to join the *eMarketplace* and either provide new services or inter-operate as a trading partner with other business entities in that *eMarketplace.*

In the current prototype, we experiment with commodity and auction market structures, as shown in Figure 12, where customers and suppliers are brought together to trade with each other and prices are set by the selected market structure. The trading behavior of the participant agents is governed by the selected market structure as described previously. An individual customer is able to participate in the market through a dedicated user interface agent possibly assigned by the *eMarketplace.* Similarly, each participating business entity is assigned to a team of CIR-Agents for the registered services and representative personnel who might have a direct contact with the market, as well as with the customers. The market ontology provides a conceptualization of the domain at the knowledge level.

The implementation utilizes the JADE platform (Bellifemine et al., 1999), which is a software framework to develop agent applications in compliance with the FIPA specifications (Foundation for Intelligent Physical Agents, 1998) for multi-agent systems. It deals with all aspects external to agents that are independent of their applications, such as message transport, encoding and parsing, and agent lifecycle. JADE supports a distributed environment of agent containers, which provide a run-time environment optimized to allow several agents to execute concurrently. This feature has been utilized to create several concurrent market sessions, such as commodity and auction sessions. A complete agent platform may be composed of several agent containers. Communication in JADE, whether internal to the platform or externally between platforms, is performed transparently to agents. Internal communication is realized using Java Remote Method Invocation to facilitate communication across the *eMarketplace* and its market sessions. External non-Java-based communication between an *eMarketplace* and its participating organizations is realized through the Internet InterOrb Interoperability Protocol mechanism or http. JADE provides support for standard FIPA ontologies and user-defined ontologies. Although our implementation takes advantage of the JADE platform and its supporting agents, such as a nameserver and a directory facilitator, the architecture of the application agent is based on the CIR-Agent model (shown in Figure 5). Java features, such as portability, dynamic loading, multi-threading, and synchronization support make it appropriate to implement the inherent complexity and concurrency in an *eMarketplace*. These features were also instrumental for executing the CIR-Agents in parallel. The design of each agent is described in terms of its knowledge and capabilities. The agent's knowledge includes the agent's self-model, goals, and local history of the world, as well as a model of its acquaintances. The agent's knowledge also includes its desires, commitments, and intentions as related to its goals.

The main capabilities of the CIR-Agent include communication, reasoning, and domain actions. Implementation of the communication component takes advantage of JADE messaging capabilities. It is equipped with an incoming message inbox, whereby message polling can be both blocking and non-blocking, and with an optional time-out mechanism. Messages between agents are based on the FIPA ACL. The agent's reasoning capabilities include problem-solving and interaction devices. The problem solving of an agent is implemented through the use of complex behaviors. Behaviors can be considered as logical execution threads that can be suspended and spawned. The agent keeps a task list, containing active behaviors. The problem-solving component varies from one agent to another. The agent behaviors can be classified as follows: behaviors that are concerned with market services, such as a market-registry service, advertisement service, mediator and auction service, and behaviors that are concerned with providing business-specific services, such as selling and purchasing.

RELATED WORK AND DISCUSSION

There have been several recent attempts to promote *eMarketplace* models by the academic and industrial communities. For example, the electronic marketplace (EMP) (Boll, Gruner, Haaf, & Klas, 1999) is an attempt to develop a business-to-business system architecture. It is viewed as a DBMS solution to support many-to-many relationships between customers and suppliers. The Global Electronic Market (GEM) system (Rachlevsky-Reich, 1999; Ben-Shaul et al., 1999) attempted to develop a logical market framework and infrastructure. A main objective was to separate system-related and market-related design issues. In GEM, the market provides trading mechanisms that include bids and offers. A more complex architecture for *eMarketplace* is MAGMA (Tsvetovatyy, Gini, Mobasher, & Wieckowski, 1997), with its special focus on the infrastructure required for conducting commerce on the Internet. In MAGMA, the *eMarketplace* has been viewed in terms of three main functionalities, namely, traders, advertising, and banking. Alternatively, OFFER (Bichler, Beam, & Segev, 1998) proposed a brokering-based architecture marketplace. In OFFER the *eMarketplace* was viewed as a collection of suppliers, customers, and brokers. A customer can search for a service either directly in the e-catalogue of the supplier or use the e-broker to search all the e-catalogues of the suppliers that are registered with this broker. E-brokers employ a simple auction mechanism. In a different approach, MOPPET (Arpinar, Dogac, & Tatbul, 2000) proposed an *eMarketplace* system as agent-oriented workflows. MOPPET viewed the market as a workflow management system carried out by several types of agents: task, scheduling, facilitator, and recovery agents.

Another approach was driven by the bottom-up modeling of market processes with self-organizing capabilities (Arthur, Holland, LeBaron, Palmer, & Tayler, 1997). The objective was to develop a computational study of economies modeled as evolving systems of autonomous interacting agents, and known as agent-based computational economics (ACE) (LeBaron, 2000; Timmers, 1999). The ACE researchers relied on computational laboratories (McFadzean, Stewart, & Tesfatsion, 2001) to study the evolution of decentralized market economies under controlled experimental conditions. The goal was to develop analysis tools that enable an economist to test economic theories developed using standard modeling approaches.

Several companies have emerged to automate logistics and resupply within specific industrial segments. For example, Ariba (2000) developed a marketplace based on procurement portals and dynamic exchanges for horizontal marketplaces. Ariba Dynamic Trade, for instance, attempts to provide dynamic trade mechanisms, such as auctions, reverse auctions, and bid/ask exchanges and negotiations. SAP Service Marketplace (SAP Services Marketplace, SAP AG) is an Internet portal for the SAP community. It provides basic online services such as catalogue browsing, matchmaking, and ordering from SAP and its partners. Other approaches were directed to support vertical marketplaces, such as PaperExchange (Paperexchange Marketplace), that enables customers and suppliers to negotiate pricing and transact directly with one another. PaperExchange also attempts to provide several supporting services, such as logistics and clearing services, industry-specific job listings, industry events, news headlines, and a resource directory. VerticalNet (VerticalNet® Marketplaces) also built a set of Web-based marketplaces for specific industrial segments, such as financial services, healthcare, and energy. Each web site forms a community of vendors and customers in a specific area. Vertical trade communities are introduced in segments with a substantial number of customers and suppliers, fragmentation on both the supply and demand sides, and significant online access.

Another direction adopted by many major software vendors is to develop Internet-based commerce platforms. Examples are IBM CommercePOINT (IBM Corporation, CommercePOINT Payment.), Microsoft Site Server Commerce Edition (Microsoft Corporation, Internet Commerce 1998), Oracle Internet Commerce Server INTERSHOP (Intershop Communications, Inc., 1998), and Sun JavaSoft JECF (Java Electronic Commerce Framework, Sun Microsystems). These proprietary attempts focus on providing infrastructure services such as security payment directories and catalogues to be integrated with existing systems and the Web.

The proposed agent-oriented BCKOA *eMarketplace*, however, provides a framework of enterprise integration that deals with several systems and business issues. Unlike the above-mentioned attempts, it is fundamentally based on business integration rather than systems integration. The objective is to develop an architecture that is semantically rich in describing an organization and the interconnection among all elements of the *eMarketplace*, including people, business services, software components, and business ontologies. Technologically, BCKOA is service-oriented in the sense that it enables business entities and their supporting systems to join the market at the highest abstraction level (service level) with minimum overhead and independent of specific technology. Utilizing BCKOA, the business object implementations of the participating services can be integrated in the execution environment. In addition, BCKOA provides an appropriate architecture for an *eMarketplace*. The form of the architecture supports *eMarketplace* functions that are inherited from real-world marketplaces. They are complex and non-deterministic, yet they characterize a real business environment. A BCKOA *eMarketplace* provides an integration environment for the broad-based services that are required for interaction and directory services, dynamic trading, cooperative supply-chain integration and management. Therefore, we believe that the BCKOA-based *eMarketplace* is appropriate for integrating horizontal business services, vertical business services, specific business functionalities, and the leveraging of legacy systems in a way that supports end-to-end integration. Furthermore, a BCKOA *eMarketplace* provides a wide variety of coordinating and trade mechanisms to fit multiple business models. In our research we have applied a flexible computational economy model for the market-services layer. Therefore, a BCKOA-based *eMarketplace* incorporates mechanisms for different types of market structures.

We believe that agent orientation is an adequate paradigm for producing the information architecture of next-generation *eBusiness* systems, especially *eMarketplaces*. Agent technology richly enables and supports the automation of complex tasks and yields systems that are reliable and able to assume the responsibilities of the *eMarketplace* in which they compete. The components of agent-based BCKOA, namely, *eMarketplaces*, business entities (products, suppliers, customers, etc.), and the foundation (integration) architecture and services that glue them together, are essential to building robust many-to-many value chains in emerging *eBusiness*.

CONCLUSION AND FUTURE WORK

This chapter presented ongoing research on developing an agent-oriented architecture for an *eMarketplace* that provides intelligent enterprise integration. The objective has been to develop a successful engineering foundation for the *eMarketplace*. To this end, several business and design issues have been identified for an *eMarketplace,* most importantly: to capture and enable many-to-many relationships between customers and suppliers, to provide services ranging from baseline interaction and directory services to specialty business-related services, and to integrate business organizations in an open market environment.

This chapter has described the agent-based Business-Centric Knowledge-Oriented Architecture (BCKOA) based on an abstraction-layered architecture for an *eMarketplace*. BCKOA is a service-oriented architecture for cooperative, distributed systems. BCKOA provides an abstraction of domain entities and applications independent of any specific technology. In putting the proposed solution into practical use, we described a methodology to map a BCKOA abstract description into the specification of target components.

A CIR-Agent model is used as the underpinning technology for the BCKOA based *eMarketplace* in which several types of agent roles were identified, namely, user-interface, business-specific service, market services, and integration services. A prototype of BCKOA using the FIPA-compliant platform, JADE is currently being developed for mutual fund management with redemption and purchasing functionalities.

The current focus is on demonstrating the feasibility and the effectiveness of our architecture as a design model for *eMarketplace*, with special attention to its foundation components, services within *eBusiness* applications, fundamental active representatives for specific business services, and leveraged legacy systems. In continuing our research, the computational effectiveness of the architecture will be our main concern. Also, we will expand the application and the implementation of our prototype *eMarketplace* to investigate the most appropriate techniques to support secure, reliable, and effective transactions.

REFERENCES

Ariba. (2000, October). *B2B marketplaces in the New Economy.* Retrieved from the World Wide Web: http://www.commerce.net/other/research/ebusiness-strategies/2000/00_07_r.html.

Arpinar, S., Dogac, S. A. & Tatbul, N. (2000, July). An open electronic marketplace through agent-based workflows: MOPPET. *International Journal on Digital Library,* 3(1).

Arthur, W. B., Holland, J., LeBaron, B., Palmer, R. & Tayler, P. (1997). Asset pricing under endogenous expectations in an artificial stock market model. In W. B. Arthur, S. N. Durlauf & D. A. Lane (Eds.), *Proceedings on the Economy as an Evolving Complex System.*

Bartelt, A. & Lamersdorf, W. (2001). A multi-criteria taxonomy of business models in electronic commerce. *Proceedings of the IFIP/ACM International Conference on Distributed Systems Platforms.*

Bellifemine, F., Poggi, A. & Rimassa, G. (1999, April). JADE – A FIPA-compliant agent framework. *Proceedings of PAAM'99, London,* (pp. 97-108).

Bichler, M., Beam, C. & Segev, A. (1998). OFFER: A broker-centered object framework for electronic requisitioning. *IFIP Conference Trends in Electronic Commerce.*

Boll, S., Gruner, A., Haaf, A. & Klas, W. (1999, April). EMP-a database driven electronic marketplace for business-to-business commerce on the Internet. *Journal of Distributed and Parallel Databases, Special Issue on Internet Electronic Commerce,* 7(2).

Chen, L., Yerneni, R., Vassalos, V., Garcia-Molina, H., Papakonstantinou, Y. & Ullman, J. (1998). Capability based mediation in TSIMMIS. *Proceedings on SIGMOD 98 Demo,* Seattle, Washington, USA.

Commerce eXtensible Markup Language, cXML 1.2.007. (n.d.). Retrieved from the World Wide Web: http://www.cxml.org.

Common Business Library (CBL) of Commerce Net. (n.d). Retrieved from the World Wide Web: http://www.commerce.net.

Davenport, T. H. (1993). *Process Innovation: Reengineering Work through Information Technology.* Harvard, MA: Business School Press.

Distributed Component Object Model (DCOM). (n.d). Retrieved from the World Wide Web: http://www.microsoft.com/com/tech/DCOM.asp.

Dooley, R. A. (1976). Repartee as a graph. In R. E Longacre (Ed.), *An Anatomy of Speech Notions* (pp. 348-358). Lisse: Peter de Ridder Press.

Dublin core. (n.d). Retrieved from the World Wide Web: http://dublincore.org.

Dubosson, M., Osterwalder, A. & Pigneur, Y. (2002). eBusiness model design, classification and measurements. *Thunderbird International Business Review*, 44(1).

Eisenberg, B. & Nickull, D. (eds.). (2001, February). *ebXML Technical Architecture Specification v1.04*.

Fensel, D., Horrocks, I., van Harmelen, F., Decker, S., Erdmann, M. & Klein, M. (2000, October). OIL in a nutshell. *Proceedings of the 12th European Workshop Knowledge Acquisition Modeling, and Management* (pp. 1-16). Springer-Verlag.

Fensel, D., van Harmelen, F. & Horrocks, I. (2002). OIL & DAML+OIL: Ontology languages for the Semantic Web. In J. Davis, D. Fensel & F. van Harmelen (Eds.), *Towards the Semantic Web: Ontology-Driven Knowledge Management*. John Wiley & Sons.

The Foundation for Intelligent Physical Agents: *FIPA '97 version 2.0 specifications*. (1998).

Genesereth, M. (1992). An agent-based approach to software interoperability. In *Proceedings of the DARPA Software Technology Conference*.

Genesereth, M. & Fikes, R. (eds.). (1992, June). *Knowledge Interchange Format, Version 3.0 Reference Manual* (Technical Report Logic-92-1). Computer Science Department, Stanford University, USA.

Genesereth, M., Keller, A. M. & Duschka, O. (1997). Infomaster: An information integration system. *Proceedings of 1997 ACM SIGMOD Conference*.

Ghenniwa, H. (2001, November). eMarketplace: Cooperative distributed systems architecture. *Fourth International Conference on Electronic Commerce Research*, Dallas, Texas, USA.

Ghenniwa, H. & Kamel, M. (2000). Interaction devices for coordinating cooperative distributed. *Intelligent Automation and Soft Computing*, 6(2), 173-184.

Hammer, M. & Champy, J. (1993). *Reengineering the Corporation*. Harper Collins.

Heflin, J., Hendler, J. & Luke, S. (1999). *SHOE: A Knowledge Representation Language for Internet Applications* (Technical Report CS-TR-4078). Department of Computer Science, University of Maryland at College Park, USA.

Huhns, M., Jacobs, N., Ksiezyk, T., Shen, W., Singh, M. & Cannata, P. (1993, June). Integrating enterprise information models in Carnot. *International*

Conference on Intelligent and Cooperative Information Systems (ICICIS), Rotterdam.

IBM Corporation CommercePOINT Payment. (n.d). Retrieved from the World Wide Web: http://www.internet.ibm.com.commercepoint.payment.

Intershop Communications, Inc. (1998). Intershop 3. Retrieved from the World Wide Web: http://www.intershop.com.

Ivezic, N., Barbacci, M., Libes, D., Potok, T. & Robort (2000, July). An analysis of a supply-chain management agent architecture. *Proceedings of the Fourth International Conference on Multiagent Systems. IEEE Computer Society Press*, Los Alamitos, CA (pp. 401-402).

Java™ 2 Platform, Enterprise Edition (J2EE™). (n.d). Retrieved from the World Wide Web: http://java.sun.com/j2ee/.

Karp, P., Chaudhri, V. & Thomere, J. (1999, July). *XOL: An XML-Based Ontology Exchange Language* (XOL version 0.3).

Lassila, O. & Swick, R. (1999, February). *Resource Description Framework (RDF) Model and Syntax Specification, W3C Recommendation.*

LeBaron, B. (2000). Agent-based computational finance: Suggested readings and early research. *Journal of Economic Dynamics and Control, 24,* 679-702.

McCabe, K., Rassenti, S. & Smith, V. (1992). Institutional Design for Electronic Trading. *Conference on Global Equity Markets, N.Y. University,* Salomon Center.

McFadzean, D., Stewart, D. & Tesfatsion, L. (2001). A computational laboratory for evolutionary trade networks. *IEEE Transactions on Evolutionary Computation, 5,* 546-560.

Microsoft Corporation. Internet Commerce. (1998). Retrieved from the World Wide Web: http://www.microsoft.com.

Nodine, M., Fowler, J., Ksiezyk, T., Perry, B., Taylor, M. & Unruh, A. (2000). Active information gathering in Infosleuth. *International Journal of Cooperative Information Systems,* 9, 3-27.

Oracle Corporation. Oracle Internet Commerce Server. Retrieved from the World Wide Web: http://www.oracle.com/products/asd/ics/ics.html.

Parunak, H. & Van Dyke. (1996). Visualizing agent conversations: Using enhanced dooley graphs for agent design and analysis. *Proceedings of the Second International Conference on Multiagent Systems, AAAI Press,* Menlo Park, CA (pp. 275-282).

Paperexchange Marketplace. (n.d). Retrieved from the World Wide Web: http://www.paperexchange.com.

Rachlevsky-Reich, B. et al. (1999). GEM: A global electronic market system. *Information Systems Journal, Special Issue on Electronic Commerce,* 24(6).

RossettaNet. (n.d). Retrieved from the World Wide Web: http://www.rosettanet.org.

Sandholm, T. & Lesser, V. (1995). On Automated Contracting In Multi-Enterprise Manufacturing. Distributed Enterprise: Advanced Systems and Tools, Edinburgh, Scotland, 33-4.

SAP Services Marketplace, SAP AG. (n.d). Retrieved from the World Wide Web: http://www.sap.com.

The Semantic Web Community Portal. (n.d). Retrieved from the World Wide Web: http://www.semanticweb.org/.

Shrivastava, S., Bellissard, L. & Lacourte, S. (2001). *Assessment of the C3DS Service Provisioning Framework.* Public Technical Report, No. 36.

Singh, M. P. (2000). Synthesizing coordination requirements for heterogeneous autonomous agents. *Journal of Autonomous Agents and Multi-Agent Systems, 3*(2), 107-132.

Smirnov, A. & Chandra, C. (2000, March). Ontology-based knowledge management for cooperative supply chain configuration. *Proceedings of AAAI Spring Symposium Bringing Knowledge to Business Processes.* Stanford, CA: AAAI Press.

Sun Microsystems. (n.d). Java Electronic Commerce Framework (JECF). Retrieved from the World Wide Web: http://www.javasoft.com/products/commerce.

Object Management Group, Inc. (1995, July). *The Common Object Request Broker Architecture and Specification (Revision 2.0).* Framingham, MA.

Tesfatsion, L. (ed.). (2001). Special double issue on agent-based computational economics. *Journal of Economic Dynamics and Control,* 25(3-4).

Timmers, P. (1999). *Electronic Commerce: Strategies and Models for Business-to-Business Trading.* John Wiley & Sons.

Tsvetovatyy, M., Gini, M., Mobasher, B. & Wieckowski, Z. (1997, September). MAGMA: An Agent-Based Virtual Market for Electronic Commerce. *Journal of Applied Artificial Intelligence, special issue on Intelligent Agents,* 11(6), 501-523.

Varian, H. R. (1995, July). Mechanism Design For Computerized Agents. The First USENIX Workshop on Electronic Commerce, New York, 11(19), 13-21.

VerticalNet® Marketplaces. (n.d). Retrieved from the World Wide Web: http://www.VerticalNet.com.

Vickery, V. (1961). Counter speculation, auctions, and competitive sealed tenders. *Journal of Finance,* 16(8), 37.

Walras, L. (1954), *Elements of Pure Economics.* English translation by William Jaffe. Allen and Unwin. (Originally work published 1874.)

Wellman, M. P. (1993). A Market-Oriented Programming Environment and Its Application To Distributed Multicommodity Flow Problems. *Journal of Artificial Intelligence Research,* 1, 1-22.

Wiederhold, G. (1992, March). Mediators in the architecture of future Information Systems. *IEEE Computer,* 25(3), 38-49.

Wiederhold G. & Genesereth, M. (1997, September/October). The conceptual basis for mediation services. *IEEE Expert, Intelligent Systems and their Applications,* 12(5), 38-47.

Chapter IV

Financial Markets in the Internet Age

Ross A. Lumley
George Washington University, USA

ABSTRACT

The chapter reviews how the financial markets historically have been affected by new technologies and shows that, time and again, technological advances have impacted the very workflow of the financial market processes including the available financial instruments. Present technologies are discussed leading to a framework for how they form the basis for building intelligent agent systems. An overview of multi-agent systems is provided followed by several examples of multi-agent systems supporting investors in financial markets.

INTRODUCTION

The age of networked intelligence along with the Internet has played a major role in formulating the financial markets of today. Dramatically increased distribution of all forms of information and near instantaneous transactions across the globe have created the opportunity for radically greater access to financial markets for all interested participants. This has led to new types of markets with greater global access to financial markets, and has allowed entirely new financial products to be offered.

Throughout history, technology has driven advances in the efficiency and liquidity of financial markets. This has led to wave after wave of innovation in the types of securities traded, the "reach" of the market participants, the distribution of news and information, and the type of market exchange auction. This chapter will show that the financial markets have been heavily influenced by Internet technology.

The chapter provides a background of how financial markets have functioned throughout history. Also, it shows that, time and again, technological advances have impacted the very workflow of the financial market processes including the availability of information, the potential for ever increasing participation, the timeliness of executing transactions and the overall increase in the efficiency and liquidity of the financial markets. As the main topic, the chapter shows the important results of Internet technologies on the financial markets in just seven years since the Internet became a commercial resource and a rapid trend toward more intelligent systems for automated transaction processing, order execution, and information filtering.

Financial markets exist to facilitate the buying and selling of financial instruments. These have traditionally consisted of stocks (equity ownership stake), options (a contract to buy or sell a financial instrument by a set date at a set price), bonds (debt obligations) and futures contracts for commodities and financial instruments. Financial markets are made up of many players, both active and passive. These include issuers of financial instruments (initial sellers), secondary buyers and sellers of financial instruments, the providers of the marketplace (exchanges and auctions), the regulators and information providers. Each of these groups can be further subdivided. For example, buyers and sellers may consist of large institutions, smaller financial organizations, professional traders and individual investors.

Technology-driven changes to the infrastructure of the financial markets have resulted in a complex, fast changing environment for the investor whether professional or amateur. Examples of such changes include instant availability of wide-ranging information, standards for financial transaction formats, online financial transaction servers ready to receive transactions over the Internet, and ever more complex hybrid financial instruments with numerous trading and investment strategies. To manage one's investments, there is a trend toward the use of a new form of expert system known as intelligent agents. By building a collection of the software intelligent agents with varying roles and specialties, it is possible to develop a coordinated team of these software experts to respond to the dynamics of the financial markets and provide the investor with balanced guidance in the management of portfolios.

This chapter focuses on the common stock of corporations as the financial instrument for examining the impact of technology on the financial markets. For clarity regarding the availability of information we will focus on two categories — information about the companies whose stock is being bought and sold and the information about the current price of a stock that is referred to as price discovery. This distinction will help to pinpoint which type of information availability various technologies have impacted.

HISTORY OF FINANCIAL MARKETS AND TECHNOLOGY

This section considers the history of financial markets from the early origins. Focus is on the more recent history of the U.S. markets including the NYSE, AMEX and NASDAQ.

Early Financial Markets

Buelens and Cuyvers (2000) chronicle the history of financial markets in Europe. They note many European "financial capitals" throughout time, most of which were located in Italy until the 15th century. These include Rome (100 AD), Genoa and Venice (11th and 12th centuries), Siena (12th and 13th centuries), and Florence (14th century). As the markets of Italy went into decline in the 15th century, the financial centers moved to Antwerp, Belgium (1531) and Amsterdam (1611). For the most part, these early "financial capitals" did not incorporate formal exchanges. Antwerp is noted as the place where the stock market was born. Many foreign merchants moved to Antwerp as other financial centers were in decline. The driving technology of the time tended to be access points to trade routes which were typically port cities. The key port cities with strategic access to trade routes and financial capital were essentially the "networks" of their day. In 1531, the city of Antwerp built a meeting place for merchants, which became the first building in the world designed as a stock exchange and trade exchange. Some of the early financial market infrastructure established in Antwerp were fixed trading hours, market regulation, and relatively low trading costs.

The beginning of modern financial trading in equity and derivative markets is often traced to 1611 when Dutch traders organized themselves to exchange shares in companies involved in overseas plundering such as the East India Company and later the West India Company. This early market eventually became the Amsterdam Stock Exchange and even introduced the concept of options.

Buelens and Cuyvers (2000) also describe the Amsterdam Stock Exchange distinction of experiencing the biggest financial market bubble in history with the "tulip mania" in 1637. Speculation drove the price up to today's equivalent of $50,000 per tulip bulb imported from Turkey. By the following year, prices plunged and tulip bulbs became virtually worthless.

Origin of the New York Stock Exchange

The New York Stock Exchange (NYSE) (2003) documents the early history of the organization. The NYSE was first chartered in 1792 when 24 brokers gathered under the famous buttonwood tree on Wall Street and signed a two-sentence statement known as the Buttonwood Tree Agreement. This agreement formed a closed trading club funding its members with a common 0.25 percent commission rate. In 1817 the New York brokers established a formal organization called the New York Stock and Exchange Board. This formalization included adopting procedures such as drawing up a constitution and electing officers as well as taking up formal residence at a room rented at 40 Wall Street. Finally, on April 22, 1903, the NYSE moved to its current location at 18 Broad Street. This trading floor is still in use today and has expanded by 60 percent to its current size of 3,600 square feet. The next section discusses the introduction of technology to the NYSE and the areas effected including order placement, price discovery, trade execution and infrastructure.

Technology on the NYSE Trading Floor

Table 1 shows a long sequence of technology that was brought into the NYSE. In most cases, this technology is providing the communication of information pre-trade (news and price discovery) or facilitating the flow of trade execution information.

As the table shows, the NYSE started using the telegraph in 1844 and telephones in 1878 to link local New York brokerage offices with the trading floor. Today, the NYSE operates on an auction basis on a trading floor of 3,600 square feet. Buy and sell orders for the listed securities are made directly on this floor at one of the 20 different trading posts. These transactions are conducted through the Specialist at the post who acts as a facilitator for the stocks listed at their post. Specialists must maintain a fair, competitive, orderly and efficient market. This means that all customer orders have an equal opportunity to interact and receive the best price. It also means that once auction trading begins, a customer should be able to buy or sell a reasonable amount of stock close to the last sale. Therefore, a Specialist works to avoid large or unreasonable price variations between consecutive sales. Each post often has a crowd of floor brokers placing their orders with the Specialist who acts as a kind of "referee" between floor brokers. Prior to the introduction of the telephone, the orders were delivered by messengers who hand carried the information to the floor brokers.

The volume of trading and the participation by many different types of investors has led to a partitioning of trading with only the largest trades going to

Table 1: Introduction of Technology to the NYSE

Year	Technology	Category
1844	Telegraph	Order placement
1867	First ticker	Price discovery
1878	First telephones	Trade execution
1881	First electro-mechanical enunciator board	Price discovery
1883	First electric lights	Infrastructure
1903	First pneumatic tubes	Trade execution
1919	Separate bond ticker system	Price discovery
1928	Quotation bureau established	Price discovery
1953	First automated quotations service	Price discovery
1962	First optical card readers	Trade execution
1966	First radio pagers	Trade execution
1966	Electronic ticker display boards	Price discovery
1976	Designated Order Turnaround (DOT) System	Trade execution
1978	Intermarket Trading System (ITS)	Trade execution
1979-80	Facilities Upgrade Program	Infrastructure
1983	Electronic Display Book	Price discovery
1984	SuperDot 250	Trade execution
1994-96	Integrated Technology Network	Infrastructure
1996	Wireless Data System	Price discovery

Source: NYSE

the Specialist post. Smaller trades are now matched by computer for more efficient high volume processing. Thus, even with the introduction of many forms of technology, the NYSE remains a human-based auction system. With the availability of advanced communication technologies, new forms of financial auction markets have developed that can be characterized as electronic exchanges.

Electronic Exchanges

While the NYSE has provided a classical human specialist-based marketplace, the National Association of Securities Dealers Automated Quotation (NASDAQ) system provides an example of how the availability of communication networks for communicating transaction information has, in fact, led to new markets. The NASDAQ is a communications network between thousands of computers. Rather than human agents (floor brokers) calling out orders at a specialist post, a registered agent of the NASDAQ, called a market maker, places their name and the prices at which they are willing to buy or sell the security on a NASDAQ maintained electronic list of buyers and sellers.

Originally, only these registered market makers could execute a trade on the NASDAQ.

The closed market maker system of the early NASDAQ has evolved into an open electronic market making function through electronic communication networks (ECNs) and the NASDAQ Small Order Execution System (SOES). The NASDAQ SOES, through the availability of communication networks, began a transition allowing extremely fast second-by-second trading to move away from this closed market maker network toward a network of leased lines with broader access. Further technological advances through the advent of the Internet then moved short-term trading possibilities to places greatly removed from the trading floor or closed network to include remote locations across the globe. These new electronic trading paradigms represent an intelligent enterprise based on technology replacing slower, less efficient traditional systems through human interaction.

Another example of a human-based auction market is the open outcry system in the Chicago Mercantile Exchange (CME) futures trading pits. The open outcry system of the CME futures trading pits has evolved through the availability of technology to the Globex electronic auction market trading 24 hours a day automatically matching buyer and seller when bid and ask prices meet.

Electronic Communication Networks (ECNs)

An Electronic Communication Network (ECN) is a decentralized, comput-erized automated order matching system that also displays the unmatched bid and ask prices (or limit orders) of the participants in a display known as the limit book. Broker-dealers provide the interface and routing to the ECN and retail investors gain access to the service through a direct access broker with a typical connection through the Internet. Table 2 shows the ECNs and their relative size.

Osterland (2000) points out that the ECNs are important because they provide competition in an environment where little existed. A number of studies in 1995 led to a Justice Department investigation into the NASD market makers and found that dealers were colluding to maintain a wide spread between the bid price and the ask price. This investigation led to a $1 billion settlement. In 1997 the SEC passed new order routing rules on the NASD dealers requiring that the dealer display customer limit orders that were better than the dealer's quote. It is this function of displaying the investor community bid and asking prices that the ECNs are performing. This, in effect, means that the ECNs are enforcing the SEC's order routing rules.

As shown in Table 2, 41.3 percent of the share volume of NASDAQ listed stocks and 57.4 percent of the trades are now conducted on an ECN rather than directly through the NASDAQ. Figure 1 shows the growth in Island's share of the NASDAQ market. Much of this growth reflects the online Internet-based trading.

Table 2: Ranking of ECN Share and Trade Volume

Rank[a]	ECN	Share Volume[a]	Trade Volume[b]
1	Island	11.2%	21.2%
2	Instinet	11.0%	12.5%
3	REDIBook	5.6%	8.6%
4	Archipelago	4.1%	5.9%
5	MarketXT	3.6%	2.6%
6	Brut	2.3%	3.7%
7	B-Trade	1.9%	2.3%
8, 9, 10	Other	1.6%	0.6%
	Total ECN	**41.3%**	**57.4%**

[a] Rank based on share volume.
[b] % of NASDAQ share volume.
[c] % of NASDAQ Trade Volume.

Source: www.isld.com/access/index

The basic steps involved in the workings of an ECN are described by Island (n.d.). This scenario involves a limit order to buy or sell a stock. A limit order identifies a specific price to buy or sell whereas a market order is filled at the current best price. The software process for processing a limit order is as follows:

1. Investor/trader sends buy/sell limit order to broker dealer.
2. Subscribing broker-dealer sends a display limit order to Island.
3. Upon receiving the order, Island first performs a series of checks (i.e., verifying the stock symbol, checking that the security is not halted, etc.).
4. After clearing those checks, Island's system is scanned instantaneously to determine if there is a matching order.

Figure 1: Island's Monthly Market Share of NASDAQ Share Volume

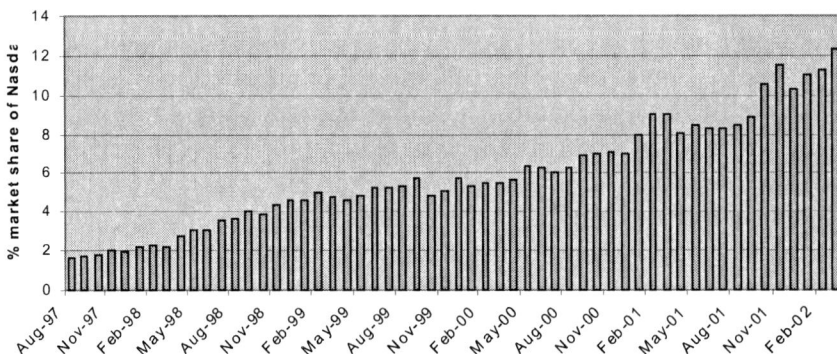

5.   If a matching order exists, the order is executed immediately.
6.   If a matching order does not exist, a display order is placed on Island's limit order book until a matching order is received or until the order is cancelled. The best-priced order on Island for a NASDAQ security is also represented on the NASDAQ quote listing, where all market participants post their best bid and ask prices.

A benefit of the ECN is that it is a more fail-safe marketplace. As decentralized systems, ECNs provide a good architecture for building a market infrastructure protected against catastrophic events such as the attacks on the World Trade Center on September 11, 2001. The events of that day demonstrated the vulnerability of physical markets with the NYSE being near the site of the catastrophe. Operations were shut down for four days (NYSE closed from September 11, 2001 through September 14, 2001, reopening on September 17, 2002).

The current trend of ECNs is toward consolidation to accomplish further cost efficiencies with greater volume. Within the past year, Archipelego announced a merger with Redibook, and Instinet announced a merger with Island.

The growth and increase in competition created by the market makers, transaction coordinators (ECNs) and regulators have resulted in more efficient and more liquid markets. Each technological change has resulted in a more efficient pricing process or price discovery as exemplified by a continual reduction in the spread between the bid price and the ask price for financial instruments. Access to a real-time transaction environment over the Internet introduces new possibilities for applying software applications with expert intelligence in automated trading and arbitrage strategies.

Assessing the Impact of Technology on Financial Markets

It is important to establish a framework for measuring the impact of technology on the financial markets. Clearly, the Efficient Market Hypothesis (EMH) is the dominant paradigm cited by economists to investigate the behavior of financial markets. The EMH offers a theoretical model of the pricing of financial assets in a world that meets the assumptions of the model. This chapter is not intended to prove or disprove the EMH. Rather, the chapter concludes that the extent to which technology has allowed real world financial markets to more closely adhere to the EMH assumptions results in a more efficient marketplace. Assumptions noted by Fama (1970) include: (a) no transaction costs, (b) costless and equal availability of information, and (c) that the implications of current information for both current price and the distributions of future prices are generally accepted by all market participants. The latter assumption also can be stated that investors behave in a rational manner.

The discussions above have shown that the introduction of new technologies has led to smaller spreads between the bid prices to buy and the ask price to sell. This is part of the cost of a transaction. If an investor bought shares at the bid and immediately sold at the ask price the difference between these prices is the spread and represents an outflow from the investor's portfolio. Also, the increased efficiency of completing a transaction automatically rather than manually leads to lower actual costs to complete the financial transaction. Thus, these technological changes have brought the markets closer to the EMH assumption that transaction costs are zero.

THE HISTORY AND TECHNOLOGIES OF INFORMATION DISSEMINATION

The EMH has an assumption that information is costless to obtain and equally available to all market participants. We will now examine that assumption over the history of financial markets in the United States. We will see that there were significant differences in the availability of information in the past and that the introduction of technologies has dramatically changed the situation.

In January 1790, several ships left New York Harbor bound for Georgia and the Carolinas. These ships carried no traditional goods or products but rather a different type of valuable freight. They carried news that Alexander Hamilton, Secretary of the Treasury, had just delivered his First Report on the Public Credit to Congress and explained his plan to reorganize the debt of the nation and refund at face value existing debt incurred during the Revolution under the failed Articles of Confederation. The early speculators sailing south, knowing that this news would take weeks to reach the local newspapers of the South, were able to buy debt certificates for 10 percent to 20 percent of face value. The speculators knew that the news of Hamilton's plan would send those values soaring, thus facilitating a hefty news lag profit.

Technology eventually took its toll on speculators profiting from such slow moving news. On May 24, 1844, Samuel F. B. Morse sent by telegraph what has become a famous message "What Hath God Wrought" from the Supreme Court chamber in Washington D.C. to partner Alfred Vail in Baltimore. The significance of this technological breakthrough is important since, for the first time, information could move almost instantaneously across potentially unlimited distances.

With one invention, Morse succeeded in eliminating such extreme news lag speculative opportunities forever. In 1861, the reach of the telegraph was further extended with the transcontinental telegraph and in 1868 the transatlantic cable. From these extensions, news in San Francisco or Europe was now quickly accessible to those near the telegraph feed and price parity between New York and London was a reality. However, to have access to information sent by telegraph, one needed to be in close proximity to a telegraph transmission station.

Daily financial newspapers extended the reach of information dissemination but clearly did not provide the rapid timing of the telegraph. However, through an ever expanding delivery network, any investor with a mailbox could receive a daily update on financial news and securities pricing as well as analysis of information. One of the best known of the financial publications is *The Wall Street Journal* which was established in 1889.

Electronic Information Dissemination

Information is a key input to most investment and trading strategies. One of the most abundant resources provided on the Internet is financial information. Every type of information is available on the Internet now, from real-time data feeds for price discovery to analysis of all kinds (technical and fundamental) and real-time breaking news. Unfortunately, the Internet also increases the ease with which misinformation and rumors can be introduced and spread globally.

When one compares the weeks that news took to travel from city to city before the telegraph and the limited number of points covered by the telegraph, a most incredible result of the Internet is a tremendous leveling of the information dissemination playing field. This essentially provides equal access from the institutional trader/investor to the retiree managing a retirement account in a remote home site with a satellite feed.

The Internet also has brought the power of more informed trading decisions to remote underdeveloped locations around the world. Kanungo (2002) discusses a research project where Internet access was brought to a tiny fishing village in India. One of the popular uses of the Internet access in that village is discovering the prices of the commodities that the village produces. Prior to the availability of the Internet, fishermen would sell all of their production to a middle-agent who knew the going market prices for the goods while the fishermen did not. With a satellite Internet feed, the fishermen now receive current market prices for their goods and, when the middle-agent comes to town, they can negotiate an appropriate price or opt to take their goods to the larger market themselves.

Electronic Documents and Markup Languages

From a pilot system begun in the mid-1980s, the SEC allows the securities issuers to file the required regulatory documents and disclosure information electronically through the Securities and Exchange Commission's Electronic Data Gathering, Analysis and Reporting (EDGAR) system. This system also results in a public database of these regulatory documents allowing securities buyers to access this information rapidly via the Internet resulting in more informed investment decisions.

The advent of markup languages permitted the SEC to receive and process required filings. The markup language (originally SGML, later XML) permitted the filing entity to tag specific sections of the document so that automated processing programs could check to make sure that required information was included. The EDGAR system thus streamlined document processing in the regulatory environment of the SEC and provides very fast dissemination of this information to large and small investors alike.

Groupware

Groupware technologies on the Internet have brought together new communities of participants. Ever advancing chat room applications, including text, voice and video through the use of high-speed communication networks, permit isolated market participants with a common interest to create a virtual trading room where ideas, techniques and strategies can be shared and taught electronically. This capability removes barriers to entry into certain forms of trading in the financial markets.

Along with the improvements in information dissemination, the Internet also has facilitated the distribution of misinformation. Thus, the user of information must validate the accuracy of information sources. In April 1999, a North Carolina man was charged with fabricating a wire-service news story that sent a company stock soaring in what prosecutors said was the first stock manipulation scheme using the Internet. Gary Dale Hoke, 25, an employee of PairGain Technologies, was arrested at his apartment in Raleigh and charged with securities fraud in connection with the posting, which claimed that PairGain was the target of a corporate takeover.

Investors must be able to judge the quality and reliability of information made available on the Internet. This is one of many areas that software technology will influence in the field of knowledge management and intelligent agents. New technology is inventing tools for filtering, classifying and validating information obtained on the Internet. We will discuss some of these tools and techniques in sections below.

THE FUTURE OF THE INTERNET AND THE FINANCIAL MARKETS IN KNOWLEDGE-BASED ORGANIZATIONS

One consistent impact of the Internet is improved access to more (but not necessarily more accurate) information and real-time streaming price data. An immediate concern for the user of this information is information overload and quality. Thus, one of the future directions of anticipated technological change is the development of tools for monitoring and processing the overwhelming stream of information. A considerable body of research that ultimately will be brought to bear on this information overload issue is the use of intelligent agents to monitor, filter, categorize and process data of all types. The impact of technology changes in the next few years will include the use of wireless networking, artificial intelligence (intelligent agents) and advanced automated electronic auction systems.

For institutional investors there is competition to further reduce middle-agent layers that add to transaction costs. This development will be facilitated by a software technology based on the eXtensible Markup Language (XML) standard and a new Internet paradigm of Web services that can be connected to and transacted with by the software interaction between the participating entities. A combination of the XML standard and industry agreement on standard transaction formats is leading to automated processing between computer systems. Some of the resulting business outcomes are Straight-Through Processing and T+1 trade clearing processing.

XML

XML is considered first in looking forward to where Internet technology will take the financial markets next. This is done because so many of the specific challenges on the radar screen today will be using XML as an underlying technology. Surveys conducted by *The Wall Street Journal* and technology trade publication show that the survey participants believe that XML is important for integrating systems (38 percent), sharing data (33 percent), integrating channels (22 percent), fulfilling industry requirements/STP (19 percent), sharing applications (18 percent), and sharing business processes/rules (17 percent).

Information disseminators can build an intelligent information resource which is totally electronic and connects a large database resource of financial information with data mining and intelligent search agents. There has been a recent move toward a standard format for the delivery of information on the Internet through the use of XML. XML is resulting in the possibility for the consumer of information to obtain information from many disparate sources in a common format and use a single intelligent analysis and presentation tool for aggregating, analyzing and visualizing the information.

An even larger role for XML is to provide a markup language for defining standard financial market transactions. Industry participants with similar business needs are collaborating in an effort to define and agree to common industry formats for these transactions. Table 3 shows a list of some of the consortia and transaction standards.

Khoshafian (2002) describes the seamless integration of processes across multiple companies as the creation of the virtual enterprise. The uses of XML technologies to provide Web services by each organization allow the entire multi-organization financial transaction workflow to be integrated into an automated

Table 3: Financial Market XML Standards

Standard	Description
BIPS	Banking Industry Technology Secretariat
DRA	Digital Receipt Alliance
ebXML	Electronic Business using eXtensible Markup Language
FinXML	A standard language for the integration and exchange of digital information in capital markets.
FISD	Financial Information Services Division of SIIA
FIXML	Financial Information eXchange Protocol
FpML	Financial Products Markup Language
FSTC	Financial Services Technology Consortium
IFX	Interactive Financial Exchange
IRML	Investment Research Markup Language
ISO 15022	Protocol for securities message types, which is being developed by the International Standards Organization Working Group 10 (ISO WG10).
• MarketsML	Markets Markup Language (Reuters)
• MDDL	Market Data Definition Language
• MDML	Market Data Markup Language
• NewsML	News Markup Language
• NTM	Network Trade Model
• OFX	Open Financial Exchange
• RIXML	Research Information Exchange Markup Language
• SDML	Signed Document Markup Language
• SIIA	Software and Information Industry Association
• STPML	Straight Through Processing Markup Language
• SWIFTML	S.W.I.F.T. Markup Language
• XBRL	eXtensible Business Reporting Language

process using Internet technologies. Khoshafian (2002) provides a description of the interaction of the front-office, middle-office and back-office functions and partners of a typical stock transaction as shown in Figure 2. This figure also shows examples of the XML standards used at different stages of the process such as RIXML, FIXML and SWIFT.

The XML standards shown in Figure 2 provide a representative example of just a few of the sometimes overlapping standards. An overview of the RIXML, FIXML and SWIFT standards are described below.

* *RIXML:* RIXML.org (2003) is a consortium of buy- and sell-side firms committed to the first open standard for investment and financial research. An increasing number of sell-side firms are producing research in RIXML format. This format is designed so that software applications can process the financial information typically locked up in a research document. With RIXML formatted files, software can process documents automatically, insert values into databases and allow for custom reporting and notification based on those values.

Figure 2: Process Flow of Trading Activity

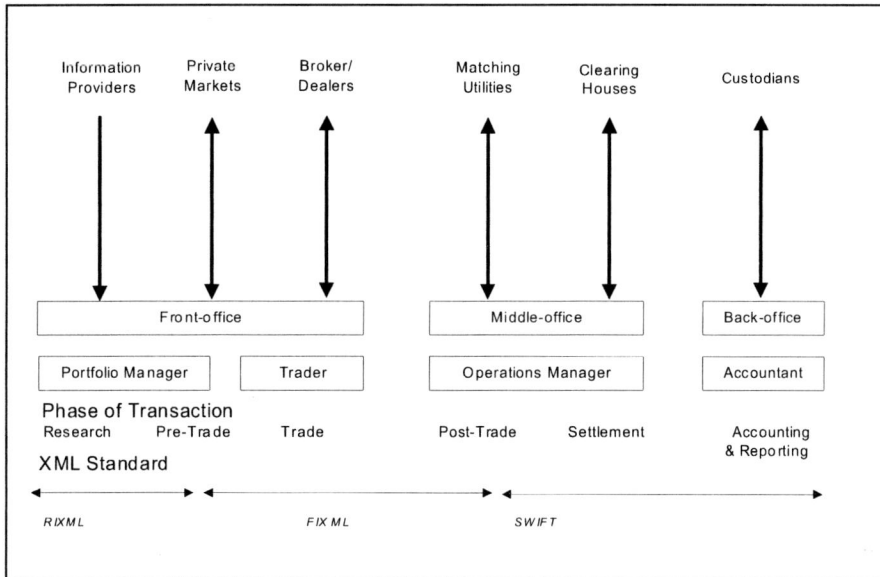

- *FIXML:* FIX Protocol Ltd. (2000), FIXML was devised in 1998 by FIX Protocol Ltd., the company responsible for the Financial Information Exchange (FIX) electronic communications protocol, as an XML vocabulary based on the FIX protocol. The original FIX protocol is a messaging standard developed for the real-time electronic exchange of securities transactions. Formatting the FIX message as XML (called FIXML) allows users to validate the message and group related fields and complements existing industry standards.
- *SWIFT:* The SWIFT consortium (2003) involves 7,000 financial institutions in 192 countries, and supports several standards. SWIFT offers a portfolio of messaging and market solutions and services. In July 2001 SWIFT and FIX announced that they would adopt the ISO 15022 XML message types. This will help link front- and back-office operations in financial institutions. SWIFT is used in the clearing and settlement phase between the back-office and custodians.

Samtani and Sadhwani (2002) provide a detailed discussion of why Web services offer advantages over more traditional enterprise integration strategies. The most relevant advantage to the topic of this chapter is that unlike the traditional integration strategies which require connection to proprietary networks and use proprietary solutions, Web services offer an open connection, platform-independent approach available on the Internet. They conclude that the ability of a financial institution to have access to real-time trade-related information spanning across multiple companies, in-house departments, applications, platforms, and systems is one of the most important driving factors behind the adoption of Web services. Through the use of a combination of these XML standards, participating organizations are attempting to automate the entire trade-processing workflow through the offering of Web services by each organization.

Straight-Through-Processing (STP)

A current trend in the processing of financial market transactions is to automate the entire trading process from order entry to final settlement and custody transfer known as STP. The transaction lifecycle of a trade flows through several firms suggesting that to successfully integrate this process requires multi-firm cooperation. This is a prime candidate for employing the XML technologies discussed previously. Intel (2002) identifies the stages of the transaction lifecycle of a trade as follows:

- *Pre-order:* information essential to making the trade decision
- *Order:* the specification and submission of the trade parameters
- *Execution:* filling the order
- *Post-execution:* recording the filled order
- *Trade confirmation:* returning filled order information to the buyer/seller
- *Clearance:* determining the stock and money obligations of participants to deliver or receive either cash or securities
- *Settlement:* securities credited or debited to participants' stock accounts and funds recorded in the participants' money ledgers on settlement day
- *Custody:* recording the official corporate record of stock ownership with the custodian

In order to build an STP system, the stages must be connected seamlessly, well-integrated, efficiently automated, and organized to ensure accuracy of trade data.

The steps and associated organizations are shown in Figure 2. As can be seen in the figure, the participants include: brokers, exchanges, custodians, clearing houses and others. Thus, standards must be developed to facilitate the execution of transactions across enterprise boundaries. With the elimination of human intervention comes the need to substitute software capable of making human-like decisions in this new environment. A software technology emerging from the academic research labs is the use of intelligent agents which are autonomous software applications capable of acting independently toward a prescribed goal. Intelligent agents will be discussed in a later section.

The acceleration in fully automated trade processing through the combination of Web services offered by participating organizations resulting in STP is making the goal of settling trades one day after they are executed a reality. This one-day settlement objective is known in the industry as T+1 processing.

T+1 Processing

The term T+1 represents the idea of settling trades the day after they are executed. This goal has been discussed in the securities industry for years. The Securities Industry Association (SIA) has announced that by June 2005 the settlement time will be reduced to one day. The goal of STP is to introduce process integration and automation as much as possible throughout the entire lifecycle of the transaction, so that the amount of human intervention is reduced, and whenever possible eliminated. Guerra (2002) notes that some have argued that the conversion is necessary to handle the increasing trade volumes and reduce risk. Others argue that the cost/benefit equation doesn't warrant the necessary work. Presently, trades must be settled within three days of the trade execution.

The combination of STP and T+1 offer the potential for yet another round of cost efficiencies leading to more efficient transactions in the marketplace and thus reduced risk through greater liquidity. Total elimination of any human intervention as well as competition between the ECNs and exchanges are driving stock trading transaction costs down to a fraction of a penny per share.

With a streamlined financial transaction processing workflow we next turn to the impact of wireless technology on the nature of how orders are entered when there is a human involved in order placement.

Wireless

Wireless networks have already permeated the trading floor with transactions now being entered through a handheld portable wireless device. The future will expand the use of wireless technologies for investors and traders off the trading floor by providing near instantaneous price discovery, breaking news and communication with automated intelligent agents.

Wireless technology has been limited in speed but there are several new levels of performance being planned for deployment in the United States, Europe and Asia. One new technology known as 3G Wireless (or IMT-2000) will provide network speeds of 144 Kbps from fast moving objects (e.g., cars), 384 Kbps from slow moving objects (e.g., walking) and 2 Mbps from fixed objects. 3G Wireless directly supports data packets and will allow global roaming — one device — anywhere in the world.

Schmerken (2000) recently noted that financial institutions are jumping on the wireless financial services bandwagon and the strategies are being driven by customer demand. He cites a July 2000 *Forrester Research* report stating that 47 percent of the firms surveyed said that customer retention was the number one reason for adopting wireless. Forrester warns that this level of wireless service soon will become a commodity and that firms will need to create more personalized financial analysis to differentiate their products. Schmerken concludes that services providing advanced analysis and alert capabilities will be a typical offering with those services often driven by complex rule-based intelligent agents.

We will now begin our discussion of knowledge management and intelligent agents. First we will establish the broader topic of knowledge management and then show where intelligent agents fit within the knowledge management technology infrastructure.

KNOWLEDGE MANAGEMENT

When beginning a discussion about knowledge management (KM) it is important to specify the meaning of the word "knowledge." The Merriam-Webster's dictionary (2003) contains the following definition:

(1) the fact or condition of knowing something with familiarity gained through experience or association; (2) a: acquaintance with or understanding of a science, art, or technique, b (1): the fact or condition of being aware of something, (2): the range of one's information or understanding <answered to the best of my knowledge>, c: the circumstance or condition of apprehending truth or fact through reasoning: COGNITION, d: the fact or condition of having information or of being learned <a man of unusual knowledge>

Clearly, the primary activity in the financial markets is making buying and selling decisions regarding financial instruments. This activity is performed to obtain the best return at an acceptable level of risk. It is performed by an extremely wide spectrum of participants ranging from the casual individual investor all the way to seasoned professionals with decades of experience. As defined in the second paragraph, this activity includes science, art and technique. Thus, the goal in constructing a KM system will be to extract this "knowledge" from the relevant experts.

Many institutional investment firms are employing KM. Santosus and Surmacz (n.d.) define knowledge management as "the process through which organizations generate value from their intellectual and knowledge-based assets." They clarify that generating value from such assets involves sharing them among employees, departments and even with other companies with a goal to devise best practices. They emphasize that the definition says nothing about technology which means that while KM is often facilitated by information technology, technology by itself is not KM.

Barnet and Migliore (2000) discuss the role of KM in the development of tomorrow's institutional investor's front office. They state that the front office remains focused on obtaining large amounts of timely and accurate data that is absorbed and used to make investment decisions. They describe the challenge as how to increase the productivity of portfolio managers and analysts by allowing them to spend less time gathering data and knowledge, and more time analyzing the data and knowledge. As an example they note that some organizations receive literally thousands of indications of interest (IOIs) — a non-binding interest in buying a security that is currently in registration (awaiting effectiveness by the SEC) — daily via the FIX transaction protocol. However, only a fraction of those IOIs might be of value. They describe the advantage of KM by noting how much time the front-office would save if it could screen IOIs based on preferences and knowledge.

Barnet and Migliore go on to say that although knowledge (know-how) must be accessible throughout the organization, in typical investment management firms knowledge is not stored in a central place for easy access. As in many types of offices, the knowledge of a typical front office is shared via meetings, paper sources, telephone calls, and so on. Thus, according to Barnet and Migliore, in a typical daily or weekly status meeting, portfolio managers and research analysts provide market updates on what's "hot" and what's not. But this knowledge typically is not captured and stored. They conclude that leading front offices now recognize KM as a strategic issue and are rapidly implementing systems to capture, share, and build on this knowledge.

Many businesses question whether KM is appropriate in their organization. Tiwana (2000) identifies key drivers that make KM a compelling case for businesses. These drivers are grouped into the following categories: knowledge-centric drivers, technology drivers, organizational structure-based drivers, personnel drivers, process focused drivers, and economic drivers. The knowledge-centric drivers result from companies not knowing what they know. The critical goal is to create a link between business strategy and KM.

Tiwana discusses a strategy for the enterprise to transition to a knowledge management technology infrastructure by leveraging the existing technology infrastructure to support the enterprise knowledge management network which reaches throughout the enterprise. Tiwana considers this to be a more realistic strategy than trying to abandon an existing technology infrastructure to build an entirely new knowledge management infrastructure. Thus, many of the components seen in Figure 3 reflect components from a traditional technology infrastructure. One category of components within this infrastructure is somewhat new and in particular, the intelligent agent components are distinct from the components found in most enterprise technology infrastructures.

Tiwana suggests that the filtering, editing, searching, and organizing pieces of knowledge are essential components of successful knowledge management.

Figure 3: Knowledge Management Technology Infrastructure

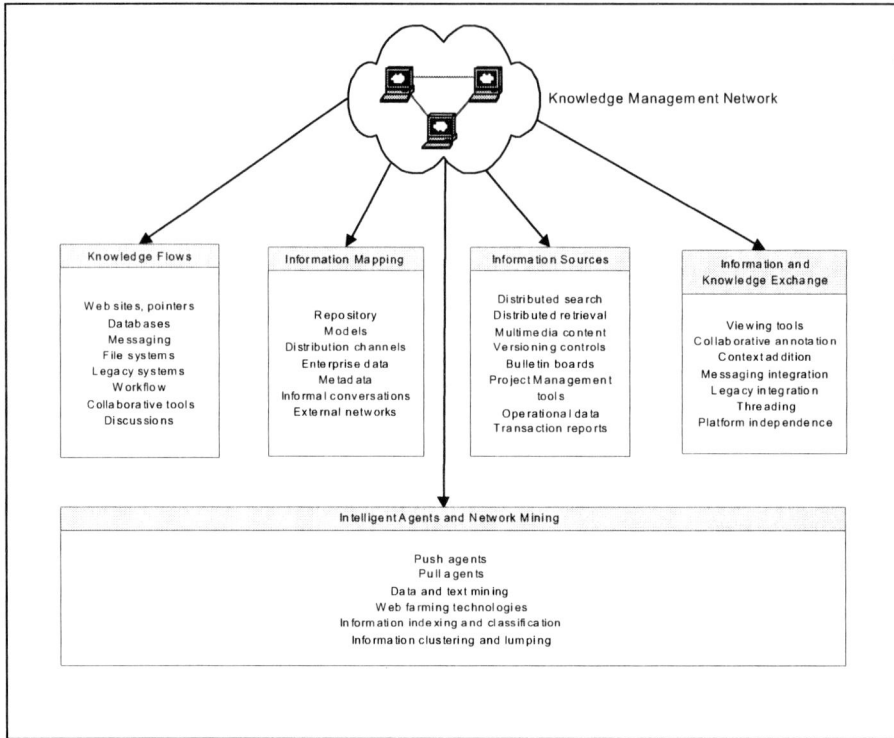

Packaging knowledge ensures that what is saved proves useful, provides value, encourages application of that knowledge to address actual business issues, and figures into critical decisions. The next section provides a much deeper investigation into the uses of intelligent agents for the securities decision-maker. Because of the widespread availability to professional traders and individual investors to much of the same information that makes up the database for the institutional investor's knowledge base system, the KM software will reach the professional trader/individual investor's toolbox in the years to come. In fact, the KM repository will provide a resource and rule-base for the intelligent agents discussed in the next section.

Intelligent Agents

One of the inescapable outcomes of the dissemination of information on the Internet is that it is creating information overload and in some cases misinformation. The near instantaneous dissemination of news and real-time price discovery information clearly eliminates the advantages financial institutions have historically enjoyed by getting an edge on the release of investment/trading relevant news. However, there is such an overwhelming stream of information that even the full-time trader cannot fully assimilate it all. Just as shoppers for retail goods on the Internet have used simple agents to search for the best available price (e.g., MySimon.com), investment decision makers will be making increasing use of such tools to search for the right stock or wait for the right entry price on appropriate securities.

Agents are a software technology that has been receiving a lot of attention in computer science research. Wooldridge (2002) describes an agent as "a computer system that is situated in some environment, and that is capable of autonomous action in this environment in order to meet its design objectives." A simple agent can perform a task for a user, thus allowing the user to avoid spending his or her own time performing the task. A higher level of sophistication or expertise in agent technology is known as an intelligent agent. Wooldridge and Jennings (1995) offer a list of properties that characterize intelligent agents:

- *Reactivity:* Intelligent agents are able to perceive their environment and respond in a timely fashion to changes that occur in it in order to satisfy their design objectives.
- *Proactiveness:* Intelligent agents are able to exhibit goal-directed behavior by taking the initiative in order to satisfy their design objectives.
- *Social ability:* Intelligent agents are capable of interacting with other agents (and possibly humans) in order to satisfy their design objectives.

Figure 4 shows a software application called Web Ferret and the results of a simple query to find information on the Internet about Intel earnings forecasts. The window in the figure shows 500 hits and this was limited by a maximum query threshold. By glancing down the abstracts on the first page, it is clear that reading through these to synthesize an opinion is a daunting task. Web Ferret is an agent that acts on the user's behalf but it is not an intelligent agent as it only presents the raw results of the search.

Seo, Giampapa and Sycara (2002) show that in the application domain of stock portfolio management, software agents that evaluate the risks associated with the individual companies of a portfolio should be able to read electronic news articles that are written to give investors an indication of the financial outlook of a company. They illustrate a positive correlation between news reports on a company's financial outlook and the company's attractiveness as an investment. However, because of the volume of such reports, it is impossible for financial analysts or investors to track and read each one. They propose a system that automatically classifies news reports that reflect positively or negatively on a company's financial outlook. To accomplish this task, they treat the understanding of news articles as a text classification problem.

This type of filtering and classification is now available as commercial Web services. YellowBrix (2003) offers news and information, company and market data in XML and HTML format. They offer filtering, editing, searching and

Figure 4: Web Ferret Query Result

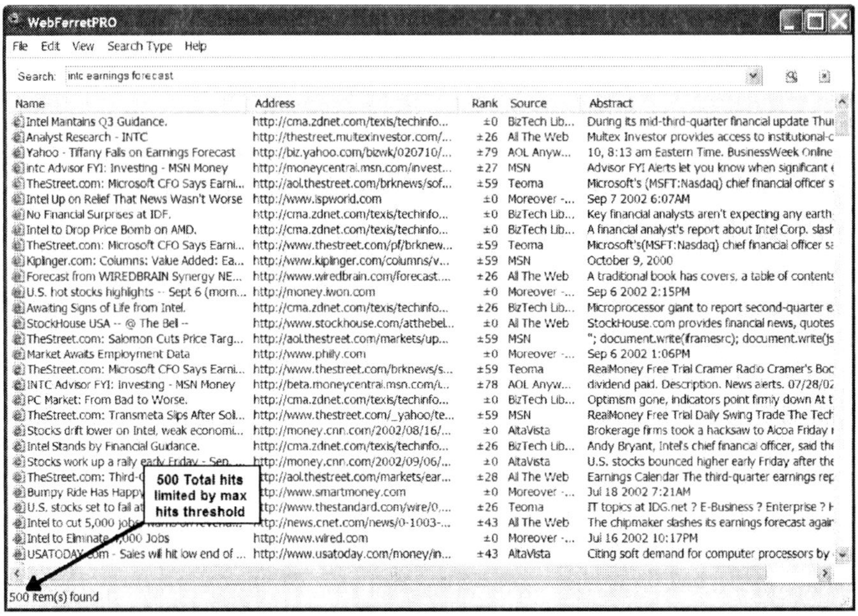

organizing of information through their YellowBrix Intelligence Engine. The YellowBrix Intelligence Engine evaluates the content to identify the key concepts in each article, then identifies redundant documents, intelligently categorizes documents to meet specified needs, generates executive summaries, and links company references to news, PR and financial data.

The general discussion of KM in the previous section did not identify the software architecture for constructing KM systems in the intelligent enterprise. Considering the broad range of information categories, transaction types, performance monitoring and record keeping required for the institutional investment house or even individual investors, a large, tightly integrated, all-inclusive software architecture will be rigid and unable to adapt to the changing environment. A software architecture involving autonomous intelligent agents is rapidly being adopted for KM and intelligent decision support in the financial services industry.

Multi-Agent Systems (MAS)

Thus far the topic of intelligent agents has focused on individual agents. A single-agent system would be simplistic and of very little value to the decision-maker. Organizations function through the interaction of teams of individuals where each possesses various specialties. Wooldridge (2001) describes a multi-agent system as one that contains a number of agents which interact with one another through communication. Each agent is able to act in the environment or domain of interest and different agents have different spheres of influence within that environment. These spheres of influence sometimes may overlap just as the expertise of individuals in an organization may overlap.

Thus, MAS are applications in which many autonomous software agents are combined to solve large problems. The cooperation among these agents allows them to pool their capabilities to solve the larger problem but this increases the complexity of the agents because they must be able to communicate with one another to coordinate their activity. This becomes an application for distributed application management and leads to a hierarchy of roles within the MAS. Some agents specialize in planning and coordination while others are more focused on retrieving specific types of information and yet other agents may filter and condense the information.

Examples of MAS in the Financial Market Domain

The Robotics Institute at Carnegie Mellon University has, under the direction of Katia Sycara, been a pioneer in exploring the possibilities of building MAS for portfolio management. A major project called The WARREN System is an application of multi-agent architecture deploying a number of different, autonomous software agents that acquire information from and monitor changes to stock reporting databases. These agents also interpret stock information, suggest the near future of an investment, and track and filter relevant financial news articles for the user to read. Since the WARREN system is designed to monitor the dynamic processes of the market, it is also designed to function under conditions of extreme uncertainty. The system is named after Warren Buffet as its goal is to implement a portfolio management strategy similar to his. Much of this research is described at the project web site at the Robotics Institute (2003).

Multi-Agent Systems for Portfolio Management

Decker, Sycara and Zeng (1996) describe some early research (1996) at the CMU Robotics Institute that focuses on the portfolio management domain. They state that their research was motivated by the voluminous and readily available information on the Internet. This is the problem discussed as information overload above. This led them to explore the use of Intelligent Agent technology for accessing, filtering, evaluating and integrating information. In contrast to most previous research that has investigated single-agent approaches, the authors developed a collection of multiple agents that team up on demand, depending on the user, the task and the situation, to access, filter and integrate information in support of user tasks. They investigated techniques for developing distributed adaptive collections of information agents that coordinate to retrieve, filter and fuse information relevant to the user, task and situation, as well as anticipate user's information needs. Their approach is based on (1) case-based

Figure 5: Project Warren System Architecture

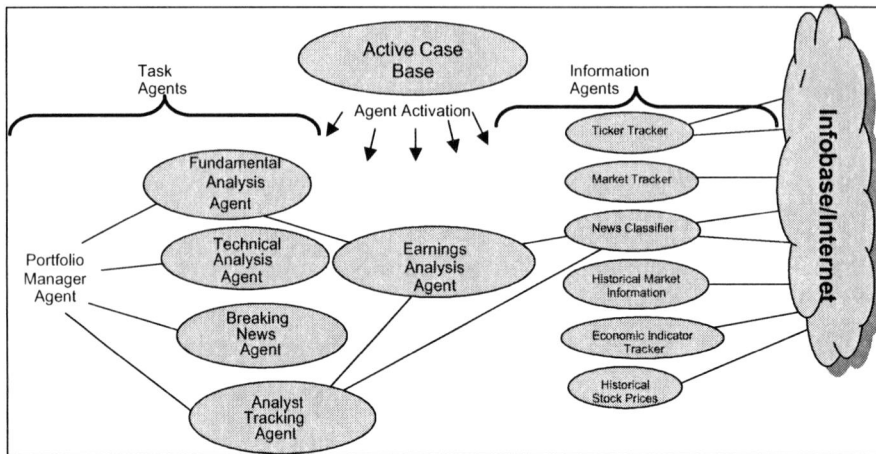

task and situation models, (2) flexible organizational structuring, and (3) reusable agent architecture. The paper describes the system in the domain of financial portfolio management.

Figure 5 shows the agent architecture of the Decker et al. (1996) MAS system. It illustrates the hierarchy of control and coordination as well as the specialization of agent roles. They categorize the agents as task agents and information agents. The task agents are focused on analysis while the information agents specialize in watching what available information is relevant and retrieving that information for the task agents.

Multi-Agent Systems for Stock Trading

Liu, Lao and Davis (2000) characterize a distributed problem-solving system as a group of individual agents running and co-operating with other agents to solve a problem. As dynamic domains such as stock trading are continuing to grow in complexity, they find it becomes more difficult to control the behavior of agents in the domains where unexpected events can occur. Their paper presents an information and knowledge exchange framework to support distributed problem solving in the stock trading domain. It addresses two important issues: (1) How individual agents should be interconnected so that their capacities are efficiently used and their goals are accomplished effectively and efficiently; (2) How the information and knowledge transfer should take place among agents to allow them to respond successfully to user requests and unexpected situations in the outside world. The focus of their paper is dynamic knowledge exchange among MAS agents. The architecture of their MAS is shown in Figure 6. While their architecture is similar to Decker et al. (1996), their design includes a risk

Figure 6: MAS for Stock Trading System Architecture

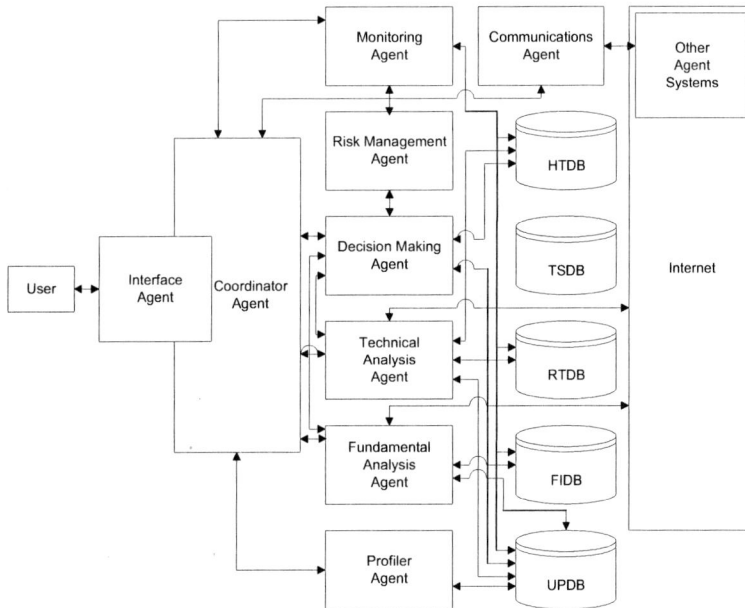

management agent; in addition, the interface to the Internet is handled by one communication agent.

Finally, Tseng and Gmytrasiewicz (2002) describe a real-time decision support system that supports information gathering and managing of an investment portfolio. Their system uses the Object Oriented Bayesian Knowledge Base (OOBKB) design to create a decision model at the most suitable level of detail to guide the information gathering activities, and to produce investment recommendations within a reasonable timeframe. They define and use the notion of urgency, or the value of time to determine the suitable level of detail for the user. Using their system can trade off the quality of support the model provides versus the cost of using the model at a particular level of detail. The decision models their system uses are implemented as influence diagrams. Using a suitable influence diagram, the system computes the value of consulting the various information sources available on the Web, uses Web agents to fetch the most valuable information, and evaluates the influence diagram producing the buy, sell and hold recommendations.

The Analytic Hierarchy Process for Identifying Information Preferences

One challenge in building intelligent agents is capturing the expert's thought process when analyzing arriving information. Of the two categories mentioned

— fundamental information and news information — the analysis of the former has a much more quantitative approach and the latter more qualitative. For processing the fundamental financial information about a company, the expert will apply a series of calculations known as financial analysis, and arrive at ratios and statistics that can be analyzed and interpreted. Even though the interpretation part of the process requires some knowledge engineering to understand the expert's approach to interpretation, the overall process of financial analysis is much more quantitative than news analysis.

The expert conducting an analysis of arriving news about a company must understand the context of the news, the source of the news, the past history of the company with respect to such news, and similar news about other companies in the industry. One approach to capturing how the expert evaluates the source of news can be quantified using a decision analysis technique known as the Analytic Hierarchy Process (AHP). AHP was introduced by Saaty (1996, 1997) and provides a methodology for generating a ratio scale of an expert's relative levels of certainty or preference over a set of choices using pair-wise comparisons. The Certainty Factors are represented by priorities and are derived from the elements of an eigenvector formed from the matrix of an expert's certainty estimates based on pair-wise comparisons of possible recommendations. Feinstein and Lumley (2000) use a technique that tracks the length of time that an expert takes in responding to financial questions in order to arrive at a set of priorities for ranking the choices offered the expert. Feinstein and Lumley describe how they implemented the AHP technique on the Internet.

Future Research in Intelligent Agents for Portfolio Management

Future research in the use of intelligent agents will explore new ways to implement and improve trade management capabilities. Some of this is already being done by brokerage systems as a value-added and competitive edge. An example of this is the ability to place an automatic stop loss order for an option based on the price level of the underlying stock. Additional topics that can be addressed in a comprehensive MAS for portfolio management could include topics such as:

- Assigning weights from a Portfolio Manager Agent according to investor strategy preference (technical, fundamental, etc.)
- Building a collection of intelligent technical analysis agents (e.g., composite technical analysis integration of techniques such as MACD, RSI, Stochastic Oscillator, etc.)
- Building diversification agents
- Building asset allocation (stocks, bonds, cash) agents
- Building hedging agents (use of option strategies)

- Building market conditions bias agents (bull/bear sentiment, extremes in Put/Call ratio, etc.)

Figure 7 illustrates a research prototype of a user interface allowing the small investor to benefit from the knowledge management and intelligent agent technology discussed above for the institutional investor. This user interface is established as an adaptable user-interface on a Web portal where either the individual investor or an intelligent agent can adapt the interface to display pertinent information to a specific decision-making activity. This research is ongoing and is known as the Rational Investor Partner Project (RIPP). Thus, the small investor will be able to benefit from the filtering, editing, searching and organizing capabilities of the knowledge management technology infrastructure discussed by Tiwana (2000). Current research with this type of service for the individual investor can be offered as a Web service with an adaptable user interface using commercial enterprise portal server software products. Filtering, editing, searching and organizing capabilities now are available commercially through companies such as YellowBrix (2003).

A prototype is under construction using a combination of the Microsoft .NET platform, Sharepoint Portal Server, Microsoft Digital Dashboard, and YellowBrix XML News Services. Intelligent agent technology is being written using Microsoft Visual Basic.NET as server side agents maintaining objectives

Figure 7: Rational Investor Partner Prototype

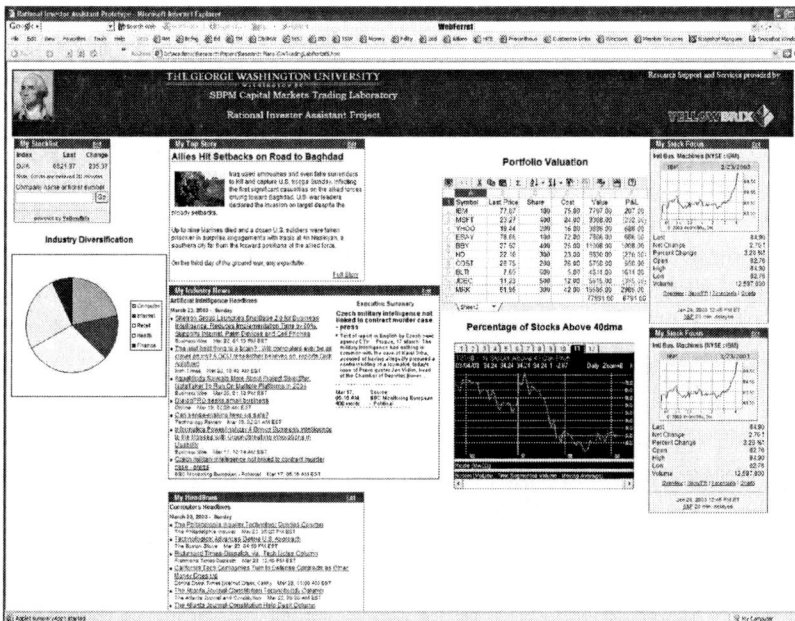

and feeding information filtered and categorized by the news and data interface agents.

CONCLUSION

This chapter has clearly shown the accelerating pace of technological advancement in the financial markets. The repeating trend is toward the efficiency of price discovery and information dissemination, improving the efficiency of executing transactions thus minimizing transaction costs, and managing the transactions and knowledge base of information and expertise.

While early technology advancement was through physical technology (devices such as the telegraph, telephone, computers, networks, etc.), the upcoming wave is much more focused on soft technologies (software, protocol, transaction standards, KM, intelligent agents, etc.). In many cases this new technology is directed to deal with the information overload caused by the avalanche of information triggered by the Internet.

Looking back at the critical assumptions of the EMH, it was noted throughout the discussion of technology that dramatic progress has been made in reducing transaction costs and increasing the availability of company information and price discovery. From the EMH this would suggest that the markets are becoming more efficient. However, with these improvements, the financial markets have continued to experience periods of extreme overpricing and underpricing as seen in everything from the "Tulip Mania" of 1637 to the Internet bubble of 2000. One conclusion that can be drawn from this phenomenon is that these technological improvements have not reduced the problem of irrational investor behaviors. Quite the contrary, technology has introduced new ways that investors can trade, most notably described as "day-trading." In some cases these changes have resulted in an increase in reckless trading activities, misinformation and rumors.

There is potential that the technology known as intelligent agents and the technologies being developed as part of the Rational Investor Partner Project may provide a stabilizing view of the ever increasing information and rapid transactions. Thus, an MAS implementation for investors may be technology that addresses the EMH assumption of a rational investor.

REFERENCES

Barnet, K. & Migliore, P. (2000). Building tomorrow's leading front office: Best practices on the trading desk. *PriceWaterhouseCoopers Perspectives Trading,* 3, 70-81.

Best, K. (2001). *XML in Financial Industries.* Retrieved from the World Wide Web: http://www.oasis-open.org/presentations/financial.pdf.

Buelens, F. & Cuyvers, L. (2000, February). *Stock Market Development and Economic Growth in Belgium: 1300-2000.* Paper presented at the University of Antwerp. Submitted to Financial History Review.

Decker, K., Sycara, K. & Zeng. D. (1996). Designing a multi-agent portfolio management system: Intelligent Adaptive Agents. *Proceedings of the AAAI-96.*

Fama, E. (1970). Efficient capital markets: A review of theory and empirical work. *Journal of Finance*, 25(2), 383-423.

Feinstein, J. L. & Lumley, R. A. (2000). *Theoretical and Practical Aspects of AHP using a Scale Derived from the Time it Takes to Decide Between Two Choices instead of one Derived from "1-9" Estimates.* Paper presented at the meeting of the ISAHP. Berne, Switzerland.

FIX Protocol Ltd., Introduction of FIX. (2000). Presentation to the Asian Pacific Region. Retrieved from the World Wide Web: http://www.fixprotocol.org/presentations/March_2000_Hong_Kong_Intro.zip.

Guerra, A. (2002). SEC to Float T+1 Conversion Proposal. *Wall Street and Technology.* Retrieved from the World Wide Web: http://www.wallstreet andtech.com/story/stp/WST20020520S0001.

Intel Corporation. (2002). Global Securities Industry: Setting a Straight Course to T+1 Trade Processing. Intel Business Computing Finance Industry Solutions White Paper. Retrieved from the World Wide Web: http://www.intel.com/ebusiness/pdf/prod/industry/ar013003.pdf.

Island Corporation. How Island Works. Retrieved from the World Wide Web: http://www.isld.com/corp/about/works.asp.

Kanungo, S. (2002). *Examining the problem of rural IT sustainability: Lessons from the field.* Working Paper. Department of Management Science, George Washington University, Washington, DC.

Khoshafian, S. (2002). Web Services and Virtual Enterprises. Web Services Architect. Retrieved from the World Wide Web: http://www.webservicesarchitect.com/content/articles/WSAVEKHOSH AFIAN220502.pdf.

Leman, J. (2000, March). *FIX Overview.* Paper presented at Introduction of FIX by FIX Protocol Ltd to the Asian Pacific Region. Retrieved from the World Wide Web: http://www.fixprotocol.org/presentations/March_2000 Hong_Kong_Intro.zip.

Liu, K., Luo, Y. & Davis, D. N. (2000). A multi-agent framework for stock trading. *Proceedings of Conference on Intelligent Information Processing, 16th World Computing Conference.*

Luo, L., Davis, D. N. & K. (2002, January/February). A multi-agent system framework for decision support in stock trading. *IEEE Network Magazine Special Issue on Enterprise Networking and Services*, 16(1).

Merriam-Webster Dictionary (2003). Merriam-Webster Online. Retrieved from the World Wide Web: http://www.m-w.com.

NYSE (2003). Historical Perspective. Retrieved from the World Wide Web: http://www.nyse.com/about/timeline/1610.html.

Osterland, A. (2000). Equity: Wall Street wired. *CFO Magazine*.

Resta, M. (2000, July). Towards an artificial technical analysis. *IEEE-INNS-ENNS International Joint Conference on Neural Networks (IJCNN'00)*, 5. Como, Italy.

RIXML Consortium (2003). Research Information Exchange Markup Language Specification 1.0. Retrieved from the World Wide Web: http://www.rixml.org.

Robotics Lab (2003). The Warren System. Retrieved from the World Wide Web: http://www.ri.cmu.edu/projects/project_77.html.

Saaty, T. L. (1977). A scaling method for priorities in hierarchical structure. *Journal of Mathematical Psychology*, 15, 79-84.

Saaty, T. L. (1996). The analytic hierarchy process: Planning, priority setting, resource allocation. *RWS Publications*.

Samtani, G. & Sadhwania, D. (2002, June). Web Services and Straight Through Processing: Web Services in the Financial Industry. Web Services Architect. Retrieved from the World Wide Web: http://www.webservices architect.com/content/articles/samtani06print.asp.

Santosis, M. & Surmacz, J. (n.d.). The ABCs of knowledge management: Knowledge management research center. *CIO Magazine*. Retrieved from World Wide Web: http://www.cio.com/research/knowledge/edit/kmabcs.html.

Schmerken, I. (2000, November). Where is wireless headed? *Wall Street and Technologies*. Retrieved from the World Wide Web: http://www.wstonline.com/story/inDepth/WST20001115S0002.

Seo, Y., Giampapa, J. A. & Sycara, K. (2002, May). Text classification for intelligent portfolio management. Technical Report CMU-RI-TR-02-14, Robotics Institute, Carnegie Mellon University.

SWIFT Consortium. (2003). Retrieved from the World Wide Web: http://www.swift.com.

Tiwana, A. (2000). *Knowledge Management Toolkit, the Practical Techniques for Building a Knowledge Management System*. Prentice Hall.

Tseng, C. & Gmytrasiewicz, P. J. (2002, January). Real time decision support systems for portfolio management. *Proceedings of the 35th Hawaii International Conference on System Sciences, HICSS-35*.

Wooldridge, M. (2002). *An Introduction to Multi-agent Systems*. John Wiley & Sons.

Wooldridge, M. & Jennings, N. R. (1995). Intelligent agents: Theory and practice. *The Knowledge Engineering Review*, 10(2), 115-152.

YellowBrix (2003). *Content Enhancement Services*. Retrieved from the World Wide Web: http://www.yellowbrix.com/pages/www/index.nsp?id=isyndicate _tech.

Chapter V

Ability of the Actor Network Theory (ANT) to Model and Interpret an Electronic Market

Murat Baygeldi
London School of Economics, UK

Steve Smithson
London School of Economics, UK

ABSTRACT

The nature of information systems is often complex and involves both human and nonhuman components. This is particularly true in an electronic market. Actor Network Theory (ANT) can be used in general to describe the actors, intermediaries, framing and power that are the most important components of such an electronic market, which we call a network. This chapter explores whether ANT can help to analyze electronic trading systems. And if so, can ANT help us to filter the success factors of a computer trading system like Eurex, the largest derivatives electronic market in the world? It highlights how ANT is useful to define the various components involved within an electronic market. Moreover, the chapter analyses ANT's limitations in modeling computer-trading systems. This chapter concludes that ANT is useful to analyze an electronic market such as Eurex.

INTRODUCTION

Globalization of financial markets has increased rapidly in the last few years due to a combination of deregulation and dramatic advances in information technology (Beck, 2000; Giddens, 1998; Kapstein, 1997; Young & Theys, 1999). Increasingly, financial institutions conduct their trades through electronic markets. Electronic trading markets like the German/Swiss European Exchange (Eurex) have had a major impact on the participants (e.g., banks) on the one hand and on the markets (e.g., exchanges) on the other hand. Electronic trading has been globally successful since 1997. Most financial products are traded electronically on a relatively few electronic trading systems such as Pats Systems and Trading Technologies.

Actor Network Theory (ANT) is introduced to describe with a specific vocabulary to what extent technology influences human behavior. ANT shows that the use and development of an information infrastructure is a socio-technical process of negotiation. ANT has been widely adopted in the social science literature and also in the information systems literature. It can provide a framework to describe global networks. ANT will help us to understand the electronic markets and, in particular, it can tell us about Eurex's success. ANT has its origins in studies of the networks of social practices within science and technology. Latour (1996) recognized that both human actors and nonhuman participants were equally actants. The neologism actant is often used as a neutral way to refer to human and nonhuman actors, thus eliminating the strong human bias in the word actor. They are defined by how they act within the networks of practices.

In this chapter, Eurex is used as a case study to analyze how a market can be interpreted as a heterogeneous network. Financial products traded on the German/Swiss electronic exchange Eurex are accessible from any location in the world. In order to understand an electronic market like Eurex, we discuss the role of an actor network. Heterogeneous actor networks will be described with the help of ANT. A network consists of different components. Analyzing such networks gives us a broader perspective and provides insight into markets based on electronic exchanges. It also allows exploring the differing interests of actors within a market. A market can also be seen as an exchange. Direct accesses from actors like institutional or private market participants to an electronic market are an important factor for the network. Without this direct access, electronic trading systems like Eurex would not exist.

Our aim is to analyze whether ANT can help us to understand the "components" involved in the "actor network" of Eurex. Relatively little literature is available on the application of ANT to new electronic markets/exchanges like Eurex, which emerged fairly recently. The aim of actors is to buy and/or sell financial products within the actor network of Eurex. Humans and artifacts are involved in this process in order to perform a transaction. Both roles within the network will be described more in detail. However, it is necessary to explain concepts like actor, black box, framing, power and intermediary in order to understand and interpret Eurex.

We explain what an electronic market and Eurex mean. Callon (1998) concludes that framing and the construction of calculative actors are essential for a market. To analyze Eurex's components, we need to describe what framing means. Aspects of power will also be mentioned for the purpose of distinguishing between actors. The main components of a network are discussed after defining the basic concept of ANT. The question, "What is an actor network?," will be discussed in section four. The framing of actors within a market will also be analyzed, before highlighting implications for theory and practice. Finally, conclusions are laid out in the last section together with areas for further research.

WHAT IS AN ELECTRONIC MARKET?

Following O'Brien (1992), Gosh and Ortiz (1994) hold that the changes of the global structure of financial markets are the result of the rapidly changing environment. The trend towards a global electronic trading platform has become a new reality for most markets or exchanges around the world (Clemons & Weber, 1996; Fan & Stallaert, 1999). We focus on Eurex, which is meanwhile the largest electronic markets in the world and is slightly different from other electronic exchanges. Eurex was formed as a result of the merger of the German and Swiss electronic exchanges.

Cunningham and Tynan (1993) tried to define electronic trading (markets) in a way that the definition needs to be sufficiently adaptable to avoid becoming obsolete because of rapidly changing technology. One of the solutions they suggest is to take perceptions of the systems in use as the starting point. As a result it would be possible to refer to "electronic trading," rather than specific communication technologies. They define electronic trading as any trading relationship that relies upon the use of computer technology for inter-organizational communications, normally involving telecommunication links. Electronic trading systems exploit information technology capabilities to improve the efficiency of communications and alter the nature of inter-organizational transactions. It can be seen as an automated process of trading financial products in a market. Trading on Eurex can be seen as the matching of bid and offer prices from different actors through translation. Eurex members can conduct trades directly through a computer link to the market or they can simply transact via the Internet. In this context, the most frequent confusion is with respect to the meaning of the term *transaction*. The relevant broker calculates how many financial products the actor can buy or sell.

When discussing transaction limits, the term transaction does not refer to the number of financial products that a given actant may trade, but rather to a processing activity within the Eurex system. From a technical point of view, a distinction is made between synchronous and asynchronous system transactions. Transactions are termed synchronous whenever an exchange participant, triggering an immediate response by the Eurex system, initiates them. Participants who have initiated such a transaction await a direct (synchronous) system response on their screen. Asynchronous system transactions are all those which cannot be directly attributed to an activity by a participant. Predominantly, this includes subsequent Eurex system processes carried out as a result of actants' activities, such as the posting of positions after the conclusion of trades or the broadcast of price information to all participants. Some authors describe an electronic market as a single or joint action of a variety of actors who are always present in a market. In the next section, we will mention two different examples of computer markets or "networks."

EUREX AND THE CBOT/EUREX ALLIANCE

The Eurex mission is to provide the customers with access to the world's most liquid financial markets. Eurex was launched in 1989 with the aim to compete against other financial markets. In order to distinguish itself from the long-established competing financial markets, Eurex decided to link actors like institutional members electronically to their local network in Frankfurt. This was possible after the German government changed its financial market legislation in 1988. The new legislation allowed financial institutions to launch the electronic market almost independently of the influence of the German Government. The role of the regional state was reduced to oversee the development with little regulatory intervention. Eurex was formerly known as Deutsche Terminbörse (DTB). Eurex was created by Deutsche Börse AG and the Swiss Exchange in December 1996 and through the merger of DTB and SOFFEX (Swiss Options and Financial Futures Exchange) was founded. The actors agreed to develop and implement a single platform for their markets and trade a harmonized product range. German banks pulled out of the major open-outcry exchanges and convinced their clients to support the electronic exchange instead of the open-outcry exchanges. Some clients were forced to conduct transactions through Eurex. The operational technical merger of the two electronic markets was completed on September 28, 1998, when all DTB and SOFFEX participants united on a common trading and settlement platform and the newly established Eurex clearing house commenced its activities.

Trading on the fully computerized Eurex platform is distinctively different from trading on traditional open-outcry markets. It transcends borders and offers actors technical access from any location, thereby creating a unique global liquidity network. Members are linked to the Eurex system via a dedicated wide-area communications network (WAN). To facilitate access to Eurex outside of Switzerland and Germany, access points have so far been installed in Amsterdam, Chicago, New York, Helsinki, London, Madrid, Paris, Hong Kong and Tokyo.

Time and space limited the expansion of the major traditional open-outcry markets. Eurex could expand with the help of technology and provide direct electronic access to a full range of products. The powerful German banks forced other participants to join the electronic exchange. They also offered their clients "fee holidays" (Franke, 1993). In other words clients did not have to pay any transaction fees for selected financial products. The success is sustainable because the banks support the system and are at the same time major shareholders. One of Eurex's other initiatives is expanding its already broad product range, either by listing innovative financial products or entering into strategic alliances. It facilitates trading of many of the world's benchmark financial products between the entire range of direct exchange users, institutional and retail investors.

For Shaw and Kauser (2000) a strategic alliance is regarded as a term that is applied to independent firms cooperating and forming alliances. Those alliances can also be seen as new "networks." The Chicago Board of Trade (CBOT) and Eurex formed a business and technology partnership in the U.S. that has resulted in a joint venture company: a/c/e – alliance/cbot/eurex. This alliance was created and launched on August 27, 2000 as one global platform. The global platform can also be seen as a "new network" or market. The CBOT exchange is modeled on open-outcry. CBOT realized that their actor network had become "unstable." More and more actors were joining the fully computerized market. Eurex realized the opportunity to extend their established and stable network through partnership. Eurex has formed an alliance with CBOT to implement and operate the Eurex electronic trading platform in the United States. CBOT and Eurex members can obtain direct access to CBOT's and Eurex's trading platforms. Every exchange participant admitted to trading is required to participate in the clearing process of Eurex Clearing AG. The participant can choose to participate as a general clearing member (GCM), direct clearing member (DCM) or non-clearing member (NCM). GCMs can participate without any limits or restrictions. It is based on a common trading platform. The alliance is open to other electronic exchanges. CBOT tried to re-stabilize their actor network through the transformation of the open-outcry exchange to a computerized exchange. Many financial firms have different network connections. The problems of different network connections are not addressed sufficiently in the literature. CBOT/Eurex have decided to link participating firms to the common platform via a wide-area communication network (WAN).

INTEGRATION OF NEW ELECTRONIC TRADING SYSTEMS

One of the bases of success for these networks is the global accessibility and low transaction costs. Transaction cost is the price a member has to pay for a matched trade. It is also called "the exchange fee." The exchange fee dropped dramatically due to lower head counts. Lower costs lead to more members or actors stimulating rising volumes. Liquidity is typically defined as the ability to convert an asset into cash equal to its current market value. In this paper liquidity is something that is easily sold in the market at current market prices. In a liquid market, an actor can sell large blocks of financial products rapidly without significantly affecting market prices. Before the integration, the CBOT open-outcry exchange network was criticized as expensive and "old-fashioned." Many market participants refused to continue trading on the open-outcry exchange. Liquidity declined in conjunction with the destabilization of the network. The open-outcry network was and still is close to a "breakdown." CBOT decided to transform their network to a computerized market. The electronic trading system is identical to the Eurex trading system. Actors can electronically transact from all over the world now. The new Eurex/CBOT global electronic system is linked to the markets in Frankfurt and Chicago. Both networks are integrated and actors have access to financial products from both exchanges. CBOT is thinking about a new alliance with different electronic exchanges such as Euronext/LIFFE. Before we continue, it is necessary to outline the main points of ANT in the next section.

ACTOR NETWORK THEORY (ANT)

Actor Network Theory evolved mainly from the authors Latour (1992), Callon (1991) and Law (1991) who were searching for an explanation for the social interaction between "us," the humans and, for example, technology, the nonhumans. Within the interaction, the actors are defined as entities that create things. Humans include all natural creatures. Nonhumans include technology, artifacts or also naturalized constructs. All of these components should be seen together in a network. Latour (1993) stresses the need for a new interpretation of our modern constitution. He is convinced that nature and culture should be treated symmetrically. The traditional view interprets nature and culture as completely opposite poles. Which view is correct, the traditional view or the view of Latour and Callon? According to Latour (1992), nature, culture and society are constructed simultaneously. These three factors should be seen as interrelated. For Callon (1991), the acceptance of a clear distinction between technical and scientific approaches should not be taken for granted. Callon (1998) focuses on the market to explain, as economists have done in a different context, "the coordination mechanism between humans, goods and technologies." Conflicts of interest are resolved by transactions. The actors are involved in transactions within the market. Callon's (1991) approach is based on the assumption that products and technology are as important as human beings in a market.

We would like to draw attention to Callon, as he is one of the few academics that are willing to answer the question, "What is a market?" in conjunction with ANT. Social aspects within economics influence theories more than many authors assumed a long time ago. This sociological aspect gives economics and information systems a more *complete* character. He discusses cognitive psychology and presumes that individual economic actors are capable of constant mental calculation. Calculation is in Callon's opinion a "complex collective practice that involves more than the capabilities granted to actors by epistemologists and some economists" (Callon, 1998). Culture, as he explains, "is frequently used to explain the appearance of rational actors." He describes it as the atom of the market economy. Actors differ in their behavior within different societies. They pursue their own interests and perform economic calculations.

Optimization and maximization of an operation can then be achieved. Actors generally have divergent interests, which lead them to engage in transactions, which resolve the conflict by defining a price. Actors are defined as calculating actors. As Akerlof stated, "I would like to ask how precisely do actors define a price?" Akerlof's idea was that if "buyers cannot tell the difference between secondhand cars by looking at them, kicking the tires or taking them for a test drive, then the price in the market will reflect the average quality of the cars on offer" (Akerlof, 1984). In order to be calculative, actors must be open to the environment. As Callon (1998) points out, actors will be calculative according to social network analysis. Actors enter and leave the exchange network like strangers after the transaction has been concluded. It is significant that he says that the actor with the greatest power of calculation is the actor whose tools enable it to have the greatest number of relations. Unfortunately, Callon (1998) does not explain the power of an actor more precisely. General clearing members in Eurex have the greatest number of relations and power. They can act in an unlimited fashion within the Eurex framework.

Human and nonhuman elements are both actors (actants). An actant should be seen as superior to just an actor. "It can be seen as an automatic door opener" (Latour, 1988) or "it can be scallops in the sea" (Callon, 1986). An actor network consists of and links together both technical and nontechnical elements. This can be easily explained from our activities, for example conducting a trade on Eurex; the buyer or seller is hereby the nontechnical element, the electronic trading system Eurex can be seen as the technical element. *"Network"* means the interaction between all actors, objects and subjects, that together determine our behavior, or in this case the market. For example, I am using a PC linked to Eurex and all the technicalities it offers in order to be able to conduct a trade. My previous experience allows me to exploit the electronic trading system Eurex in more depth and continuously develop my own skills. All these surrounding factors, myself as the user, the PC, the advancing technology, my experience, are related or connected to how I act now. All these influencing components should be interpreted together to produce a framework or "network" as defined in ANT. Networks will be explained in more detail within the next sections.

Actors share the scene in the reconstruction of the network of interactions. This leads to the stabilization of the system. Only actors are able to put actants in circulation within the system, although uncertainty about the stability of a network does exist. A possible solution (Granovetter, 1992) to reduce uncertainty "is provided by the network, a network that configures anthologies." The actors, their dimensions, and what they perform, depend on the morphology of the relations in which they are involved. The number of connections that an actor has with different networks determines what the actor is.

For Law (1999), an actor network "is a name, a term which embodies a tension." A tension, which lies between the centered actors on the one hand, and the decentralized "network" on the other. The actor-network insists on the preformative character of relations (Law & Hassard, 1999). Translation does not tell us how links are made. Similarity and difference are unclear. If we assume that ANT is alive, then we can also assume that it transforms itself. So there should be no identity or any fixed point. We can assume that relations are in general uncertain and can be reversed by actors.

ACTORS AND BLACK BOXES

Callon and Law (1986) define an actor as an element, which bends space around itself and makes other elements dependent upon it. The aim of an actor is to translate its will into a language of its own. In another definition Latour (1992) sees actors as entities that do things. Accordingly he emphasizes that what an actor is, is not as important as the action itself and the competences it performs within the chain. An actor is also defined as an element, which performs through trial and error (Akrich & Latour, 1992). For example, a coin is an actor and performs as a mechanism for exchange. The coin is acting and is being represented. Actors show that the elements represented in a market do act. A computerized market can be seen as a network. The coin as an exchange mechanism depends on the strengths of the network. In other words, its performance and success as an accepted exchange mechanism depend on the strength of the network. A coin in this sense can also be seen as a "black box."

Thus, it is not possible to break up the world into discrete objects, events or persons (Introna & Whitley, 1999).

Electronic trading participants in offices and the actions they perform confirm that the technology is well advanced and that human-actors such as traders or stakeholders decide which system they use and support. An example of two different electronic trading systems clearly supports the idea that human actors use their power unexpectedly. LIFFE (London International Financial Futures Exchange) used to trade all derivative products (options and futures) on the open-outcry market. If we look more specifically to the short-term three-month interest rate futures we realize a very interesting behavior of human actors. In spite of the immense success of the electronic trading system Eurex, one specific product remained in "London," the Euronext/LIFFE Connect system, namely the three-month Euribor futures and options. The social relationship within the actors including the pit traders was so robust that the transformation has been to the electronic trading system of Euronext/LIFFE instead of Eurex. The "leading" actors and social environment animated them to switch to LIFFE Connect. Pit traders, for example, socialize on a regular basis and often make their decisions during a dinner or a drink after work. The network in this case was still intact and difficult to change. As we know, all fixed income and equity derivative products are traded on the LIFFE-electronic trading system Connect. Actors trading the short-term interest rate sterling futures on the pit simply supported the LIFFE electronic trading system and switched over and continued conducting trades via this new heterogeneous electronic network. The German electronic exchange Eurex "took over" the five-year Government Futures and Options (BOBL) and also the 10-year Government Futures and Options (BUND). All actors moved from the LIFFE pit to the German electronic trading system in a very short period. The actors now act differently and translate their activities in an electronic environment.

The reasons for using an electronic trading system rather than an open-outcry exchange are mostly costs, time and transparency. Now, back to the unexpected and unusual behavior of the actors in one specific area. The three-month Euribor futures can be traded on both the LIFFE electronic trading system/exchange and the German electronic trading system/exchange. There are no major differences between those two exchanges, except for the difference of clearinghouses. The German clearinghouse gives the actor some advantages because it is integrated to the exchange. But the actors do trade Euribor products via the LIFFE trading system. It is important to mention that the German electronic exchange did offer the service — trading three-month Euribor derivatives- long before LIFFE on their electronic exchange. The actors did not support the German electronic trading system for one specific product, namely the Euribor products. This finding supports our hypothesis that human actors have the power to support or reject existing trading systems. The explanation can only be found if we analyze social issues, which influence actors' activities.

A black box can be treated as a fact where only the input and output counts. A black box contains that which no longer needs to be considered, those things whose contents have become a matter of indifference (Callon & Latour, 1986). Law (1999) states: "ANT removes the productive non-coherence even further from view. The black boxing and punctualizing that we have witnessed as we have named it made it easily transportable. They have made a simple space through which it may be transported. But the cost has been heavy. We have lost the capacity to apprehend complexity. What we are trying to do is to argue against simplicity-and a notion of theory that says that it is or should necessarily be simple, clear, and transparent."

EMERGENCE OF INTERMEDIARIES

Networks are created by or through actors. In some cases a sustainable development is interrupted by new developments like new inventions (e.g., open-outcry market versus computer market). A new invention can result in new networks. These new networks develop out of existing networks. Another example is the failed electronic market Jiway (*Financial Times*, October 2001).

As soon as an actor tries to increase power (Introna, 1997; Foucault, 1983) a starting point of a different network can emerge. If actors follow the "leader," it is likely that a new network can emerge. The stability of the network depends on the number and commitment of each actor. If the actor is very active he can be very powerful. Two aspects of power should be mentioned: the micro politics of power and the semiotic power structure. In the micro politics of power, technologies can be used as instruments to build up networks of influence (Kapstcin, 1997; Walsham, 1993). Walsham also uses the term domination. The semiotic power is a result of the "fixity" of meanings. It is built-up during the creation of a technological frame. After spending a lot of time on the key technology, the technology's meaning becomes settled or fixed. It is not easy to revert to a new technological frame. Framing will be further analyzed in the next section.

Intermediaries are not always accepted in markets, because they can slow the process between two transactions, although intermediaries may be necessary to create a network. An intermediary connects actors into a network and defines the network itself. Actors create networks by implementing intermediaries between each other. An intermediary is anything that "passes between actors in the course of relatively stable transactions" (Bijker & Law, 1992). Intermediaries are the language of the network. Through intermediaries, actors communicate with each other within the network. For example, one bank employee communicates with a broker and asks him to find a buyer for the product within the "network." The financial institution employee prefers to conduct the trade via an intermediary due to his or her limited time.

NETWORKS

A network can be described as a dynamic system of communication, co-operation and partnership between individuals and groups. The concept of the network is found in biology, politics, telecommunications, business, and sociology. The products of these networks could be nature in the form of scientific facts (Latour, 1987), society (Castilla, Hwang, Granovetter, & Granovetter, 2000; Rosen, 1993) or technology (Bijker, 1992; Law & Callon, 1992; Latour, 1991). They can be "hybrids" (Latour, 1993) or in a different word, "cyborgs" (Richard & Whitley, 2000). Callon (1993) defines the term network as a "group of unspecified relationships among entities of which the nature itself is undetermined." A network can be seen as two systems of alliances (Wasserman & Faust, 1994): "Firstly, people who are involved in the usage, construction, distribution and implementation of an artifact. And secondly things (nonhumans) like coins or computers." People and things are interconnected (Latour, 1987). This view should be developed further.

An actor cannot act without a network, since networks consist of actors (Callon, 1987). Actor and network redefine each other permanently. The size or the power of an actor is not necessary dependent on the size of the network. For example, the Jiway electronic market is very small compared to Eurex. But an actor within the smaller electronic market can be more powerful. The power of an actor is defined by the position within the network. Actors are not necessarily equal (Latour, 1992). It can be criticized that he also says that there is no structural difference between large and small actors.

Benjamin and Wigand (1995) discuss the unspecified relationship between things and people within a network. They are convinced that networking technologies can reduce the costs in exchange transactions. With the decline of costs, business activities previously carried out within vertically integrated firms will be shifted to the marketplace. Some authors claim that transaction costs can be crucial for ANT. The market structure depends on network characteristics and the economies of the network. Part of the development within a network is the process of translation. It is possible to have two directions within the network. The first one is leading to convergence and the other one to divergence. New actors within a network can lead to higher divergence. Those new actors are already involved in other networks. Translation is a process that is performed by at least two different actors. Actors are as mentioned engaged in other networks. This engagement can lead to different translation between actors and can lead to various results. It is not clear enough in the literature which role intermediaries have in networks in terms of increasing the success rate of translation in networks.

MARKET AS A NETWORK

The motivation behind an actor's actions is not predetermined (Callon, 1998). To show the strength of ANT and one of the reasons why it was created we use the example of the "market" which mixes humans and nonhumans and controls their relations. Actors are active and able to make difficult decisions to achieve their objective. As mentioned earlier in this paper, actors are calculative, pursue their own interests, and make informed decisions. Their roles are defined in the computer market Eurex. We can use ANT to understand micro-processes of this market. Actors are interested in the outcome of their economic calculations. This is caused by the fact that a discord regarding a price during a transaction between actors can generally be transformed into consensus.

The ideal situation to be able to calculate is an environment with low uncertainty. Callon (1998) uses the term contingent contract to solve the problem of uncertainty in a market. In this context contingent means, contingent to the precise market situation. For example: I am offering a product A in the Eurex network for a price of X1, contingent to Y. If the price of Y changes to Y1, I will ask the actor to cancel the order to sell X1. Here the actor can be seen as an artifact and/or as a human being. The contracts offered between actors are constantly revisable during the social interaction. Shared culture, rules, procedures and routines can reduce uncertainties for actors and increase the predictability of electronic markets. Unfortunately, behavior is not always predictable, although interaction and negotiation can help to reduce misleading interpretations.

One solution to the question of coordination would be the notion of embeddedness (Granovetter, 1985). Actors can calculate their decisions because they are entangled in relations. For Granovetter the solution that is provided by the network is a network that configures ontology. The actors, their dimensions and their actions depend upon the morphology of the relations in which they are involved. An actor's power rises with the number of relations within different networks. General Clearing Members (GCM) have more power than Non-Clearing Members (NCM) in Eurex. Teamwork and trust lead to a network, which can improve performance (Luhmann, 1988). We have seen this behavior of locals switching to the LIFFE electronic trading system rather the German Eurex system. This view can be criticized. Many networks "breakdown" even if they are entangled in relations. But it takes time and the rejection of many human actors with different power structures before a heterogeneous already established network becomes vulnerable. The global financial system can become vulnerable over time. As soon as an actor's activities change, their power supporting existing infrastructures becomes uncontrollable and not stoppable. Those human actors will — after an unknown time — support a different heterogeneous network or heterogeneous networks which have different actors and which are possibly in place already. Those networks consist of actors and behave like atoms which always remain but which appear in various locations.

FRAMING OF ACTORS

Actors and goods conducting calculations should be framed and disentangled. Therefore, it is necessary to implement boundaries. Actors' activities are within these boundaries. The notion of externality has been developed in economic theory to show one of the shortcomings of the market (Aumann, Hart, & Neyman, 1995). Callon (1998) uses the notions of framing and overflowing to explain what he means by constructing a market. According to Callon framing is an operation that helps to define actors. He distinguishes actors from other actors and goods from other goods. Framing is a tool to create a market. Rules and regulations helped Eurex to frame relations. Relations outside the frame are externalities. Framing is a continuous procedure. Calculations are not possible without framing as explained by Garcia (1986). Garcia's study of the transformation of the strawberry market in the Sologne region of France explains the development of framing and the construction of calculative actors very well and is a good example of how an electronic market can be framed. This framing allows actors belonging to the Eurex network to calculate. Transactions within this newly created market started in line with the existence of the product (strawberries) and a sustainable supply and demand (bid and ask) between actors. The different components help framing and lead to transactions within Eurex. The strawberry market can also be created electronically and is similar to the electronic market Eurex.

Ciborra (1996) emphasizes that the modern form of economic organizations as alliances or networked or federated firms is considered to be at the forefront in terms of combinations of routines and transactions. The actors' intention is to stabilize the network in order to reduce uncertainty. Stabilization or closure means that the interpretive flexibility diminishes (Callon, 1992). A stable network is able to resist competing translations. It is also able to avoid further possible future translations because it is already "settled" (Star, 1995). Latour (1992) sees the description of a network as finished when it is "saturated" and an explanation emerges. But how can we measure a saturated market? Is Eurex the — electronic market — saturated and not vulnerable to a breakdown?

PRACTICAL IMPLICATIONS

Financial products are either traded on open outcry exchanges or on electronic exchanges. Both markets can be seen as different heterogeneous actor networks. The shift from traditional exchanges towards electronic exchanges can result in uncontrollable networks. Risks are involved because many questions regarding electronic exchanges are not answered. One of the risks involved is a "breakdown" of a network and the appearance of a new one.

ANT has its limitations because it is not seen as a fixed theory. This "theory," a very interesting and exciting one, is on the other hand also controversial (Richard & Whitley, 2000). Sometimes it is partly rejected (Walsham, 1995) and can be seen as a methodology rather than a theory.

It is very useful to explain markets or networks based on electronic trading systems in order to understand the complexity of a market. Unfortunately, it is also necessary to develop or define the "components" (e.g., actor, power and framing) within ANT further. It is also necessary to know more about how IT shapes and constrains changes within an electronic market. Callon (1998) interprets a market as an actor network. The available literature does not clearly support this hypothesis. It has been said that computers can cause the collapse of a market. We need to know not only that there is a correlation between human and nonhuman behavior, but also how it works. ANT has been used in a few interpretative case studies (Monteiro, 2000). ANT does not clearly distinguish between small and big networks, or between micro and macro level. The question of power between actors is also not analyzed well enough. The way the authors interpret an electronic market like Eurex as a heterogeneous actor network is controversial.

CONCLUSION AND FUTURE WORK

This chapter has attempted to bring together a range of different literature. The aim was to investigate what an actor network is and conclude what kind of further research is necessary in order to describe networks. The nature of information systems is complex and involves both human and nonhuman components — no less so than in an electronic market. We explored whether ANT can help to analyze electronic trading systems. An electronic market depends on the outlined components or elements of a network. The authors interpret a market or an electronic exchange as an "actor network."

ANT is a tool for the analysis of socio-technological development. Intermediaries are passed among the actors to assure a certain degree of convergence among them. This convergence allows the heterogeneous network Eurex to act in an understandable way, which is to translate one actor's objectives through different actors to achieve the goal via a transaction. A goal of an actor within Eurex's network can be seen as the attempt to find a counter party who is willing to buy or to sell. The importance of an actor within the transaction procedure is defined by his/her/its position within the network. Power rises in correlation to the degree of convergence. In a situation where we can see high convergence, the network seems to be stable. In this situation it can be seen as a black box. Black boxes can be seen as artifacts or structures.

There have been various "breakdowns" of *networks* (Taurus, LIFFE "open-outcry," Jiway). A "breakdown" of a network (market) can be seen as the result of the move of actors to different networks. In many ways, ANT seems to offer a useful approach to studying such breakdowns and, in particular, it seems especially suited to studying the creation of new networks.

ANT enables us to go further than traditional socio-economics or analyses in terms of networks proposed by authors like Granovetter (1992). Eurex as an electronic market is the result of operations of disentanglement, internalization, externalization and framing. To understand a market we need to understand the construction of calculative actors. Framing can be possible only if there are connections between actors. Eurex does supply these connections. ANT assumes social relations are "in-forged" into the technology. It can be system-theoretically presumed that there are different types of electronic trading systems. They differ in complexity levels. During a system transformation complexity enlarges (e.g., a/c/e, the new electronic market that resulted from the alliance of Eurex and CBOT).

One particular benefit of the ANT approach is that it offers a relatively straightforward and systematic way of formalizing much of the tacit knowledge regarding social behavior. This type of knowledge is held by all of us, in our particular fields of expertise, but it is not easily formalizable, unlike much of a knowledge-based organization's low-level data. We have shown how this type of knowledge concerning the formation of Eurex can be captured in a reusable form, using ANT.

The nature of ANT analysis is such that it is very detailed and comprehensive, which means that an analysis of a large market like Eurex, with all its traders, operators and regulators, becomes very complex. The number of actors shaping Eurex's network is so high that it is difficult to identify all of them. Furthermore, although ANT provides the tools to track the process of change in networks, it does not seek to explain the behavior of actors. Thus, the use of ANT alone makes a network change unpredictable and a change to the network causes new changes. Callon (1998) criticizes that, "ANT is so tolerant that it ends up presenting an actor, which is anonymous and not well defined." Nevertheless, with further development, or perhaps in combination with other social science theories, the tools of ANT may become the basis of a more effective approach to explaining changes in social and business networks.

REFERENCES

Akerlof, G. (1984). *An Economic Theorist's Book of Tales: Essays that Entertain the Consequences of New Assumptions in Economic Theory.* Cambridge, MA: University Press.

Akrich, M. & Latour, B. (1992). *A Convenient Vocabulary for the Semiotics of Human and Nonhuman Actors.* In W. Bijker & J. Law (Eds.), *Shaping Technology - Building Society Studies in Sociotechnological Change.* Cambridge, MA: MIT Press.

Aumann, R. J., Hart, S. & Neyman, A. (1995). *Game and Economic Theory.* University of Michigan Press.

Beck, B. (2000). *What is Globalization?* Cambridge, MA: Polity Press.

Benjamin, R. & Wigand, R. (1995). Electronic markets and virtual value chains on the information superhighway. *Sloan Management Review.*

Bijker, W. (1992). *The Social Construction of Fluorescent Light, Or How an Artifact was Invented in its Diffusion Stage.* In W. Bijker & J. Law (Eds.), *In Sociotechnological Change.* Cambridge, MA: MIT Press.

Callon, M. (1986). The sociology of an actor net-network: The case of the electric vehicle. In M. Callon, J. Law & A. Rip (Eds.), *Mapping the Dynamics of Science and Technology.* London: MacMillan.

Callon, M. (1991). Techno-economic networks and irreversibility. In J. Law (Ed.), *A Sociology of Monsters: Essays on Power, Technology and Domination.* New York: Routledge.

Callon, M. (1993). Variety and irreversibility in networks of technique conception and adoption. In D. Foray & C. Freemann (Eds.), *Technology and the Wealth of Nations: Dynamics of Constructed Advantage.* London, New York: Pinter.

Callon, M. (1998). *The Laws of the Market.* Oxford: Blackwell Publishers.

Callon, M. & Law, J. (1986). *How to Study the Force of Science.* In M. Callon, J. Law & A. Rip (Eds.), *Mapping the Dynamics of Science and Technology.* London: MacMillan.

Castilla, E. J., Hwang, H., Granovetter, E. & Granovetter, M. (2000). *Social Networks in Silicon Valley.* Stanford University Press.

Ciborra, C. U. (1996). The platform organization: recombining strategies, structures, and surprises. *Organization Science,* 7(2), 103-116.

Cunningham, C. & Tynan, C. (1993). Electronic trading, interorganizational systems and the nature of buyer-seller relationships: the need for network perspective. *International Journal of Information Management.*

Financial Times. (2001). London. October 11.

Foucault, M. (1983). The subject and power. In H. L. Dreyfus & P. Rabinaw (Eds.), *Beyond Structuralism and Hermeneutics.* Chicago, IL: The University of Chicago Press.

Franke, J. (1993). Eurex, Grüneburgweg, 61306 Frankfurt.

Garcia, M. F. (1986). *"La construction sociale d'un marché parfait: le marché au cadran de Fontaines-en-Sologne."* Actes de la recherche en sciences sociales.

Giddens, A. (1998). *The Third Way.* Cambridge, MA: Polity Press.

Gosh, D. K. & Ortiz, E. (1994). *The Changing Environment of International Financial Markets.* London: The MacMillan Press.

Granovetter, M. (1992). Problems of explanation in economic sociology. In N. Nohria & R. Eccles (Eds.), *Networks and Organizations: Structure, Form, Action.* Boston, MA: Harvard Business School Press.

Hedesstrom, T. & Whitley, E. A. (2000). What is meant by tacit knowledge: Towards a better understanding of the shape of actions. *Eighth European Conference on Information Systems* (pp. 46-51). Vienna.

Introna, L. D. (1997). *Management Information and Power.* London: Macmillan Press.

Introna, L. I. & Whitley, E. A. (1999). *About experiments and style: A critique of laboratory research in information systems.* Working Paper Series 68, Department of Information Systems, London School of Economics and Political Science.

Johnson, G. & Scholes, K. (1999). *Exploring Corporate Strategy.* London: Prentice Hall Europe.

Kapstein, E. B. (1997). *Regulating the internet: A report to the president's commission on critical infrastructure protection.* Humphrey Institute of Public Affairs, University of Minnesota, USA.

Land, F. (1999). *Evaluation in a Social-technical Context.* Working paper series 76. London School of Economics, Department of Information Systems.

Latour, B. (1987). *Science in Action: How to Follow Scientists and Engineers Through Society.* Open University Press.

Latour, B. (1988). *The Pasteurization of France.* London: Harvard University Press.

Latour, B. (1991). Technology is society made durable. In J. Law (Ed.), *A Sociology of Monsters: Essays on Power, Technology and Domination.* New York: Routledge.

Latour, B. (1992). The sociology of a few mundane artefacts. In W. Bijker & J. Law (Eds.), *Shaping Technology/Building Society Studies in Sociotechnological Change.* Cambridge, MA: MIT Press.

Latour, B. (1993). *We Have Never Been Modern* (C. Porter, Trans.) London: Harvester Wheatsheaf.

Latour, B. (1996). *Aramis, or, The Love of Technology* (C. Porter, Trans.) Cambridge, MA: Harvard University Press.

Law, J. (1991). *A Sociology of Monsters: Essays on Power, Technology and Domination.* New York: Routledge.

Law, J. & Callon, M. (1992). The life and death of an aircraft: A network analysis of technological change. In W. Bijker & J. Law (Eds.), *Shaping Technology/Building Society Studies in Sociotechnological Change.* Cambridge, MA: MIT Press.

Law, J. & Hassard, J. (1999). *Actor Network Theory and after.* Oxford: Blackwell Publishers.

Luhmann, N. (1988). Familiarities, confidence, trust: Problems and alternatives. In D. Gambetta (Ed.), *Trust: Making and Breaking Cooperative Relations.* New York: Blackwell.

Monteiro, E. (2000). Actor-network theory and information infrastructure. In C. Ciborra (Ed.), *From Control to Drift, The Dynamics of Corporate information Infrastructures.* Oxford: University Press.

O'Brien, R. (1992). *Global Financial Integration: The End of Integration.* London: Pinter Publishers.

Richard, M. & Whitley, E. A. (2000). *Addressing the cyborg: A useful concept for information systems research?* Working paper series (89). Department of Information Systems, London School of Economics.

Rosen, P. (1993). *The Social Construction of Mountain Bikes: Technology and Postmodernity in the Cycle Industry.* Social Studies of Science.

Shaw, V. & Kauser, S. (2000). The changing patterns of international strategic alliance activity by British firms. *Journal of General Management*, 25(4).

Star, S. L. (1995). *The Cultures of Computing.* Oxford: Blackwell Publisher.

Walsham, G. (1993). *Interpreting Information Systems in Organizations.* Chichester, UK: John Wiley and Sons.

Walsham, G. (1995). The emergence of interpretivism in IS research. *Information Systems Research*, 6(4).

Wasserman, S. & Faust, K. (1994). *Social Network Analysis: Methods and Applications.* Cambridge, MA: University of Cambridge Press.

Young, P. & Theys, T. (1999). *Capital Market Revolution.* London: Financial Times Prentice Hall.

Chapter VI

An Explanatory Approach to the ASP Industry Evolution Where IT Services Move from P-service to E-service

Dohoon Kim
Kyung Hee University, Korea

ABSTRACT

This chapter introduces the ASP (Application Service Provider) industry which provides essential infrastructure for the Internet-based e-business transactions. First introduced is the current status of the ASP industry with some industry analysis focusing on the driving forces shaping the evolutionary changes. Then, emerging ASP business models are classified and analyzed in order to assess their positions in the competitive landscape based on the economies of scale. We also explore the prerequisites for the success of each ASP business model. Lastly, a conceptual model is provided to predict some possible scenarios of the evolution of the industry structure. For example, we identify the prerequisites for the ASP business models to develop themselves into XSPs (eXtended Service Providers), and develop a scenario for that evolutionary path. The proposed framework will present a deep insight into the e-transformation and a way to improve enterprise intelligence and performance through ASPs.

INTRODUCTION:
BACKGROUND AND MOTIVATION

Innovative Race to Enterprise Intelligence and Departure from the Old

The enterprise intelligence through e-transformation will be one of the cornerstones of the next generation e-business era where the Internet constitutes the core business resource. The competitive landscape of the e-business is changing from the head-to-head competition between companies to one between network organizations formed around competing value chains. Under this circumstance, the capability of taking full advantage of IT (Information Technology) becomes one of the essential prerequisites to attain a competitive edge. Accordingly, enhancing intelligence and synergy through IT outsourcing is now at the heart of the issue of building core competence.

However, it is ASPs (Application Service Providers) that accomplish the IT outsourcing in the Internet economy. Furthermore, ASPs provide a way to redesign the value chain, thereby, enabling corporate e-transformation in order to maximize the benefits around the value chain. ASPs' functional role in the e-business context is to make companies view the collaboration over the value chain from a different angle and raise the make-or-buy decision issue from a new perspective. The success of an ASP first depends on the extent to which its client companies are likely to streamline their business process and utilize outsourcing to reduce costs. In addition, the technical and/or legislative factors like SLA (Service Level Agreement) will become another key success factor in building a seamless value chain.

This chapter first introduces the ASP industry in its early stage of the development, its expected role as one of the most important service industries in the e-business era, and various types of the ASP business models. The primary purpose of this study is to present a systematic framework to generate meaningful viewpoints on the next generation e-business world with focus on the ASP industry. To achieve the research goals, provided is a conceptual model to analyze the industry evolution, which requires understanding of the dynamic market mechanisms. The proposed model is also expected to serve as a strategy development tool for the incumbent or prospective companies in the ASP industry.

Fundamental Questions To Be Addressed

This chapter will highlight and answer the following three key questions that are integral to the understanding of the next generation e-business process and possible changes.

1. How does the ASP industry contribute to value creation of network organizations? Why do we need IT outsourcing? What factors influence the way that APSs organize the value chain for delivering IT outsourcing services to their clients?

2.   What brings forth a structure for the ASP industry? That is, what will be the key factors shaping the ASP industry and how do they affect the industry value chain structure? What are the emerging forms of the ASP business models with the dynamic capability and strategy? Where on the value chain does the most viable ASP model position itself? For example, is it always necessary for an ASP model to develop itself into a XSP (eXtended Service Provider) to survive in the end?

3.   How can we model and analyze the complicated interactions among interrelated decision-making entities on the ASP value chain? And how can we gain insights from these collective behaviors and complex interactions? What will be the environmental and technological prerequisites to the success of each ASP type? And what kind of ASP business models will survive in the future under what conditions? Finally, how will the ASP industry evolve and be clustered?

The following sections will be devoted to addressing and answering these questions one by one. The organization of this chapter is as follows. We first review the ASP industry and its dynamic evolution process around the value chain of the industry. In the next section, we construct conceptual models that put together *ex post* historical lessons as well as *a priori* theoretical predictions. This explanatory approach presented here will shed light on the issues. Leveraging this conceptual framework, provided are some propositions and their implications in the industry structure and strategy development. Lastly, we conclude this chapter by reviewing the key findings highlighted in conjunction with their implications and discussing the future research opportunities.

INDUSTRY DEVELOPMENT TRENDS AND BASIC ANALYSIS

Industry Definition and Value Chain

An ASP is generally defined as a third-party service firm which deploys, manages, and/or remotely hosts a software application through centrally-located servers in a lease agreement. ASPs started their business with providing online application programs such as ERP (Enterprise Resource Planning) and CRM (Customer Relationship Management) solution packages to corporate customers. The first customers were small companies or local branches of multinational companies where IT outsourcing was the only option to deploy IT resources due to financial or regional constraints. As seen in these cases, the biggest merit of employing ASPs is the fact that corporate customers no longer should own the applications and take responsibilities associated with initial and ongoing support and maintenance. In sum, ASPs are differentiated from the existing IT services in that ASPs provide IT resources to multiple corporate clients on a one-to-many basis with a standardized service architecture and pricing scheme.

Figure 1 shows the Internet-based e-business value chain around the ASP industry. This value chain does not allow a single service provider to control the entire service delivery process. Even if we confine our attention to the software delivery process in the value chain, the complexity does not reduce significantly. In order to deliver applications over the Internet, we need a mechanism to establish and maintain collaboration among independent functional divisions.

This study will focus on this nature of the value chain to show how the industry is likely to evolve and to interpret the strategic meaning of its specific convergence pattern. We will also point out the critical aspects of the value chain, which are required for an ASP business model to survive in the market: a large customer base and stable relationship with other functional divisions. For example, some survey results shows that an ASP should provide ERP packages to more than 20 clients to reach the break-even point. This number is quite challengeable to many ASPs under the current sever competition for market share. And due to the system market nature (Katz & Shapiro, 1994) of the ASP industry, the partnership structure in the value chain is one of the major elements to classify emerging ASP business models. These unique features constitute essential ingredients of the conceptual model to be presented in the following sections.

Figure 1: The Internet-Based e-Business Value Chain Around the ASP Industry

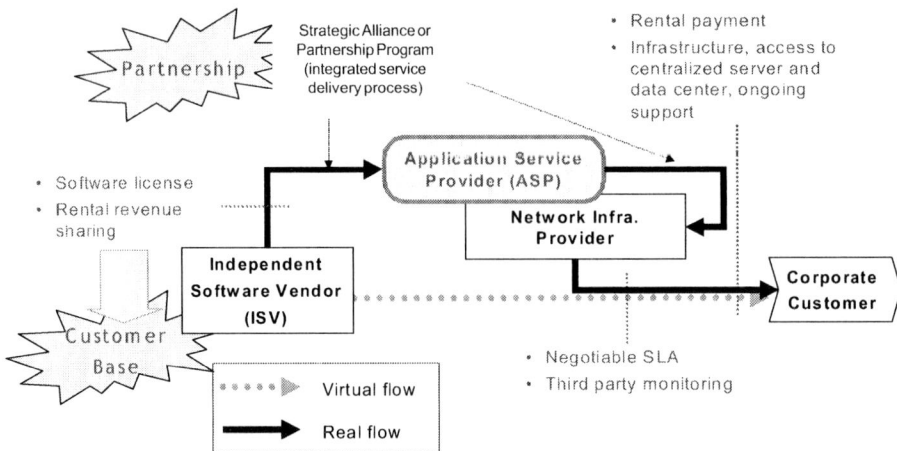

An Outlook of the ASP Industry: Historical Inevitability of the ASP Emergence

IT service outsourcing through ASP made its debut in the market around 1998. Since then, as seen by the below numbers, the ASP market has been recognized as a promising emerging market with explosive growth potential. In the U.S., there were more than 480 ASPs that achieved a sales record of $986 million in 2000. With other infrastructure or service providers such as network service providers, contents providers, and system integration companies included in the ASP industry category, the market size in 2000 amounted to $106 billion. This growth pattern was unparalleled relative to other IT industry classes whose average annual growth rate amounted to about 10%. However, after the hype in the market, some ASPs have been hit particularly hard amid reports of management turnover. Currently, the ASP market seems to have moved beyond the hype stage and into a more substantial restructuring stage. Although the stock price has significantly increased, many ASPs continue to struggle to keep their market share.

On the other hand, despite the current downturn, the industry size is projected to reach $392 billion in 2005. These numbers represent over 30% annual growth rate, which still outperforms by almost three times the average growth rate of the entire IT industries (Gartner, 2001a; IDC, 2001a). As the industry has a mixed outlook, the most plausible scenario tells us that only a few ASPs will survive and lead the market in the end. Some market research reports support this view and predict that more than 60% of current ASPs will be forced out of the market by the end of 2002 and that only 4% of current ASPs will remain in the near future because of the limitation of customer base (Gartner, 2001a). Figure 2 depicts the early stage of the industry life-cycle together with the fluctuation in the related stock market.

Indeed, the ASP business models are beginning to face serious challenges to their viability and broader market acceptance. This somewhat pessimistic view has arisen from the fact that many ASPs do not seem to have clear positioning strategy and target market segment. Such a misplaced positioning is likely to jeopardize the ASP's business opportunities which require huge initial fixed costs at the very early stage in the product life cycle. In this situation, it is almost impossible to set the service price that could assure sufficient profits, so that ASPs are focusing on expanding the customer base by driving down the service price at the expense of quality. In addition, many ASPs do not have enough room to combine their service delivery process together with the clients' business process. Subsequently, most ASPs still put the competitive priority on the cost leadership rather than stable service quality and reliability. Last but not least, ASPs have yet to succeed in earning trust from customers on the technology. Concerns over the network and systems security have not been fully

Figure 2: The ASP Industry Life Cycle

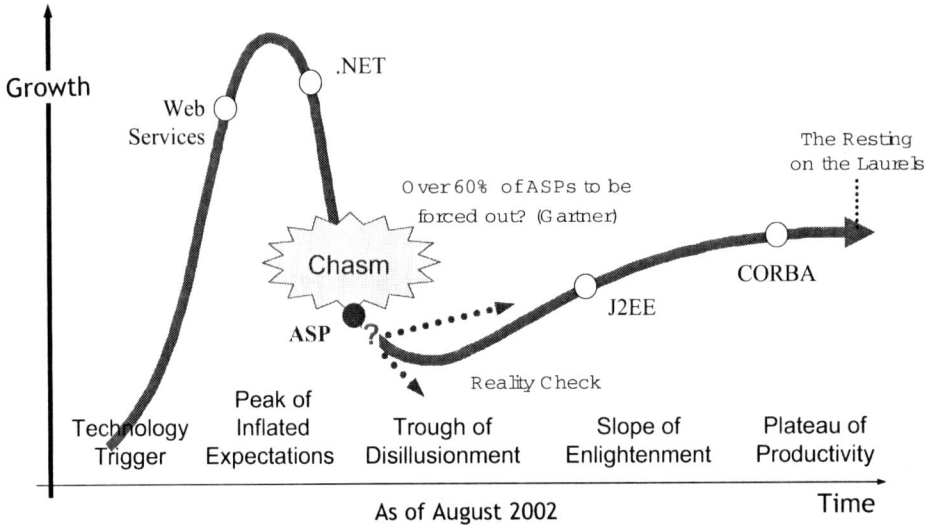

Growth

.NET

Web
Services

The Resting
on the Laurels

Over 60% of ASPs to be
forced out? (Gartner)

Chasm

CORBA

J2EE

ASP   ?

Reality Check

Technology   Peak of   Trough of   Slope of   Plateau of
Trigger   Inflated   Disillusionment Enlightenment   Productivity
           Expectations

As of August 2002   Time

addressed yet. There has been little progress in establishing a standard process of establishing SLA including a penalty mechanism when a service failure occurs.

As the industry has undergone market chasm and is about to move toward uphill in the early stage of the life-cycle, the competitive landscape and industry environment is changing. First, the traditional ASP offerings are commoditized, repackaged, and diversified into new ones, thereby making the original concept and industry boundary fuzzy. In consequence, new relationships among the players in the industry value chain are emerging with new, diverse ASP business domains and models. This phenomenon attributes to shortened service life cycle and changing rankings of leading providers. Furthermore, this market share race is highly likely to result in a dynamic process where winners get richer and losers get poorer.

In order to abstract the essential feature of the ASP industry dynamics and market mechanism and to build a conceptual model to predict the industry evolution, we first investigate and identify the market drivers and challenges as well as potential ASP variations in the following sections.

Market Drivers and Challenges

There are a number of factors that are frequently cited as fueling or dashing the growth of the ASP market. Though there has been a little ASP-related literature, most of them deal with market drivers and challenges (for example, Factor, 2002). Thus, in this study we present only the literature survey results rearranged from the perspective of our research objectives to construct an analytical conceptual model to capture the industry dynamics. More detailed and somewhat different views on the industry can be found in Factor (2002), Kim (2002a), Kim and Choi (2001), etc. Table 1 gives a summary of market drivers and challenges which are classified into three categories: (1) technical factors, (2) market/economic factors, (3) other business environment factors including institutional/regulation issues.

One of striking characteristics observed so far is that immaturity of the industry is the most representative challenge in terms of the market factor. In particular, the uncertainty persists as to whether existing and emerging ASPs are winning enough customers to validate the basic ASP delivery model for highly sophisticated enterprise applications. For instance, while many ASPs are gaining momentum with early adopters, there are still many companies that are unwilling to rent ERP applications due to the lack of trust in the industry itself. Moreover, it is security control and remote monitoring systems, SLA management, and global open system architecture and standardization processes that should be further developed to support the proliferation of ASPs. We will revisit this facet in the discussion section.

ANALYTICAL FRAMEWORK OF THE EMERGING ASP BUSINESS MODELS
ASP Taxonomy with the Emerging Business Models

We are indeed witnessing a large number of variations on the ASP value propositions that represent a promising future for companies that properly align their hosted solution offering. However, these observations cannot be explained

Table 1: The Drivers and Challenges of the ASP Industry

Category	Drivers	Challenges
Technology[1]	– Reduce risk of technological obsolescence due to rapidly changing IT – Provide a chance to utilize best-of-breed applications – Avoid IT staffing shortage	– Unsolved security concerns – Emerging new technological requirements from the clients: e.g., SLA with client participation – Unproved service reliability: e.g., network problems, system scalability and performance
Market	– Minimize up-front TCO (Total Cost Ownership) – Provide predictable cash flows	– Unproved client momentum – Failure in giving clients sufficient trust due to unstable ASP industry
Other business environment	– Standardized IT supports around the world due to increasing global competition	– Economic downturn

without mentioning the typical aspects of the early stage in the system market (Church & Gandal, 2000; Farrell, 1998; Katz & Shapiro, 1994) where a service product of a firm should be tied to complimentary products or services provided by another firm. Furthermore, the current value chain has not settled down yet, and any key player other than the pure ASPs can develop itself beyond a simple supplier and into a variation of the ASP business model, thereby resulting in a different value chain structure in the end.

The industry's short history raises the following questions: what changes will happen and who will be the winners and the losers? To answer these questions, this section will first clarify the currently emerging ASP business domains and classify them based on their partnership structure over the industry value chain. This classification will play a key role in identifying and analyzing the collaborative network architecture where the ASP business models support the next generation e-business at the bottom. Then, with the analysis of the emerging ASP business models, we will identify dynamic capacity of each business model in the following section.

The surviving ASPs will be different species from the current main stream in that they will supply differentiated services focusing on various niche markets. The new models have given rise to real e-transformations and proliferate in diverse forms such as HSP (Hosted Service Provider), IDC (Internet Data Center), AIP (Application Infrastructure Provider), MSP (Management Service Provider), VSP (Vertical Service Provider), and so on (Factor, 2002; Kim, 2002a; Kim, 2002b; Kim & Choi, 2001). When an ASP as a market enabler maintains a collaborative network infrastructure with its partners, it is called XSP (eXtended Service Provider) to stress the difference between ordinary ASP and this new species (Kim, 2002a; Kim & Choi, 2001). ISVs (Independent Software Vendors), network infrastructure providers, and virtually all kinds of other players in the value chain can now take advantage of XSP that creates an integrated value proposition. Thus, XSP will be at the center of implementing e-transformation and the virtual firm.

Table 2 and Figure 3 represent the simplified version of the classification in alignment with the research objective. In particular, Figure 3 depicts the procedure where the diverse provider types presented so far are rearranged into four business models in Table 2 based on the relationship among the key players in the value chain.

Analytical Approach and Framework
Guiding Principles of the Industry Evolution

From the market drivers and challenges, abstracted are the fundamental principles which seem to shape the major trend of the ASP market evolution and consequently the industry structure around the value chain.

Table 2: The Emerging ASP Business Models

Basic Types	Characteristics	Variations
H-ASP (Horizontally-specialized ASP)	– Develop deep expertise within a given functional area (as opposed to one-stop shop) – ISVs' need of partnership with systems integration and distribution companies – Should be Web-based software provider	– Examples: PeopleSoft, Oracle (esp. in ERP), Sibel (esp. in CRM) – Mission-critical application providers: e.g., security infra. providers (Interliant)
V-ASP (Vertically-specialized ASP)	– Industry-specific applications (in contrast to one-stop shop)	– Vertical exchange for B2B market – Examples: Trizetto
AIP (Application Infrastructure Provider)	– Originated from telecommunication company that owns networks and has operations experience – Provide infra. management to ASPs	– Examples: AT&T, Exods, Qwest Cyber, Korea Telecom, G&G Network
XSP (eXtended Service Provider)	– Provide total services from front-end to back-end with systems integration consulting – Create new business process by rearranging suppliers and customers – Help customers and even other service providers enter new markets, deploy services, and improve profitability easily while minimizing risk	– Examples: EDS, Corio, Jamcracker, USInternetworking

First, it is the economies of scale or increasing return that serves as the core economic guiding principle for ASPs. First note that in many cases, the breakout for the TCO of a traditional client/server ERP package is roughly 20% for the up-front license fee and the remaining 80% for all of the implementation and ongoing maintenance service. And ASPs should do their best to cut this 80% portion of the TCO down upon the notion of one-to-many sales points. For instance, since standardizing solutions across multiple clients makes the over-head costs dispersed over many clients, it is a great leverage to obtain cost leadership which establishes core competence by decreasing prices. Attaining demand momentum to create network externality is another major economic motivation. That is, increasing the customer base tends to build a positive feedback mechanism that intensifies the market share and control power of a leading ASP. Accordingly, the competition basically keeps going for expansion of customer base or market share which provides a good surrogate measure of profit for this case.

Second, the competitive landscape shows the unique nature of a service system market where independent hardware and software resources are combined and reorganized into a new package in alignment with partnerships

Figure 3: ASP Business Models with Key Drivers

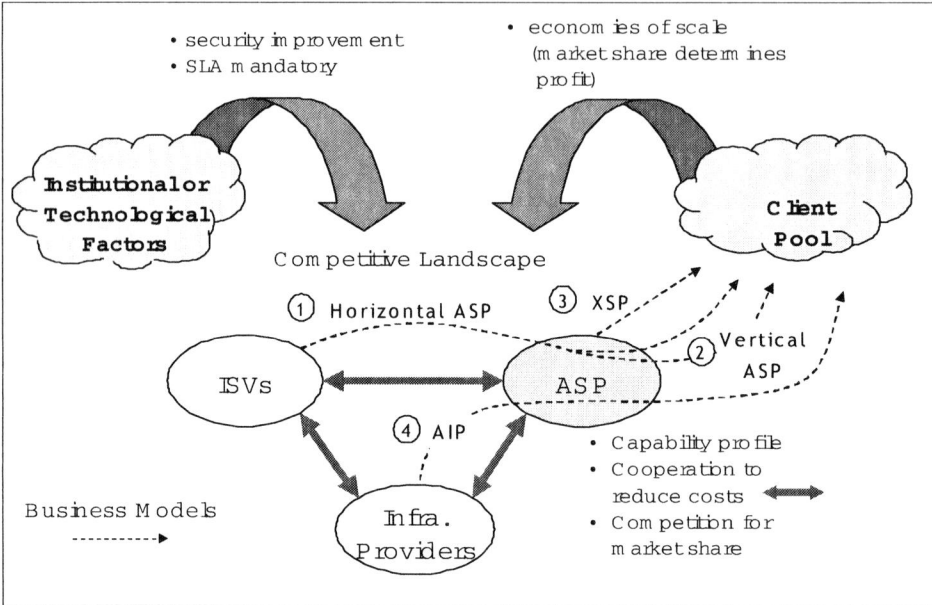

over the value chain and/or even a customer's business process. These offerings aim at designing a seamless and proprietary service delivery process to sharpen the competitive edge while raising the entry barrier. This essential feature of integration in the service delivery process makes the various possible business models reduce into the different types of service product combinations along the value chain as presented in Table 2. However, since it is not easy to measure the size of the cost reduction by a certain partnership structure or the integration process, each ASP receives mixed signals of success from the market. Accordingly, the cut-throat competition fueled by business domain integration not only drives down the price to an acceptable market price but also creates multiple market segmentations based on the service product differentiation.

To put these arguments in perspective, it is useful to introduce the skeleton of our conceptual model by arranging them. First, in terms of supply side, the common goal pursued by all types of emerging ASPs is to create and focus on the target market segment that fits the most with their value propositions. This enables ASPs to develop a differentiation strategy to maximize client's utility and gain greater focus of key capability, thereby bringing forth various trials in designing the service product, each of which corresponds to a business model summarized in Table 2 and 3. On demand side, the dynamic mechanism of the market provides greater opportunities to ASPs better positioned to win market share competition through network externality. In sum, two regimes, (1) partnership structure and characteristics for differentiation and (2) economies of scale through positive feedback, will guide the evolution of the industry where we now witness the proliferation of different types of ASPs.

With these distinct regimes taken into consideration, the following is a preliminary conclusion: at the early stages of the industry life cycle, a wide variety of ASP business models emerge and they are uniformly distributed over each niche market. However, in the course of the evolution, the guiding principles will influence the development path and give rise to a market concentration around ASPs which achieve a series of successes in the market share competition. However, it is not yet easy to answer to the questions such as whether the evolutionary paths are symmetric over the various ASP types or not and which type of the ASP model will win the race in the end. These questions may not be fully addressed without a systematic model that at least conceptualizes and mediates guiding principles leading the industry evolution.

Along this line, the following sections carefully examine and formalize the conceptual relationship patterns among various elements and principles to grope for both existing and new opportunities. If the proposed conceptual model is correct, some logical conclusions drawn from the model will provide us with deep insights on the dynamic capabilities of each ASP type. We also expect that this explanatory approach will offer a solid foundation on which the dynamic evolution process could be empirically tested.

Research Methodology

The complexity embedded in the value chain hinders a clear mathematical analysis from providing practical results. For example, the typical approach in industrial organization economics is highly likely to miss some important aspects of the dynamic mechanism since it simplifies many interdependent functional elements in the course of abstraction of the reality. In particular, not only the variety of key player types but also the number of players usually generates many possible combinations of different strategies from the players, which also makes a traditional approach like Church and Gandal (2000), Farrell, Monroe and Saloner (1998), and Hotelling (1931) difficult. Accordingly, paying too much attention to a static notion of market equilibrium may end up with ignorance of fundamental features in the competitive process that tend to produce winners and losers. On the other hand, it was the nontraditional approach by Nelson and Winter (1978) that showed how dominant firms may emerge from competitive struggles under the assumption of firm heterogeneity.[2]

ASP industry researchers are also often hampered by a lack of meaningful data regarding market size, customer demand, or actual application outsourcing revenues generated by companies positioning themselves as ASPs. Furthermore, it is not easy to test outcomes from the interrelated behaviors among players in the industry since a cause becomes an effect, which in turn becomes a cause recursively in this type of endogenous process. Therefore, sample data alone may not meaningfully uncover an underlying process of this sort, which makes statistical analysis or forecasting hard to present keen prospects on the industry evolution. Accordingly, required here is an explanatory approach to develop a conceptual model that will capture the endogenous features, thereby providing more plausible and richer analytical results.

Conceptual Model

A key concern in this explanatory research is how the race in the ASP industry will shape the industry structure around the value chain: in particular, the expected market share of each ASP business model, whereupon the overall pattern of industry concentration and behavior can be predicted. To this end, we will build a conceptual model and seek some propositions which are associated with the business models. In this section introduced first are the essential ingredients comprising the conceptual model. The proposed conceptual model is expected to offer an unusual opportunity to not only gain deep insight into the industry evolution but also analyze and evaluate the dynamic capability of each emerging ASP business model. Moreover, the model may serve as a basis for future empirical research to test core industry factors with their relations and dynamic features in the way our conceptual model describes and suggests.

Capability and Strategy Profile of Each Business Model

We have seen that the goal of every ASP business model is somehow identical: acquisition of market share through creation of proprietary and sustainable customer relationship. To attain this goal in the current circumstance, differentiation is an inevitable option. Hence, we have seen many different ASP business models, which were reorganized into four classes in the previous section. However, each business model should be further analyzed in connection with various types of differentiation strategies, each of which takes a unique value creation path to the customers. The second column of Table 3 summarizes differentiation focus, or strategic choice of each ASP model with its implications.

For example, the XSP's strategic profile shows a distinguishing nature of a commercialized service architecture wherein combined and reorganized are independent applications into a new package in alignment with customer's business process. Thus, ISVs and other service providers of virtually all kinds can take advantage of XSPs that create an integrated value proposition. These offerings supply seamless and the most efficient service delivery process, and thereby help customers and other service providers enter new markets, deploy services, and improve profitability while minimizing risk. As these features and potentials are at the center of realizing the e-transformation and virtual firms, the XSP model has been in the spotlight.

However, all of the emerging ASP business models have a common feature in their differentiation strategies, which overlaps with XSPs: developing a proprietary service product and delivery architecture to integrate a client's business logic into its commodity. As in many intermediary commercial services, many Internet services are bundled to provide not only value to the customer but also channels to the customer's attention. In the light of this trend, ASP's success first depends on the extent to which a company is likely to streamline its business process and utilize outsourcing to reduce costs. Accordingly, required is a minute observation on the dynamic capability of each ASP model in order to check the possibility that the corresponding model renders its value component sustainable, thereby signaling its strong position to the market. That is, the chance to survive the competition will be primarily determined by the degree of proper match between the provider's strategic focus and its capability. In Table 3, we present the profile linking the dynamic capacity of ASP business models with its value component or strategic focus.

Competitive Landscape and System Dynamics

All of the diverse business models tied with unique differentiation strategies cannot succeed in the market. In the end will survive only a few successful kinds that adapt themselves to the market requirements and take the most advantage of the competitive landscape of the industry. We propose in this section a more definite form of the competitive landscape and its dynamic mechanism, whereby the key guiding principles in the previous section play a fundamental role.

The dynamically changing nature of the landscape tends to prevent the ASPs from receiving a clear signal from the market. This interference makes

Table 3: Strategy and Capability Profile of ASP Business Models

Basic Types	Value-added Components	Dynamic Capability
H-ASP	− Either own the software or develop proprietary integration in a specific field − Substantial consulting services	− Well positioned to expand customer basis quickly − Hard to copy the domain-specific knowledge
V-ASP	− Vertically-oriented, template methodology: easily deploys across multiple clients in the same industry	− Strong advantage in customized solutions (e.g., lead time) − Hard to copy the industry-specific knowledge
AIP	− Provide system management services including SLA − Alleviate client concerns regarding network reliability, etc.	− High investment costs as an entry barrier: easy to protect their market share
XSP	− Build and integrate customized applications − Enable clients to avoid the need to handle multiple ASP solutions − Has its own IDC	− Going back to one-stop-shop idea: Improved flexibility will be the core competitive edge for XSP

providers concentrate their capability on the differentiation area, thereby successively generating additional value-added components to the clients and raising the entry barrier against both incumbent and potential competitors. Subsequently, the resulting competition can be characterized by large customer switching costs and high barrier to entry. New value propositions from the emerging ASP business models disclose this underlying mechanism in the competitive landscape. For example, while the original value components of the traditional ASPs were to provide online applications with ongoing supports, those of the emerging business models are now to utilize domain-specific knowledge, focus on vertical industry applications, integrate applications across the client's resources, and so on. All of these value propositions aim at the creation of proprietary and sustainable customer relationship.

Moreover, economies of scale enable early success in terms of the market share, leading to further success primarily because of a positive feedback loop. The feedback loop is working via either more diversified strategic options, that is, resource flexibility to try various combinations, or extended partnership and a revised business model to enter new market segment, or a strengthened dominant position in the current market niche. Therefore, successful business models or providers grow faster than the average providers and consolidate them, resulting in a few dominant types of providers emerging over time. The following propositions from the conceptual model investigate how positive feedback may affect the emergence of a certain pattern of industry structure. The analysis results based on the propositions reveal the aspects of the dynamic evolution process in the ASP industry, in which a small historical event like partner selection (thereby determining its business model) can change the course of evolution through a self-reinforcing mechanism if the prerequisites and environmental conditions are on the right track.

The capability and strategy profile of each business model and the underlying mechanism in the competitive landscape derived from the evolution guiding principles will constitute the fundamental ingredients of our framework to conceptualize the industry dynamics and evolution. Figure 4 depicts the skeleton of this model and sets forth some key differentiation factors and the competitive landscape. The conceptual model highlights the substance that has led the industry to face proliferation of ASP business models, which in some cases makes it difficult to draw the boundary of the industry and to properly classify types of business models. In the next section, we present some propositions derived from this explanatory research, which are followed by assessment and interpretation of their strategic implications to the ASP business models as well as the entire knowledge-based network organizations. Some technical factors that may affect the evolution path, for example, SLA regulation to complete a seamless value chain, will be considered in the discussion section.

Figure 4: Conceptual Model of the ASP Industry Dynamics and Evolution

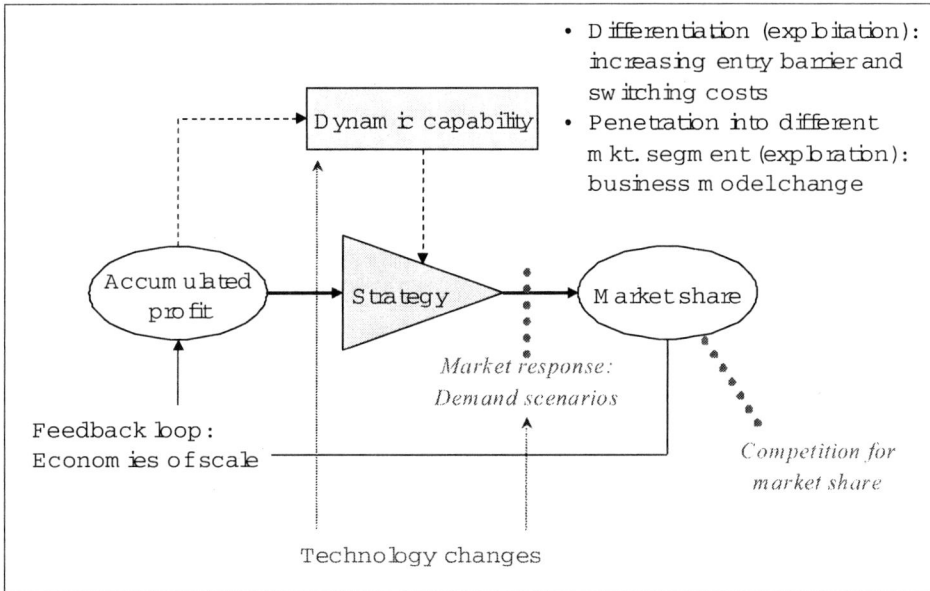

ANALYSIS AND DISCUSSIONS
Propositions with Strategic Implications

Proposition 1: The total number of ASPs in the industry will reduce. However, consolidations of different business models will not occur on a large scale.

We start with a simple, general proposition looking somewhat trivial at the first glance since the customer base is not large enough to keep all the incumbent ASPs alive. Internally generated cash flows from success in this market share competition give winners resilience to possible occasional failures and allow them to better manage risk by diversifying a portfolio of value components to open a new market niche. It is this kind of positive feedback loop, or economies of scale, that accelerates driving the losers out of the market and shaping the industry structure.

However, it is hard to guarantee that only some specific types of the ASP business models will survive in the end. Two basic activities regarding the competitive landscape, increasing switching costs and raising entry barriers are common to all the business models defined in the previous section. As a result, penetrating into a different market segment and building new relationships with the customers at the niche necessarily run into strong resistance from the incumbents. Some events like technological breakthroughs are likely to be required in order for a specific ASP model to consolidate another. Therefore, various business models will thrive over a long period of time before some giant players in each business model emerge.

Proposition 2: The market will concentrate more around horizontally-and/or vertically-specialized ASPs (i.e., H-ASPs and V-ASPs) than around the pure ASPs (that is, a simple partnership with ISV).

This proposition is another direct consequence of the logical reasoning based on our conceptual model. According to the conceptual model, the primary concern of the emerging ASPs is to build some value-added components to their service architecture, thereby making it hard for competitors to replicate the business model as well as for customers to replace the current provider. However, reliance on third-party ISVs could make it more difficult to resolve many of the underlying performance issues that have been the subject of customer scrutiny. On the other hand, looking up the capability profiles of the ASP business models, we can conclude that both H-ASPs and V-ASPs hold a dominant position from this standpoint. If some technical constraints such as SLA and security requirement from the clients come to rise to the surface, AIP will also be able to gain technological competitiveness. More details will be dealt with in proposition 3.

Proposition 3: ASPs that originally developed their proprietary solutions will be better positioned in terms of ultimate performance and scalability.

ASPs that are offering proprietary solutions will increase the chance to succeed in the market irrespective of how critical a given solutions is to their client's day-to-day operations. One example of the essential features that this kind of proprietary application should have is that it should be built from scratch for the Internet environment. That is, the application delivery process may be much more critical to success than the level of sophistication of the service product. This assertion is sustained by the current trend that many companies are conducting a test-drive with non-mission critical applications before signing with an ASP to host large-scale enterprise applications. Actually, we have witnessed that many ISVs have been withdrawing from the IT outsourcing market. This phenomenon reflects the importance of the underlying architecture of the application services, in particular at the early introduction stage of the product life cycle.

Thus, ASPs are required to develop proprietary applications for delivery via a hosted service approach, which will give the AIP model a good opportunity. Even though the AIPs are usually far behind the other ASP models in terms of domain expertise or application development, they have a strong position in assuring network security, scalability, and other performance-related concerns that are foremost among underlying architectural issues. This proposition is also supported by the fact that relinquishing the control of core enterprise applications to an external provider demands ASPs to prove their capability to provide reliable and stable operations. In these regards, the AIP model clearly increases the chance to take the top rank among other provider types as technical leadership is being divided along various dimensions in developing proprietary service products, for example, technological advantage at the service delivery process in the case of AIPs. As a result, we will see a unique coexistence of the diverse ASP business models.

Proposition 4: The rate of demand increase will affect the industry structure, the pattern of market segmentation, market share of each ASP type, etc.

The speed of the market expansion will affect ASPs' selection of competitive priorities and hence the overall market structure. For example, success of the XSP model which is the most cost sensitive among other types of ASPs, should presume the rapid proliferation of the ASP services in an overly complex market. If we observe a trend of steady but slow adoption of the ASP services across a wide spectrum of corporate functions, XSPs will be in a financial predicament since the costs to provide total solution cannot be recovered from cash inflows. In this case, XSP will emerge only after the market demand for the ASP services become sufficient enough and the number of XSPs will not be significant. However, if the ASP service demand grows explosively in a short period of time, the XSP model will debut in the market earlier on, increasing the possibility of XSPs dominating the industry as they have scale advantage in terms of cost. This will result in other ASP business models concentrating on relatively small market niches.

Discussions about Future Trends and Research Opportunities

Until now, the ASP services have been confined to online applications for enterprise or other corporate organizations (that is, business-to-business area). However, with IMT-2000 era near at hand, emerging are a lot of new ASP business models which execute billing services on behalf of individual users (that is, business-to-consumer area) and support mobile offices to let employees access their intranet regardless of location and time (that is, business-to-employee area). This trend is evidenced by the emergence of new WASPs (Wireless ASPs) born almost every hour in the U.S. in 2001 (Gartner, 2001b). The above examples will definitely be a new opportunity for ASP business, and we expect that wireless applications for general users are to form a new niche in the near future. In the mean time, as of early 2002, general understanding about

IMT-2000 is not so popular to become a mainstream of the ASP services in many major countries. Hence, we decided it would be premature to include WASP business model in the conceptual model even though the proposed framework could be extended to cover this case without any significant modification.

We have seen so far that ASP will garner economies of scale to achieve a large customer base. However, given some performance and scalability issues that are likely to arise as the number of clients increases, it is quite unclear where the optimal number of customers will lie to achieve the sufficient customer momentum not only needed to drive economies of scale but also required to maintain a certain level of service quality. Furthermore, it will make the analysis framework far more complicated to incorporate a SLA regulation which is predicted to be a common practice in a few years, thereby becoming another key success factor which cannot be overlooked. We can now only speculate that some SLA requirements will lead to higher costs on a customer-by-customer basis, which in turn potentially disturbs the basic one-to-many leverage that ASPs need to succeed in the long haul. We may need a different approach to estimate the impacts of these technological and political changes and verify or revise our research results presented in the propositions.

Lastly, though the embedded complexity in the current industry value chain disturbs a neat empirical research, we will need some simplified models to test a set of propositions empirically as the industry evolves and converges to a specific configuration. As time goes by, the industry's development path will accumulate time series data enough for both a longitude and a cross-sectional empirical study to reveal significant results.[3] There is some related research in progress toward this direction [for example, Kim (2003a), Kim (2003b), etc.]. In order to develop a quantitative approach to model the industry evolution, future research may employ a simulation technique similar to Lee (2002).

CONCLUDING REMARKS

ASPs, as a fundamental building block of the next generation e-business infrastructure, provide a way to redesign the value chain, thereby, enabling the corporate e transformation. The ASP concept started as a value proposition of IT outsourcing which offers hosted ERP or other similar applications. However, much attention is now paid to vertical or domain-specific expertise, flexible capabilities, or other value-added components in addition to the basic offerings. Accordingly, the competitive landscape has changed dramatically, and a sustainable ASP business model should provide far more than hosted third-party solutions from ISVs.

While many ASPs are gaining momentum with early adopters, there still remains uncertainty as to when and how the existing and emerging ASPs win a sufficient number of customers to validate their business model. However, the

ASP industry research is often hampered by a lack of meaningful data regarding market size, customer demand, or actual revenues generated by companies positioning themselves as ASPs. It is this short historical background together with complexity inherent in the industry value chain that puts some limits on the traditional statistical analysis or industrial organization models. This also explains the reason why questions about emerging new sorts of ASPs have rarely been raised in the literatures although the emergent economic properties are important.

To address these issues, provided here was an explanatory approach and conceptual model to capture and analyze the essential features around the industry evolution which is now at the early stage of the industry life cycle. The proposed model was developed from thorough examination and deep understanding of the dynamically evolving market mechanisms, in particular, economies of scale and value-added components in the emerging ASP business models. The analysis on the competitive landscape also disclosed that the capability of an ASP model to win the race hinges on differentiation of service products to a large degree. With this framework, presented are some propositions regarding overall predictions on the industry structure and some prerequisites that should be met for an ASP model to succeed in the market share competition.

Lastly, we conclude this chapter by referring back to the implication of proliferation of ASP services to the corporate e-transformation. The ASP industry will shape the future e-business transactions, thereby, on the one hand providing a great flexibility in redeploying a firm's resources and on the other hand reconfiguring the structure of network organizations. Under this circumstance, the emerging ASP models like XSP in an e-marketplace will become the hub of business transactions. By extending and improving the framework presented in this chapter, we believe that we can comment on some fundamental issues and prospective changes that deserve further consideration. Subsequently, this kind of conceptual model is expected to serve as a window to predict the possible architecture of the next Internet-based business world.

REFERENCES

Arthur, W.B. (1989). Competing technologies, increasing returns, and lock-in by historical events, *Economic Journal*, 99.

Chang, S.J. (1996). An evolutionary perspective of diversification and corporate restructuring: Entry, exit, and economic performance. *Strategic Management Journal*, 17.

Church, J. & Gandal, N. (2000, Spring). Systems competition, vertical merger and foreclosure. *Journal of Economics and Management Strategy*.

Factor, A. (2002). *Analyzing Application Service Providers.* Sun Microsystems Press.

Farrell, J., Monroe, H. & Saloner, G. (1998, Summer). The vertical organization of industry: systems competition versus component competition. *Journal of Economics and Management Strategy.*

Gartner Group Technical Report. (2001a, November). ASPs in 2002: Disappoint 2001 market goes mainstream.

Gartner Group Technical Report. (2001b, July). Telecommunication carriers and ASP.

Gilder, G. (2002). *Telecosm: The World After Bandwidth Abundance.* Touchstone Books.

Greenstein, S. (2000). The evolving structure of commercial Internet markets. In E. Brynjolfsson & B. Kahin (Eds.), *Understanding the Digital Economy.* MIT Press.

Hotelling, H. (1931, April). The economics of exhaustible resources. *Journal of Political Economy.*

IDC Report. (2001a, August). Dynamics of the ASP: How to build, price, and sell ASP services.

IDC Report. (2001b, July). A study of major ASP expenses.

IDC Report. (2001c, June). XSP Market: Preliminary World Wide Forecasting and Analysis 2001-2005.

Katz, M.L. & Shapiro, C. (1994, Spring). Systems competition and network effects. *Journal of Economic Perspectives.*

Kim, D. (2002a). ASP and collaborative network infrastructure for global enterprise intelligence: An explanatory approach to identify prerequisites and challenges. In J. Chen (Ed.), *Global Supply Chain Management.* International Academic Publication.

Kim, D. (2002b). The evolution of the next generation collaborate e-business: An analysis of the ASP industry (Translated in Korean). *Proceedings of Corporate Management Conference* (June), Seoul, Korea.

Kim, D. (2003a). Developing a cost estimation model for systems operations in the ASP industry (Translated in Korean), Working Draft.

Kim, D. (2003b). A study on the changes in ASP revenue structure and the networking architecture (Translated in Korean), Working Draft.

Kim, M.S. & Choi, Y.C. (2001). The Current Status of ASP Market Development (Translated in Korean). Korea Information Society Development Institute.

Lee, J. (2002). Innovation and strategic divergence: an empirical study of the U.S. pharmaceutical industry from 1920 to 1960. *Management Science* (unpublished).

Lewis, L. (1999). *Service Level Management for Enterprise Networks.* Artech House.

Nelson, R.R. & Winter, S.G. (1978). Force generating and limiting concentration under Schumpeterian competition. *Bell Journal of Economics*, 9.

Zuscovitch, E. & Justman, M. (1995). Networks, sustainable differentiation, and economic development. In D. Batten, J. Casti & R. Thord (Eds.), *Networks in Action*. Springer-Verlag.

ENDNOTES

[1]   The greatest driving force in the technology dimension is abundance of bandwidth and storage, which makes it possible for network to be a computer as supported by the Gilder's law (Gilder, 2002) and asserted in the famous and long-promoted slogan from Sun Microsystem.

[2]   In their research, Schumpeterian competition numerically demonstrates that successful technological leaders who pay the price of innovation earlier tend to enjoy further advantage over time as their capital accumulates; declining firms tend to further decline as their capital runs out through the process. Consequently, a small number of dominant firms emerge from the initial industry condition of identical firm sizes.

[3]   Remark that time is critical not only to gather sizable data but also to simplify a research model. That is, the industry evolution fixes some endogenous mechanisms so that a model can simplify and capture an essential aspect in the real world. Similar argument can be found in Lee (2002) and Nelson and Winter (1978).

SECTION III:

KNOWLEDGE MANAGEMENT

Chapter VII

Management of Knowledge in New Product Development in Portuguese Higher Education

Maria Manuel Mendes
Deloitte and Touche - Quality Firm, Portugal

Jorge F. S. Gomes
Instituto Superior de Psicologia Aplicada (ISPA), Portugal

Bernardo Bátiz-Lazo
Open University Business School, UK

ABSTRACT

This chapter uses key concepts in the knowledge management literature to analyse the procedures and practices used by a team during a new product development project. More precisely, the knowledge process or knowledge cycle is used as a means to examine issues relating to knowledge identification, creation, storage, dissemination, and application in new product development.

Results from the case study also suggest that the knowledge process may be valuable in assessing the structural elements of knowledge management, but fails to provide a more comprehensive explanation of the dynamics and complexities involved. This suggests that more elaborate models are needed to explain how knowledge is created, shared and used in knowledge-intensive processes.

INTRODUCTION

Recent focus on knowledge management (KM) has been stimulated by the idea that companies must increase their ability to learn if they are to operate successfully in an environment characterised by rapid technological and societal change, globalisation, and increased competition (Senge, 1990). However, despite the attractiveness of the concept, there is no consensus on how knowledge can be efficiently managed. This is not surprising since knowledge is a pervasive and difficult concept to observe in organisations.

This chapter tries to overcome shortcomings associated to the practical observation of knowledge in organisations by focusing on a specific new business-project: the implementation of an e-Learning portal using new product development (NPD) tools and systems.

Our aim is to explore KM practices used by the project participants during development of the new business, therefore offering an interpretation and understanding of the sequence of events upon which participants in the project team assessed the relative success of the new business development process.

This chapter proceeds as follows: the first section reviews central concepts in the KM literature and offers a framework to analyse and assess the implementation of effective KM practice within an e-Learning project. The following section encompasses the method and study design, as well as the context of the case material. The case material is then evaluated in light of the notions and main ideas behind the current thinking in KM. The final section puts forward a summary and tentative conclusions.

KNOWLEDGE MANAGEMENT
AND SYSTEM DEVELOPMENT
Knowledge Management: A Strategic Imperative?

In recent years, the management literature has emphasised the prominent role of knowledge in organisations. This distinction has led to reassessing previous contributions to the broad areas of management and economics as well as resulting in the development of new research streams, e.g., the knowledge-based view of the firm (Brown & Duguid, 1991) and learning in organisations (Argyris & Schön, 1978). Much of this interest has been triggered by two trends. The first one suggests that organisations rely more and more on massive information transfers and consequent intensive use of information and communication technologies (ICT). The second indicates that emerging organisational forms are based on collaborative networks, which cross department, functional, firm, physical and national frontiers (e.g., Drucker, 1991).

A number of assumptions are made in the above views. Firstly, knowledge is conceived as a manageable asset, just as cash flow, raw materials, or human resources (Spender, 1996). As a consequence, KM becomes the set of activities and practices used by an organisation to harness the brainpower within it and therefore achieve its goals (Davenport & Prusak, 1998). In other words, the *raison d'être* for companies investing in KM is not so much because they want to work smarter, but because they need to efficiently exploit any recently implemented systems and practices in areas such as innovation at the product, services, and organisation levels.

Secondly, knowledge cannot be dissociated from the particular context in which it is generated and used. Different contexts have distinct knowledge requirements and, as a result, distinct forms of managing knowledge are needed in order to cope with the specific situation (Demarest, 1997). Therefore, the first step in understanding KM is to choose a focus for analysis (e.g., a knowledge-intensive process) after which an investigation on knowledge creation and use is carried out.

Finally, knowledge can only be understood within a social system, in which the individual is its core element. In such a social network, knowledge is transferred from the individual to the organisation and back to the individual through the collaboration dynamics between all parties involved in a business process (Kim, 1993). Value is created by individual action but also via group and organisational actions. Without this assumption, there is only information and communication. Knowledge is what is used by a human agent to meaningfully organise information through intuition, experience, communication, or inference (Blackler, 1995).

Concepts in Knowledge Management

Given the widespread interest on knowledge and KM, the emergence of a wide variety of definitions, theories, and models is not surprising. In order to understand how knowledge can be managed in organisations, it is first necessary to define and delimit some key concepts. This section briefly addresses this need by establishing a reference for: (a) knowledge and knowing, (b) forms of knowledge, (c) level of observation, and (d) knowledge types.

With regard to the first distinction, knowledge is associated with the content of what is known, which can be stored and manipulated. Knowing refers to the process of giving meaning to information, and transforming that meaning into action with value for the organisation. Knowledge is regarded as something that people have, whereas knowing is regarded as something that people do (Blackler, 1995; Cook & Brown, 1999). In KM terms, this distinction implies that organisations should concentrate on knowledge both as an object and as a process.

Another useful theoretical tool is that of knowledge forms, of which the terms tacit and explicit have gained extensive acceptance (Polyani, 1966; Nonaka, 1994). Explicit knowledge is formal, systematic, easy to communicate, store and share, while tacit knowledge is highly personal, hard to formalize and to communicate to others, and context-dependent. Tacit knowledge consists partly of technical skills (the know-how) and partly of mental models, beliefs, and perspectives (a cognitive dimension). Mechanisms that transform tacit into explicit knowledge or other combinations between the two are discussed in Nonaka (1994).

The level of observation refers to the concepts of individual, group, and organisational knowledge. At the individual level, researchers focus on how individuals develop new understandings and acquire and interpret knowledge (Argyris & Schön, 1978; Lyles et al., 1996). At the group and organisation level, authors usually propose that knowledge is dependent upon the ability to share common understandings and to exploit them. Consequently, mechanisms and processes at an individual level may differ from those at a group and organisation level. Furthermore, it also becomes important to know how the interaction between the three levels operates in the organisation.

Knowledge can be general or specific (Whitaker, 1996). General knowledge is broad and independent of particular events. The context of general knowledge is usually shared, therefore it is relatively easy and meaningful to codify and exchange. Specific knowledge, in contrast, is context-specific. The codification process becomes more difficult as both knowledge and its context must be described and managed.

A final distinction is made between procedural and declarative knowledge (Cohen & Sproull, 1996). The first type characterizes individual knowledge of well-practiced skills, both motor and cognitive. It is about *how* something occurs or is performed. Declarative knowledge relates to facts and propositions. It is about knowing *what* do to.

These and other concepts are currently the focus of much research as there is a need to both define their meaning with greater precision, and to assess their usefulness in understanding life within and of organisations. A final element in understanding KM is the knowledge process, which not only aims to explain the relationships amongst the aforesaid concepts, but it also provides an operational tool for using knowledge and KM notions in a practical context.

The Knowledge Process and Research Goals

Central to KM is a description of the process explaining how knowledge is created and shared in organisations. Based on the work of, among others, Brown and Duguid (1991), Denning (1998), Huber (1991), Kerssens-van Drongelen et al.

(1996), and Nonaka (1994), as well the practices observed at various organisations during the 1980s and 1990s at Arthur Andersen, Ernst & Young and the World Bank (Denning, 1998), the knowledge process can be depicted as a cycle or spiral with five sections, as illustrated in Figure 1.

- *Identification of the Knowledge Base* consists of mapping the organisation's existing knowledge, that is, identifying what is the knowledge base in a particular business situation.
- *Knowledge Creation and Capture* identifies the sources of information and ideas, and it focuses on individual information and the creation and capture of ideas.
- *Knowledge Storage and Retrieval* identifies the repositories of individual and organisational knowledge. This phase seeks to organise, structure, and maintain a knowledge warehousing and mining system, which are required to index and document the organisation's memory.
- *Knowledge Sharing and Dissemination* are mechanisms that link individual knowledge to group and organisational knowledge. As previously indicated, knowledge is created via sharing and disseminating processes that occur within a social context.
- *Knowledge Application, Trading, and Exploitation* of new knowledge has the aim of improving both the intra- and inter-company activities and ultimately the firm's efficiency and effectiveness.

The above-mentioned knowledge-related concepts can be used to improve understanding of organisational processes, especially knowledge-intensive ones, such as the NPD process.

Figure 1: The Knowledge Process

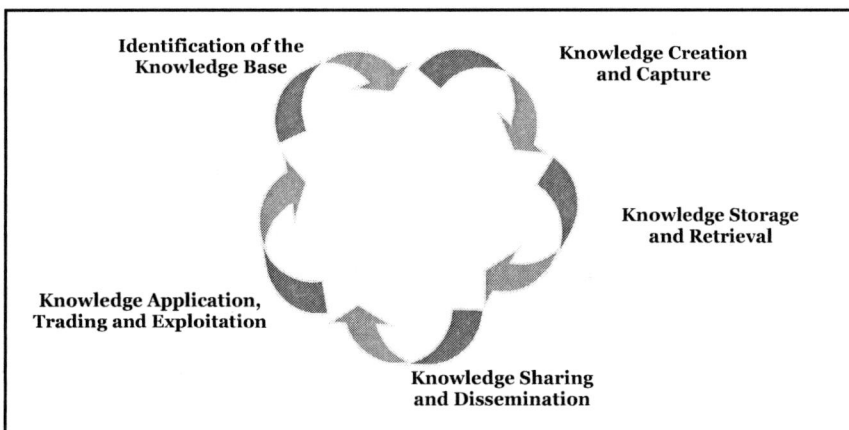

NPD can be defined as a process that requires the capability to obtain, transform and interpret large amounts of market, technical, financial and other internal and external information, in order to develop product ideas and evaluate their technical soundness, manufacturability and economic feasibility (Ancona & Caldwell, 1990). This usually requires the efforts of various individuals from a number of functional areas, hence turning NPD into a collective achievement, more than an individual activity (Emmanuelides, 1993).

In line with these views, NPD is, therefore, a knowledge-creation process, in which new ideas and concepts are transformed into new or improved products. In the process, knowledge is used and new knowledge is created, which can be used for generating more ideas and concepts. Conceiving the NPD process in these terms requires a progressive focus shift from structures and functions, to individuals and teams, and finally to knowledge and KM.

The aim of this chapter is to use the knowledge process cycle as a framework to assess the implementation of an NPD project, i.e., the implementation of an e-Learning portal.

THE NEWLEARNING PROJECT
Research Design and Methodology

This chapter is based on a methodology of a single case study. As explained by Yin (1994), the case study is the most suitable strategy when the researcher wishes to understand the relationships between a phenomenon and its context. Reconstruction of the case study was made through documentation analysis and successive in-depth interviews with the NPD project coordinator. Early versions of the case description were submitted to project managers from the entities involved for cross-checking and refinement. Feedback received was used to clarify narratives and descriptions. Analysis of the case material was informed by the concepts outlined around the knowledge process cycle, and limited to an exploration of KM issues that were used within the project.

Fieldwork in this chapter is exploratory and partially inductive. This approach was chosen due to the fragmented and scanty knowledge with regards to the use of KM practices in the context of e-Learning NPD projects [after recommendations on theory-building and case study research by Eisenhardt (1989) and Robson (1999)]. Nonetheless, a deductive approach was not completely discarded. In fact, it is not possible to prevent the work on KM practices previously presented from influencing the research, hence the research approach aimed at combining the benefits of a thorough description of the case material with the conceptual framework described above. In sum, instead of testing pre-defined hypotheses, the study used fieldwork examples to identify management challenges and to generate and refine ideas for future research.

Case Description

NewLearning Project's Goal

The final goal of the project is a conceptual design of a vertical portal for top executives, university students, and university lecturers. The main components of the system's architecture are: News and Events; Forums; Recruitment (specific for companies and students); Company's Training Catalogue (a catalogue for all of the company's existing courses, especially for new online courses); BrainSpace (for knowledge sharing between executives and experts); Intranet space (specific for e-Learning resources for the University lecturers); Knowledge sharing about the disciplines from the university and from the company; Academic Services); and the company's presentation.

The Organisations

Project NewLearning is the result of a need felt by the customer organisation — *the customer* — to distribute its teaching courses, specifically by implementing an e-Learning solution. This need was captured by the consultant organisation — *the consultant* — which recognised a business opportunity and therefore got involved in the project right from its inception.

The customer is an organisation that is part of a large public university. The customer is well established in the Portuguese higher education sector and executive-training sectors, offering educational courses for undergraduates, post-graduates and executive training. It has long-standing experience with courses delivered in a traditional way: attendance of students and executives at structured and programmed classes (i.e., face-to-face, synchronous delivery), but lacked significant know-how with regards to the provision of educational services through a Web portal. NewLearning was designed exclusively for the executive-training market, due to the shorter length of these courses and to the constraints of adult learners, such as less free time to attend teaching sessions than undergraduate students.

The consultant was a global, multi-disciplinary professional services organisation operating in areas such as business consulting, corporate finance, human capital, legal services, and tax services. In Portugal, the consultant had experience in implementing e-Business solutions, but was less familiar with the strategic definitions and detail of implementing e-Learning projects.

Team Members

Team composition and team members' involvement varied throughout the project. The following people had direct responsibility over the project:

- From the Customer: director of the Company's Executive Centre (project coordinator in the first phase of the project), director of ICT, several lecturers, senior decision-makers, and a project coordinator (in the second phase of the project).

- From the Consultant: three experts in project management and one in distance learning. The latter came from a foreign office elsewhere in the consultant's organisation, because he was the only one in the European division to have both the experience and specific competencies in e-Learning.

The NewLearning Project

The project started in the first quarter of 2000, with the concept generation and definition phase. After several months of changes and negotiation, the project concept was accepted by the customer during the third quarter of the year. The second phase — project feasibility and financial viability — started in 2001, and was concluded by the summer of the same year. The project then entered its third phase — implementation of the business plan — and was expected to run for at least five more years.

The Process

The project was characterised by intense contacts and enduring communication between the customer and the consultant. Notwithstanding the consultant's extensive experience in project management, some of the practices described below were new in NewLearning.

First Phase – Concept Generation and Definition

The consultant had little experience in the executive training market, therefore started by conducting a survey in order to identify and explore similar experiences (e.g., events where Internet delivery had allowed an organisation to develop a significant presence in the market). Information was gathered through internal and external searches. The internal search was based on the company's intranet and contacts with other European offices. This search showed the unique and novel features of such a project, which made it new for the consultant worldwide. The external search involved studying existing e-Learning models in Europe and North America, as well as informal interviews with key informants (e.g., people working for other companies similar to the customer's organisation).

A team composed of people from the customer and the consultant started working right from the project kick-off to gather information regarding the customer's needs, culture, practices, concerns, and problems, and to deliberate on the project goals, purposes, and concepts. In addition, the consultant interviewed several University lecturers, to capture their unique and experienced accounts in relation to a traditional educational model and their opinions and comments with regards to alternative learning models based on the Web.

Shortly after the official project start-off, the consultant invited the customer's project coordinator to attend its annual international conference, held in the US, on new learning technologies. Two reasons explain this unusual invitation: firstly, it was an opportunity to improve the customer's — and the consultant's — knowledge on e-Learning matters; and secondly, since the consultant is also involved in the development of teaching contents worldwide, this seemed to be an interesting way of sharing the consultant's corporate university with the customer.

Towards the end of the third quarter of 2000, the consultant decided to take a stake on e-Learning. As a result, some project team members were sent out to visit the European office, which had more experience in e-Learning issues, resulting in additional knowledge brought to the Portuguese group and the inclusion of consultant team members in an international learning and KM network.

Second Phase – Project Feasibility and Financial Viability

After the go-ahead for the second phase and still during the negotiation period, another internal conference on best practices in business consulting was organised by the consultant. The customer's project coordinator was invited to talk about NewLearning's uniqueness and novelty, and to show how collaboration and integration between the customer and the consultant had shaped the project from the outset.

When the second phase started in the beginning of 2001, other practices were implemented.

Another person came to the team representing the customer. This person was in direct and continuous contact with one of the key consultant members, holding long-term working meetings throughout the second phase. These intense contacts aimed to create and share ideas with regards to the financials of the project, the systems' architecture, and potential problems for learners, amongst others. Meanwhile, the consultant's company had also brought financial experts into the team.

By his own initiative, this new team member — project coordinator — registered to an online course offered by an international e-Learning provider. The aim was to experience the difficulties of distance learning from a learner perspective, the disadvantages of this method, and so on. He also got involved in an international virtual learning community.

The perceived boundaries between the customer's and the consultant's organisations dematerialised because of the activities of key individuals, which were the operational "faces" and "names" of NewLearning. For quick reference, these persons were the two customer-project coordinators (one in the first phase and another in the second phase) and the consultant-project coordinator (involved in both phases).

Until the end of the second phase, two more conferences served to disseminate NewLearning. In the first one the consultant presented NewLearning to its customers, highlighting the shared experiences and lessons learned throughout the process. The purpose of this meeting was to explore the potential market for new e-Learning projects, which had become a strategic issue for the consultant. In the second meeting, the consultant's European HQ sponsored yet another international academic and industrial conference on e-Learning, in which both customer and consultant had another opportunity to share experiences.

Throughout both phases several presentations were made by the consultant to the customer, to inform customers about the progress of the project and to show successive prototypes. A prototype in this context encompassed a "dummy" demonstration of what the NewLearning concept would look like. These sessions were very dynamic, with an intense information exchange between the consultant and a demanding customer, and allowed the consultant to refine graphical interfaces as well as the system's functionality.

CASE ANALYSIS AND DISCUSSION: KM IN PROJECT NEWLEARNING

A First Move

Project NewLearning represented a first move in the Portuguese e-Learning market because it aimed to deliver a solution based not only on online training supporting materials — characteristic of existing e-Learning projects — but also on the building of a full online training programme. The new product's web presence included a corporate portal aimed at improving the organisation's external responsiveness. This aim was met by the learning portal offering a focal point for a set of innovative interactions that resulted from key contact points between the consultant's customer and the customer's customers.

The novelty of the project, the relatively low experience of both parties, and the lack of benchmarks in the Portuguese market meant that this was a risky and uncertain project. The challenge for the project team was to translate market and technical intelligence, learning offerings, and legacy knowledge into a newly effective product design and distribution configuration that could meet and exceed the few competitive benchmarks in the evolving global market. In general terms, the process was characterised by an immediate and wholesale destruction of the "walls" between the working parts of the extended enterprise (i.e., the perceived boundaries between the customer's and the consultant's organisation). The traditional NPD process based on clearly-market boundaries between two separate entities each with well-defined roles, was not followed. Instead, it was substituted by an NPD process based on blurred and fuzzy frontiers between two entities — which at times functioned as *one* single entity — each with a reservoir of knowledge that was continuously transferred between individuals. In this sense, project NewLearning resembled less the case of clear role-definition and structured stage-gate processes, as traditionally put forward by authors like Clark and Wheelwright (1993), and Cooper (1990) than that of flexible and evolving roles and responsibilities, as suggested by Hill et al. (2000), Kamoche and Cunha (2000), or Nonaka (1990).

Both entities realised that they required a higher-order comprehension of matters than that underlying more traditional or less knowledge-intensive projects. These matters included the specific product contents and the wider context represented by the novel business activity. Both parties focused their efforts on the innovation at hand using a number of practices, which although may not have been labelled KM practice, were in fact directed at elevating the degree of understanding and knowledge about a common goal, i.e., delivery of a new product. More than advanced integrative practices between two distinct parties, these mechanisms were used to deconstruct the whole NPD process with regards to the distinctions between *internal-external*, *in-out*, and even *customer-consultant*.

Business Practices as KM Practices

Cycle Stage 1: Identification of the Knowledge Base

The first important element in the knowledge process is the identification of the project's knowledge content, i.e., what knowledge is required in a particular situation. This corresponds to digging out the existing intellectual capital (Wiig, 1997) or knowledge base (Zeleny et al., 1990).

The NewLearning project can be pictured as a two-phase process — strategic definition and implementation, which required distinct but complementary capabilities of the project's team members. The consultant had strong competencies in implementing e-Businesses, but less experience in the strategic definition of a business model in the distinct higher education and executive training markets. The customer was a leader, with well-built capabilities to deliver teaching contents, as well as for the strategic analysis of Portuguese higher education and executive training markets. The complementary nature of diverse capabilities opened opportunities to develop joint competencies in order to create synergies which would result in the first project in Portugal to integrate the strategic definition of an e-Learning concept with its implementation. In structural terms, the process was aimed at widening and deepening the knowledge base for NewLearning in the following categories:

Project management: project NewLearning was a complex interplay of activities, with a highly interdependent set of tasks involving inputs and outputs of each member. Knowledge about the project was embedded in the phases and in the objectives of each stage, timing and deadlines, existing subprocesses, and risks and costs associated with changes.

The team: knowledge about team members' roles, their personal characteristics, location of informants, and team functioning. This is knowledge about who is who in the team and about other people's knowledge. A substantial part of this knowledge is likely to be tacit and vulnerable to changes in the project, as it is mostly stored in individuals.

Product/solution: this category included several dimensions of the product/solution: technical requirements, applications, end users, performance in the marketplace, objectives of the project, and so on. This knowledge is relatively easy to record and retrieve.

The companies: structure, strategy, goals and mission, organisational routines, rules and accepted behaviours, informal organisation, information gatekeepers, and culture and politics.

External environment: market and end-customers' characteristics, market trends, competitors, similar products/solutions in the marketplace, legislative constraints, suppliers, other companies that may have been involved in a partnership, and other entities.

These two last categories provided both parties with information regarding the environment in which both companies operate. It is general knowledge, as opposed to specific knowledge (the first three categories, i.e., project management, the team, and product/solution), which is more context-dependent. Despite its more general character, knowledge about the companies and the environment seemed to have played an important part in NewLearning, since not only has it helped to define strategic intents but also because it shaped relationships between people.

Cycle Stage 2: Knowledge Creation and Capture

An important section of the cycle involves the creation and capturing of knowledge, aimed at locating or generating the information and ideas required to carry out the project. As mentioned above, this category considers knowledge produced as the result of individual efforts only, and not of the social dynamics between project team members. As far as NewLearning was concerned, there was an important gap between what was known and what needed to be known, due to the incomplete competencies of the parties and to project novelty.

Some of the project management tools were standard practice. For example, within the consultant's organisation there were templates, protocols, procedures, project management techniques and software, and a stage-gate system (Cooper, 1990), detailing the type of tasks to be carried out by individual consultants when working with a customer. One such pre-set task was the undertaking of a survey of organisations with similar capabilities to those of the customer. Specifically for NewLearning, this survey attempted to identify successful and unsuccessful e-Learning projects elsewhere in Europe and in the U.S. as well as assess lessons learned by teams in other similar projects.

These tools were part of the consultant's framework for business-analysis and they had one purpose: to collect, process and compile information with regards to established industry practice in e-Learning. Key information areas included: strategic positioning of the customer, internal supporting processes of the new business, technologies to be used, and human resources and organisational structure, amongst others.

However, there were also some new practices that emerged during NewLearning. For instance, in the second stage of the project the new team member enrolled in an online course at his own initiative. The spontaneous registration in virtual networks was also an attempt by this project coordinator to localise sources of ideas and information. Both these actions denoted elements of individual inspiration and improvisation, which were triggered by project needs.

Active use and participation of project members in an online learning environment was consistent with the customer's "reflective practitioner" teaching approach, and illustrates a complex interplay between knowing and knowledge. In fact, enrolling in an online course is an action of *knowing*, which generates insights — *knowledge* — about the final-customers' views on distance learning.

Succinctly, required knowledge can be created through numerous ways: assessment tools (e.g., framework for business-analysis used by the consultant), best practices (e.g., internal search), lessons learned (e.g., other projects), non-competitors (e.g., external search), yellow pages (e.g., the expert in distance learning), and hands-on experience (e.g., the team member that embarked on a distance course).

Cycle Stage 3: Knowledge Storage and Retrieval

With regards to storage and retrieval, data analysis suggests that despite the efforts to stock up all the information of an NPD project in a hardware format, some knowledge was not easily transformed into a readable layout. The following is a brief discussion of knowledge repositories in NewLearning and the types of knowledge stored in them.

Documentware: output documents (e.g., reports, communication logs), procedures, guidelines and business models that instructed how to deliver a project in process (e.g., main milestones), technological (e.g., technical requirements) and financial terms (e.g., commercial targets).

Humanware: project team members from the consultant and customer organisations, including participants that had a brief, yet crucial, input (e.g., the expert in distance learning). Elements stored in humanware include: lessons learned from the project (e.g., the information-procurement routines in the beginning of the project), the wrongdoings (e.g., bad practices), procedural knowledge (e.g., who to contact for a specific question on e-Learning), and intuition (e.g., a feeling for potential problems in a similar project).

Hardware: intranet and Internet, project management software, internal databases, and tele-, video- and computer-conferences. Included in this category are also presentations and successive prototypes that served to communicate the realisation in visible terms of the project.

Groupware: cultural identity and image of the customer organisation, its informal features, and the attributes of the higher education and executive training sectors. Groupware also includes the consultant's corporate university. Similarly to humanware, the groupware exists in the collective minds of groups, and in organisational routines and structures.

Documentware and hardware are tangible elements, which are relatively easy to use by authorised and competent individuals. They are important repositories if the project is to be replicated, corrected or assessed. By the same token, they are easy to copy and imitate.

Conversely, the knowledge contained in humanware and groupware repositories is difficult to code and record in a written format because much of that knowledge is tacit (Nonaka & Takeuchi, 1995). This knowledge is what gives a particular project its unique and exclusive character, and is usually extremely difficult to copy and imitate.

One difficulty in KM is the conversion of tacit into explicit knowledge, due to the technical problems that may be involved, but especially due to the paradox that it brings to bear on the company. In fact, on one hand, any sudden unavailability of a key individual would probably lead to that knowledge being inaccessible. On the other hand, it is this difficulty of coding and transferring that makes these repositories hard to imitate and use by other entities (Cunha et al., 1999), therefore creating advantages over competitors. It is interesting to note, however, that the current text is an attempt to convert parts of this uncoded and tacit knowledge into an explicit format.

Cycle Stage 4: Knowledge Sharing and Dissemination

A central step in the cycle is knowledge sharing and dissemination. The importance of this step derives from the fact that most of the knowledge-in-context necessary for a project such as the one under analysis is created during the intense social and network activity between all parties (Huber, 1991).

Overall, the data suggests that this cycle stage is better described as an ongoing process, rather than a phase with clear start and end points.

Significant sharing and distribution means used in NewLearning are: the mixed team composed of customer and consultant members, the successive interviews between individual consultants and University lecturers, the various conferences and presentations, international learning and KM networks, joint work by team members, and prototypes.

These means illustrate the use of key concepts in KM, some of which were described in the theoretical sections in this chapter. For example, the mixed teams and the international virtual learning and KM networks, are forms of communities of practice (Brown & Duguid, 1991), or communities of knowing (Boland & Tenkasi, 1995). Projects such as NewLearning are characterised by a process of distributed cognition in which multiple communities of specialised knowledge workers, each dealing with a part of an overall project problem, interact to create patterns of sense-making and behaviour displayed by the project as a whole. Therefore, developing a new project can be regarded as a working-innovating-learning cycle, in which different communities of individuals bring their knowledge and past experience together in order to transform an idea into a final product. The essential link between adjacent communities is made through individual actors who belong to several groups at the same time, such as the consultants that are part of the mixed team and of the international learning and KM network.

The joint work by key team members, especially the team composed of the customer and consultant project coordinators in the second phase of the project shows how knowledge is transformed from tacit into explicit/tacit (Nonaka, 1994) throughout NewLearning. This team of two is a powerful way of tapping the tacit and highly subjective insights, intuitions, and hunches of both customer and consultant and making those insights available for testing and use by the project team as a whole (explicit knowledge) or by other individuals (tacit knowledge). A similar role is played by prototypes. A prototype is a technology or product — explicit knowledge — that symbolises the consultant's commitment and embodied tacit knowledge regarding the project, and requires that the customer is comfortable with and understands the images and symbols used by the other entity.

Cycle Stage 5: Knowledge Application, Trading, and Exploitation

The final section of the process is knowledge application, trading, and commercialisation. However interesting the generation of new knowledge may be, the final goal of the process is to use that knowledge in favour of the organisation. Both companies involved in NewLearning operate in highly competitive markets, hence knowledge is regarded as a resource that if well managed should contribute to achieving the firm's goals and mission. The most obvious knowledge application in the present case is the e-Learning solution, which is the main deliverable of the whole project and represents its most important tangible output. However, other project spin-offs can also be linked to KM concepts. These include: new strategic focus and new organisational routines, which are detailed next.

Towards the end of the first phase, the consultant decided to focus on the emergent e-Learning market. Several direct and indirect actions were taken thereafter, such as the team members that visited the European office with more experience in e-Learning, their enrolment in an international learning and KM network, the internal conference on best practices in business consulting that was held during the negotiation period, and another conference organised by the consultant, already in the second phase, aimed at publicising organisational learning and KM topics by its customers. The purpose of some of these measures was to explore a potential market that had become strategically pertinent for the consultant over the previous six months. Although a definite causal link cannot be established, there was an interesting relationship between the creation of a new market focus on e-Learning by the consultant and the initiation of the NewLearning project. One can argue, at the end, that NewLearning played at least an important role in creating a new business area for the consultant company.

A final significant output of NewLearning is the possible institutionalisation of some practices used during the project, which were initialised by the people involved. For example, the participation of a customer in the consultant's internal conference was not a common procedure; however, after NewLearning other similar actions took place in other projects. This try-and-learn process illustrates how individual knowledge can become organisational knowledge via learning, as predicted in some literature. For example, March (1991) theorised that the product of the organisation process is the institutionalisation of an organisation schema reflected in organisational systems and routines. Routines are the places where the lessons of experience are accumulated. They are embedded in the organisation and are reflected in an organisation's consistency in behaviour (Kim, 1993).

Assessment of the Knowledge Process

Overall, the knowledge process is a useful conceptual tool to analyse the issues encountered during NewLearning from a KM perspective. However, it provides a static, hence incomplete, picture of what is actually going on in a knowledge-intensive process. In fact, the five stages described above do not seem to capture the highly dynamic and complex character of knowledge creation, sharing and use in a project such as NewLearning. This evaluation is based on three observations:

Firstly, some of the explained practices cannot be satisfactorily inscribed in one single stage of the cycle. For example, enrolling in an international virtual learning community is both a knowledge-creation and sharing mechanism. This suggests that cycle stages may be not mutually exclusive.

Secondly, each cycle stage interacts in a very complex manner with other stages, with interdependencies amongst them. Taking the example above, enrolling in an international virtual learning community allows ideas to be shared, and in turn creates new ideas, which are again shared. One cannot avoid creating new ideas and concepts when sharing information and knowledge.

Thirdly, starting and ending points of each cycle stage are neither fixed nor clearly discernible. Knowledge sharing and dissemination, for instance, is a mechanism operating every time individuals communicate. Likewise, storage and retrieval are non-ending procedures throughout a project lifetime.

These observations suggest that instead of describing the knowledge process as a number of sequential stages, it is more valuable to define it as a set of continuous interdependent sub-processes, or as multiple inter-reliant knowledge cycles, each relating to particular phases in an NPD project.

CONCLUDING REMARKS

Empirical evidence documented in this chapter points to how organisations and teams involved in NPD create the brainpower needed to transform an idea into a final product/solution. The concepts and especially the notion of knowledge cycle seemed to provide an interesting lens for analysing complex organisational processes such as the NPD process.

The analysis suggests that the knowledge base necessary for an innovative project covers areas such as project management, the team, product/solution, the companies involved in the project, and external environment. This base represents a complex set of elements to be managed and is permanently evolving during a project. In fact, this base can be regarded as the ideal intelligent infrastructure of an NPD project, but it does not suffice, per se, to successfully take a project to market. Other dynamical elements play a crucial role, which were observed in NewLearning.

Firstly, the project showed how two entities consciously combined efforts in order to improve understanding of an area where there was an evident and significant gap. This collaboration was characterised by an exemplar process of trust building, mutual confidence, and openness to information and ideas exchange, from two companies used to operating under two apparently irreconcilable philosophies: on one hand, the more information-and-knowledge-protection oriented paradigm of the consultant organisation and, on the other, the information-and-knowledge-sharing oriented paradigm of the customer organisation.

A second important factor that emerged from the case is the intense use of new ICTs, which allowed the creation and recreation of the conditions for faster, easier, and cheaper access to information. However, as suggested by Handy (1995), information is only useful if transformed through corporate intelligence into new ideas. This transformation was accomplished by actions of key individuals, such as the three project coordinators, who to a large extent shaped the acquisition, circulation, dissemination and application of new and existing knowledge in NewLearning. In addition to the specific technical skills, the analysis suggested that these knowledge workers relied on a certain level of creativity and improvisation to achieve the project's goals.

With regards to the knowledge cycle itself, the findings suggest that, although the concept is a useful one to analyse the structural elements of knowledge creation, sharing, and use, it has limited value when looking at the dynamics and complexities involved. This is an issue deserving further research.

The observations reported in this study illustrate how the highly abstract field of KM and its concepts can be used to examine a central process in modern innovative organisations. The findings need confirmation in other settings and situations, as only one case was reported in this chapter. More projects would permit one to perform a cross-case analysis and hence refine the aspects described above and highlight others not captured by this research. Furthermore, the lack of benchmarks and the fact that the project has only concluded up to its implementation stage (i.e., resilience to environmental turbulence and acceptance by potential users is still to be thoroughly tested), does not allow a thorough evaluation of the KM practices used in NewLearning.

To conclude, knowledge and KM are topics still in their infancy, especially as far as practical evaluation and assessment is concerned. Organisations and individuals can only benefit from the recent theoretical developments in the knowledge literature if the models, theories and concepts put forward are tested for their usefulness and validity in the real world. Failing to acknowledge this will probably lead to the creation of another management fad.

ACKNOWLEDGMENTS

Helpful comments from participants at the 13th ISPIM 2001 Conference, Lapperaanta, Finland, and anonymous referees are gratefully acknowledged. The usual caveats apply.

REFERENCES

Ancona, D. G. & Caldwell, D. (1990). Beyond boundary spanning: Managing external dependence in product development teams. *The Journal of High Technology Management Research*, 1(2), 119-135.

Argyris, C. & Schön, D. (1978). *Organizational Learning: A Theory of Action Perspective*. Reading, MA: Addison-Wesley.

Blackler, F. (1995). Knowledge, knowledge work and organizations: An overview and interpretation. *Organization Studies*, 16(6), 1021-1046.

Boland, Jr., R. J. & Tenkasi, R. (1995). Perspective making and perspective taking in communities of knowing. *Organization Science*, 6(4), 350-372.

Brown, J. S. & Duguid, P. (1991). Organizational learning and communities of practice: Toward a unified view of working, learning, and innovation. *Organization Science*, 2, 40-57.

Clark, K. B. & Wheelwright, S. C. (1993). *Managing New Product and Process Development: Text and Cases*. New York: The Free Press.

Cohen, M. D. & Sproull, L. S. (1996). Editors' introduction. In M. D. Cohen & L. S. Sproull (Eds.), *Organizational Learning*. Thousand Oaks, CA: Sage.

Cook, S. D. N. & Brown, J. S. (1999). Bridging epistemologies: The generative dance between organizational knowledge and organizational knowing. *Organization Science*, 10(4), 381-400.

Cooper, R. G. (1990). Stage-gate systems: A new tool for managing new products. *Business Horizons*, 33(3), 44-54.

Cunha, M. P., Gomes, J. F. S. & Cunha, R. C. (1999). Recursos Humanos e Vantagem Competitiva: A Perspectiva da Organização Baseada nos Recursos. *Revista Portuguesa de Gestão*, 1, 57-66.

Davenport, T. K. & Prusak, L. (1998). *Working Knowledge: How Organisations Manage What They Know*. Boston, MA: Harvard Business School Press.

Demarest, M. (1997). Understanding knowledge management. *Long Range Planning*, 30(3), 374-384.

Denning, S. (1998). What is Knowledge Management? *World Development Report*, World Bank.

Drucker, P. F. (1991, November/December). The new productivity challenge. *Harvard Business Review*, 69, 69-76.

Eisenhardt, K. (1989). Building Theories from Case-Study Research. *Academy of Management Review*, 14(4), 532-550.

Emmanuelides, P. A. (1993). Towards an integrative framework of performance in product development projects. *Journal of Engineering and Technology Management*, 10, 363-392.

Handy, C. (1995, May/June). Trust and the virtual organisation. *Harvard Business Review*, 40-50.

Hill, S., Martin, R. & Harris, M. (2000). Decentralization, integration and the post-bureaucratic organization: The case of R&D. *Journal of Management Studies*, 37(4), 563-585.

Huber, G. P. (1991). Organizational learning: The contributing processes and the literatures. *Organization Science*, 2, 88-115.

Kamoche, K. & Cunha, M. P. (2000). Minimal structures: From jazz improvisation to product innovation. *Organization Studies*, 22(5), 733-764.

Kerssens-van Drongelen, I. C., Weerd-Nederhof, P. C. & Fisscher, O. A. M. (1996). Describing the issues of knowledge management in R&D: Towards a communication and analysis tool. *R&D Management*, 26(3), 213-229.

Kim, D. H. (1993). The link between individual and organizational learning. *Sloan Management Review*, 35(1), 37-50.

Lyles, M., Krogh, G. von, Roos, J., & Kleine, D. (1996). The impact of individual and organizational learning on the formation and management of organizational co-operation. In G. von Krogh & J. Roos (Eds.), *Managing Knowledge: Perspectives on Co-operation and Competition* (pp. 82-99). London: Sage Publications.

March, J. G. (1991). Exploration and exploitation in organizational learning. *Organization Science*, 2(1), 71-87.

Nonaka, I. (1990). Redundant, overlapping organization: A Japanese approach to managing the innovation process. *California Management Review*, 32(3), 27-38.

Nonaka, I. (1994). A dynamic theory of organizational knowledge creation. *Organization Science*, 5, 14-37.

Nonaka, I. & Takeuchi, H. (1995). *The Knowledge-Creating Company: How Japanese Companies Create the Dynamics of Innovation*. New York: Oxford University Press.

Polyani, M. (1966). *The Tacit Dimension*. New York: Doubleday.

Robson C. (1999). *Real World Research: A Resource for Social Scientists and Practitioners-Researchers*. Oxford: Blackwell.

Senge, P. M. (1990). *The Fifth Discipline*. New York: Doubleday.

Spender, J. C. (1996). Competitive advantage from tacit knowledge? Unpacking the concept and its strategic implications. In B. Moingeon & A. Edmondson (Eds.), *Organizational Learning and Competitive Advantage* (pp. 56-73). London: Sage Publications.

Whitaker, R. (1996). Managing context in enterprise knowledge processes. *European Management Journal*, 14(4), 399-406.

Wiig, K. M. (1997). Integrating intellectual capital and knowledge management. *Long Range Planning*, 30(3), 399-405.

Yin, R. (1994). *Case Study Research: Design and Methods* (2nd ed.). Thousand Oaks, CA: Sage.

Zeleny, M., Cornet, R. J. & Stoner, J. A. F. (1990). Moving from the Age of Specialization to the Era of Integration. *Human Systems Management*, 9(3), 153-172.

Chapter VIII

An Interactive System for the Collection and Utilization of Both Tacit and Explicit Knowledge

Karen Neville
University College Cork, Ireland

Philip Powell
University of Bath, UK

ABSTRACT

This chapter outlines the proposed development of a "Knowledge Base Support Environment" for a university. The system is completely interactive allowing every end user the opportunity to extract from and add to the system. As well as providing a support system for both students and staff alike, the system or environment (see Figure 1) will profile both the academic and technical interests of its end-users. The environment will test student's problem-solving skills with "real world" simulations and cases providing feedback to both lecturers and students. The environment will grow and change as both staff and students collaborate to add and extract material from the system. Duplication of work by staff will be dramatically reduced, freeing staff to concentrate on other tasks. The environment itself can be used by organizations in training, and in the management and creation of knowledge.

INTRODUCTION

The World Wide Web in its entirety offers the learner access to a seemingly endless supply of information, captivating graphics video and audio, making it an effective, user-friendly, method of delivering training or educational material to learners (McCormack et al., 1997; Driscoll, 1998). The delivery of material over the Web is commonplace in today's technological environment. The Web provides access to a tremendous amount of information, therefore, an education or knowledge system must be customised to the needs of the learners (McCormack et al., 1997; Driscoll, 1998) to ensure use of the system (Sano, 1996). As an instructional technology, the Web offers the learner access to resources such as search engines and discussion forums to collaborate with other learners or experts in the field queried. The WWW, therefore, has the potential, if used carefully, to become the most comprehensive communication tool (Crossman, 1997) and ultimately the knowledge Web. It could be argued that advances in technology, such as multimedia and virtual simulations, have left the traditional classroom trailing behind with learners expecting more and more. The WWW is the latest challenge to the education and knowledge "norm." Web-based education is described as an education delivery system in which the WWW is its medium of delivery (Driscoll, 1998). The WWW can enable instructors to generate new environments to cope with the limitations of the old. While the two approaches are different, both require careful planning to deliver effective education. The traditional approach requires as much thought in its design as does the Web-based format, however it is limited by both time and space as student numbers continue to escalate. Web-based education cannot replace the traditional approach but it can provide a necessary balance to its limitations (Driscoll, 1998) and allow users to access a Web of knowledge.

BACKGROUND

This chapter focuses on the design of a knowledge base environment to support students and academics in the pursuit of both tacit and explicit knowledge. The research outlines the different components necessary to assemble the different types of knowledge created in an environment such as a university. It also highlights the potential of the knowledge base (KB) to overcome the physical barriers of the traditional classroom.

THEORETICAL FOUNDATION

Cuban (1993) argued that the traditional classroom, with the instructor at the head of the room, has been in place since the early 1900s and nothing has changed since. The widely accepted criticism of the teacher-centered model is that the *"what"* rather than the *"how"* of the instruction is delivered (Goodlad, 1984). However, it is also argued that problem solving and other intellectual skills are difficult to incorporate into the traditional environment due to the very nature of the educational system. Factors such as space, the grouping of students according to grades and the duration and size of classes all hinder the desired environment. The WWW is regarded by many as the solution to the problem. The attributes of the Web can enable the educator or the teacher to redesign the classroom to incorporate what the traditional classroom lacks. Web education is defined *"as the application of a selection of intellectually stimulating lessons implemented within a creative and collaborative learning environment that utilises the resources of the World Wide Web"* (Lebow, 1993; Perkins, 1991, McCormack et al., 1997). The formula used can take any of the following forms:

- As both a source of information and as an assessment mechanism;
- As a medium for sharing information, participating in discussions and simply communicating;
- As a medium for participating in simulations and cognitive partnerships;
- As a global platform for the sharing and acquisition of knowledge.

Traditional training, as described by Goodlad (1984), occurs in a structured environment. However, the virtual classroom operates under a number of assumptions. The first of which is that it is assumed that the student has access to the Internet and that the learner can work independently of the instructor. Given these assumptions of the system the following are some of the numerous advantages gained through the utilization of the Web:

- The classroom is no longer bound by space and time; the learners have constant access to the learning material, regardless of geographic location.
- The Web can be used to promote experimental learning, for example students can view real-world examples of what they are learning.
- The environment encourages social interaction that is geared towards learning (Johnson & Johnson, 1990).
- The content of the information under study becomes more dynamic. For example students learning about information systems can view and operate examples through the Web-based environment.
- Students can also, through the environment, contribute to the class by using facilities such as discussion forums.

Learning Networks and Groups

Learning networks are computer networks that are used for both educational and training purposes (Harasim, 1995). They consist of groups of people working together online to educate both themselves and others. The hardware and software that forms the network system is the only limitation to these groups. This type of learning system introduces new options available to aid education in both universities and organizations alike. It has been determined that network technologies can improve traditional teaching through the use of new communication techniques, collaboration and knowledge building, (Harasim, Hiltz, Teles, & Turoff, 1995). However, there are both advantages and disadvantages to this approach to learning. There are a number of benefits to the use of learning networks (Wells, 1992). Educators have discovered that through the use of learning networks students can interact with their peers (Kaye, 1991) to create and improve group work in distance education (Davie & Wells, 1991) and to provide the learners with access to online resources and relevant information (Teles & Duxbury, 1992). Education is built around the use of textbooks, classrooms and assignments. Learning networks make the interactive textbook a reality (Harasim et al., 1995). A network, itself, is defined as a shared space (Peterson et al., 1996). Telephone and satellite signals form a vast web or network of computers to enable communication to anywhere in the world. Networks can therefore be used by trainers to create a learning environment (McCormack et al., 1997; Driscoll, 1998). Educators and students from any location in the world can share their knowledge and collaborate with each other (Harasim et al., 1995). Learning in a traditional classroom can be intellectually engaging, as it produces a competitive and collaborative environment. Learning networks strive to support the same environment. Groups of individuals work together to share knowledge and resources, the difference being that those individuals could be from different countries working together, through a learning network that connects their computers. Groups are defined as people who are aware of one another and have the opportunity to communicate (McGrath, 1984). Gustave Lebon (1896) investigated the absorption of individuals into a crowd, losing their personality and adopting the collective mind of the group (Huczynski & Buchanan, 1985). The behaviour of individuals will change in the presence of other individuals (Argyle, 1994; Adam, 1999). It has long since been established that individuals can be expected to perform better or worse when they are observed or supported by others (Baron & Byrne, 1977). The word "group" seems to suggest co-operation and collaboration in any environment. However, research is full of as many examples of conflicts as co-operation (Putnam & Poole, 1987; Easterbrook, 1991). Communication doesn't necessarily encourage collaboration. For example, discussion forums can, if not properly structured, result in information overload and therefore structural chaos. Ten threaded replies can result in ten thousand unstructured responses and queries. Learning networks are used at the different levels of education from primary, secondary to third-level (Harasim, 1990) in order to facilitate the group and the individual and therefore encourage collaboration. At third-level education students use learning systems to support lecture material or participate in courses delivered online (McCormack et al., 1997). Learning networks are based on a number of learning models. These designs or approaches aim to construct a process of learning to support both the educator and the learner (Harasim et al., 1990). The learning models do not, however, focus on the educator as the central figure in the learning process but emphasise the interaction between all the participants and the access to the resources needed. The following are some of the different types of network models available: mentorship, access to experts, access to key information and collaborating groups.

The traditional classroom environment emphasizes the interaction between the educator and the learner (James, 1958; Laurillard, 1993), however collaboration is not as emphasized as it is in learning communities (Kaye, 1991; Dede, 1996). Mentorship is also a traditional method of teaching that strengthens the concept and objectives of learning (Benton et al., 1995). Mentorship is a method of teaching that has been used for hundreds of years. This design is incorporated into learning networks to develop more effective learning practices (Eisenstadt & Vincent, 1998) and provide additional support and mediation to the learners (Alexander, 1995). "Access to experts" is one of the many advantages provided through learning networks (Harasim, 1995). Networks are, in fact, modelled on this method (Harasim et al., 1995). Therefore, learning environments allow students to communicate with experts in a field and collaborate with their peers (Dick & Reiser, 1989; Crossman, 1997). Another component intertwined in the learning methodology is group collaboration (Wells, 1992). The collaborative model assigns specific roles in the learning environment, and each participant communicates through the network (Luetkehans et al., 1996; Driscoll, 1998). The roles of educators and students are changing (Jonassen et al., 1996; Driscoll, 1998). Learning networks enable both the student and the educator to expand the time, place and pace of education (Harasim et al., 1995). This method is more individualized when compared to the traditional classroom (Teles & Duxbury, 1992) while peer interaction and collaboration are also emphasized (Wells, 1992). The Web-based learning systems are designed to provide greater support to the individual learner allowing everyone with the opportunity to speak without conforming to the pressures of "face to face" communication and conflict. But it also allows the learners to anonymously share ideas and pose queries to one another (McCormack & Jones, 1997).

Knowledge

Organizations and universities alike depend on the collection of the data pertaining to the purpose (Curtis, 1998) of the domain in which they operate. Internally each functional part of the organization works with data collected from the different types systems used (Laudon & Laudon, 2000). Organizations, therefore, use technology to collect and store data (Whiten et al., 1994) to be processed by the rules formulated to produce valuable information (Connelly &

Begg, 2002) and eventually knowledge. Universities too, collect data, process it and endow it with relevance and importance (Drucker, 1993). Most organizations use knowledge, for example regarding their target audience, to gain a competitive advantage. Knowledge and knowledge workers are theoretically the "products" produced by universities. However, they face the same dilemma as the majority of firms, that is, too much data and information but not enough knowledge. Buckingham et al. (1987) define information as "explicit knowledge," the significance of which is that information has meaning and it is clearly understood. Knowledge is regarded as volumes of relevant information but, importantly, in addition to experience (tacit knowledge) in the form of an expert (Avison & Fitzgerald, 1997). An expert, to be effective, must use extensively both formal (quantitative) and informal (qualitative) information (Earl & Hopwood, 1980; Land & Kennedy-McGregor, 1987) in decision-making. Knowledge is regarded as a strategic asset and therefore the creation of which is often an enterprise-wide goal. Alavi and Leidner (1999) argued that the importance of knowledge is based on the hypothesis that the barriers to the transfer and duplication of knowledge award it with enormous strategic importance. Universities, with the technological capability necessary, are developing systems that can collect and manage knowledge. The combination or integration, along with the capability to combine an expert's experience in the form of a system is regarded as a strategic tool. Systems capable of combining both explicit and tacit knowledge are referred to as Knowledge Management Systems (KMS). Research in this area is not very detailed due to the fact that organizations (not universities) have only been implementing the systems in the last few years. These systems are used to acquire and manage knowledge and distribute it among the different functional units as well as with any external collaborating groups. The idea of disseminating knowledge is not a new concept, be it in education or in industry. Like the classroom, the traditional approach such as paper-based knowledge sharing and the virtual are used, depending on factors such as the numbers of students or the type of decisions to be made. An organization creates a knowledge base to reduce the level of experience needed by managers and to improve the effectiveness of their decisions (Peters, 1992). Industry invests an enormous amount of capital in the training of its employees and therefore in the creation of so-called "experts in the field," a "true" knowledge base will allow the acquisition of the experience of experts to reduce the loss of investment should the employee leave (Curtis, 1998).

A Knowledge Base Support Environment (KBSE)

Nonaka and Takeuchi (1995) define knowledge as *"just true belief."* Knowledge is regarded in this information-driven economy (Drucker, 1993) as *power* or a source of competitive advantage (Laudon, 2000; Barua, 1996; Grant

1996; Drucker, 1993). Powell (2001) and Casey (1995) describe knowledge as a combination of both information and expertise. Knowledge is acquired or created when an individual, with expertise in a field, uses relevant information productively (Hertog & Huizeneg, 2000). The training and the experience that academics amass over the years (knowledge) allows them to both teach and collaborate to produce additional knowledge. Therefore, a knowledge base support environment (KBSE) can be described as a dynamic repository of existing learning and processing systems such as discussion forums, virtual libraries and research to allow academics and students to retrieve knowledge (either tacit or explicit) based on individual profiles. The possibilities of such a system are limited only by constraints imposed by the university in question, such as technological or managerial support (Neville, 2000). Innovative universities could use this implementation for a number of reasons, specifically to keep staff and students abreast of research and emerging technologies in their fields (Khan, 1997). Designing the system requires a thorough investigation into the use of the Web as a medium for delivery (Ritchie & Hoffman, 1996; McCormack et al., 1997; Driscoll, 1998). The designer must be aware of the attributes of the WWW and the principles of instructional design to create a meaningful learning environment (Gagne et al., 1988; Driscoll, 1997). The Web-based classroom is viewed, as already stated, as an innovative approach to teaching (Relan & Gillani, 1997). Like the traditional method, it requires careful planning to be both effective and beneficial (Dick & Reiser, 1989). As stated by McCormack et al. (1997), *a Web-based classroom must do more than just distribute information...* it should include resources such as discussion forums to support collaboration between learners and ultimately it should also support the needs of both the novice and advanced learner (Sherry, 1996; Willis, 1995). A KBSE is composed of a number of components that are integral to the success of the environment (Banathy, 1992): (1) a student mentoring system to support both full and part-time learners, (2) an exam domain to test both practical and cognitive abilities, (3) a virtual library to allow easy access to conference papers and journals, and (4) finally, the knowledge base facilitated by an agent to integrate all of the components and automate the retrieval of information for the end-users.

RESEARCH OBJECTIVE

The practical objective of this research is to provide an interactive environment for both students and staff to facilitate collaboration in the creation and management of knowledge created by the different actors involved and by the proposed system. The support environment will provide staff with the necessary tools to automate manual tasks that currently necessitate long hours and can never give an accurate picture of the resources (books, journals, research interests) available both on and offline. This research will also provide the reader with strategic information regarding the creation of knowledge through the promotion of group collaboration and cooperation.

RESEARCH APPROACH

The research approach is action-oriented in nature as it is focussed on both the development and evaluation of an interactive system that will allow users to utilise both tacit and explicit knowledge. The virtual environment consists of four separate components, which will undergo intensive software testing, as well as quality assurance testing before the environment is made available to its intended users. Once the system has been in operation for a period of time, the evaluation process will begin to determine the effectiveness of the knowledge base support environment (KBSE). Every user of the system (both students and staff) will be asked to provide feedback through both postal and online questionnaires as well as personal interviews. The findings from these evaluation tools will determine the success of the overall system.

THE TARGET CASE STUDY

In order to validate the goal of this research, the researcher chose University College Cork (U.C.C.) which is one of Ireland's leading third level institutes. The researcher is an employee of the university lecturing in business information systems. The university is a learning institution as opposed to a competitive organization. The success of a university is not based on stock prices or profit margins but on the quality of the graduates and the research or knowledge created. However, U.C.C., like other universities, is just as complex, if not more so. It, too, is composed of departments (both academic and non academic), however these combine to form faculties, committees and boards with management composed of governing bodies, each generating data, information and knowledge. Like organizations, universities create systems to collate data concerning both students and academics and support systems such as learning networks. Again, like organizations, work is duplicated and knowledge is rarely dispersed throughout the enterprise. The purpose of the KBSE is to integrate all of the systems in operation and allow users to pull the knowledge relevant to them.

THE SYSTEM

The "Knowledge Base Support Environment" (KBSE) is in the process of development with the objective of supporting a (generic) university environment.

As well as providing a support system for both students (postgraduate/under-graduate) and staff, the system will produce a large amount of reports for managing and expanding research within departments. The environment will test students' problem-solving skills with "real-world" simulations and MCQs proving feedback to both lecturers and students. The environment will grow and change as both staff and students collaborate to add and extract material from the system. Duplication of work by staff will be dramatically reduced, freeing staff to concentrate on other tasks. The environment itself can be used by the university in training and in the management and creation of knowledge. The system will enable or automate four of the many components that constitute a university and therefore support virtual learning and research. The four components of the system are as follows:

Student Mentoring System

Web-Based Mentoring Systems (WBMS) can be described as learning delivery environments in which the WWW is its medium of delivery (Crossman, 1992; Driscoll, 1998). Due to the increase in student numbers there is a need for greater student support, which can be provided through the Web. The mentoring component of the system allows students to log in and view lecture and tutorial material. In addition, a discussion forum will enable both the mentors (lecturers and tutors) and students to exchange ideas and add to the environment, eliminating constraints such as time and location and making the knowledge base available to each type of student.

- To allow lecturers and tutors to update the content segments of the web site (for example, course homepages and online reading lists) through a Web browser on or off-campus.
- To provide 24-hour online support to students.
- To facilitate group collaboration, e.g., discussion forums.
- To allow students to have positive input into courses.
- To provide students with the ability to add to the environment through discussion forums, links and papers.
- To enable anonymous feedback and questioning, e.g., feedback forms.

Exam Domain

Students attend tutorials and demonstrations for practical subjects, for example programming languages and computer networking. However, due to security systems in place to protect network resources (for example, worksta-tions and servers), students' access rights are restricted. Therefore, written exams are used in universities to test practical skills when industry itself tests the student's practical ability rather than the student's ability to memorise material. A domain (server) with user accounts allocated to test material will enable lecturers to fully evaluate the skills gained through practical work. The exam domain will be designed:

- To give students and lecturers the opportunity to both test and evaluate skills in a simulated environment where they can assume roles such as a network or database administrator without risk to departmental resources.
- To house written exam material for IT and other courses.
- To reduce the duplication of course materials (MCQs and research) on the part of teaching staff.
- To enable students to assess their own understanding of the course material and prepare for summer assessment.
- To supply lecturers and instructors with case examples to expand students' understanding of a particular topic.

Virtual Library

Every college department and individual lecturers archive material in the form of journals and books related to specific topics. However, few use systems to track departmental and individual repositories to facilitate research and budgeting. This component will:

- Track research material within departments.
- Automate the lending of research material to staff and students.

Figure 1: A Knowledge Base Support Environment

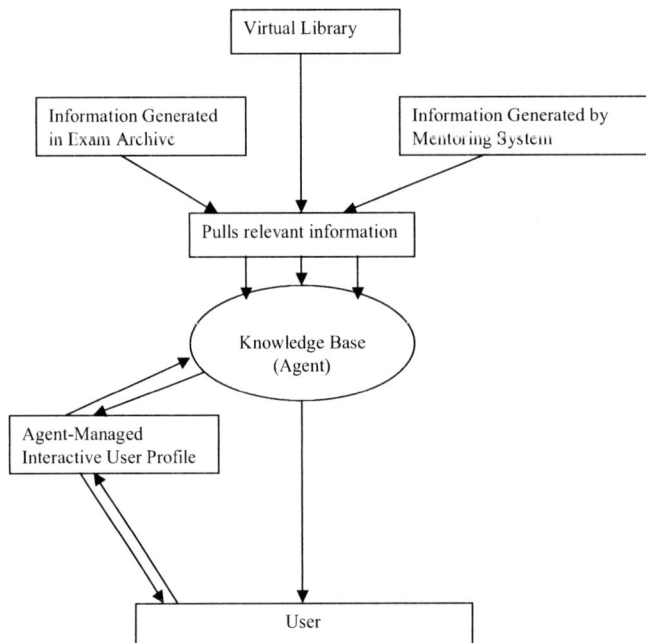

- Enable inventory and budget reporting.
- Assist lecturers in managing their personal resources (journals, books and proceedings).
- Eliminate duplicate purchases of material.
- Reduce the workload of administrative and academic staff.

The Knowledge Base

This is the integrating component of the environment to act both as a repository and as the channel enabling the ongoing process of knowledge creation. It is intended to extend and compliment the other parts of the system as well as adding the ability for users to automate the task of retrieving research and technical papers relevant to their areas of interest. The knowledge base (KB) will generate profiles of users relating to their areas of interest. The KB will intermittently build indexes based on the content collected from the different components, and the system will notify the users when items of interest are added based on the different profiles. The KB will have the following functionality:

- Search out users' particular areas of interest on the Web.
- Automatically provide users with links and updates of online material.
- Profile users' areas of research from which the agent can learn more about what information the users would find helpful in the pursuit of their specific research interests.
- Build a knowledge base of research, as defined by the individual users, to support research acquisition and collaboration.

EVALUATING THE KBSE

Evaluation is the final stage in the development of a KBSE. However, it is an important component of the process. Evaluation is defined as *"the value or merit of something"* (McCormack et al., 1997; Driscoll, 1998). KBSE is a relatively new phenomenon. Therefore, the evaluation stage of the development life cycle will provide valuable insight into the success and failures of both the development of the system and the value of the system as a knowledge management tool (McCormack et al., 1997; Driscoll, 1998). The data gathered during this phase will aid in the development of future environments. Evaluation should not be viewed simply as a process of measurement and estimation but a method of learning about the end product: the learner's acceptance of the system and its effectiveness in creating knowledge. Rowntree (1992) states that:

1. Evaluation is not an assessment.
2. The unexpected should not be ignored.
3. Evaluation is a planned systematic and open endeavour.

Evaluation and assessment are often confused. However, the processes refer to different levels of the investigation into the success of the environment. Evaluation involves all of the factors that influence the acceptance of the system. However, assessment measures the level of understanding of a learner. The developer can perform a number of different evaluations, each of which seeks to elicit specific information. The developer can evaluate the platform used to deliver the system to determine if it provided adequate support. The second type merely involves determining if the system addressed the goals and objectives of the research. Evaluating the impact of the environment on academics and students alike provides the developer or researcher with valuable data regarding its use. Questionnaires are the easiest method used in the evaluation process. The researcher can design a questionnaire to elicit the desired information regarding the system. The questionnaire provides a number of advantages, such as anonymity, which usually provides genuine responses. It enables the researcher to collect large amount of data in a simple format. It is easy to administer to the target group under review, usually by post, and it is relatively easy to analyse. However, the technique cannot be utilised as the only method of evaluation. Follow-up interviews are necessary. Semi-structured interviews allow the researcher to obtain an elaboration of issues identified as a result of the questionnaires. However, interviews tend to collect large quantities of data that is difficult to analyse. Evaluation provides rich data only if designed properly. It is an ongoing process that should be an integral component of the methodology used to develop the system (Breakwell & Millward, 1995). The use of knowledge base environments is increasing in importance. Therefore, a suitable method of evaluation is necessary to collect information regarding both the effectiveness and the ineffectiveness of the different components and the system as a whole to continue to add to the value of this knowledge approach. The virtual support environment will initially be offered to a sample of end-users (both staff and students) who will manage and use the system for a period of time before the environment is made available to all potential users. The purpose of this pilot study is to uncover any potential issues arising from the daily use of the environment.

CONCLUSION

Pressures of the Information Age are forcing organizations and universities to turn to knowledge systems to provide a strategic advantage in this global economy. Effective support environments help create and maintain the knowledge base of a university or organization. There are numerous technologies available to support educational needs. Technologies such as Distributed Desktop Training and Computer-Based Training offer a number of advantages to both universities and organizations. However, these methods can be expensive to maintain as they become out of date relatively quickly. Therefore, more and more universities are turning to learning networks to support their knowledge workers. Academics and students alike can share information and access resources over the World Wide Web, without restrictions such as geographic location, time or the platform used. The utilisation of the Web as an educational tool is not an innovative approach to the needs of the learners. However, the use of the Web and software agents as facilitating technologies in the creation of knowledge is.

Web-based learning allows *"educators and students alike to perform learning-related tasks"* (McCormack et al., 1997). The development of knowledge base support environments require careful investigation into the requirements of the problem case. The developer must consider factors such as the method employed by the student to learn, incentives to ensure use, the identification of goals and objectives and the different roles that are needed to support this new approach to training and ease of use. However, the advantages far outweigh the limitations, which through careful planning can be reduced.

REFERENCES

Alavi, M. & Leidner, D. (1999). *Knowledge Management Systems: Issues, Challenges, and Benefits.*

Alexander, S. (1995). Teaching and Learning on the World Wide Web. Retrieved from the World Wide Web: http://www.scu.edu.au/ausweb95/papers/education2/alexnder/.

Argyle, M. (1994). *The Psychology of Interpersonal Behaviour (5th Edition).* Penguin, Harmondsworth.

Avison, D. E. & Fitzgerald, G. (1995). *Information Systems Development: Methodologies, Techniques and Tools (2nd Edition).* New York: McGraw-Hill.

Baron, R. A. & Byrne, A. (1977). *Social Psychology Understanding Human Interaction (2nd Edition).* Boston, MA: Allyn and Bacon.

Barua, M. K. (1996). *An Empirical Study of Network and Individual Performance in Distributed Design Groups.*

Benton, V., Elder, M. & Thornbury, H. (1995). *Early Experiences of Mentoring: Design and Use of Multimedia Material for Teaching.* OR/MS Working paper 95/5, Department of Management Science, University or Strathcycle.

Casey, C. (1995). Exploiting expert systems for business. *Executive Business Review.*

Connolly, T., Begg, C. & Strachan, (1996). *Database Systems: A Practical Approach to Design, Implementation and Management.* Addison-Wesley.

Crossman, D. (1997). *The Evolution of the World Wide Web as an Emerging Instructional Technology Tool.* Englewood Cliffs, NJ: Educational Technology Publications.

Cuban, L. (1993). *How Teachers Taught (2nd Edition).* New York: Teachers College Press.

Damarin, S. (1993). Schooling and situated knowledge: Travel or tourism? *Educational Technology*, 33(10), 27-32.

Davie, L. & Wells, R. (1991). Empowering the learner through computer-mediated communication. *American Journal of Distance Education*, 5(1), 15-23.

Dede, C. (1996). *The Transformation of Distance Education to Distributed Learning.* Retrieved from the World Wide Web: http://129.7.160.78/InTRO.html.

Dick, W. & Reiser, R. (1989). *Planning Effective Instruction.* Englewood Cliffs, NJ: Prentice-Hall.

Driscoll, M. (1998). *Web-Based Training: Using Technology to Design Adult Learning Experiences.*

Drucker, P. (1993). *Post-Capitalist Society.* New York: HarperCollins.

Easterbrook, (1991, July). *CSCW: Co-operation or Conflict.* New York: Spring Verlag.

The Economist Intelligent Unit, Executive Information Systems, Special Report No. S123.

Eisenstadt, M. & Vincent, T. (1998). *The Knowledge Web, Learning and Collaborating on the Net.*

Gagne, R. M. Briggs, L. J. & Wagner, W. W. (1988). *Principles of Instructional Design (3rd Edition).* New York: Holt Reinbank Winston.

Goodlad, J. (1976). Schooling today. In J. S. Golub (Ed.), *Facing the Future*, (pp. 3-22). New York: McGraw-Hill.

Goodlad, J. (1984). *A Place Called School.* New York: McGraw-Hill.

Grant, R. M. (1996). The resource-based theory of competitive advantage: Implications for strategy formulation. *California Management Review.*

Guba, N. K. & Lincolin, Y. S. (1994). Computing paradigms in qualitative research. In N. K. Denzin & Y. S. Lincoln (Eds.), *Handbook of Qualitative Research.* CA: Sage Publications.

Harasim, Hiltz, Teles & Truoff (1995). *Learning Networks.*

Harasim, L. (1990). Computer learning networks: Educational applications of computer conferencing. *Journal of Distance Education*, 1(1), 59-70.

Hertog, J. F. & Huizenga, E. (2000). The Knowledge Enterprise. Implementation of Intelligent Business Strategies.

Huczynski, A. & Buchanan, D. (1985). *Organizational Behaviour* (2nd Edition). Kidlington, Oxon: Prentice Hall International.

James, W. (1889). *Talk to Teachers.* New York: W. W. Norton. (Original work published 1958.)

Johnson, D. & Johnson, R. (1990). Cooperative learning and achievement. In S. Sharon (Ed.), *Cooperative Learning Theory and Research* (pp. 22-37). New York: Praeger.

Jonassen, D. H. & Reeves, T.C. (n.d.). Learning with technology: Using computers as cognitive tools. In D. Jonassen (Ed.), *Handbook of Research on Educational Technology*. New York: Macmillan.

Kaye, A. (1991). Computer networking in distance education: Multiple uses many models. In A. Fjuk and A. E. Jenssen (Eds.), *Proceedings of the Nordic Electronic Networking Conference* (pp. 43-51). Oslo, Norway: NKS.

Khan, B. (1997) *Web-Based Instruction*.

Laudon, K. C. & Laudon, J. P. (2000). Management Information Systems: Organization and Technology in the Networked Enterprise.

Laurillard, D. (1993). *Rethinking University Teaching*. London: Routledge.

Lebon, G. (1986). *The Crowd – A Study of the Popular Mind*. London: Fisher Unwin.

Lebow, D. (1993). Constructivist values for instructional systems design: Five principles for a new mindset. *Educational Technology Research and Development*, 41(3), 4-16.

Lin, X., Bransford, J. D., Hmelo, C. E., Kantor, R. J., Hickey, D. T. & Secules, T. (1996). *Instructional Design and the Development of Learning Communities*.

Lucas, H. C. (1994). *Information Systems Concepts for Management* (5th Edition). New York: McGraw-Hill.

Luetkehans, L., Hill, J. R. & Hagan, T. (1996). Science connections: Problem solving at a distance. In M. P. Driscoll (Ed.), *Proceedings of Getting It Together: Collaboration in Distance Education*. Conference held at the Florida State University, Tallahassee, Florida, USA.

McCormack, C. & Jones, D. (1997). *Building A Web – Based Education System*.

McGrath, J. E. (1984). *Groups: Interaction And Performance*. Englewood Cliffs, NJ: Prentice-Hall.

McGrath, J. E. (1986). Studying groups at work: Ten critical needs for theory and practice. In P. S. Goodman and Associates (Eds.), *Designing Effective Work Groups*. CA: Jossey-Bass.

Neville, K. (2000). A Web-based training (WBT) system development framework: A Case Study. *Business Information Technology Management* (BIT) 2000, 10th Annual Conference, Manchester, UK.

Nonaka, I. (1995). *The Knowledge Creating Company: How Japanese Companies Create the Dynamics of Innovation*. Oxford: Oxford University Press.

Peterson, L. L. & Davie, B. S. (1996). *Computer Networks: A Systems Approach*. Morgan Kaufmann.

Powell, P. Loebbecke, C. & Levy, M. (2001). SMEs, Co-opetition and Knowledge Sharing: The IS Role. *Global Co-operation in the New Millennium, ECIS*.

Relan, A. & Gillani, B. (1997). *Web-Based Information and the Traditional Classroom.*

Rowntree, D. (1990). *Teaching Through Self Instruction.* London: Kogan Page.

Sano, D. (1996). *Designing Large-Scale Web Sites: A Visual Design Method-ology.*

Sherry, L. (1996). Raising the prestige of online articles. *Interom*, 43(7), 25-43.

Teles, L. & Duxbury, N. (1992). T*he Networked Classroom: Creating an Online Environment for K-12 Education.* Burnaby, BC: Facility of Education, Simon Fraser University (ERIC ED348 988).

Wells, R. A. (1992). Computer-Mediated Communication for Distance Education: An International Review of Research Monographs 6. American Centre for the Study of Distance Education, State College, PA: Pennsylvania State University.

Whitten, J. L. Bentley, L. D. & Barlow, V. M. (1994*). Systems Analysis and Design Methods* (3rd Edition).

Willis, J. (1995). A Recursive, Reflective, Instructional Design Model Based on Constructivist-Interpretivist Theory. *Educational Technology*, 35(6), 5-23.

Chapter IX

Inducing Enterprise Knowledge Flows

Mark Nissen
Naval Postgraduate School, USA

ABSTRACT

The knowledge-based organization appears to offer great promise in terms of performance and capability. Indeed, many researchers are actively working to understand how organizational strategy, structure and technology can be combined and integrated to harness the competitive power of knowledge. However, knowledge is not evenly distributed through the organization, so rapid and efficient knowledge flow is critical to enterprise performance. This chapter builds upon the current state of the art pertaining to knowledge flow, and it develops a model to help induce the flow of knowledge through an organization. Because of the time-critical nature of most knowledge work in the modern enterprise, we focus in particular on knowledge dynamics, to enable rapid and efficient flow, and to help the enterprise become more knowledge-based. Using a global manufacturing firm as an example to illustrate how the knowledge-flow model provides practical guidance, we identify knowledge elements that are critical to effective performance in an unpredictable, dynamic business environment, and we use the multidimensional model to illustrate how to identify specific knowledge flows required for success. Further analysis reveals that different knowledge flows require different approaches in terms of IT and process changes — with the attendant insight that one size does not fit all in terms of knowledge management — and a specific focus on clumped knowledge and constricted flows enables the experienced manager to work through the necessary interventions—often with the set of tools and processes already present in the organization. We also illustrate how the multidimensional model can be augmented to depict the relative flow times associated with various knowledge elements, which provides a rough schedule as well as a roadmap to use for planning requisite knowledge flows for the knowledge-based organization.

INTRODUCTION

It is axiomatic to say, "knowledge is power" when referring to individuals in the workplace, but the practice of **knowledge management** (KM) purports to take the power of knowledge to the group, organization and even enterprise level (Davenport & Prusak, 1998). Although this potential benefit of KM is not viewed universally (cf. Gore & Gore, 1999; McDermott, 1999), many scholars (e.g., Drucker, 1995) assert that knowledge represents one of the very few sustainable sources of **competitive advantage**. Hence the **knowledge-based organization** — one that competes on the basis of its differential knowledge [e.g., see Grant (1996) for discussion of the knowledge-based view of the firm] — appears to offer great promise in terms of performance and capability. Indeed, many researchers are actively working to understand how organizational strategy, structure and technology can be combined and integrated to harness the competitive power of knowledge [e.g., see Augier et al. (2001), Birkenshaw et al. (2002), Brown and Duguid (1991), Hargadon and Fanelli (2002), Kogut and Zander (1992), Leonard and Sensiper (1998), Levitt and March (1988), Nonaka (1994), Swap et al. (2001), and Thomas et al. (2001)].

The knowledge-based organization must be able to apply substantial knowledge, when and where it's needed, to effect organizational goals. However, knowledge is not evenly distributed through the organization, so rapid and efficient **knowledge flow** is critical to enterprise performance. The larger, more geographically dispersed, and time-critical an enterprise (e.g., global manufacturing firms, telecommunication and software companies, military forces), the more important knowledge flow becomes in terms of efficacy. Unfortunately, our collective knowledge of how knowledge flows is quite primitive (Alavi & Leidner, 2001). Lacking knowledge-flow theory and application for guidance, even enterprises with multimillion-dollar KM projects have difficulty seeing past *information* technologies such as intranets and Web portals. Further, Nissen et al. (2000) note such KM projects rely principally upon trial and error, one of the least effective approaches known.

Although computer networks and systems now enable a flood of data and information, managerial time and attention remain highly constrained, and a dearth of information systems (IS) is available to induce the flow of knowledge. Notwithstanding the many contemporary information systems labeled "KM tools" (e.g., groupware, Web portals, document databases, search engines) that are available and being employed in hopes of enhancing the flow of knowledge through many enterprises, few such tools even address *knowledge* as the focus or object of flow. Rather, nearly all contemporary information systems focus instead of the transfer of information and data, which is qualitatively different across numerous dimensions (Davenport et al., 1998; Nissen, 2002; Teece, 1998).

This chapter builds upon the current state of the art pertaining to knowledge flow, and it develops a model to help induce the flow of knowledge through an organization. Because of the time-critical nature of most knowledge work in the modern enterprise, we focus in particular on knowledge dynamics, to enable rapid and efficient flow, and to help the enterprise become more knowledge-based. For instance, leveraging the good understanding of flows in physical (e.g., electronics, aerospace) and organizational (e.g., manufacturing, logistics) domains, in which many flow-enhancing devices (e.g., amplifiers, engines, assembly lines, distribution hubs) have been developed and demonstrated, we extend models that may someday lead to "devices" (e.g., knowledge amplifiers and engines) of comparable utility in the knowledge-based organization domain.

The chapter is organized into five sections, beginning with this introduction. The second section summarizes key background on knowledge flow, with particular emphasis on the kinds of information systems employed in knowledge-based organizations. Section 3 discusses knowledge-flow mechanics and the multidimensional model. This knowledge-flow model is then used in Section 4 to articulate and graphically illustrate key insights into knowledge-based organizational design that emerge through practical application in the domain of global manufacturing. The chapter closes with important conclusions and implications for managers of knowledge-based organizations in the 21st century. A list of selected references is included to guide the reader to other sources of information on this topic.

BACKGROUND

This section draws heavily from Nissen (2002) to summarize key background work pertaining to knowledge flow. It focuses in particular on important concepts from the emerging knowledge management literature. For the purposes of this chapter, five important concepts from the KM literature are summarized: (1) knowledge hierarchy, (2) information technology, (3) knowledge-based systems, (4) knowledge management life cycle, and (5) current knowledge-flow theory.

Knowledge Hierarchy

Many scholars (e.g., Davenport & Prusak, 1998; Nissen et al., 2000; von Krough et al., 2000) conceptualize a hierarchy of knowledge, information, and data. As illustrated in Figure 1, each level of the hierarchy builds on the one below. For example, data are required to produce information, but information involves more than just data (e.g., need to have the data in context). Similarly, information is required to produce knowledge, but knowledge involves more than just information (e.g., it enables action). We operationalize the triangular shape of this hierarchy using two dimensions — abundance and actionability — to differentiate among the three constructs.

Briefly, data lie at the bottom level, with information in the middle and knowledge at the top. The broad base of the triangle reflects the abundance of data, with exponentially less information available than data, and even fewer chunks of knowledge in any particular domain. Thus, the width of the triangle at each level reflects decreasing abundance in the progress from data to knowledge. The height of the triangle at each level reflects actionability (i.e., the ability to take appropriate action, such as a good decision or effective behavior). Converse to their abundance, data are not particularly powerful for supporting action, and information is more powerful than data. But knowledge supports

Figure 1: Knowledge Hierarchy

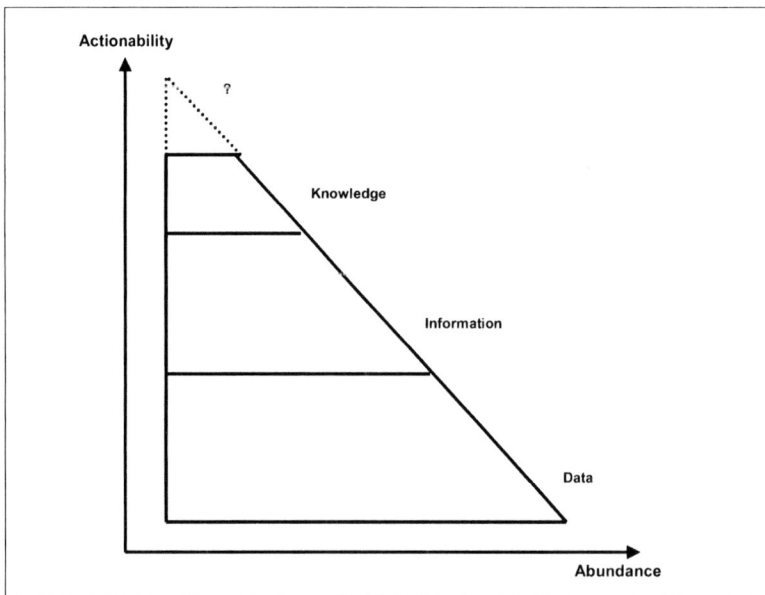

action directly, hence its position near the top of the triangle. Curiously, there is current speculation as to one or more additional levels "above" *knowledge* in such hierarchies (e.g., *wisdom,* cf. Spiegler, 2000), which also receives speculation in the trade press (Angus, 1998; Mullins, 1999). The present chapter does not attempt to address "wisdom flow."

Information Technology

Current information technology (IT) used by enterprises is limited primarily to conventional database management systems (DBMS), data warehouses (DW), intranets/extranets, portals, and groupware (O'Leary, 1998). Arguably and as noted above, just looking at the word "data" in the names of many "knowledge management tools" (e.g., DBMS, DW), we are not even working at the level of information, much less knowledge. Although (especially, Web-based) Internet tools applied within and between organizations provide a common, machine-independent medium for the distribution and linkage of multimedia documents, current intranet and extranet applications focus principally on the management and distribution of information, not knowledge per se.

Along these same lines, groupware offers infrastructure support for knowledge work and enhances the environment in which knowledge artifacts are created and managed, but the flow of knowledge itself remains indirect. For example, groupware is widely noted as helpful in the virtual office environment (e.g., when geographically dispersed knowledge workers must collaborate remotely), and it provides networked tools such as: shared, indexed, and replicated document databases and discussion threads (e.g., Lotus Notes/ Domino applications), shared "white boards," joint document editing capabilities, and full-duplex, multimedia communication features. These tools serve to mitigate collaboration losses that can arise when rich face-to-face joint work is not practical or feasible. But supporting (even rich and remote) communication is not sufficient to guarantee knowledge flow.

One notable exception to the comment above pertains to data mining (DM). Although it too has the word "data" in its name, DM is focused on filtering massive volumes of data to extract useful patterns and relationships that are not readily apparent from the data themselves. Such patterns and relationships certainly qualify as knowledge, and DM represents one the few IT approaches that can effectively support knowledge creation (see Nissen et al., 2000, for discussion).

Knowledge-Based Systems

Construction and use of knowledge-based systems (KBS) appears to offer excellent potential for knowledge-based organizations, because KBS can make knowledge explicit and its application direct. Key KBS technologies include applications such as: expert systems and intelligent agents; infrastructure and support tools such as ontologies, knowledgebases, inference engines, search algorithms, list and logic programming languages; and a variety of representational formalisms (e.g., rules, frames, scripts, cases, models, semantic networks). Much deeper than just their names' sake, KBS are predicated on the capture, formalization and application of strong domain knowledge. The use of KBS for knowledge organization and distribution is well known, widespread, and now the subject of textbook application (Russell & Norvig, 1995; Turban & Aronson, 2001).

Unlike the extant IT tools noted above, the substance of KBS is knowledge itself — not just information or data — and KBS are designed to interpret and apply represented knowledge directly. These capabilities and features make KBS distinct from most classes of IT applications presently employed for KM (Smith & Farquhar, 2000). However, expert system development — through classic knowledge engineering — requires explicit capture and formalization of tacit knowledge possessed by experts. This is just the kind of tacit knowledge that researchers (e.g., Leonard & Sensiper, 1998) stress "underlies many competitive capabilities." However, such knowledge has long been known as being "hard to capture."

Knowledge Management Life Cycle

Nissen et al. (2000) observe a sense of process flow or a life cycle associated with knowledge management. Integrating their survey of the literature (e.g., Despres & Chauvel, 1999; Gartner Group, 1999; Davenport & Prusak, 1998; Nissen, 1999), they synthesize an amalgamated KM life cycle model as outlined at the bottom of Table 1.

Briefly, the creation phase begins the life cycle, as new knowledge is generated within an enterprise. Similar terms from other models include *capture* and *acquire*. The second phase pertains to the organization, mapping, or bundling of knowledge, often employing systems such as taxonomies, ontologies, and repositories. Phase 3 addresses mechanisms for making knowledge formal or

Table 1: Knowledge Management Life Cycle Models

Model	Phase 1	Phase 2	Phase 3	Phase 4	Phase 5	Phase 6
Despres and Chauvel	Create	Map/ bundle	Store	Share/ transfer	Reuse	Evolve
Gartner Group	Create	Organize	Capture	Access	Use	
Davenport & Prusak	Generate		Codify	Transfer		
Nissen	Capture	Organize	Formalize	Distribute	Apply	
Amalgamated	Create	Organize	Formalize	Distribute	Apply	Evolve

Adapted from Nissen et al. (2000)

explicit. Similar terms from other models include *store* and *codify*. The fourth phase concerns the ability to share or distribute knowledge in the enterprise. This also includes terms such as *transfer* and *access*. Knowledge use and application for problem solving or decision making in the organization constitutes phase 5, and a sixth phase is included to cover knowledge refinement and evolution, which reflects organizational learning — and thus a return to knowledge creation — through time. It is important to note, as in the familiar life cycle models used in IS design (e.g., System Development Life Cycle), progression through the various phases of this Life Cycle Model is generally iterative and involves feedback loops between stages; that is, all steps need not be taken in order, and the flow through this life cycle is not necessarily unidirectional.

The cyclical nature of KM is more readily discernible when the life cycle model is presented as a circle (see Figure 2). Notice the three "sharing" activities from above — knowledge organization, formalization, and distribution — are adjacent on the right-hand side of the cycle. Nissen et al. (2000) show how these activities correspond with greater support from extant information technologies and hence represent more of a localized view of knowledge management; thus, the grouping under the "Class I" heading in the figure. We note such localized knowledge management systems are inherently supportive in nature; that is, this class of implementations to organize, formalize, and distribute knowledge in the enterprise *support* people in the loop, who in turn apply, evolve, and create knowledge in the organization.

Alternatively, the latter three non-sharing activities are adjacent on the left-hand side of the cycle. But these activities do not correspond well with support from extant information technologies and hence represent an expanded view of knowledge management; thus, the grouping under the "Class II" heading in the figure. We note such expanded knowledge management systems are inherently performative in nature; that is, this class of implementations to apply, evolve, and create knowledge in the enterprise *perform* knowledge management activities, either in conjunction with or in lieu of people in the organization. We thus observe a relative abundance of systems and practices available to support three phases of the KM life cycle and a dearth for the other three phases.

Current Knowledge-Flow Theory

One of the best known models of knowledge flow stems from Nonaka (1994) in the context of organizational learning. This work outlines two dimensions for knowledge: (1) *epistemological* and (2) *ontological*. The epistemological dimension depicts a binary contrast between explicit and tacit knowledge. Explicit knowledge can be formalized through artifacts such as books, letters, manuals, standard operating procedures, and instructions, whereas tacit knowledge pertains more to understanding and expertise contained within people's minds. The ontological dimension depicts knowledge that is shared with others

Figure 2: Knowledge Management Life Cycle

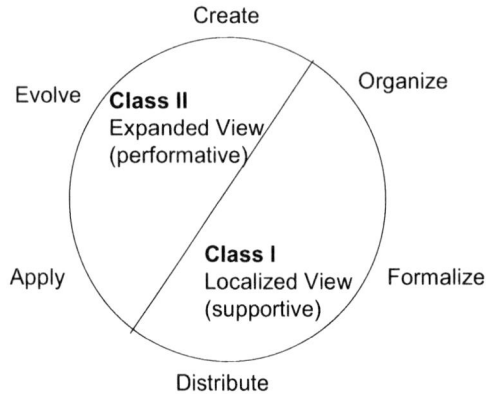

in groups or larger aggregations of people across the organization. Although this aggregation of organizational units appears arbitrary, in the enterprise context it could clearly apply to small teams, work groups, formal departments, divisions, business units, firms, and even business alliances or networks.

As delineated in Figure 3, Nonaka uses interaction between these dimensions as the principal means for describing knowledge flow. This flow is characterized by four enterprise processes: socialization, externalization, combination, and internalization. Briefly, socialization denotes members of a team sharing experiences and perspectives, much as one anticipates through tightly knit workgroups and communities of practice. Externalization denotes the use of metaphors through dialog that leads to articulation of tacit knowledge and its subsequent formalization to make it concrete and explicit. Combination denotes coordination between different groups in the organization — along with documentation of existing knowledge — to link and combine new intra-team concepts with other explicit knowledge in the enterprise. Internalization denotes diverse members in the organization applying the combined knowledge from above — often through trial and error — and in turn translating such knowledge into tacit form at the organization level (e.g., through work practices and routines). As suggested by the repeating pattern delineated in the figure, the four flow processes enable a continuous spiral of knowledge.

KNOWLEDGE-FLOW DYNAMICS

This section summarizes the dynamic model developed by Nissen (2002). It begins by building upon Nonaka's work to conceptualize an extended model of knowledge-flow dynamics. This extended model is intended to help managers to

Figure 3: Nonaka Knowledge-Flow Model

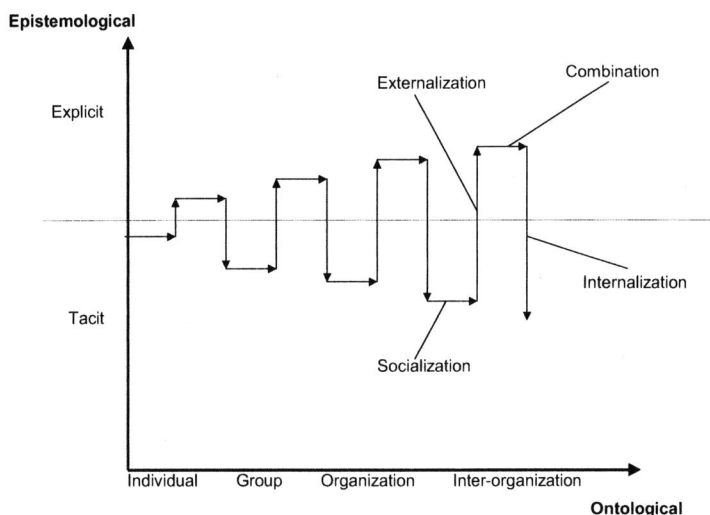

Adapted from Nonaka (1994)

understand better how enhancing knowledge flow can increase enterprise intelligence. The first step is to augment Nonaka's two-dimensional framework by incorporating a third dimension, the *KM life cycle*. We operationalize the construct using the life cycle stages from the Amalgamated Model presented in Table 1.

The second step requires relabeling the epistemological and ontological dimensions. Because the terms *epistemological* and *ontological* can be confusing when used in the present context, we relabel them as *explicitness* and *reach*, respectively, to target directly the principal focus of each dimension (i.e., differentiating explicit vs. tacit knowledge; indicating how broadly knowledge reaches through an enterprise).

In Figure 4, we note a few notional vectors for illustrating and classifying various dynamic patterns of knowledge as it flows through the enterprise. For example, the simple linear flow labeled, "Policies and Procedures" depicts the manner in which most enterprises inform, train, and attempt to acculturate employees: explicit documents and guidelines that individuals in the organization are expected to memorize, refer to, and observe. As another example, the cyclical flow of knowledge labeled "KM life cycle" reflects a more complex dynamic than its simple linear counterpart. This flow describes a cycle of knowledge creation, distribution, and evolution within a workgroup, for example.

Further, Nonaka's dynamic model of knowledge flow can also be described in this space by the curvilinear vector sequence corresponding to the processes

Figure 4: Notional Knowledge-Flow Vectors

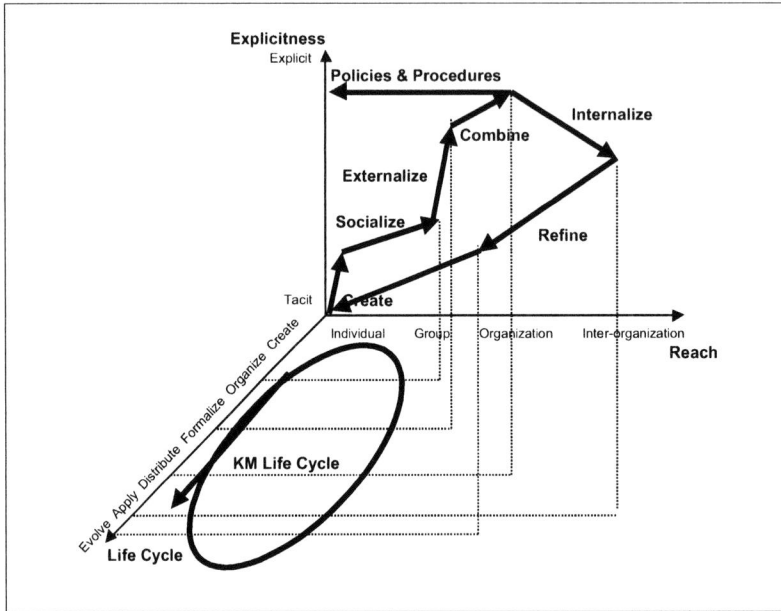

Adapted from Nissen (2002)

labeled "socialize," "externalize," "combine" and "internalize." Thus, our model subsumes the one proposed by Nonaka and shows a complex dynamic as knowledge flows along the life cycle. Moreover, examination of this space suggests also including (and connecting) the "create" and "refine" vectors, which are not part of Nonaka's theory but represent key elements of the empirically derived Life Cycle Model (e.g., the key to knowledge generation and evolution). Clearly, a great many other flows and patterns can be shown in this manner.

APPLICATION EXAMPLE – GLOBAL MANUFACTURING

The business environment now changes very rapidly, and the frequency of such changes is only expected to increase through time. Business processes must change even more rapidly for the knowledge-based organization to anticipate — not simply react to — new competitive requirements and market opportunities. Hence, the days of fixed business rules (e.g., embedded in static workflow or ERP systems) are long gone, as enterprises must be able to quickly reconfigure processes to capitalize on often-ephemeral advantages. To accomplish such agile reconfigurability, enterprise knowledge must quickly and efficiently flow across space, time, and organizational units as process changes dictate. Again, enterprise knowledge flow is critical to performance.

To help ground in practice our knowledge-flow model from above, we illustrate its application through an example of global manufacturing in 21st century. We can similarly ground the knowledge-flow model in other application domains (e.g., banking, consulting, telecommunications) — in which some of the specifics vary, but the principles hold constant. However, this example should convey clearly the key ideas. Typically heavy investments in manufacturing plant and equipment confine most physical capital to specific geographical locations and processes based upon such plant and equipment are very resistant to short-term changes. Yet global customer markets and supplier bases demand just such short-term changes. This represents a challenging context in terms of knowledge flow. Further, for most firms with global markets and operations, the demand for specific products is unpredictable and continually shifting, new-product design cycles can barely keep up with such demand shifts, and dynamic supplier networks change with each new product offering. What knowledge is important for success, and how can the firm enhance its efficacy through attention to knowledge flow? Such questions are important for the knowledge-based organization.

Having long observed and worked with such firms, here we discuss four areas of knowledge that appear to be critical: (1) customer demands, (2) competitor products, (3) design processes, and (4) supplier capabilities. In Figure 5, we use our multidimensional model to depict and examine such critical knowledge. Beginning with customer demands, the three-dimensional plot point corresponding to such knowledge is labeled "CD" in the figure. Notice it is plotted at the tacit end of the explicitness axis (e.g., future customer wants are generally not explicitly stated), the individual level in terms of the reach dimension (e.g., customer preferences are developed by individuals), and evolve stage of the life cycle (i.e., customer tastes evolve through time). Even with this single step of classifying and plotting customer-demand knowledge in terms of our multidimensional model, we have identified a critical knowledge element and can visually compare and contrast it with other key elements of knowledge.

In similar fashion, knowledge of competitor products is labeled "CP" in the figure and plotted at the point denoting explicit knowledge (i.e., presuming the products have been articulated and designed), with reach at the organizational level (i.e., known within the competitor's organization but not ours), at the distribution stage of the life cycle (i.e., product knowledge is distributed through the competitor's organization). Notice such knowledge of competitor products is very different than that associated with customer demands. This suggests a different flow of knowledge is required, and different kinds of IT and business processes are applicable.

Figure 5: Current Enterprise Knowledge

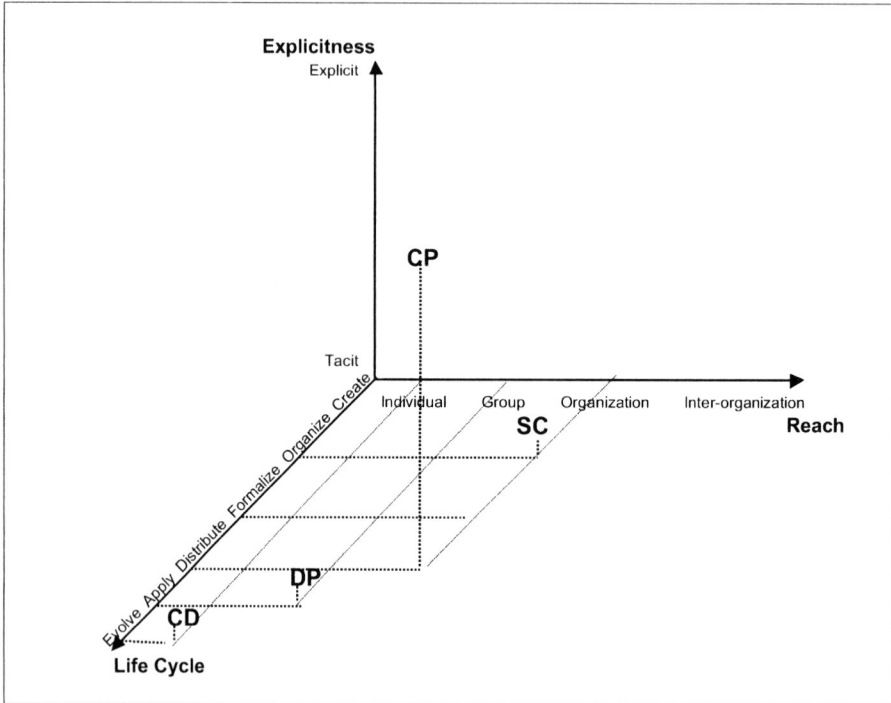

The plot point corresponding to (internal) design processes is labeled "DP" and depicts tacit knowledge, at the group level, which is applied to design new products. This too provides some contrast with both customer demands and competitor-products knowledge, as does the knowledge associated with supplier capabilities, the latter of which is labeled "SC" and plotted as tacit (e.g., new capabilities may only be emerging), at the organization level (e.g., known within the supplier organization), and organize stage of the life cycle (e.g., new product capabilities may not yet be formalized in terms of development processes). This set of points provides us with a view of the firm's critical knowledge as it exists today. We explain below how such knowledge is *not flowing* to where (and when) a knowledge-based organization needs it to be, even though it is deemed critical. This motivates the need for inducing knowledge flow.

In Figure 6, we plot these same four points along with their counterparts depicting how knowledge in each area needs to flow in terms of our three model dimensions. For instance, customer-demands knowledge needs to be made explicit, and its reach must extend at least to the level of a marketing group within the firm. The question of where along the life cycle depends upon how agile and proactive the firm wishes to be. As depicted in the figure (i.e., point CD'), ideally the firm would want to *create* customer demand through new-product innovation

Figure 6: Required Knowledge Flows

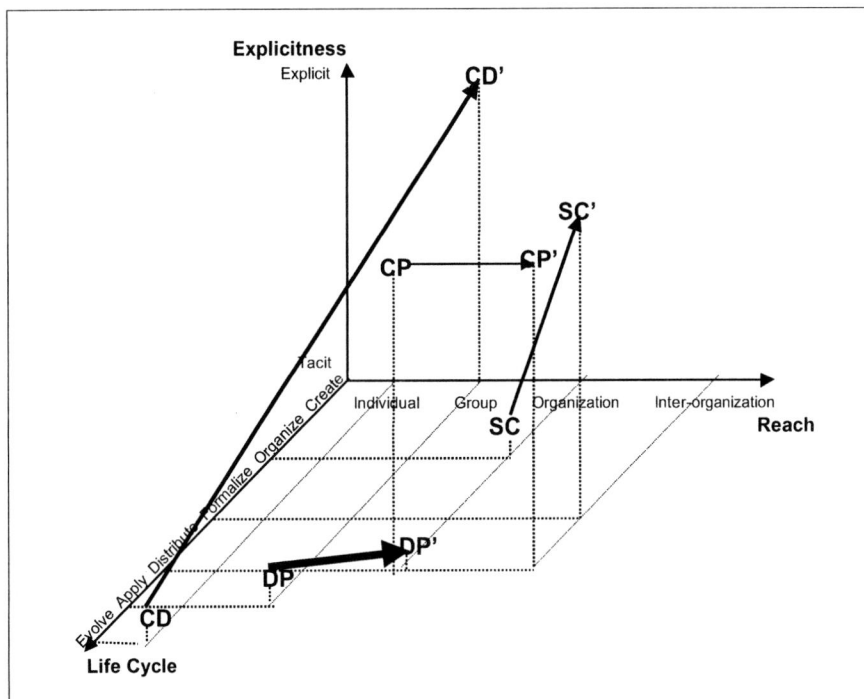

and brand loyalty. A vector connecting the current and desired knowledge points (i.e., CD-CD') is shown to delineate the corresponding knowledge flow requirement. Here we understand now what knowledge is critical, the state of such knowledge, and how it must flow to enable new product innovation.

Points and vectors corresponding to necessary knowledge flows in terms of competitor products (i.e., CP-CP'), supplier capabilities (i.e., SC-SC'), and design processes (i.e., DP-DP') are classified, identified, and plotted in similar fashion in Figure 6. For instance, unlike (tacit) customer demands, knowledge of competitor products is already explicit and distributed. But the requisite knowledge flow shows such knowledge must also be made explicit *across* organizations (i.e., within our firm as well as the competitors'). This requires business intelligence to identify what competitors are doing in relevant market spaces.

The knowledge flow corresponding to supplier capabilities is similar (e.g., required to flow beyond the supplier and into our firm), except such capabilities (e.g., in terms of new product development) must also be made explicit (i.e., not left as unarticulated potential) through formalization. This requires competitive sourcing to identify and help develop promising suppliers. Finally, design-process knowledge is required to flow beyond a specific design group, which suggests organization-wide distribution. However, distributing tacit knowledge as such remains a difficult undertaking, as it is often referred to as "sticky" in the product-development context (von Hippel, 1994; Szulanski, 1996).

What kinds of knowledge-flow "devices" are suggested by this analysis? Each of the four knowledge-flow vectors is somewhat unique, so clearly each calls for a different set of (IT) tools and process changes than the other knowledge flows. This provides insight into the reality that one size does not fit all in terms of KM and IT. The key to analysis lies in focus on how the requisite knowledge associated with each vector can be induced to flow in situations where it is currently "clumped" or "constricted." For instance, the marketing flow associated with creating customer-demands knowledge requires "devices" to satisfy current customer expectations, anticipate future customer needs, and develop and advertise new products to meet such needs.

Most successful firms have the tools and processes available to meet such requirements, but they are often isolated in different organizations and unfocused in their targeting. To induce the knowledge flow, such tools and processes must be integrated and targeted to focus specifically on the key knowledge required to understand customer demands. The manager must ask what is preventing this specific knowledge from flowing today and reconfigure the enterprise's tools and processes to obviate the problem. The experienced manager can then work from this knowledge-flow understanding to effect the necessary process changes to induce such flow. This same kind of analysis and problem solving can also be applied to other knowledge flows (e.g., involving business intelligence, competitive sourcing, design distribution).

Notice in this example the manager already possesses the tools and processes necessary for inducing knowledge flow. Analyzing the knowledge flows in the manner illustrated above does not require the invention and acquisition of new tools — nor even necessarily radical change to enterprise processes — to become knowledge-based. Rather, analyzing knowledge flows in this manner serves to highlight "clumped" and "constricted" flows, which can help the manager identify where the enterprise's tools and processes can be applied best to enhance the flow of knowledge. This provides actionable guidance for today's manager, who wants to know what can be done to make his or her organization more knowledge-based. Hence we offer the means for practical application as well as theory development.

One other feature of our knowledge-flow classification and visualization approach requires comment at this point: flow time. Notice arrows used to represent the four knowledge-flow vectors depicted in Figure 6 have different thickness. In this representation, the thickness of the vector arrow is proportional to the expected time required for each corresponding knowledge flow to take place. Thus, the flow time associated with competitor-products knowledge (e.g., weeks) is expected to be shorter than that required to identify and help develop supplier capabilities (e.g., months), which in turn should be shorter than that required to create customer demand (e.g., years). The flow time associated with the transfer of tacit design expertise is seen as the longest of all. This provides the manager with a rough schedule as well as a roadmap to use for planning requisite knowledge flows for the knowledge-based organization.

CONCLUSION

The knowledge-based organization appears to offer great promise in terms of performance and capability. Indeed, many researchers are actively working to understand how organizational strategy, structure and technology can be combined and integrated to harness the competitive power of knowledge. However, knowledge is not evenly distributed throughout the organization, so rapid and efficient knowledge flow is critical to enterprise performance. This chapter builds upon the current state of the art pertaining to knowledge flow, and it develops a model to help induce the flow of knowledge through an organization. Because of the time-critical nature of most knowledge work in the modern enterprise, we focus in particular on knowledge dynamics, to enable rapid and efficient flow, and to help the enterprise become more knowledge-based.

Using a global manufacturing firm as an example to illustrate how the knowledge-flow model provides practical guidance, we identify knowledge elements that are critical to effective performance in an unpredictable, dynamic business environment. We also use the multidimensional model to illustrate how to identify specific knowledge flows required for success. Further analysis reveals that different knowledge flows require different approaches in terms of IT and process changes — with the attendant insight that one size does not fit all in terms of knowledge management. A specific focus on clumped knowledge and constricted flows enables the experienced manager to work through the necessary interventions — often with the set of tools and processes already present in the organization. We also illustrate how the multidimensional model can be augmented to depict the relative flow times associated with various knowledge elements, which provides a rough schedule as well as a roadmap to use for planning requisite knowledge flows for the knowledge-based organization.

Despite such techniques, insights, analyses, and illustrations, however, this dynamic knowledge-flow approach to enterprise problem solving is only just beginning to emerge from the research lab, where it has been principally the focus of scientific investigation into the phenomenology of knowledge flow. Only now is the promise of dynamic knowledge-flow analysis being applied in terms of knowledge-based organization process design. It is clear that substantial work along these lines remains to be done. For instance, many practicing managers (particularly those not possessing relatively great experience) will require additional guidance to understand how to induce knowledge flows in circumstances marked by clumping or constrictions, and a set of enterprise diagnostics is being developed to support just such managerial uses.

Nonetheless, we still offer something new to the manager: a new way to look at the enterprise, a new way to identify its knowledge-flow needs, and a new way to increase enterprise intelligence through knowledge flow. Although the progress associated with this work may appear to represent a relatively small step, every step in the right direction moves us closer to our destination. By focusing on dynamic knowledge flows, the manager can choose a destination appropriate for the 21st century knowledge-based organization.

REFERENCES

Alavi, M. & Leidner, D.E. (2001). *Review*: Knowledge management and knowledge management systems: Conceptual foundations and research issues. *MIS Quarterly,* 1(25), 107-136.

Angus, J. (1998, September). Executive report: The organization and knowledge. *Informationweek Online,* 14.

Augier, M., Shariq, S.Z. & Vendelo, M.T. (2001). Understanding context: Its emergence, transformation and role in tacit knowledge sharing. *Journal of Knowledge Management,* 5(2), 125-136.

Birkinshaw et al. (2002). Knowledge as a contingency variable: Do the characteristics of knowledge predict organization structure? *Organization Science,* 13(3), 274-289.

Brown, J.S. & Duguid, P. (1991). Organizational learning and communities-of-practice: Toward a unified view of working, learning, and innovation. *Organization Science,* 2(1), 40-57.

Davenport, T.H. & Prusak, L. (1998). *Working Knowledge: How Organizations Manage what they Know.* Boston, MA: Harvard Business School Press.

Davenport, T.H., De Long, D.W. & Beers, M.C. (1998). Successful knowledge management projects. *Sloan Management Review,* 2(39), 43-57.

Despres, C. & Chauvel, D. (1999, March). Mastering information management: Part six — Knowledge management. *Financial Times,* (8), 4-6.

Drucker, P.F. (1995). *Managing in a Time of Great Change.* New York: Truman Talley.

Gartner Group. (1998). *Knowledge Management Scenario.* Conference presentation, Stamford, CN, presentation label SYM8KnowMan1098Kharris.

Gore, C. & Gore, E. (1999). Knowledge management: The way forward. *Total Quality Management,* 10(4/5), S554-S560.

Grant, R.M. (1996). Toward a knowledge-based theory of the firm. *Strategic Management Journal,* 17, 109-122.

Hargadon, A. & Fanelli, A. (2002). Action and possibility: Reconciling dual perspectives of knowledge in organizations. *Organization Science,* 13(3), 290-302.

Kogut, B. & Zander, U. (1992). Knowledge of the firm, combinative capabilities, and the replication of technology. *Organization Science,* 3(3), 383-397.

Leonard, D. & Sensiper, S. (1998, Spring). The role of tacit knowledge in group innovation. *California Management Review,* 3(40), 112-132.

Levitt, B. & March, J.G. (1998). Organizational learning. *Annual Review of Sociology,* 14, 319-340.

McDermott, R. (1999). Why information technology inspired but cannot deliver knowledge management. *California Management Review,* 41(4), 103-117.

Mullins, C.S. (1999, March). What is knowledge and can it be managed. *The Data and Administration Newsletter,* 8.0. Retrieved from the World Wide Web: www.tdan.com/i008fe03.htm.

Nissen, M.E. (1999). Knowledge-based knowledge management in the re-engineering domain. *Decision Support Systems,* (27), 47-65.

Nissen, M.E. (2002). An extended model of knowledge-flow dynamics. *Communications of the Association for Information Systems,* 8, 251-266.

Nissen, M.E., Kamel, M.N. & Sengupta, K.C. (2000). Integrated analysis and design of knowledge systems and processes. *Information Resources Management Journal,* 1(13), 24-43.

Nonaka, I. (1994). A dynamic theory of organizational knowledge creation. *Organization Science,* 1(5), 14-37.

O'Leary, D.E. (1998). Enterprise knowledge management. *Computer,* 3(31), 54-61.

Russell, S.J. & Norvig, P. (1995). *Artificial Intelligence: A Modern Approach.* Englewood Cliffs, NJ: Prentice Hall.

Smith, R.G. & Farquhar, A. (2000). The road ahead for knowledge management. *AI Magazine,* 1(24), 17-40.

Spiegler, I. (2000). Knowledge management: A new idea or a recycled concept? *Communications of the Association for Information Systems,* 14(3), 1-24.

Swap et al. (2001). Using mentoring and storytelling to transfer knowledge in the workplace. *Journal of Management Information Systems,* 18(1), 95-114.

Szulanski, G. (1996). Exploring internal stickiness: Impediments to the transfer of best practice within the firm. *Strategic Management Journal,* 17, 27-43.

Teece, D.J. (1998). Research directions for knowledge management. *California Management Review,* 3(40), 289-292.

Thomas et al. (2001). Understanding 'strategic learning': Linking organizational learning, knowledge management, and sensemaking. *Organization Science,* 12(3), 331-345.

Turban, E. & Aronson, J. (2001). *Decision Support Systems and Intelligent Systems* (5th Edition). Upper Saddle River, NJ: Prentice-Hall.

von Hippel, E. (1994). 'Sticky information' and the locus of problem solving: Implications for innovation. *Management Science,* 40(4), 429-439.

von Krough, G., Ichijo, K. & Nonaka, I. (2000). *Enabling Knowledge Creation: How to Unlock the Mystery of Tacit Knowledge and Release the Power of Innovation.* New York: Oxford University Press.

Chapter X

Developing and Maintaining Knowledge Management Systems for Dynamic, Complex Domains

Lisa J. Burnell
Texas Christian University, USA

John W. Priest
University of Texas, USA

John R. Durrett
Texas Tech University, USA

ABSTRACT

An effective knowledge-based organization is one that correctly captures, shares, applies and maintains its knowledge resources to achieve its goals. Knowledge Management Systems (KMS) enable such resources and business processes to be automated and are especially important for environments with dynamic and complex domains. This chapter discusses the appropriate tools, methods, architectural issues and development processes for KMS, including the application of Organizational Theory, knowledge-representation methods and agent architectures. Details for systems development of KMS are provided and illustrated with a case study from the domain of university advising.

INTRODUCTION

An effective knowledge-based organization is one that correctly captures, shares, applies, and maintains its knowledge resources to achieve its goals. Knowledge Management Systems (KMS) enable such resources and business processes to be automated. Possibly the greatest benefits, but with the biggest challenges, emerge from creating KMS for environments with dynamic and complex domains (DCD). If knowledge is viewed as information applied in a particular context, then a dynamic domain is one in which information such as policies and procedures are subject to frequent change. A complex domain is one in which many interrelated policies exist with informally defined and tacit exceptions.

Typical parameters used to describe or classify organizational structures in any environment are centralization, hierarchy, and standardization. Dynamic and complex environments tend to coerce organizations into highly centralized, hierarchical structures with many strictly enforced standards-based rules of operation. This environment results in organizations wherein only a few experienced individuals have the knowledge and experience to cope with frequent change, exceptions, and their complex interrelationships. The rest of the organization is thus poorly informed and subject to making errors when employees must make decisions. Obviously, this highly centralized, hierarchical structure is the wrong approach for a knowledge-based organization. The organizational goal is to get the right knowledge to the right person at the right time so better decisions and fewer mistakes will be made. The knowledge management challenge is to support this goal through the development of KMS that can readily adapt to change while dealing with complexity. The emerging science of knowledge management should preserve and build upon literature that exists in other fields (Alavi & Leidner, 2001). We believe, and research on knowledge as a contingency variable (Birkinshaw, Nobel et al., 2002) indicates, that any KMS will benefit from the application of Contingency Theory (CT) and Information Processing Theory (IPT), both well established in the field of Organizational Theory (OT).

The chapter begins with the role of CT and IPT in examining the organizational aspects of dynamic, complex environments, followed by an overview of classic knowledge management and tools for KMS development. Next, the organizational, domain, development, maintenance, and KMS issues for dynamic, complex domain environments are presented. The recommended strategies and tools are illustrated through a case study of a recently developed university advising system, a classic case in which a few knowledgeable individuals (departmental advisors) attempt to serve a large population (students) in a dynamic, complex domain. Additional recommendations and future trends conclude the chapter.

CONTINGENCY THEORY

A basic tenet of CT is that organizations are structured according to their situational environment. OT is a field of study that examines an organization's structure, constituencies, processes, and operational results in an effort to understand the relationships involved in creating effective and efficient organizations. Countering the "one best" organizational structure approach of classical organization theory, the subfield known as CT (Galbraith, 1973; Pfeffer & Salanick, 1978; Dess & Beard, 1984; Thompson, 1967) recognizes that environment influences appropriate structure. CT has been applied to a wide variety of fields including software design (Lai, 1999). In CT an organization's environmental context may be described by two characteristics: (1) the complexity and heterogeneity of the entities in the environment and (2) their rate and predictability of change (dynamicism). Successful organizations survive by adapting to the demands of their task environments (March & Simon, 1958). There may be more than one equally effective organizational design, as each varies by degree of centralization, hierarchy, and standardization. Fortunately, due to interdependencies between components, organizational configurations tend to fall into a limited number of coherent patterns, and thus the set of possibilities is limited. In proposing IPT-aiding application of this theory, Galbraith proposed that complexity, predictability, and interdependence actually measure one underlying concept, that of task information processing requirements (Galbraith, 1973; Galbraith, Downey et al., 2001). Thus, the basic concept to be analyzed is the task and its information processing requirements. A task may be defined as a relatively independent sequence of activities that serves a purpose for some user.

The more heterogeneous, unpredictable, and dependent upon other environmental resources a task is, the greater the information processing that the organization must be able to do in order to successfully accomplish it. IPT shows that as diversity and unpredictability increase, uncertainty increases due to incomplete information. As diversity of resources, processes, or outputs increase, inter-process coordination requirements and system complexity increase. As uncertainty increases, information-processing requirements increase because of management's inability to predict every situation. Thus, the basic premise of IPT is that the greater the uncertainty in the overall tasks in an organizational system, the greater the amount of information that the system must process. When a task environment is stable with few or no exceptions, then standard operating procedures, hierarchical control, and specific goal-setting can be used to coordinate activities. When a task environment is less stable or more diverse, alternative organizational structures must be used either to reduce information processing requirements or raise information processing capability. Organizational structures are therefore a result of attempts to deal with uncertainty, the result of which is complexity and dynamicism.

As an example of how organizational structures can limit the effectiveness of KMS, consider the situation in Figure 1 in which the worker at Line 1 needs knowledge held by the employee at Line 5. In this simplified example using a traditionally structured, hierarchical organization, the knowledge request would have to be propagated up the organizational hierarchy until a common departmental shared knowledge space was reached (in this example, the CEO) then down to the employee, and then back up through the hierarchy. This communication sequence is lengthy primarily because it relies only on tacit knowledge and hierarchical control. However, following IPT guidelines allows the use of this "exception" to create a much more direct path using a technical-level knowledge space. Once this vocabulary is encoded into the KMS by either a human or by the KMS's learning module, future communication is greatly facilitated.

As shown in the above example, a conceptual transformation must take place in order to apply CT and IPT to the design of KMS in a dynamic, complex environment. The technological complexity-information processing relationship from the viewpoint of the IS and KMS as a whole must be examined. Among the factors a designer should consider are: (1) how this interaction affects organizational control structure, (2) how this interaction is affected by organizational control structure, (3) the importance of the development groups, (4) the time constraints on the results, and (5) management's viewpoint. This complex analysis is aided by first developing the basic relationship, then examining limitations and effects by the listed factors one at a time.

A series of questions must be considered related to the individual concepts and their interactions. What exactly does technological complexity mean when it is considered as part of a KMS rather than as a separate construct? How does the nature of information processing in a KMS change when it is part of a single team, which is part of other organizational systems? How long has this level of technological complexity been used in this industry, and how well standardized is its infrastructure? All of these questions relate to the constraints that are placed on this one system by other systems within the organization.

The primary determinants in this relationship are the environmental variables of heterogeneity and stability. In distributed IS design for KMS the concept of heterogeneity can be measured in terms of output requirements, IS familiarity and ability, physical location, connectivity method and type of device; data — in terms of location, source, rate of change; and processes — in terms of both business and software; and system hardware. These indicators, along with the stability or predictability of each constituency, provide a means for concept categorization.

In the following sections the knowledge management and KBS tools overviews provide the necessary background and then the case study demonstrates how these concepts are applied to a real project. Additional details on the application of CT and IPT to KMS design, along with examples, may be found in Durrett, Burnell and Priest (2003, 2002a, 2002b, 2001).

Figure 1: Knowledge Vocabularies Based on Shared Knowledge Spaces

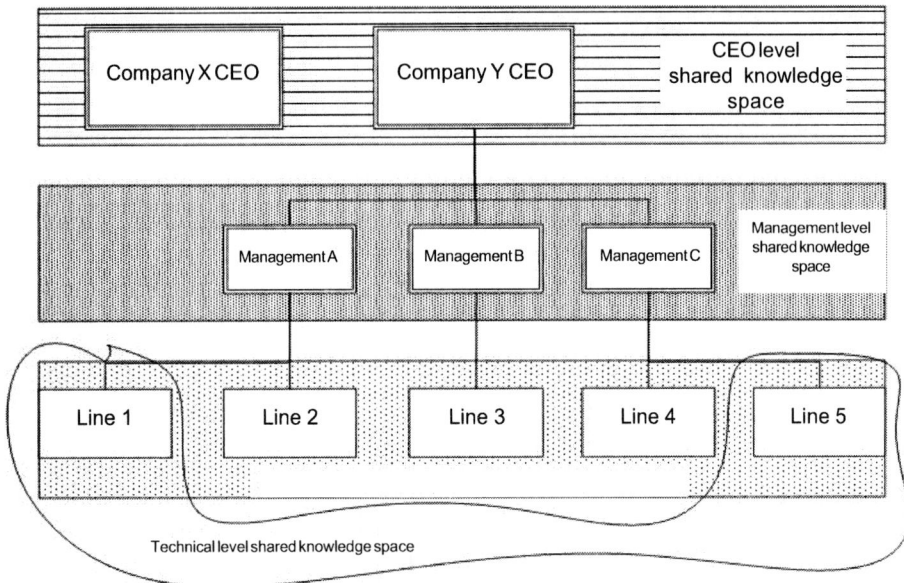

KNOWLEDGE MANAGEMENT OVERVIEW AND CHALLENGES

Knowledge management focuses on knowledge creation, storage, sharing, and application. Knowledge management systems are then developed to support these tasks. The specific types of knowledge needed will determine the organizational structure. A full review of knowledge management and KMS are beyond the scope of this chapter. The focus is on how KM and KMS can improve knowledge in a dynamic, complex environment. Properly implemented KMS can provide the following benefits to an organization: (1) fewer mistakes, (2) less redundancy, (3) quicker problem-solving, (4) better decision-making, (5) increased worker independence, (6) enhanced customer relations, and (7) improved products and services.

KMS are a class of information systems used to manage organizational knowledge (Alavi & Leidner, 2001). While information systems are not absolutely required in KM, they can be an important enabler for finding, storing, and distributing information quickly and efficiently throughout the organization. KMS can extend an individual's knowledge beyond formal communication lines (Alavi & Leidner, 2001).

Knowledge management classifies knowledge into two types:

- Tacit Knowledge (informal) — knowledge held by an individual or organization, but which has not been documented and is not widely known.

- Explicit Knowledge (formal) — information that has been documented and shared for others to use. This type includes procedures, manuals, policies, guides, and customer databases.

The goals of transfer, creation, and expansion of knowledge require that knowledge be transformed from tacit to explicit and back to tacit again as it is utilized. Unfortunately in a DCD environment the amount of tacit information is widespread, large, complex, and constantly changing. In this environment, a KMS needs to (Tiwana, 2000):

- Have a shared knowledge space which provides a consistent, well-understood vocabulary;
- Be able to identify, model, and explicitly represent their knowledge;
- Share knowledge among employees and re-use knowledge between differing applications; and
- Create a culture that encourages knowledge sharing.

Databases (DB) and other technologies such as data mining, bulletin boards, best practices, expert directories, expert systems, and case-based reasoning are just some of the methods used. However, knowledge does not thrive by IT alone. The challenges of a dynamic, complex environment require the organization to recognize change and complexity as normal and use these technologies accordingly. A review of the knowledge literature shows several mentions of flexibility and scalability as development objectives but almost no mention of "designing for change and complexity."

TOOLS FOR KMS DEVELOPMENT

In order to develop software that manages change and complexity, sophisticated methods and data representations need to be applied appropriately. A number of these tools are summarized in this section. The three basic categories described are Data Base Management Systems (DBMS), Artificial Intelligence (AI), and distributed communication. For each, recommendations and limitations are given.

DBMS

Much of the basic data needed for creating a knowledge-based organization will reside in databases. A DBMS takes care of concurrent access, security, and data integrity, and can handle large data items, such as audio or video. Processing can be performed by small programs (triggers) to respond to events like deleting a row in a table. Database design and performance-tuning methods are well developed, and personnel with such skills are readily available. Most companies will already have, and should use, a relational DBMS. Pure object-oriented DBMS have essentially found use in a small number of niche markets. Furthermore, major relational DBMS vendors are continuing to expand the capabilities of their products to include object-oriented support.

Not all data is best suited for storage in a DBMS. While a particular DB design can accommodate moderate amounts of change over time, such as adding new tables or attributes, large changes to the schema or processing requirements are difficult to accommodate. While standard relational databases should be employed for some domain knowledge and facts, declarative representations such as rules are the better choice for dynamic or complex policies and procedures. When trying to represent complex policies, a database solution (commonly attempted) becomes too complex or incomprehensible for system designers to understand or for anyone to try to modify. The same is true for hard-coding business logic into programs, which not only creates a confusing system, but also possesses great inflexibility to change. A combination of rules and relational database management systems, sometimes called an active DBMS, allows both declarative and relational representations to be defined using a single product. While this model can be useful, it is not required to integrate both paradigms into one solution. Later, in the case study, we show how separate DBMS and knowledge-based tools are integrated to provide a solution. But first we discuss powerful tools and methods from Artificial Intelligence (AI) that are used to capture an organization's knowledge.

Knowledge-Based and Expert Systems

Systems that represent and reason with knowledge are generally referred to as knowledge-based systems (KBS). While the term KBS can be used to describe any system that uses or delivers knowledge in some way, a KBS is traditionally defined to be a program or collection of programs that represents and reasons with declaratively specified knowledge. Current KBS often integrate the knowledge component with other processing so that the knowledge-based part of the system is hidden from the user and may be a small, though critical, part of overall system functionality. Within this section, the term KBS will refer to the specific knowledge component or components within a larger system. A KBS is sometimes referred to as an Expert System if the performance matches or exceeds that normally found in experts within a discipline.

A number of methods for constructing KBS are available. We will discuss a few of these. Developing KBS typically requires advanced training and experience, but some vendor tools provide specific support for staff without such training. A given problem may require combining multiple KBS methods to obtain a satisfactory solution. Some important methods are rules, cases, belief networks, fuzzy systems and business-rule systems.

Rule-based systems represent knowledge in an IF-THEN format. The inputs for solving a problem are the rules plus facts that represent a current situation. An inference engine executes by finding patterns in the rules that match the facts, "firing" (executing) the rule, and repeating these two steps until no more patterns match facts (Figure 2). Each cycle through the rules may result in changes to current facts, so dynamic behavior can be achieved. As an example, with facts that state that a student has a GPA of 3.7 and has taken a DB course, the following rule will fire.

IF the student has a GPA>3.5 AND has taken the DB course
THEN approve student for the AI course

A number of commercial and free shells exist that provide the inference engine, supporting functions for string and numeric processing, and required format for creating rules. Examples include JESS (JESS, 2002) and CLIPS (CLIPS, 2002).

Case-based reasoning (CBR) attempts to solve problems by comparing them to those that have previously been solved. The reasoner searches a case-base of problems and their solutions to find those that best match the description of a current problem, then attempts to adapt the stored solution to the new problem. The new problem and its solution may be stored into the case-base for future reference. A common application of CBR is to support help-desks.

Belief nets, also known as Bayesian belief networks, are used to represent uncertainty, specifically the probabilistic causal relationship between objects or attributes. For example, the relationship between a person's age, weight, blood pressure, and other factors influences the belief that the person is at risk for heart disease in the future. An extension to belief nets, called influence diagrams, adds decision nodes to the representation to recommend a choice among actions that maximizes value to the decision-maker. Using the same example above, a decision node could be added to recommend if the person should undergo the expense of a stress test. Rather than trying to represent a complete model of some phenomena, probabilities are used to summarize knowledge. The result is that computationally tractable large models can be constructed. Taking another example, consider the need to represent that most birds fly. Using a logic-based representation, we would need to describe all the exceptions to the most likely case that if something is a bird, then it flies. Exceptions include the species, if the bird is dead, or has its wings clipped. We can group these exceptions into one or more belief net nodes, depending on how the knowledge is to be used in the overall system. A belief net for the simplest case is shown in Figure 3.

Fuzzy systems, which can extend the representational power of rule-based systems, commonly are used to represent vagueness, not uncertainty, such as is found in the statement "Elton is tall." Here, the statement is certain, but the term

Figure 2: Execution Cycle in a Rule-Based System

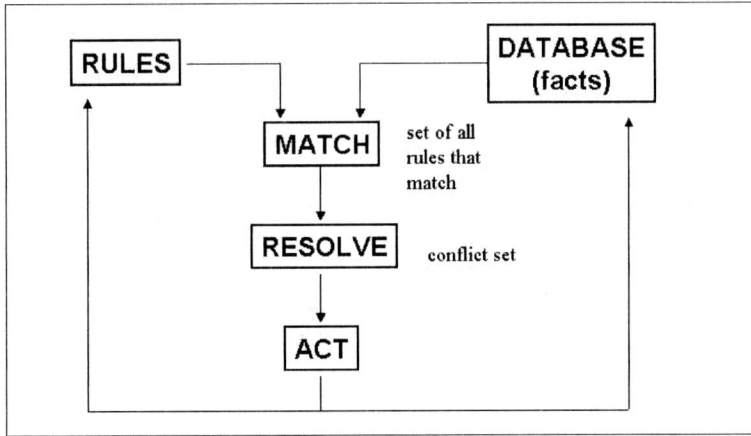

"tall" is vague. A fuzzy calculus is used to map natural language terms to numbers, and to combine those numbers in a meaningful way to determine if a rule should fire.

Business-rules systems (BRS) are a subcategory of KBS that encode particular kinds of knowledge. BRS capture, disseminate, and enforce the current explicit and tacit policies, procedures, and guidelines of an organization. Because such knowledge must be adaptable to changing market and economic demands, business rules must be easily identifiable and maintainable. While the term "rules" is part of the BRS acronym, and standard expert system style "If-Then" rules are often used, this encoding is not a requirement. Other declarative knowledge-representation systems, such as cases (as in case-based reasoning systems), are appropriate. The rationale for choosing a declarative representation is to give end-users (knowledge-workers) the ability to comprehend and modify the business logic.

Other Techniques from AI

Two important techniques that can be used with the methods of the previous section are neural networks and machine-learning methods. By adding the

Figure 3: A Belief Net for the Simplest Case

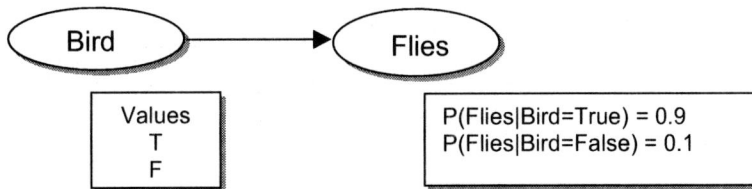

capability to learn autonomously from past data, these methods can be used to create knowledge components or to adapt the behavior of a system to changes over time. This capability allows tacit knowledge to be more easily encoded into explicit knowledge.

Complex problems with multiple input and output values can also be modeled using neural networks. Patterned conceptually after the human brain, this technique allows weighted linkages between value nodes to transform input data to output knowledge. Neural nets (networks) learn a mathematical function that describes the relationship between variables by using example data. Common uses include classification, speech, and vision tasks. Complex functions can be learned that, unlike statistical models, do not require the user to specify the expected type of function. Unlike the other representations discussed here, neural nets are a "black box" — it is not possible to uncover the model learned. In a rule-based system, for example, a user can view the chain of reasoning (rule firings) used to solve a problem. Despite this disadvantage, neural nets are powerful problem solvers that can tackle problems the other reasoning methods have difficulty solving.

Machine learning methods can be employed with many representations, including databases, precise and fuzzy rule-based systems, belief nets, and case-based reasoning. The learning can be used to enhance system capabilities (be able to create new explicit knowledge) or performance (solve problems faster). In data mining, machine learning and statistical methods can be used to discover new knowledge. For example, a grocery store could discover that customers who buy lots of fresh fruit also tend to buy soy milk. Using knowledge of buyer patterns of behavior, product selection and display can then be adjusted to maximize profits. Rules can be learned by supplying past data, for example, to classify the creditworthiness of persons seeking loans. Belief net learning algorithms either learn the basic structure of the belief net or improve the accuracy of the results. CBR learning algorithms, often integrated within the CBR tool, learn new cases or combine several specific cases into general ones that can solve a wider range of problems.

Web Services and Distributed Communication

More systems development is becoming distributed across computers. Part of the reason for this shift is a desire to take advantage of the trend in using many computers instead of one big mainframe. Systems have become developed by individual departments or divisions that need to work together. This trend toward distributed computing is necessary because the systems being developed are much too complex to consider as one monolithic system, and must be decomposed into subsystems so developers can understand them. Further, the trend is towards piecing together components, some custom developed, some purchased, where each component performs some specific tasks, such as credit card processing. Finally, intercompany processing means that disparate computing systems need to communicate. A Web service is a software entity that is capable of inter-application communication over any local or wide area network. Web services enable the creation of dynamic intra- and intercompany systems.

Standards exist, and are continuing to be developed. There is a confusing and overwhelming array of communications protocols. The old EDI (Electronic Data Interchange) for intercompany communication is giving way to many other standards, including but not limited to XML. WSL, CORBA, KQML, FIPA, SOAP, UPNP are a few of the standards. Some of the newest standards target security (XML Signature), requirements (Web Services Description Usage Scenarios), and design (Web Services Architecture and Descriptions Requirements). These and other standards documents are published by the World Wide Web Consortium (W3C).

Currently, XML and some of the protocols built on top of it are reasonably safe choices. XML can be used to share data between databases and programs running across the Internet. Unlike HTML, which simply describes the formatting of data within a web browser, XML describes what data items are. Like a database scheme, an XML tag describes what a piece of data is, for example <price>$19.99</price> uses the <price> tag to identify the data $19.99 as the price of some item. In order to use XML for communication, the programs sharing the XML data must agree on what the tags mean. Some communities, like medicine, have created XML vocabularies, with the expectation that any program wishing to communicate about medical data will use this standard vocabulary. Creating these standards, and then using with existing programs and databases, is a major challenge.

Having reviewed CT/IPT and key software technologies, the following section shows how these concepts and methods can be used in the development of a KMS in a DCD. Software development phases, each with specific issues when applied to dynamic and complex domains, are presented, then demonstrated by the example KMS currently being developed.

DEVELOPING KMS FOR DCD

There are a number of fundamental work phases, each with issues and choices, in the development of a complete KMS solution. The domain analysis phase involves acquiring an accurate model of business processes including data elements, policies, and their stability over time. The requirements phase entails eliciting, analyzing, and specifying the system behavior, including interaction with users and other systems. In architectural design, the blueprint for the system is constructed to define major components and their interactions. In detailed design, the components are fully specified, including data representation and algorithm selection. Implementation translates the design into executable code.

Testing is an integral part of each phase and continues throughout the lifecycle of the product. Once the system is in place, maintenance is necessary to correct errors and to respond to changes in the domain and operational environment. This process is especially important for a DCD where needed changes are frequent. The goal of designing for systems in DCD is to reduce the maintenance burden, which accounts for up to 80% of system lifecycle costs in many instances.

The work phases are performed within a software engineering methodology and generally require a number of iterations through each phase. For DCD systems, an agile methodology, such as FDD (Palmer & Felsing, 2000) or XP (Beck, 2000), should be considered because it provides better support for change throughout development. The standard notation for describing artifacts of software development is the Unified Modeling Language (UML). An easy-to-use guide to the UML is Fowler and Scott (2000). Computer Aided Software Engineering (CASE) tools are available to support collaborative development of one or more phases. Commercial and free tools include products from Rational, TogetherSoft, and Gentleware.

Domain Analysis

Knowing your domain is vital to successful knowledge management. For DCD, it is not enough to only look at your current operation. The best thing to do is to collect three types of data from (1) your current domain, (2) your domain history, and (3) other organizations. The data you should collect includes the language (terms used and their precise definitions), business policies and processes, and specific overrides to those policies and processes. A primary benefit of CT/IPT-based KMS is the utilization of situations not covered by existing policy. In traditional systems, such exceptions are propagated up a control hierarchy to eventually land in a log file and thus on a human's desk. In a KMS utilizing IPT's organizational model, common exceptions are sent to a learning module and are used to create new knowledge. This structure allows tacit knowledge to be more easily encoded into explicit knowledge. For example, the policy for offering a book discount may be that the discount is only given if a person presents a discount card, with a learned exception to offer a discount if the person spends more than $100 on their first purchase and turns in an application for a new discount card at the cash register.

Following this advice obviously will take more time, but the result in a DCD will be much easier maintenance. Designers must understand which items are likely to change and which can be abstracted. For example, terms may change over time. What is called a "general education requirement" may later be called an "undergraduate core requirement." Abstract the term in the ontology to use internally, and add specific terms as synonyms for display to users (each synonym can be augmented with an audience and date range to determine when appropriate to use). Users need to see the terms they know, but finding and changing them throughout a database and programs is time consuming and error prone. Policies and processes also change over time, often with more frequency than language.

Policies are the guiding principles by which the organization operates. These principles can be stated succinctly in a single statement or a series of if-then-else clauses. An example policy is, "Senior level electives require completion of the software engineering course and a GPA greater than 3.2." A more complex policy is, "If the student has the course prerequisites, then they may take the course; else if they get departmental approval, then they may take the course; else they may not take the course." Notice the many terms used within these two simple examples — course, prerequisite, departmental approval, GPA, elective, (course) completion.

Processes describe steps that need to be performed. These steps may involve many data changes or the execution of multiple policies and can be quite complex. Example processes are purchasing books online or getting approval for a college degree plan.

Within all these three areas — language, policies, processes — the domain can change. In a DCD, the goal is to develop systems that can be easily modified when needed.

Requirements

There are three major tasks in the requirements phase. These are elicitation, in which you get the requirements from the users; specification, in which you record these requirements; and analysis, in which you organize and correct the specification. Each is discussed in this section, including how to deal with change during and after initial requirements are gathered.

Eliciting requirements is a similar process to domain modeling, but the focus is different. In domain modeling, designers are trying to understand the domain — what the users do and how they do it. This process facilitates communication with the users, in their language, to determine what they need the system to do. There are many structured and unstructured methods for requirements elicitation, including interviews, process tracing, and user interface prototyping (McGraw & Harbison, 1989). Prototyping is a particularly powerful method for eliciting requirements that have significant user interaction, since it is generally easier for a user to critique a simulation than to construct a comprehensive list of their needs. The process almost always starts with interviewing and some initial specification before the prototype is developed. Further elicitation and specification then proceed iteratively.

A powerful technique for capturing functional requirements is the use-case model. A use case describes the interaction of a user with the system to perform a task of value to that user. For example, entering a PIN number into an ATM is not of value to the user; getting cash from a bank account is. Use cases specify

Figure 4: Example Use Case with Multiple Scenarios for Buying Groceries

---

Buy Groceries using self check-out
1. Customer goes to check out with items to purchase
2. Customer scans each item and places it in a bag
3. Customer indicates last item has been scanned
4. System displays total
5. System requests payment information (credit, debit)
6. Customer inputs payment information
7. System confirms purchase

Alternative: Card authorization failure
At step 7, system requests customer to re-enter information up to two more times, then notifies store employee for assistance.
Other Possible Alternatives: dealing with coupons, discount cards and scan failures are described in alternative scenarios.

---

the external systems and types of users, collectively called actors; preconditions that stipulate the required system state for the use case to be valid; and possibly post-conditions, or changes to system state after the steps of the use case have been completed. Use case *scenarios* describe particular sequences of steps involving interaction with the system. A use case with multiple scenarios for buying groceries is shown in Figure 4. Nonfunctional requirements that do not fit into a single use case, such as specification of platform or performance needs, are recorded in a supplementary document. The use-case model and supplementary documentation together form the requirements specification.

An important facet of using use cases for requirements determination in DCDs is that they allow an analysis of the potential exceptions that will be generated out of a particular process. In use cases where there are a great many alternative scenarios, the IPT guidelines tell us that support objects and rules created should be very flexible, containing more functionality and thus minimizing the inter-object communication requirements. In some cases, these guidelines can dictate violations to traditional software development models.

In requirements analysis, the specification is examined to identify missing, conflicting, or incorrect requirements and to organize the specifications to aid understanding and communication with potential users (Priest & Sanchez, 2001). Use cases that perform similar tasks may be combined, or complex use cases may be decomposed into multiple user cases. Another analysis task is to find steps that occur in multiple use cases and extract them into a single use case. This process often results in the specification of basic system utilities like retrieving student transcript data. The collection of use cases, actors, and their relationships may be represented in a graphical format to communicate a high-level view of the total system capabilities. While early analysis aims to capture all the requirements, this goal is not usually possible, especially in DCD environments.

Copyright © 2004, Idea Group Inc. Copying or distributing in print or electronic forms without written permission of Idea Group Inc. is prohibited.

As in all the phases of development, dealing with change must be built into the process.

To account for later change, the analysis model must be readily maintainable. Extremely detailed and large numbers of use cases are too hard to keep current. Instead, limit use-case specification to major functions. Alternative scenarios can be summarized as brief text statements instead of a detailed sequence of steps. Identify each use case using a project standard identification scheme. As development progresses, each developer should know which use case she is designing, implementing, or testing. Each artifact produced and each milestone scheduled should be tied to specific use cases. Each use case should also reference any related artifacts produced in domain analysis. This traceability is key to maintaining a live requirements specification — one that accurately reflects the current purpose of the system.

Design and Architectural issues for DCD

With maintainability as a major design goal for DCD, general software design principles are just the first consideration in selecting an appropriate architecture. Two important general principles are high cohesion, where each component is responsible for a related set of tasks, and low coupling, where the communication between components is small. Using these principles provides a starting point from which CT and IPT principles are applied to examine the concepts, and their interactions, stability and heterogeneity. In the resulting architecture, the number of required specialized components (agents) increases with the number of dynamic and/or unique processes. While this negatively effects coupling, the advantage is that policy and language changes are simpler to implement.

Two design issues of particular relevance to design for DCD are ontology creation and agent-based architectures. Ontology creation, begun in domain and requirements analysis, is fully developed during design to create a central repository for the domain language. Agent-based architectures are a means for structuring a software system that adhere to Contingency Theoretic principles. Contingency-theoretic system development (CTSD) adapts contingency theory to development and maintenance of software systems (Burnell, Durrett, & Priest, 2002; Durrett, Burnell, & Priest, 2001). A summary of CTSD is given in Table 1.

Ontologies are specifications of conceptualizations, used to help programs and humans share knowledge. They are sets of concepts — such as things, events, and relations — that are in some way congruous (such as specific natural language) and thereby create an agreed-upon vocabulary for exchanging information. They allow one group's knowledge to be understood by and shared with other groups. The DCD environment requires the ontology to be a

Table 1: CTSD Design Principles

Design Principle	Rational
Isolate dynamic concept names in ontology	As terms change over time or across organizations, updating only needs to be performed in the ontology.
Isolate external systems connections	Subsystems that interface with external databases and systems tend to be highly dynamic, both in connection method and format of returned data.
Create agents for specialized complex processing; each agent performs a tightly related set of tasks	Changes to processes are localized in specialist agents, thereby aiding reuse of components.
Software Teams	IPT suggests to minimize communication requirements by combining agents into "teams."
Exception Management	To follow CT guidelines and quickly identify exceptions to existing policy, overrides are propagated to human and AI-based knowledge creation modules.
Do not use DBMS for dynamic policies or processes	Makes DBMS structure overly complex and difficult to modify, especially after system has gone into production.
Incrementally design and deliver fully tested functionality	Waiting for a complete system can result in delivery of an obsolete system.

continuously evolving effort. Keeping a well maintained ontology facilitates the continued use of and even allows the expansion of existing knowledge spaces

There are many definitions of and arguments over agents. Agents can be autonomous, mobile and/or intelligent. A generally agreed upon viewpoint is that an agent is a program or collection of programs that lives (continuously runs) for some purpose (is goal-based) in a dynamic environment (changing access to resources) and can make decisions to perform actions to achieve its goals. Agents have been created to schedule meetings, to find and filter news items, and to perform military reconnaissance. To illustrate how an agent operates, consider meeting scheduling. I simply notify my agent that I need to meet with my staff this week about a new project. My agent then automatically contacts the agents of each of my staff members, coordinates a suitable time, arranges the meeting room, places the meeting on my calendar, and notifies me at the appropriate time. Like the best administrative assistants, agents both know and adapt to their boss.

Multi-agent systems are those in which multiple agents (usually) cooperate to perform some task. In the meeting example above, the agents for each employee communicate directly to negotiate a time to meet. The agents may or may not be developed together. A vision for the future is that agents will seek out other agents anywhere on the Internet to find the information or resources they need to achieve a goal. This interaction will all be transparent to the user and completely secure. A less ambitious goal for multi-agent systems is to decompose a complex task into a collection of interacting agents that together solve some problem. In a military reconnaissance application, separate agents may be responsible for collecting images, navigation, and detecting threats.

The design of an individual agent is flexible. It may be object-oriented, a rule-based expert system, a neural net, or any other design. Legacy software may be "wrapped" with an agent interface. The key point is to design the agent using good design principles. This requirement means that the interfaces to the agent are clearly defined and the internal operation is hidden from all external software.

A thorough analysis of tasks and the environment are used to guide architectural design issues. Tasks capture the actions that need to be performed by the system. Often, it is necessary to create a task hierarchy (Figure 5) so that the appropriate level of task is assigned to a computational component (or software team of multiple components), which is performed later. For each task, a *predictability* metric is assigned to indicate the expected stability of the task over time. This predictability metric allows us to follow IPT guidelines and create components for high predictability tasks and software teams for low predictability tasks. From domain analysis in our case study, approving a semester schedule is dynamic — the process changes over time and across universities. Conversely, checking for scheduling conflicts is static — the task of checking if there are time conflicts between two courses must always be done. Maintenance is driven by measuring the frequency with which manager (exception-handling) modules are employed to complete processing tasks.

Testing

The test effort should demonstrate that the product satisfies the customer, meets the design requirements, performs properly under all conditions, and satisfies the interface requirements of the hardware and other software components. The product is incrementally validated using the use-case scenarios. Since each scenario provides a complete description and can be immediately prototyped, this testing allows user validation to begin very early in the development process. The validation process also uses scenarios for documentation, training, and user

Figure 5: Example Task Hierarchy for Approving a Semester Schedule

Task Hierarchy

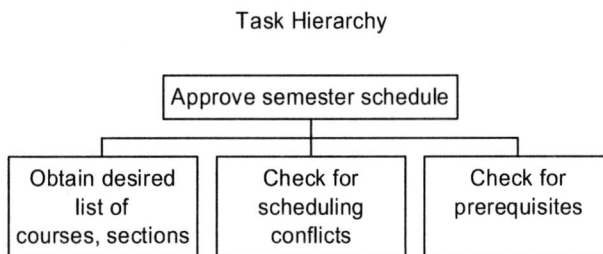

manual purposes. Feedback is gathered from users as they learn to use the system. Issues are efficiently defined within the scenario task context and task ontology and problems can be automatically traced back to the appropriate design area. Analysis of the system by users may result in new scenarios. The best approach is to use several test methods continuously throughout design and coding. Testing rules adapted from Myers (1976) are shown below:

- A good test is one that discovers an undiscovered error.
- The biggest problem in testing is knowing when enough testing has been done.
- A programmer cannot adequately test his or her own program.
- Every test plan must describe the expected results.
- Avoid unpredictable testing.
- Develop tests for unexpected conditions as well as expected conditions.
- Thoroughly inspect all test results.
- As the number of detected errors increases, the probability that more errors exist also increases.
- Assign the most creative programmers to the test group.
- Testability must be designed into a program. Do not alter the program to make tests.

Well designed code and a development process that recognizes the importance of near-continuous testing will result in fewer schedule delays and software that performs to its specifications. One of the tenets of extreme programming is to write the test cases before writing code and to perform regression testing as part of frequent code integration.

CASE STUDY: A VIRTUAL ADVISOR

A recently designed expert advising system will be used to illustrate the process for developing a KMS for a DCD application. The student advising process found at most universities is an example of a knowledge-intensive process within a dynamic, complex environment. The process can prove to be tedious, time-consuming, inconsistent, and error-prone. From a student's perspective, the task of deciding what courses to take and when to take them can leave many students frustrated and confused. Students only need advising a limited number of times throughout their college experience, so their level of knowledge varies and is often incomplete. Designing a degree plan for a given time period and creating a schedule for each semester requires an understanding of all the policies and regulations within a university, college, and department. Student objectives and preferences mean that some semester schedules or degree plans are preferred over others, i.e., optimization. These users want a quick, effective process with limited training required.

From a faculty member's perspective, the advising process includes not only an understanding of the documented policies and rules of the university, i.e., explicit knowledge, but also an understanding of the rules and exceptions or choices that may not be explicitly stated within her own department. Many of the interrelationships between the rules are confusing, and many exceptions are often not documented. Because of this dynamic complexity, most departments identify a few individuals as departmental advisors. The departmental advisors become the knowledge center for the advising process. This organizational structure results in tacit knowledge only being known by a few individuals. The overall goal is to ensure that a student takes the appropriate courses mandated for his graduation and appropriate for his capabilities, interests, and scheduling constraints. However the level of knowledge both tacit and explicit between different faculty and faculty advisors can vary greatly. Faculty objectives focus on time management, consistency, and minimizing mistakes. Students depend on faculty advisors to know all of the rules and exceptions, as well as the students' preferences, in order to guide them appropriately.

Administrators have to manage data for each student, each semester, and each degree plan. With numerous rules and the exceptions and interrelationships between rules that are constantly changing, complexity increases exponentially. Administrators need up-to-date information about each student's course schedule and transcript, departmental schedules, lists of classes that are full, and degree, course, or section changes. Their objectives are time management, responsiveness, and maintenance.

The purpose of the Virtual Advisor (VA) system is to quickly and accurately aid students and faculty advisors in selecting courses for a semester and planning courses needed for graduation. Furthermore, the system is end-user customizable across departments and universities. Because the data, policies and procedures change frequently, are heavily interrelated, and vary widely across universities and departments, the environment is dynamic and complex. Any system built with hard-coding constraints will become obsolete within a matter of months after implementation. A university or department cannot rely upon inflexible and non-customizable systems in adapting to the dynamic nature of curriculum changes and university rules. In the following, the major KMS development tasks are described. These tasks are performed in an iterative, not purely sequential fashion, for reasons discussed in the prior section.

Domain Analysis

In domain analysis, we first analyzed several existing departmental advising systems, including those we had used ourselves as advisors. This analysis yielded a number of important insights. First, the existing systems were either tightly integrated with external systems, in which calls to external databases were embedded within processing code, making maintenance difficult, or they were not integrated at all, requiring downloading and manual reformatting of data before use in the system. Second, maintenance, if it occurred at all, was passed around to novice personnel with heavy workloads resulting in shoddy patches just to keep the code running. One system analyzed was so brittle that only a few of the many functions worked at all, and these required much manual effort to input and maintain accurate data. Finally, none of the systems had the capability that students want, including the ability to specify preferences for course times, or spreading difficult courses evenly over multiple semesters.

According to CTSD principles, a domain with frequent changes like this one requires a measure of the type and frequency of changes. We examined two departments at two universities, then looked at the changes that had occurred at each over the past five years. We found that an initial decomposition of terms and policies was useful (Table 2). Static concepts are those that are not subject to change. These concepts describe the fundamental terms and processes within a domain, e.g., students, instructors, and courses. This data is generally already represented in a database system. Dynamic concepts are those that have shown to change over time or are new concepts. The stability of such concepts is uncertain, and therefore the representation needs to be amenable to change. In education, policies for curriculum and admissions requirements change over time. New programs for distance education, which may have little or no history, might be categorized as dynamic, since changes are likely after the organization gains experience with the new model for education delivery. Static and dynamic concepts may be either common or unique. Common concepts are those found widely across organizations, whereas unique concepts are specific to a small percentage of organizations. Looking at these two dimensions by which a concept can be categorized, a student is a static, common concept. A require-ment for an undergraduate thesis may be a static, unique concept. How the four decompositions are related is shown in Figure 6.

An important task for ontology development was the creation of abstract names for common concepts. The prior concept analysis activity showed that some concepts change slightly over time within departments, and others are

Table 2: Categories of Domain Concepts

Decomposition of Domain Concepts	Example
Static	A student ID; classification (e.g., freshman)
Dynamic	General curriculum requirements and exceptions
Common	Courses have prerequisites
Unique	Requirements for admittance into upper division technical program

static, but are named differently by different organizations. In order to support maintainability, we needed to represent these differences in the ontology. For a simple example that illustrates both these characteristics, consider the static concept of a set of courses that are required for all students graduating from a particular university. In one university, the name for this concept changed from UCR to CUE. The same concept was called GEC or had no specific name at two other universities. Previous systems hard coded these names into databases, variable names, and user interfaces. The better approach is to use the abstracted name wherever invisible to the user and translate to the appropriate specific term for display. Changes are thus isolated to changing the ontology, a key tenet for supporting maintainability.

Based on the understanding gained from the domain analysis and additional interviews with domain experts, the use-case model was then prepared. Here the focus is on clearly demarcating the desired functions of the system. Since each use case describes an interaction with the system to perform a task of value, a use case can be assigned measures to rank its priority and implementation difficulty. Analyzing the preconditions and post-conditions, a graph showing the dependencies between use cases is also developed to show, for example, that checking a degree plan is dependent upon being able to select courses for a single semester. The dependency graph and ranking measures are then used to prepare an implementation schedule, in which major milestones result in the delivery of a core set of functionality to the user. A sample use case for the virtual advisor is shown in Figure 7.

Design

To transition to design, two major activities occur that shift the focus from the external, or behavioral, view of the system, to the internal system construction. One activity is the construction of an initial class model containing only the objects and attributes that describe the major entities and their relationships. The other activity is the extraction of tasks, which will become the object methods.

Figure 6: Relationship of Domain Concept Categories

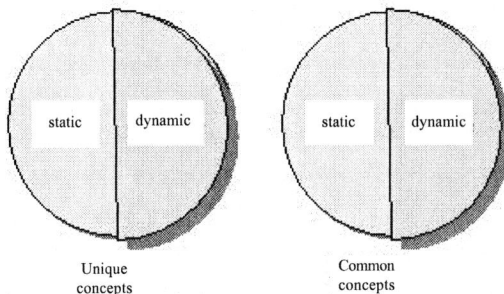

Figure 7: Use Case for Checking Student Degree Plan

USE CASE: USER-DEFINED DEGREE PLAN CHECKER
Use Case ID: A13
Priority: 1   Implementation difficulty: 3
Description: The student can chose to create their degree plan for a selected number of semesters. The student is given a list of courses offered within the university. The student can then assign courses to specific semesters. The student then submits the degree plan created for system verification.
Precondition: Student logged in; in academic good-standing

Actors: Student, Online Enrollment System

Primary Scenario:
1.   Student selects Degree Planner option
2.   Student selects what type of degree plan he/she wants to perform
3.   Student enters desired number of semesters to plan for and college/major info
4.   System retrieves information on student courses and displays them
5.   Student assigns desired courses into appropriate semesters
6.   Student repeats step 5 as often as desired
7.   Student submits created degree plan for verification
8.   System checks rules and prerequisites
9.   System returns with approval or an error message for any conflicts

A useful technique for extracting these items from the use cases is to use Class-Responsibility-Collaboration (CRC) cards. A card is filled out that contains a class name, the major tasks this class is responsible for, and the other classes with which this class interacts. The strength of CRC cards is that, when utilized by a team, the interaction between the members (in simulating the execution of the system) can highlight missing or incorrect fields in a class, whether attributes or methods (Schach, 2002).

Following CTSD for the design of VA, the design grouped related classes from the CRC cards according to the considerations given below. The related classes are implemented as major modules in the systems and, if processing or communications requirements are complex, are designated to be implemented as "employee" or "manager" agents. Factors to consider when selecting the grouping of tasks, classes, and modules are:
1.   the predictability/stability of the task environment and business processes involved;
2.   the diversity of the task environment in terms of each relevant constituency;
3.   scope or granularity of "line-level" software teams;
4.   inter-team coordination techniques used and business knowledge involved; and
5.   "management-level" control teams.

In the system architecture design phase CT design guidelines tell us that domain policies must be specified declaratively and grouped according to predictability to minimize the impact of change. We used relational database tables to store raw data, downloaded from external systems. This design choice isolates legacy system interface tasks. Domain policies are categorized and stored as rules. These rules are implemented in JESS. JESS rules represent and check prerequisites, degree requirements and other university rules. The Java degree planner manager interfaces with the rules and internal database to provide a degree of isolation of policy and implementation. The degree-planner manager controls the mechanics of supplying data to and storing data supplied by the degree planner rules. Thus, individual rule bases that behave as employee specialists are strictly focused on solving specific domain problems, such as creation of a degree plan based on student and university constraints. Managers handle the mundane tasks of acquiring and distributing resources (data) from the appropriate sources. A separate user interface again isolates domain policies and procedures from mechanics of implementation. Graphical rule editors, templates and parameter-setting forms allow an administrator, typically a department chair or lead advisor, to maintain the system to meet their needs and to provide portability across departments and universities. The resulting architecture for the system is shown in Figure 8.

Figure 9 shows one option for the semester scheduler that allows the student to select courses that match a set of preferences, and for which the student has prerequisites. As courses in the desired subject areas are selected, they are checked for time conflicts with those already selected. In the display, generic terms used internally within the system have been mapped to the specific terms used at this student's university, as specified in the ontology.

Figure 8: Virtual Advisor Architecture

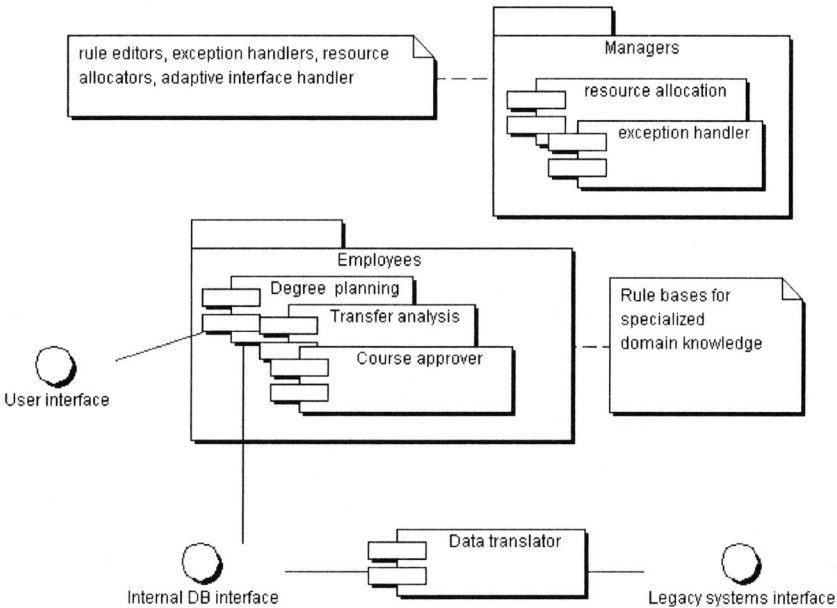

Figure 9: Semester Scheduler with Student Preferences

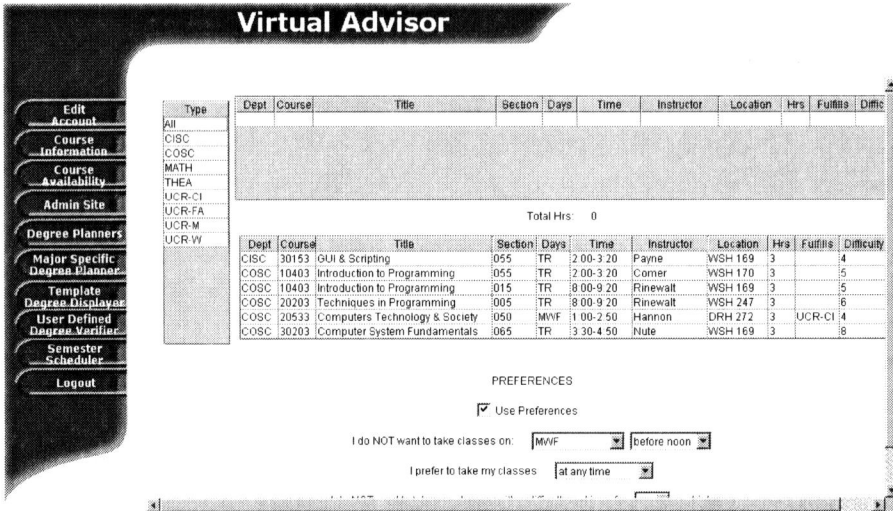

FURTHER RECOMMENDATIONS AND CONCLUSION

The development of an effective knowledge management system in any organization is a complex process. This fact is especially true in an environment subject to rapid and unpredictable changes and with many differing and interrelated resource, processing, and output requirements. However, in this type of dynamic complex environment, KMS can be extremely beneficial and can be used to create a true knowledge-based organization.

The initial design steps in any project are especially important. In developing tools to support an organization's evolution toward a flexible, knowledge-based organization the first and most important step is the creation of a vision. The vision statement for our example advising system is:

To provide accurate, timely, specific guidance to students, faculty, support staff, and others about the services provided by and the rules, requirements, and procedures of the university while remaining flexible to changing requirements and as easy to learn and use as possible.

As with all such statements, one stating the motivation for a KMS should be in terms of benefits to company, customers, and other stakeholders, not in terms of technology. It should motivate designers and users of the system toward cooperation in the realization of a greater goal. This motivation is potentially the most important part of the design of a KMS.

Equipped with the right processes, methods, and tools, it is the people that create a knowledge-based organization. It takes an upper-management champion for the system vision, the right team of developers, a good team leader, and enthusiastic users, all within an environment that encourages and rewards knowledge sharing. Developers, chosen for their creativity and flexibility as well as their technical talent, should be given the resources to learn and experiment. A team leader acts primarily in the role of coach, i.e., providing guidance, motivation, resources, and a common vision. An upper-management champion works to keep the projects funded and to garner support for larger scale efforts. Enthusiastic users are critical as well, for without their knowledge and feedback, developed products will not solve the correct problems, nor will they be used.

REFERENCES

Alavi, M. & Leidner, D.E. (2001, March). Review: Knowledge management and knowledge management systems: Conceptual foundations and research issues. *MIS Quarterly*, 25(1), 107-136.

Beck, K. (2000). *Extreme Programming Explained*. Reading, MA: Addison Wesley.

Birkinshaw et al. (2002). Knowledge as a contingency variable: Do the characteristics of knowledge predict organization structure? *Organization Science*, 13(3), 274-289.

Bukowitz, W. R. & Williams, R. (2000). *Knowledge Management Fieldbook*. Upper Saddle River, NJ: Prentice Hall.

Burnell et al. (2002, May). A business rules approach to departmental advising. *Proceedings of the 15th International Florida Artificial Intelligence Research Society Conference (FLAIRS-2002)*, Pensacola Beach, Florida (May 14-16, pp. 305-309).

CLIPS: C Language Integrated Production System. (2002). Retrieved March 29, 2002 from the World Wide Web: http://www.ghg.net/clips/CLIPS.html.

Davenport, T. & Probst, G. (2000). *Knowledge Management Case Book, Siemans Best Practices*. New York: John Wiley & Sons.

Dess, G.G. & Beard, D.W. (1984). Dimensions of organizational task environments. *Administrative Science Quarterly*, 29(1), 52-73.

Dixon, N. M. (2000). *Common Knowledge*. Boston, MA: Harvard Business School Press.

Durrett, J.R., Burnell, L.J. & Priest, J.W. (2001, July/August). An organizational behavior approach for managing change in information systems. *Proceedings of PICMET, Vol. 1*. Portland, Oregon (pp. 74-75) and CD-ROM.

Durrett, J.R., Burnell, L.J. & Priest, J.W. (2002). A hybrid analysis and architectural design method for development of smart home components. *IEEE Wireless Communications Special Issue on Smart Homes*, 19(5), 85-91.

Durrett, J.R., Burnell, L.J. & Priest, J.W. (2002, May). SARA: Smart, agent-based resource for virtual advising. *Proceedings of 2002 International Resources Management Association International Conference Issues and Trends of Information Technology Management in Contemporary Organizations.* Seattle, Washington (May 19-22, pp. 344-348).

Durrett, J.R., Burnell, L.J. & Priest, J.W. (2003). A virtual advisor utilizing multi-agent software teams and contingency theoretic coordination models. In F. Albalooshi (Ed.), *Virtual Education: Cases in Learning and Teaching Technologies,* (pp. 50-62). Hershey, PA: IRM Press.

Fowler, M. & Scott, K. (2000). *UML Distilled Second Edition (page 40).* Reading, MA: Addison-Wesley.

Galbraith et al. (2001). *Designing Dynamic Organizations: A Hands-On Guide for Leaders at All Levels.* New York: Amacom.

Galbraith, J.R. (1973). *Designing Complex Organizations.* Reading, MA: Addison-Wesley.

JESS: Java Expert System Shell. (2002). Retrieved July 22, 2002 from the World Wide Web: http://herzberg.ca.sandia.gov/jess/.

Krough, G. V., Ichijp, K., & Nonaks, I. (2000). *Enabling Knowledge Creation.* New York: Oxford Press.

Lai, V. S. (1999). A contingency examination of CASE-task fit on software developer's performance. *European Journal of Information Systems,* 8(1), 27-39.

Levesque, H. J. & Lakemeyer, G. (2000). *Logic of Knowledge Bases.* Cambridge, MA: MIT Press.

Loshin, D. (2001). *Enterprise Knowledge Management.* San Mateo, CA: Morgan Kaufmann.

March, J.G. & Simon, H.A. (1958). *Organizations.* New York: John Wiley & Sons.

McGraw, K. & Harbison, K. (1989). *Knowledge Acquisition: Principles and Guidelines.* Englewood Cliffs, NJ: Prentice Hall.

Palmer, S.R. & Felsing, J.M. (2002). *A Practical Guide to Feature-Driven Development.* Englewood Cliffs, NJ: Prentice Hall.

Pfeffer, J. & Salanick, G.R. (1978). *The External Control of Organizations (Chapters 1, 3, and 6).* New York: Harper and Row.

Priest, J. W. & Sanchez, J.M. (1998). Design for producibility: A key concept in product live-cycle engineering (Chapter 15). In A. Molina, J.M. Sanchez & A. Kusiak (Eds.), *Handbook of Life Cycle Engineering.* Dordrecht: Kluwer Academic Publishers.

Priest, J. W. & Sanchez, J.M. (2001). *Product Development and Design for Manufacturing: A Collaborative Approach for Producibility and Reliability.* New York: Marcel Dekker.

Schach, S.R. (2002). *Object-Oriented and Classical Software Engineering*. Boston, MA: McGraw-Hill.

Sowa, J. F. (2000). *Knowledge Representation*. Pacific Grove, CA: Brooks/ Cole.

Thompson, J. D. (1967). *Organizations in Action: Social Science Bases of Administrative Theory*. New York: McGraw-Hill.

Tiwana, A. (2000). *The Knowledge Management Toolkit*. Englewood Cliffs, NJ: Prentice Hall.

W3C. (2002). *World Wide Web Consortium*. Retrieved from August 13, 2002 from the World Wide Web: www.w3c.org.

Chapter XI

Virtual Communities as Role Models for Organizational Knowledge Management

Bonnie Rubenstein Montano
Georgetown University, USA

ABSTRACT

Knowledge management serves to create value from an organization's intangible assets. Many organizations have adopted knowledge management practices in recent years. Some of those organizations have achieved success at knowledge management, but others have not. The focus of this chapter is on those organizations that have not been as successful at knowledge management as they originally planned. This chapter posits that organizations can look to virtual communities as role models for successful knowledge management because many of the features that have been identified in the literature as important for successful knowledge management are present in virtual communities. The very nature of virtual communities — their sense of community, the desire they create to share knowledge, the automatic archiving of knowledge for future use, etc. — are used in this chapter to support the claim that virtual communities can serve as role models for knowledge management in organizations.

INTRODUCTION

Organizations worldwide have embraced knowledge management as a way to create value from an organization's intangible assets, thus improving their bottom line (O'Dell & Grayson, 1998). Typically, organizations undertaking knowledge management initiatives treat knowledge as an important organizational resource, with the assumption that employees need incentives for sharing their knowledge with others in the organization (Gupta & Govindarajan, 2000). Under this model for knowledge management, there have been many success stories (e.g., Buckman Laboratories, The World Bank, Nucor Steel, KPMG Peat Marwick, Accenture, and Ford Motor Company). However, knowledge is often an individual, rather than organizational, resource residing within the minds of members of the organization, and the critical success factors of organizational culture, trust, and reward systems aligned with the principles of knowledge management remain difficult to attain in many cases. Organizations can expend significant resources to develop a culture, high levels of trust, and reward systems necessary for enabling effective knowledge management.

In contrast, virtual communities, which seem to emerge fairly effortlessly on the Internet, possess these critical success factors as inherent parts. Virtual communities are "social aggregations that emerge from the Net when enough people carry on public discussions long enough, with sufficient human feeling, to form webs of personal relationships in cyberspace" (Rheingold, 2000). According to this definition, knowledge sharing is the very essence of virtual communities. Thus, it can be assumed that both a potent culture (along with at least some minimum level of trust) and incentives for sharing knowledge have developed within virtual communities. Otherwise, sharing would not occur and virtual communities would cease to exist.

A key question that emerges from this realization that virtual communities are essentially entities established for the sole purpose of knowledge sharing revolves around what virtual communities do that traditional organizations do not do to facilitate knowledge sharing. This serves as the general theme of this chapter, with specific research questions to address this theme detailed below.

It should be noted that knowledge sharing is selected as the focus of this study since it is a cornerstone of successful knowledge management (Davenport & Prusak, 1998; Hansen et al., 1999). A number of organizations have recognized the potential of knowledge sharing for enhancing organizational performance. Buckman Laboratories and Ford Motor Company have begun developing knowledge networks to facilitate knowledge sharing (Ruggles, 1998).

American Management Systems has established knowledge centers where one of the center's four goals is to learn and share knowledge (Sensiper, 1997). KPMG Peat Marwick restructured its organization around its lines of business in order to facilitate knowledge sharing (Alavi, 1997). The World Bank reorganized to create horizontal relationships between staff in an effort to facilitate the sharing of knowledge (Valor, 1997).

Although some organizations have embraced virtual communities as a way to provide customer support (e.g., Microsoft), virtual communities and more traditional types of organizations are very different entities. As mentioned above, virtual communities are primarily concerned with social aggregations and personal relationships. Business organizations are primarily concerned with competing in the marketplace. Also, while organizations often have electronic components to supplement physical ones, virtual communities are strictly electronic. The typical model for knowledge management adopted by organizations, where knowledge is treated as a commodity, appears to be at odds with the critical success factors for knowledge management because this approach often results in those who possess knowledge seeking to keep it to themselves for personal leverage. In contrast, virtual communities seem to have already obtained the key characteristics for successful knowledge management. The specific research questions that this chapter seeks to answer, then, are:

1.   What attributes of virtual communities show promise for knowledge management?
2.   How can the attributes that make virtual communities successful at knowledge sharing be carried over to traditional organizations and used in knowledge management?

Because virtual communities exist only in cyberspace, technology is a fundamental part of them, and thus a fundamental part of the communication and knowledge sharing that occurs in virtual communities. The view of virtual communities as exemplars for knowledge management seems to counter recent work indicating that technology is more of an enabler of knowledge management than an essential component (Alavi & Leidner, 2001; Davenport & Prusak, 1998; Rubenstein-Montano et al., 2001). This chapter addresses the two primary research questions listed above while considering this "issue" of technology. Secondary research questions in this chapter include the following:

1.   What is the role of technology in a virtual community versus a traditional organization?
2.   What aspects of technology make it a better or worse enabler of knowledge management?
3.   What barriers to knowledge management does technology add? What barriers does technology remove?

VIRTUAL COMMUNITIES

Internet sites have shifted from the static presentation of material to interactive communities, involving the members of the community in ongoing public dialog (Levitt et al., 1998). Sponsors of interactive sites hope such interaction will encourage individuals to spend more time at the site and return more frequently (Levitt et al., 1998). While information sharing over electronic networks, especially with relative strangers, has been examined in organizations (Constant et al., 1996), on the Internet sharing occurs outside of an organizational context in what are commonly termed "virtual communities" (VCs).

Virtual communities consist of people with shared interests or goals for whom electronic communication is a primary form of interaction (Dennis et al., 1998). Traditionally, the word "community" suggests a geographic area, such as a neighborhood (Wellman & Gulia, 1999), but the "virtual" part of the term "virtual community" indicates communities lacking a physical place as a home (Handy, 1995). Formally defined, VCs are groups of people that use a location on the Internet such as a listserv, chat room, newsgroup or bulletin board to communicate regularly. The groups have common practices and interests, and often have a notion of membership, formal or informal, and form personal relationships with others in the community. An example of a VC would be a Usenet newsgroup in which a group of people communicates regularly through the newsgroup and therefore forms personal relationships and bonds. VCs usually center on some common interest, hobby, or life event, such as surf fishing, collecting decorator plates, dealing with colon cancer, or raising a child with Down syndrome.

Not all virtual meeting forums can be considered VCs. For example, a bulletin board on the Web for selling used cars, where most of the postings simply advertise a car and do not have replies, and where people do not return after they sell or buy their car, would not constitute a VC. Authors have proposed certain minimum levels of interactivity in order for virtual spaces to qualify as VCs (Jones, 1997; Liu, 1999). These criteria are as follows: 80% of postings must have responses, a minimum of 15 different members must post over a three-day period, a minimum of ten postings a day per during any random three-day period must be posted, and at least 50% of the posters must post more than one time. It is important to note that individuals participate when they know many others are participating. Although the literature does not specify a particular frequency, a VC is generally understood to consist of persistently interacting members (Smith, 1999). VC sites can quickly fail when the membership, and therefore the usage, drops below some threshold (Ackerman & Starr, 1995).

Figures 1 through 4 provide samples of VC exchanges, illustrating the types of knowledge shared in these communities, with specific examples identified below each figure.

Figure 1: Down Syndrome VC

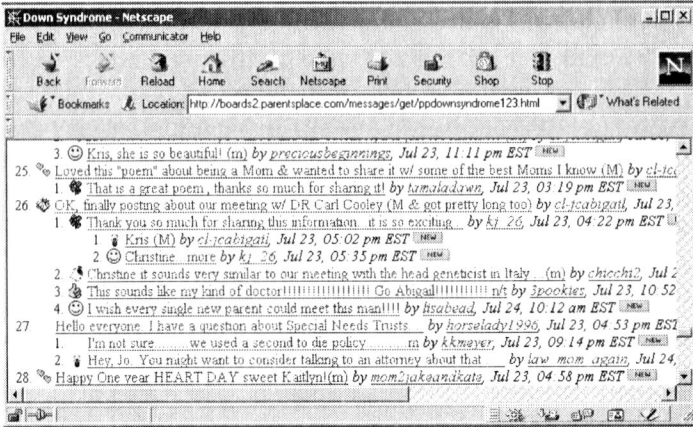

Explicit knowledge — "OK, finally a posting about out meeting w/ DR Carl Cooley"
Innovative knowledge — "we used a second to die policy"

Figure 2: Gardening VC

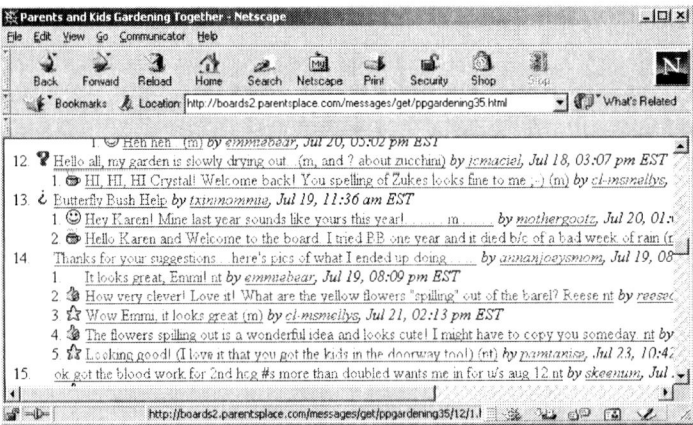

Explicit knowledge — "Mine last year sounds like yours this year!"
Feedback for previously shared knowledge — "Thanks for your suggestions ... here's pics of what I ended up doing... ."

Figure 3: Surf Fishing VC

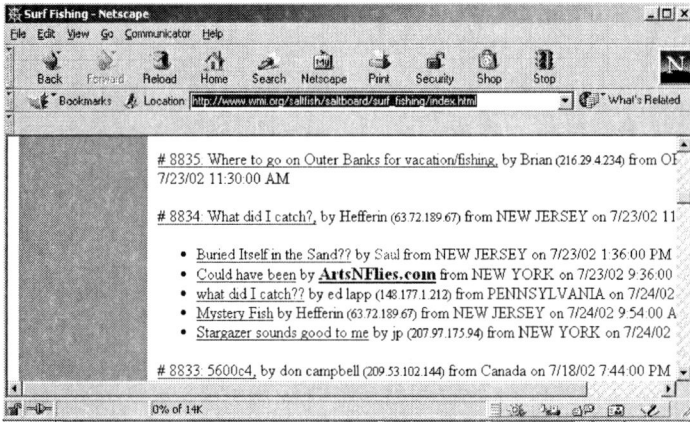

Explicit and tacit (storytelling) knowledge — "Where to go on Outer Banks for vacation/fishing"

Explicit knowledge — "Could have been"

Figure 4: Bow Hunting VC

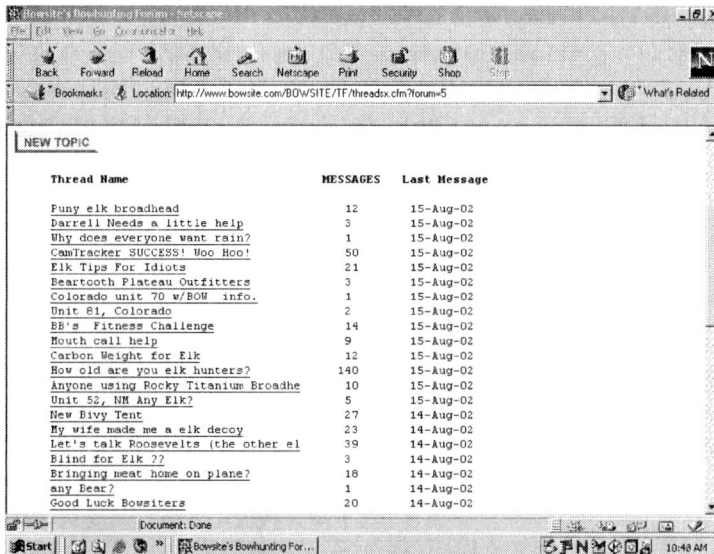

Tacit knowledge — "Why does everyone want rain?"

Explicit and tacit knowledge — "Mouth call help"

PROMISE OF VIRTUAL COMMUNITIES FOR ORGANIZATIONAL KNOWLEDGE MANAGEMENT

The description of VCs, and the included figures, given in the preceding section provides the basis from which the claim, "VCs can serve as role models for organizational knowledge management" is made. The overriding attribute of VCs that lends support to this claim is the fact that they are social aggregations established for the purpose of sharing knowledge. In organizations, the goal of KM is directly in line with the purpose of VCs — to get members of the organization to interact and share knowledge so the knowledge can be leveraged for organizational benefit. In addition to the fact that the primary purpose of VCs is to share knowledge, several specific features of VCs that lend themselves to knowledge management are discussed below. The features can be categorized as pertaining to members of the VC (people), interaction in the VC (communication), or means of communication in the VC (technology).

Communication

1. VCs are emergent communities that develop in a grassroots fashion (Rubenstein-Montano & Ridings, 2002). Conversations on a message board can grow naturally over time as knowledge of their existence and quality of conversation is disseminated. In this way, success of the VC is a result of direct need for the VC and the knowledge it generates. Site sponsors cannot "make" a site successful.
2. The definition of a VC indicates that social ties must exist between members of the VC for the online forum to be considered a VC. Thus, the social ties necessary to facilitate knowledge creation and sharing (Hansen, 1999) are in place when such creation and sharing occurs in a VC.
3. Members of the VC communicate when they want to, without pressure to communicate a certain number of times or at regular intervals. This feature of VCs allows members of the VC to generate and share knowledge when it is most appropriate and efficient for the member to do so. Thus, the knowledge sharing process is self-regulating and streamlined to some degree.
4. The focus of VCs is communication, with concern over how to profit from such communication as secondary, or at least transparent to VC members. That is, while VC sponsors depend upon the communities for revenue in some way, either in the form of selling advertising, selling products to members, providing market research, collecting subscriptions, or using them for customer support, seeking revenue does not change the underlying functioning of the VC as an online discussion forum. Focus of the VC remains on knowledge sharing.

5. The ongoing nature of discussion among users provides an incentive for members to repeatedly return to the VC to read others' comments and to respond, thus, continuing the process of knowledge generation and sharing. The very features that classify online entities as VCs — 80% of postings must have replies, a minimum of 15 different members must post over a three-day period, a minimum of ten postings per day per any random three-day period, and at least 50% of posters must post more than one time — dictate that ongoing discussion and repeat returns will be the norm.

6. The criteria for determining if virtual spaces qualify as VCs, membership levels, number of postings, and number of responses to postings (Jones, 1997; Liu, 1999), indicate that VCs are, by definition, successful in knowledge dissemination (Rubenstein-Montano & Ridings, 2002). World Wide Web sites are public and therefore viewable by anyone with Internet access. Knowledge dissemination can occur regardless of whether individuals actively participate in the site (e.g., lurkers).

People

7. Members of VCs have direct control over the VC since their contributions and exchanges with other members serve as a part of the site's content (Levitt et al., 1998). Thus, VC members have a vested interest in the success of the VC.

8. VCs have low barriers to entry. Typically, individuals only have to click on a link, or enter a URL, possibly completing an online registration form. The infusion of people results in the infusion of new ideas and expertise, which are in turn shared with members of the VC.

9. Members of a VC are initially strangers to one another, allowing them to create any persona they choose. Members often choose to provide accurate information, but this is not required to participate in most VCs. The ability to remain unknown supports the need for anonymity, which has long been the focus of research on group decision-making (DeSanctis & Gallupe, 1985) and often leads to VC members feeling more comfortable participating and sharing knowledge with others in the VC.

10. Oversight and moderating of VCs tends to be somewhat transparent to users. Moderators, who vary from laizze-faire to heavy-handed, tend to adopt more of the laizze-faire attitude. This promotes an environment with some level of freedom from censorship and a sense of privacy (Levitt et al., 1998). Guidance that is visible to members of the VC tends to be in the form of knowledgeable responses to posted queries or gentle reminders to stay "on topic."

11. Oversight and moderation of VCs tends to be handled by individuals with some level of expertise in the domain area of the VC. This enables moderators to not only oversee interaction on the sight, but to provide

knowledgeable responses (as mentioned above) on occasion. Moderators also allow other members of the VC to provide answers. This avoids the problem of the VC becoming dependent on the moderator to answer all questions, which is not consistent with the definition of "community." Allowing others to answer questions also increases the number of "experts" in the community, which is important for valuing the community overall.

12. Moderating responsibilities are typically assigned to more than one person so that moderating is coordinated and covered at all times.

Technology

13. The electronic nature of VCs makes storage of past discussions straightforward. VCs typically archive discussions and allow members to search archives when they are interested in retrieving knowledge that has already been generated by the VC.

14. VCs exist on the Internet and are therefore accessible from anywhere and anytime. This allows knowledge to get to the right people *at the right time*, which is an important part of knowledge management (O'Dell & Grayson, 1998).

15. The use of different technologies enables robust communication similar to that in face-to-face settings. Bulletin boards allow serial discussion, but chat rooms allow for real-time communication that includes feedback and interruptions. Multimedia auditoriums allow for sharing of non-text knowledge such as video clips.

TRANSFERRING ATTRIBUTES OF VIRTUAL COMMUNITIES TO KNOWLEDGE MANAGEMENT IN TRADITIONAL ORGANIZATIONS

A number of attributes of VCs were identified in the preceding section as important reasons why VCs are successful at knowledge sharing. Some of these attributes are already a part of organizational knowledge management initiatives, and some may not be appropriate for an organizational setting. The VC attributes of particular interest, however, are those which are not typically adopted by organizations at present, but could be used to enhance knowledge management in traditional organizations. There are five attributes identified as critical for knowledge sharing success in VCs but not currently part of the typical organizational knowledge management initiative.

First, VCs were described as emergent communities. This counters the typical top-down establishment of work groups and teams in organizations.

Formation of groups in a top-down fashion means members of the group are assigned to work together rather than allowing individuals to come together on their own, simply because they want to. While organizations cannot force the development of grassroots groups, they can work to nurture those that do develop without trying to control them in a heavy-handed manner. Organizations can also allocate space (physical or virtual) for gathering to talk about topics *not* related to work. Relationships that develop from these informal places may carry over to collaboration and knowledge sharing on work-related projects.

The second attribute of VCs, regarding social ties, can be handled in much the same way as nurturing grassroots groups. That is, employees should be encouraged, within reason, to develop personal relationships with other employees that do not necessarily revolve around work-related issues. Again, a location for social gathering can facilitate this and, in fact, many organizations already have this in place in the form of an employee lounge, cafeteria, or simple water-cooler/coffee pot. For social ties to develop, though, the organization must truly encourage such relationship building, with the focus on social and personal issues and not on work issues.

Third, there has been a trend in organizations to "encourage" knowledge sharing by mandating that individuals participate in communities of practice or write-up summaries of projects and contribute them to databases. This is very different from allowing individuals to contribute knowledge when they want to, without pressure to contribute a certain amount of knowledge. Rather than redesigning employee evaluations to account for how many times an individual contributes to an organizational knowledge base, businesses ought to illustrate how the knowledge base can help individual employees so they will want to participate on their own, perhaps include a reputation management system so participants will be benefiting by developing a better reputation without linking participation to specific employee evaluation processes. This would allow individuals to share knowledge only when they desire. Reputation has been shown to serve as a strong motivation to excel at a task (Nowak & Sigmund, 1998; Lotem et al., 1999) and there is no reason to assume such a motivating factor would be anything but successful for knowledge sharing.

This will require the implementation of new evaluation models in much the same way that the Internet has led to new business models. Although still evolving, the banner-ad model for Internet businesses is successful, not necessarily profit-wise, but in the sense that they enable countless people to view a site free of charge. The banner-ad model places the burden of revenue generation on advertisers rather than customers. Similarly, organizations can shift their focus from employees and the quantity of knowledge they share, to a support infrastructure that encourages knowledge sharing. Web sites that have adopted the banner-ad model gain through advertising, without requiring anything specific from users. Similarly, organizations can use a similar template and gain by filtering, organizing, updating, or "pushing" knowledge, without requiring employees to make predefined knowledge contributions.

Unfortunately, the idea of a reputation management system counters the concept of anonymity. Organizations can examine their culture and determine which approach is most appropriate for them — reputation-based or anonymous.

Fourth, in organizations, the focus is on money with communication and sharing as a way to achieve increased revenues. This makes sense for organizations since organizational self-interest depends on revenues. However, individual self-interest does not always revolve around wealth (Sloan, 2002) and VCs are capable of exploiting other drivers beyond self-interest. It is easy to say that organizations should focus on communication and knowledge sharing in their own right without considering economics, but this is an attribute of VCs that may not be realistic for organizations.

Fifth, because of the top-down approach and presence of managers typical in organizations, moderating any sites sponsored by the organization receives more oversight than typical VCs. This point spans several of the success factors of VCs that are lacking in organizations. Specifically, this can inhibit employee participation (especially when a sense of privacy is not engendered) and removes some of the control individuals have over which contributions are allowed to remain on the site for others to view. Several issues need to be addressed by organizations here. Since it is unlikely that management will be disbanded in order to create an organizational environment that better mimics the VC environment, resources ought to be allocated to building trust between management and staff. Also, oversight of organizational sites should shift toward the laizze-faire end of the scale rather than the heavy-handed end, and participants should have control over admissible content. If a reputation system is implemented as mentioned above, contributions should over time increase in quality and relevance so that oversight by a heavy-handed moderator will not be necessary.

The attributes of VCs already present in organizations, indicating what organizations are already "doing right," include: (1) the ongoing nature of discussion, (2) dissemination of knowledge, (3) individual control over their contributions (to some degree and depending on the organization), (4) low barriers to entry, (5) storage of knowledge in archives, (6) continual access to knowledge, and (7) multiple technologies for sharing knowledge. Most of these are straightforward, but I will comment on a couple of them. First, if knowledge is added to a company intranet site, it is disseminated the same way knowledge is disseminated in VCs. Second, individual control over contributions was discussed above, but can easily be adopted by organizations by allowing employees to upload information directly, with more transparent moderation similar to that of VCs. Significant scrubbing of submissions should not occur.

Continual access to knowledge is easily achieved if employees can access intranet sites with knowledge from work, home, or while traveling.

The key feature of VCs, which may prove difficult to transfer to organizational KM, is that of anonymity. The World Wide Web is a much bigger place than a single organization, and fake information can be used to register for participation in a VC. However, in organizations a list of all employees is typically accessible via an intranet search, and anonymity may not be desirable if an individual is trying to obtain "credit" for participating in knowledge sharing. Even if anonymity is allowed by the organization, employees may not trust they are truly anonymous to superiors.

MODELING ORGANIZATIONAL KNOWLEDGE MANAGEMENT AFTER VCS

Table 1 summarizes the VC features discussed in the preceding two sections, and Figure 5 depicts how the three classes of VC features presented in this chapter relate to each other and influence organizational KM. As shown in Figure 5, technology serves as the basis upon which VCs can exist. People create the community, and communication among people sustains the community. The success of organizational KM rests upon these three classes of VC features.

Table 1: Applying VC Features to Organizational KM

Feature	NOT Currently Present in Organizational KM	Currently Present in Organizational KM	Probably Cannot be Easily Transferred to Organizational KM
Communication			
Emergent communities	✓		
Social ties	✓		
Self-motivation	✓		
Ongoing discussion		✓	
Successful knowledge dissemination		✓	
Communication prioritized over money	✓		✓
People			
Vested interest by members		✓	
Low barriers to entry		✓	
Anonymity possible	✓		✓
Transparent oversight	✓		
Technology			
Knowledge archiving		✓	
Anywhere-anytime access		✓	
Combinations of technologies		✓	

Figure 5: VC Features for Organizational KM

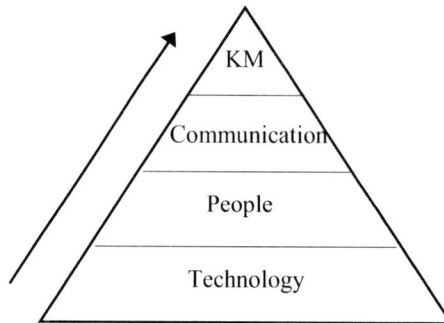

ISSUES AND CONCERNS

While the attributes of VCs that enable them to serve as role models for organizational knowledge management have been outlined above, VCs are not without limitations. Because knowledge sharing in VCs occurs strictly through technology, the emphasis is on sharing explicit knowledge. Some tacit knowledge may be shared (Rubenstein-Montano & Ridings, 2002), but the majority of knowledge shared will be explicit since it can be written down. Some have argued that tacit knowledge is where much of the value added comes in (Sveiby, 2001), and this is lost if VCs emphasize explicit knowledge.

Also, quality control in VCs is questionable since anyone anywhere can contribute knowledge. The low barriers to entry and ability to create a fictional person mean there is no way to verify the expertise of contributors, and Internet fraud is becoming more commonplace (National White Collar Crime Center & FBI, 2000; National Consumers League, 2002). For example, web sites on which individuals have purposefully posted false stock information to drive up prices of stocks they own for personal gain have received a fair amount of media attention on. Also, comparison of two web sites — http://www.wto.org and http://www.gatt.org — illustrate how easy it is to publish false information online. Http://www.wto.org is the official web site for the World Trade Organization, but http://www.gatt.org appears the same as the official site with manufactured stories.

Because participation in VCs is technology dependent, only those with Internet access can contribute to a VC. Theoretically, this can limit the pool of available expertise. Enough people do have access that this probably is not a real concern, but it is mentioned for completeness. This is an issue that should not apply to organizations if we assume all relevant employees would have access to the company intranet. Of course, restrictive access rules for different classes of employees could lead to an artificial constraint on the amount of expertise available to others in the organization.

Lastly, some of the limitations of VCs for serving as knowledge management systems have been pointed out by Rubenstein-Montano and Ridings (2002). Fairly simple knowledge is shared, explicit rather than tacit knowledge is typically shared, and knowledge is archived by date rather than subtopic making location of stored knowledge difficult. Therefore, VCs cannot serve as a panacea for organizational knowledge management. Instead, they can serve as a starting point for future enhancements to organizational knowledge management.

FUTURE TRENDS

Both VCs and KM continue to evolve. In this section VC trends that can be applied to KM are presented. The first trend involves knowledge organization in VCs using semantic networks. Typically, knowledge is stored in VCs according to the date the content is added to the VC (Rubenstein-Montano & Ridings, 2002), but a newer approach for VCs is to use semantic networks. Semantic networks enable the organization of knowledge around topic areas. This is a change to knowledge organization that enhances search and retrieval of knowledge from storage locations. Consulting firms have already created knowledge management systems that employ semantic techniques for organizing knowledge about customers and their industries, projects, and competitors (Alavi, 1997).

Second, it is expected that emphasis will be on more *anticipatory* responses from the organization members who need to carry out the mandate of a faster cycle of knowledge-creation and action based on the new knowledge (Nadler & Shaw, 1995).

Third, community members must be able to find and bring to bear the relevant knowledge in the repository. In both today's VCs and knowledge management systems, the search engine is the main workhorse for finding stored knowledge. Search engines apply rudimentary natural language-understanding techniques. Over time, lessons learned about indexing and retrieval in case-based reasoning systems will be applied to KM. Furthermore, agents and distributed problem-solving technology will play an increasingly important role (Smith, 2000).

A couple of recent trends in KM involve enterprise portals and employee relationship management. Enterprise portals provide unified access across business units and enterprise boundaries to just about any resource an employee might need, including front-end and back-end resources, personal workspaces, and the World Wide Web. Individuals can customize their view of the enterprise portal (SAP & PriceWaterhouseCoopers, 2001). Employee relationship management (ERM) is aimed at getting employees, managers and senior executives on the same level and using the same vocabulary for increased productivity, efficiency and customer and market awareness (Ericson, 2002).

CONCLUSION

This chapter has outlined some of the key features of virtual communities that suggest they can serve as role models for knowledge management initiatives in traditional organizations. Because the primary purpose of virtual communities is sharing knowledge, there are prerequisites for the existence of a culture, along with at least some minimum level of trust, and effective incentives for facilitating knowledge sharing. The nature of virtual communities suggests that traditional organizations can look to virtual communities to learn what virtual communities do that traditional organizations do not do for facilitating knowledge sharing. However, there is no claim that virtual communities will serve as a panacea to solve all of the problems organizations face when implementing knowledge management. Instead, this chapter reviewed some of the features of virtual communities that show promise for improving upon current knowledge management practices in traditional organizations.

First, the chapter reviewed the attributes of virtual communities that support knowledge sharing and can thus help traditional organizations. These attributes include the presence of social ties, the emergent nature of virtual communities, the self-motivation present in members of virtual communities, the ongoing nature of discussion, low barriers to entry, community member control over content, some degree of anonymity, transparent oversight, anywhere-and-anytime access to the community, and technologies that enable robust communication.

The chapter then went on to note that traditional organizations already do many things "right" when it comes to knowledge management. However, since there is always room for improvement, organizations can adopt features of virtual communities that do not currently characterize them. Of the features of virtual communities that encourage knowledge sharing, those that traditional organizations do not typically possess, but that can be transferred to organizations to some degree include the following:

- Emergent, instead of top-down, development of communities for sharing knowledge.
- Development of social ties ought to be encouraged and nurtured.
- The emphasis on required contributions should be replaced by an emphasis on employee choice. Individuals should contribute knowledge when they feel self-motivated to do so. Perhaps a reputation system would serve as an effective motivator instead of employee evaluations that link knowledge contributions to pay raises and promotions.
- Exploit the drivers behind self-interest of employees to encourage knowledge sharing instead of placing the entire focus on wealth.

Although virtual communities cannot solve all of the problems of knowledge management that traditional organizations encounter, their very nature serves as a goal to which traditional organizations can strive.

REFERENCES

Ackerman, M.S. & Starr, B. (1995). Social activity indicators: Interface components for CSCW systems. *Proceedings of Computer Supported Cooperative Work Conference* (pp. 159-168).

Alavi, M. (1997). *KPMG Peat Marwick U.S.: One Giant Brain* (case #9-397-108). Boston, MA: Harvard Business School Publishing.

Alavi, M. & Leidner, D. (2001). Knowledge management and knowledge management systems: Conceptual foundations and research issues. *MIS Quarterly*, 25(1), 107-136.

Constant, D., Sproull, L. & Kiesler, S. (1996). The kindness of strangers: The usefulness of electronic weak ties for technical advice. *Organization Science,* 7(2), 119-135.

Davenport, T. & Prusak, L. (1998). *Working Knowledge.* Boston, MA: Harvard Business School Press.

Dennis, A.R., Pootheri, S.K., & Natarajan, V.L. (1998). Lessons from the early adopters of web groupware. *Journal of Management Information Systems*, 14(4), 65-86.

DeSanctis, G. & Gallupe, B. (1985). Group decision support systems: A new frontier. *Data Base*, 16(2), 3-10.

Ericson, J. (2002). Is ERM a Contender? *KM Magazine.* Retrieved July 23, 2002 from the World Wide Web: http://kmmag.com/articles/default.asp?ArticleID=954.

Gupta, A.K. & Govindarajan, V. (2000). Knowledge management's social dimension: Lessons from Nucor Steel. *Sloan Management Review*, 42(1), 71-80.

Handy, C. (1995). Trust and the virtual organization. *Harvard Business Review*, 73(3), 40-48.

Hansen, M., Nohria, N. & Tierney, T. (1999, March/April). What's your strategy for managing knowledge? *Harvard Business Review*, 106-116.

Jones, Q. (1997). Virtual-communities, virtual settlements & cyber-archaeology: A theoretical outline. *Journal of Computer Mediated Communication*, 3(3). Retrieved from the World Wide Web: http://www.ascusc.org/jcmc/vol3/issue3/jones.html.

Levitt, L.M., Popkin, L. & Hatch, D. (1998). *Building online communities for high profile Internet sites*, ISOC 1998. Retrieved March 2002 from the World Wide Web: http://www.magicpub.com/presentations/Isoc98/virtualcommunities.html.htm.

Liu, G.Z. (1999). Virtual community presence in Internet relay chatting. *Journal of Computer Mediated Communication*, 5(1). Retrieved from the World Wide Web: http://www.ascusc.org/jcmc/vol5/issue1/liu.html.

Lotem, A., Fishman, M.A. & Stone, L. (1999). Evolution of cooperation between individuals. *Nature*, 400, 226-227.

National Consumers League. (2002). *2001 Internet Fraud Statistics*. Retrieved June 27, 2002 from the World Wide Web: http://www.fraud.org/internet/2001stats.htm.

National White Collar Crime Center and Federal Bureau of Investigation. (2000). *Internet Fraud Complaint Center (IFCC) Six-Month Data Trends Report*. Retrieved June 27, 2002 from the World Wide Web: http://www1.ifccfbi.gov/strategy/6monthreport.PDF.

Nowak, M.A. & Sigmund, K. (1998). Evolution of indirect reciprocity by image scoring. *Nature*, 393, 573-577.

O'Dell, C. & Grayson, C. J., Jr. (1998). *If Only We Knew What We Know*. New York: The Free Press.

Rheingold, H. (2000). *The Virtual Community*. Cambridge, MA: MIT Press.

Rubenstein-Montano, B., Liebowitz, J., Buchwalter, J., McCaw, D., Newman, B., & Rebeck, K. (2001). A systems thinking framework for knowledge management. *Decision Support Systems*, 31(1), 5-16.

Ruggles, R. (1998). The state of the notion: Knowledge management in practice. *California Management Review*, 40, 80-89.

SAP & PriceWaterhouseCoopers. (2001). *The E-business Workplace: Discovering the Power of Enterprise Portals*. New York: John Wiley & Sons.

Sensiper, S. (1997). *American Management Systems: The Knowledge Centers* (case #9-697-068). Boston, MA: Harvard Business School Publishing.

Sloan, A. (2002, June). The verdict is in: Greed isn't good. *The Washington Post*, 195, June 18, E3.

Smith, A.D. (1999). Problems of conflict management in virtual communities. In M. A. Smith & P. Kollock (Eds.), *Communities in Cyberspace* (pp. 134-163). New York: Routledge.

Smith, R.G. (2000). The road ahead for knowledge management. *AI Magazine*.

Sveiby, K.E. (2001). A knowledge-based theory of the firm to guide strategy formulation. *Journal of Intellectual Capital*, 2(4).

Valor, J. (1997). *Information at the World Bank: In Search of a Technology Solution (B)* (case #9-898-054). Boston, MA: Harvard Business School Publishing.

Wellman, B. & Gulia, M. (1999). Virtual communities as communities. In M. A. Smith and P. Kollock (Eds.), *Communities in Cyberspace* (pp. 167-194). New York: Routledge.

SECTION IV:

LEARNING ORGANIZATIONS

Chapter XII

Learning Maturity: Incorporating Technological Influences in Individual and Organizational Learning Theory

Gary F. Templeton
Mississippi State University, USA

ABSTRACT

An explosion of research on the organizational learning paradigm has caused a great need for continued theoretical development to enable a more complete understanding of how to manage the concept for strategic advantage. At the same time, learning theory has not adequately addressed the technology variable in its framework, models, or propositions. The body of theory derived here centers around "learning maturity," the capacity of an actor to effectively exhibit intelligent behavior in a wide range of situated actions. The theory is significant because it uniquely includes technology as a meaningful element in learning and intelligence. The research methodology uses over a century of published literature to serve as a "learning history" of an observed organization: the learning research community. The theory extends decades of cumulative research by focusing on the capabilities of actors to succeed in their interactions (use and development) with technology.

INTRODUCTION

An explosion of research on learning has recently been observed in the organization and information sciences. The concept has served as a theoretical foundation for studies involving adaptive behaviors of organizations and their members who strive to compete in the ever-turbulent information society (Templeton & Snyder, 1999). At the same time, learning theory has not adequately addressed the technology variable in its framework, models, or propositions. This incompleteness of theoretical application is evidenced by several problems in the field, such as relatively few accepted definitions and measures of learning (Templeton, Lewis, & Snyder, 2002), despite its long tradition. The crisis can only be alleviated by attempts at providing more complete theories on learning.

The purpose of this chapter is to report on a theory that respects the profound influences that technology has had on learning theory and report what this means to both individual and organizational learners. A synthesis of the literature resulted in several conceptualizations about learning. Among them:

- a history of learning research at both individual and collective levels of analysis
- the major periods and eras of theoretical development in learning research
- some major specific contributions upon which prominent learning theory is based
- effects of technological change on the evolution of learning theory
- a theory of learning maturity

The technology-inclusive theory of learning presented here is called *learning maturity*, the capacity of an actor to effectively exhibit intelligent behavior in a wide range of situated actions. In the spirit of Kleiner and Roth's (1997) "learning histories" methodology, this chapter attempts to document major events, contributions, and themes found in individual and organizational learning theory. In this vein, the presented "learning history" of the learning field of research serves as the empirical basis upon which theory is developed. Throughout the discussion, several major contributions are made through the synergistic construction of themes found in the history of discourse on learning theory.

The derived theory and its associated concepts are important because they help explain the essence of learning at both levels of analysis. It is a unique investigation into the causes of change in thought about learning. In addition, the research synthesizes the long tradition of learning research into an encapsulation about what we currently know about entity[1] learning capability. A recurring theme resulting from this investigation was that the concept of *technology* consistently influenced, and continues to influence, the evolution of learning research. Thought on learning theory has evolved based on observations about entity behavior that ranges from simple to complex.

This chapter is useful to managers of aspiring "learning organizations" and organizational theorists for five primary reasons: (1) to clarify the relationship between the organization and its members in learning organizations (Argyris & Schon, 1978), (2) to educate change agents about the traditional foundations of learning theory during the implementation of the organizational learning (OL) ideal (Kiernan, 1993), (3) to build an understanding of the past so that the future of thought on learning can be more easily anticipated, (4) to understand the role of technological advancement and proliferation in dictating organizational design changes, and (5) to understand higher-order learning processes, relationships, and outcomes in the "learning maturity" construct. The study has been inspired by the significant differences between the cultures, structures, and behaviors found in learning organizations, as compared to traditional hierarchical models. The topic is timely because of the increased interest in OL, and the inherent interdependency between the organization and its members during collective learning. The theory extends decades of cumulative research on how organizations and individuals interact with (use and develop) technology by focusing on the issue of capability.

Grounded theory development builds the general features of a topic using empirical observations of recurring real-world phenomena (Martin & Turner, 1986). This poses several problems in the pursuit of theory about individual and organizational learning maturity, which can take decades to materialize. The idea of learning maturity implies changes in skills and technologies over time by the members of an organization as well as the collective, which is not always easily defined over long periods of time. Thus, learning maturity is a very difficult concept to observe and support through traditional observational techniques.

This chapter involves an innovative method for theory development in organization studies. As in any learning endeavor (whereby a change to the preexisting learning history is attempted), the sourcing, prioritization, and reframing of a collective body of knowledge represents the contribution of this research. Challenges included finding an observable and ongoing example of an interactive cluster of technology and actors (individual or organizational) that have "learning matured" in the past. The *knowledge* that is shaped and observable from the scientific literature was chosen as the technology under study. The cumulative existing base of literary contributions serves as the "learning history" from which to observe recorded discovery, and the published set of organization and behavioral scientists serve as the actors.

I assume that the actors (institutions and scholars) are seeking "learning maturation." From this description, it is easy to see that any discipline or stream with a respectable cumulative tradition can be observed as a learning organization. While any topic could be interchanged in the discussion, I find that the documented history in the field of learning is an ideal subject from which derive the foundation of general organizational learning theory. The field has a long and vast tradition of theoretical and empirical research as well as periods of revolutionary and normal science (Kuhn, 1962). A convenient by-product is the use of developments and terminology that is generally familiar to readers of a manuscript on "learning maturity." In summary, I observed the organizational (an academic field) and individual (researchers) treatment of a technology (knowledge about the learning concept) over a century of development. By deploying this observational method, I am assuming that lessons learned about a particular type of technology (such as knowledge in this case) are generalizable to other types (such as tasks, tools, and techniques). Also, I assume that the findings of this research about learning theory are generalizable to any topic or discipline. Using the example of how learning theory has evolved over time has the added benefit of reinforcing how knowledge about any subject progresses during the natural progression of organizational and individual life.

The body of this chapter is organized into three sections: a case presented as a learning history of individual and organizational learners in the field, a discussion about the influence of technology on that history, and a discussion on learning maturity. An overview of conclusions and implications for further research follows.

A LEARNING HISTORY OF
LEARNING THEORY

Table 1 depicts the various periods and eras of learning theoretical development at both levels of analysis, and serves as a guide to the organization of the chapter. Since the earliest scientific inquiries into learning initially occurred at the individual level of analysis, it is appropriate to explain its developmental path first.

A History of Individual Learning Theory

There were three distinct periods in the long tradition of theoretical development on individual learning: pre-learning, mechanistic, and organismic. Each successive period introduced greater explanations for environmental interaction.

Table 1: Periods and Eras of Learning Theory at the Two Prominent Levels of Analysis

Period	Individual Level Era	Organizational Level Era
Pre-learning	• Master Teacher • Introspection	Emergent Learning
Mechanistic	Behaviorism	• Tool Implementation • Learning Curves
Organismic	• Cognition • Social learning	• Self-Redesign • Learning Organization

The Pre-Learning Period

Drucker (1989) noted that *master teaching*, not learning, was the societal focus of the educational process for thousands of years. This was due to the presence of very few scholars, who were justifiably the focal point of interest in the educational process. Despite the traditional focus on teaching, very few meaningful gains were realized in the profession. Drucker (1989) stated that, "master teachers today teach the same way master teachers taught three thousand years ago." By the late 1800s, society had changed due to the new technologies[2], wealth, and opportunities brought about by the world-class *organizations* of the Industrial Revolution. This spawned a lasting growth of societal interest in learning research, as international corporations were faced with a new and growing need to hire, train, and disseminate knowledge to diverse and widely dispersed workforces. As a result of the relative absence of inquiry about learning prior to this time, the focus shifted from the teacher to the learner just prior to the outset of 20th century.

Pioneering philosophers of learning theory initially subscribed to the traditionally accepted *introspectionist* analysis methodology, which uses self-examination of one's own consciousness as the data collection method. Since the subject and observer is the same person during this method, introspection requires less interpretive capability on the part of the researcher.

Although the introspection era represents the birth-time of thought on learning, within a couple of decades, two primary deficiencies associated with introspection surfaced. First, data associated with self-examination was believed to be highly inaccurate. This is because subjects were unqualified to interpret or communicate about psychological phenomena. Second, some mental states are inaccessible to the self-examiner upon data collection. This is because often, humans are not aware of, do not recall, or cannot associate rationale with, behavior.

The Mechanistic-Individual Learning Period

Shortly after the turn of the century, researchers developed better ways for explaining behavior and examining the phenomenon of learning. Introspection fell into obsolescence due to the development of operational theories for describing human behavior. This stimulated an interest in the mechanics of human behavior, a philosophical viewpoint that serves as the foundation for structured theory on learning: the mechanistic period of individual learning.

Learning theory at varying levels of analysis began to take significant shape during the rapid adoption of *behaviorism* in the 1930s. Inspired primarily by John B. Watson (1913, 1924), behaviorist methodologies offered new opportunities to study learning in the fields of philosophy and psychology. By allowing the trained researcher to systematically interpret observed subject behavior, behaviorist methodologies represented a radical departure from introspective methods. Human behavior was quickly linked to one's ability to achieve desired consequences. Behaviorism argues that the only important subject matter in social sciences is behavioral action, not beliefs, attitudes, or other mental states. In studies about human learning, behaviorists attempted to change conditions that maintain or lead to maladaptive behavior. These were the first attempts at providing structure to the "black box" of learning behavior.

Theories deriving from pure behaviorism are termed *mechanistic* in nature, because they assume that the subject is essentially reactionary; absent of the ability for planning and self-modification. The Mechanistic Period denies the relevance of subject consciousness by espousing the belief that the unobservable mind could not be studied. Thus, subjects in mechanistic studies are assumed to be simple, unconscious and automatic reactors to the environment.

For data collection, mechanistic theories emphasize identifiable and measurable subject behavior. While convenient, the approach is biased towards behavioral *outcomes* and *results* while ignoring internalized *causes*. Heavily environmental, the mechanistic approach views the learning subject as a reactive organism, in which behavior is viewed as outward, reflex-responsive acts initiated by external forces. In this sense, learning occurs through a *reinforcement* process known as *conditioning*, during which *stimuli* are manipulated to take the form of either reward or discouragement. To researchers and managers, environmental stimuli are selected based on the desired *response*. In empirical studies involving mechanistic models, stimuli and responses represent researcher and subject behavior, respectively.

The mechanistic view introduced the important concept of *reinforcement*, which suggested that learning is a continuous, repetitive process. Luthans (1995) defines the reinforcement of behavior as, "anything that both increases the strength of response and tends to induce repetitions of the behavior that preceded the reinforcement." Reinforcement is externally controlled in the case of mechanistic learning, and relates to two major influences in learning theory: *classical* and *operant* conditioning.

Classical Conditioning

The first major influence in classical conditioning theory was established by Thorndike, who conceptualized learners as discrete, empathetic organisms who behave in the form of random and automatic responses to contrived external stimuli. This work influenced Pavlov's (1927) famous "stimulus-response" (S-R) experiments on dogs for understanding the classical conditioning process (the process by which new S-R connections are established to form reflex behavior). In his experiment, the dog learned that a conditioned, learned stimulus (the ringing of a bell) would soon be followed by a reward (feeding). Thus, classical conditioning occurs when subjects learn about the association between a previously neutral stimulus and another response stimulus.

Learning theory began taking shape as behaviorists watched their subjects learn new associations between conditions, situations, and contingencies in their environment. A tremendous amount of interest in learning theory was generated, because of its new-found ability to explain simple tasks. However, a major constraint to learning research was the reflexive nature of responses. To fill the need for a new set of theories that take into account voluntary, intentional behavior, the operant conditioning set of theories was formulated.

Operant Conditioning

In *operant conditioning*, stimuli serve the same role as in classical conditioning, but behavior is dictated through the subject's interpretation about consequences of that behavior. The ideas surrounding operant conditioning directly derived from the work of Thorndike (1911), who believed that individuals learn according to the *law of effect*, that subjects tend to repeat behaviors that are followed by good effects. In addition, they tend to stop behaviors that are not rewarded as such. B.F. Skinner (1938) translated Thorndike's law of effect into *operant conditioning*, which states that operant behaviors are learned when desired responses are either ignored or punished. Skinner replaced the idea of "good effects" with the *reinforcement process*.

There were two primary advances of operant conditioning over its classical conditioning foundation. First, operant conditioning offered a heavier emphasis on the subject's environment. Subject behavior was shaped by the utility of artifacts in its surroundings. Second, it introduced the notion of subject control over its environment. Both of these contributions advanced understandings about how to better manage behavior by manipulating environmental conditions.

The Organismic-Individual Learning Period

This class of learning theories sees the subject as an active organism performing independent, self-determining acts. Shani and Lau (1996) described the organismic approach as representing, "a universe that is a unitary, interactive, developing organism." Cognition and information processing models were developed in attempts at explaining *precursors to behavioral outcomes*. These models showed that subjects had important higher-order qualities that led to their observable behavior.

Two prominent streams of research were born from organismic considerations of behavioral preconditions. First, *cognitive learning theories* attempt to associate mental processes (perceptions, memory, attitudes, decision-making, etc.) with social behavior. Second, *social learning theories* focus on how the behavior of human subjects is affected by social peers. These two powerful branches of organismic thought are described in the following two sections.

The Cognition Era

Cognitive psychologists, like pioneer Hans Eysenck, found that learning models that included cognition and information use and handling were more powerful than mechanistic models in their prediction of behavior. The theory suggests that beings actively select stimuli and interpret stimuli-derived information, making behavior dependent on cognitive abilities. Human cognition is, "the process of knowing (thinking), sometimes distinguished from affect (emotion) and conation or volition (striving), in a triad of mental processes" (Marshall, 1994). The thinking/cognition realm of mental behavior emphasizes the continual evolution of a mental map through internalized mental *processes* that interpret environmental cues.

Cognitive models supplanted the S-R models because they were found to explain more human behavior by including mental operations such as *thought, perception, memory, attitudinal*, and *decision-making* processes (Worchel & Shebilske, 1992). More complex and dynamic models of learning are now dominant because they view learning in the form of variously proposed cognition and information handling processes. It is prominently believed that learning processes are so dependent upon context, that using highly generalizeable learning models (like the stimulus-response model) are incompatible with behavior in practice. For example, an emerging theory is "social learning theory," which includes the ability for subjects to observe and emulate others.

The Social Learning Era

Social learning theories evolved to integrate behaviorist and cognitive approaches by demonstrating how individuals learn by observing and imitating the behavior of social peers. Primarily limited to humans, social learning is experienced when the subject tries new behavior by observing others in social situations (Bandura, 1977). During successful trials, the behavior yields favorable results and is retained. During more negative situations, the subject may ask that others change. Social learning theory is unique because it attributes power to both the subject and the environment: they can affect one another. Behavior is determined by the continuous interaction between cognitive, behavioral, and environmental elements.

Social learning theories contributed greatly to the understanding of at least four important learning processes: vicarious learning, symbolism, self-control (Bowditch & Buono, 1989; Luthans & Kreitner, 1975), and *self-efficacy*. *Vicarious learning* derived from the belief that humans can imagine themselves in the place of peers. In many situations, learning by observing and imitating others can be more beneficial and easier than trial and error (systematic learning found in operant conditioning). *Symbolism* derived from the human ability to anticipate the responses of other humans. Human performers typically desire anticipating events before they experience them firsthand through mental, symbolic modeling. Social learning theories showed that managers could change results by *self-controlling* cognitive processes (e.g., symbolic models) and the environment. As a consequence, they could intervene in the organization by positively or negatively reinforcing worker behavior through organizational "self-reinforcement." Thus, internalized behaviors of the subject became commonly viewed as stimuli for external behavior. Finally, social learning theory emphasized subject *self-efficacy*, defined as one's judgment about his ability to perform well in a given situation (Bandura, 1982). One's self-efficacy is highly situation-dependent, and relies heavily on response-outcome expectations during the trial. Response-outcome expectations, the subject's judgment of likely outcomes associated with particular behaviors, is a more permanent perception than self-efficacy.

A History of Organizational Learning Theory

To this day, researchers continue to draw from other disciplines to seek better frameworks for envisioning how the modern organization should work. The following sections describe the evolution of thought on the organizational learning paradigm.

The Pre-Learning Period

The history of organizational learning begins with the origin of the organization, at one time a novel mechanism for enabling human survival. Alec Lee (1970) traced the origin of the organization concept back to the city of Jericho, a city of 3,000 members that dated back to 8,000 B.C. This first-known organization convened for the purpose of exploiting new collaborative agricultural techniques to better ensure the survival of its members. This began a long tradition of hierarchical rule in empires, nations, and organizations throughout history. During these early times of extreme hierarchical rule, organizations sought to survive with very little emphasis on intellectual cultivation, operating in the emergent learning era.

The *emergent learning era* represents a period in which organizations were unplanned structures that necessitated an emergent, natural state of OL. Although the evolution of organizational thought was in its infancy, the era has made contributions that are applicable to practice today. For example, Lee (1970) noted that the people of Jericho probably had a greater capacity for information memory than did members of modern literate societies. This is because they relied less on information stored in writing, a new information technology at that time. The trend of reliance upon technology, and its influence on changing the nature of human and organizational life, continues today.

The pre-learning era completely ignored the nature of, and existing differentials in, organizational and individual experiences and knowledge. As a result, the pace of innovation and technological adoption was the slowest during this era, as was necessary. As technologies became more advanced, new models for their organizational assimilation became apparent and articulated in mechanistic paradigms.

The Mechanistic-Organizational Learning Period

Similar to the mechanistic period of individual learning, the Mechanistic-Organizational Learning Period began a long tradition of observing organizational entities. However, it was the development of industrial tools that made observations about changes in collective behavioral performance possible. The need for organizational survival and prosperity hinged on the organization's ability to implement large, collectively used tools in the *Tool Implementation Era*.

The Tool Implementation Era

Adam Smith's Wealth of Nations (1776), the seminal literary contribution to the industrial revolution, was also the impetus for the *tool implementation era* for organizational learning theory. Smith introduced powerful organizational concepts that greatly impacted international wealth distributions, employment, and the outcomes of wars. His theories espoused division of labor, mass production, line assembly, economies of scale, and government-sponsored education. These radically new concepts were based upon the implementation of large, industrial-sized tools that were used to determine collective success.

The introduction of thinking about continuous organizational change can be attributed to the work of Fredrick Taylor (1911), whose scientific management concepts improved organizational efficiency in the early 1900s. Taylor considered management to be a science in itself, and suggested the use of quantitative analysis methods using objective data in order to achieve incremental efficiency gains. By using these techniques successfully, managers became more receptive to the notion that organizations can be test subjects for new tools.

The implementation and use of large tools were fairly long-term projects, enabling the retention of top-down, autocratic management styles that resisted systematic change. In the presence of static competitive environments, methods for organizing for greater work efficiency became popular in the form of bureaucracy (Weber, 1995) and functional management (Fayol, 1949). In order to make these rigid structures more ergonomic, management began implementing techniques aimed at fostering human relations (McGregor, 1960) between workers and the organization. However, much of the interactions between management and workers were based on the premise of avoiding disputes related to labor policies, and not capitalizing on member knowledge that might result in worker empowerment, or organizational improvement.

The Learning Curve Era

The *learning curve era* represents the first attempts at quantifying collective learning. First formulated and documented by Wright (1936)[3], (organizational) learning curves empirically showed that the average cost of producing airplanes decreased as production increased. He attributed this to the learning enacted by workers, who learned through repetition with the task, workstation, and tools. Thus, this era explicitly attributed gains in organizational production outcomes to worker knowledge and learning. The tradition of learning curve research extends to many important genres in modern organizational research, due to the convenience of data brought about by information technologies embedded in modern production and operations facilities.

The Organismic-Organizational Learning Period

Pursuant to internalized precursors and contexts that affect desired outcomes, the Tool Adoption Era was subsequently outdated by more robust approaches to technology assimilation. The *redesign* and *organizational learning* eras focused on the organizational factors that enhance effective organizational adaptation.

The Redesign Era

The continuous redesign era signifies the first organismic view of competitive firms. This era suggested that organizations should proactively research, manage, and design organizational change in perpetuity. Lippitt, Watson and Westley's *Dynamics of Planned Change* (1958) was the first in-depth investigation of change as a discipline in itself. Although the OL concept was not the focus of their book (the term *"organizational learning"* did not exist at the time), Schein (1996) states: "the field of planned change and organization development is all about learning."

The continuous redesign era focused on improving the quality and effectiveness of organizational operations. Management programs such as total quality management (TQM) and business process reengineering (BPR) surfaced to help top managers learn as never before about areas in the organization that were candidate subunits for change. TQM, espoused by Deming (1986), was characterized by "bottom-up" communication from operations, operations workers, and customers to top management, a radical departure from the traditional mechanistic protocol.   BPR signified a top-down enforcement of change (Hammer & Champy, 1993), a risky and unpopular technique that necessitates a reinstatement of temporary hierarchy so the organization can overcome severe misalignment between structure and environment.

The contribution of the continuous redesign era was two important organizational disciplines: incremental and radical change. These change mechanisms allowed organizations to formulate and reformulate themselves into a desired state over time. Born from change management was *benchmarking*, the ability for managers to compare quantified abstractions with those of other firms. Benchmark measures proliferated because they enlightened management about organizational efficiency and effectiveness that greatly enhanced competitive sustenance. Organizations proactively and incrementally improved processes that led to the outcome performance measures so heavily emphasized in mechanistic eras. However, its most important contribution is an organizational awareness to improve change mechanisms.

This era was characterized by two managerial concerns: (1) implementing organizational designs that facilitate learning, and (2) getting employees to adopting a learning culture (Schein, 1996).   These efforts have recently convened to treat OL as a useful means for explaining the behavior of organizations and their members, providing stimulus for the second organismic era: behavioral enactment of OL.

The Learning Organization Era

Dodgson (1993) credited Cyert and March (1963) with the explicit introduction of the term "organizational learning" to organizational theorists. Stimulus for the topic derived from pressure on U.S. companies to compete with a Japanese cultural tradition that paid particular attention to OL (Pucik, 1988).   The prescriptions described by Cyert and March assumed that worker *behavior*, not propitious to organizational learning, was the primary deficiency in the global marketplace.

This era introduced the notion that organizations change incrementally and radically as an expected and natural function of organizational life. Thus, TQM and BPR are cyclical behaviors, inherent within the organizational culture. Most descriptions of OL describe two modes of cyclical processing: single- (SLL) and double-loop learning (DLL). These learning modes correspond directly to the *continuous redesign era* techniques of TQM and BPR, respectively.   The primary difference is that during the OL era, these two behavioral alternatives were not techniques to be implemented, but normal organizational functions. Refer to Templeton and Snyder (1999)[4] for an integrative model of organizational learning processes, modes, and intelligence.

Specific behaviors that manifest OL were described in the work of Huber (1991), who developed a taxonomy of behaviors enacted through the members of successful learning organizations. According to Huber, the four primary phases of OL are knowledge acquisition, information distribution, information interpretation, and organizational memory. Researchers in the organizational learning era have also proposed a myriad of factors that facilitate, precede, and result from organizational learning processing (Templeton & Snyder, 2000). Used in combination with organizational aspects (i.e., politics, hierarchy, structural rigidity, etc.) that work counter to the organizational learning effort, these factors provide powerful explanations for managing for OL success.

In summary, the behavioral enactment era is significant because it empowers individuals to improve organizational learning, a construct that includes top management concerns of radical and incremental adaptation. Furthermore, organizational learning theory is intended to influence *organizational intelligence*, the firm's competency in self-controlling learning processes (Huber, 1991; Templeton & Snyder, 1999). This speaks to the significance "learning to learn" through experience gained by coordinating the organization's learning processes. This skill is known as *deutero learning*, the highest order of intelligence available to competitive entities.

TECHNOLOGICAL INFLUENCES IN THE EVOLUTION OF LEARNING RESEARCH

One primary factor that has caused a need for organizational learning is the increasing dynamicity of technological proliferation in societies. An analysis of the two cumulative traditions of learning research teaches us that *technology*[5] has greatly impacted its theoretical development. This can be seen clearly by observing the history of organizations in the 20th century. In modern organizations, we might find that robotics support operations, computer-aided design supports reframing, CASE tools support radical change, and the Internet supports knowledge acquisition.

Described in order of increasing complexity and hence evolutionary ascension, technology categories (tasks, tools, knowledge, and techniques) are used as a framework in the ensuing sections to describe the influence technology has had on society's view of entity learning. Over time, theorists have attempted to describe entity interactions with increasingly more complex technologies. Figure 1 illustrates a hierarchy of technology, as differentiated along two dimensions: *ease of learning* and *complexity*. The figure shows that as the epistemological complexity of a given technology increases, ease of learning tends to decrease. *Tasks* are epistemologically least complex, while *techniques*, which require an understanding of each of the three more simple technologies, is most complex.

Ease of learning is the level simplicity in understanding the contents of a given technology category. The ease of learning a given technology has impacted the evolution of theoretic interest by human and organizational theo-

Figure 1:   The Technology Hierarchy

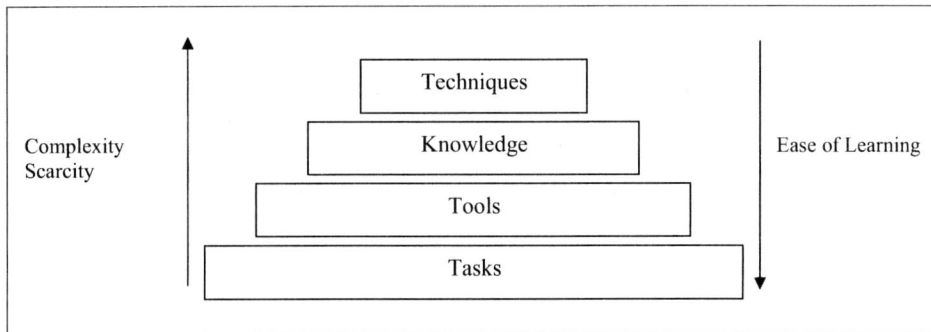

rists. For instance, researchers were first interested in simple tasks, because they were easily observable, and not yet explained. Epistemological complexity is the degree of difficulty required in, or the extent to which there are barriers associated with, obtaining a level of understanding about a given technology. Technologies that are more complex are inherently more economically beneficial, but are scarce because they are difficult to learn and distribute. Researchers focused on entity interaction with more complex technologies in later research, because those types of interactions were scarcer, and it was necessary to build the foundations of learning theory upon easily observable tasks.

Ease of learning and epistemological complexity impact other attributes of a given technology, such as scarcity and diffusion rate. For instance, we do not expect understandings about techniques to be readily prevalent in a given society, since it is most complex, and more difficult to learn. Since complex technologies are more scarce and in greater economic demand, greater uncertainty exists about their acquisition and use. This uncertainty inevitably causes heightened levels of environmental dynamicity, as community participants are unsure about the economic and operational costs associated with their adoption.   This uncertainty causes an increased need for entity interaction with the environment. Since the nature of demands placed on entities in technologically complex environments are systemic, subjects seek models for self-design and behavior that explain heavy environmental interaction. This is why theories will continue to place greater emphasis on the environment as the more simple technologies progress into the technique category.

Tasks

Deriving from that mindset, the first part of the Mechanistic Period was heavily influenced by the desire to understand basic tasks. A *task* is a simple undertaking involving labor or difficulty. A task is a burdensome, straining, overtaxing act that is not usually associated with skill, cognitive requisite, the use of specialized tools, or thinking. For this reason, tasks are usually assigned to, or required of, subordinates. The planning, directing, and controlling of tasks was the nature of work and organizational management for the first half of the Mechanistic Period.

At the individual level of analysis, the Master Teacher, Introspection, and part (Classical Conditioning) of Behaviorism are based on understanding the human performance of simple tasks. The Emergent Organizational Learning Era focused on the enabling, and often controlling, of greater productivity by large numbers of people. The idea was to achieve greater outcomes of simple tasks by accumulating larger numbers of workers. This was the impetus for the creation of organizational life. For instance, the Jericho account informs us of the need for collectivism at that time. The organizational concept began as a coincidence of necessity, with very little organizational formality. Members relied heavily upon tasks, and had a relatively diminutive reliance upon the sharing, development, and use of tools, knowledge, and techniques.

Tools

Later in the Mechanistic Period, it was found that for humans, the conception, development, and use of new *tools* are innate endeavors. A tool is anything that serves in the manner of an instrument, implement, device, or utensil. It is any foreign object designed and constructed to help an entity accomplish its purposes.

Behaviorism evolved into a mindset aimed at understanding the human operation of tools in the form of Operant Conditioning models. Behaviorists developed operant conditioning theories because it was observed that subjects commonly "operate," or manipulate environmental structures proactively to help them achieve an intended goal. Thus, operant conditioning, by considering the *use* of environmental structures to achieve objectives, introduced a more complex technological concept to individual learning theory.

At the organizational level of analysis, the Tool Implementation Era began to change the nature of organizational and societal life. Adam Smith's (1776) work offered organizations the first meaningful opportunity to adopt performance-enhancing tools. However, the propositions by Smith retained an extremely hierarchical structure, since there were still very few varying tools to adopt. The number of available tools gradually grew as information technologies increased rates of scientific progress.

The Tool Implementation Era espoused a piecemeal approach to technology assimilation that caused a great deal of inter-unit segregation and infrastructural inefficiency that was difficult to quantify. By promoting hierarchy, the Tool Implementation Era necessitated and assumed almost perfect knowledge in top management and very little knowledge elsewhere.

The Learning Curve Era was made possible due to advances in the embedding of information technology in tool-based operations. The Learning Curve Era continues to proliferate today (Uzumeri & Nembhard, 1998), due to the radical advancements in the expedition of data via modern information technologies. However, the nature of the data used in learning curve analyses remains biased towards organizational and collective worker outcomes. By definition, learning curve analyses ignore higher-order organizational experiences that translate to a great deal of healthy innovation.

Knowledge

As humans became familiarized with tasks and tools, they realized that knowledge was the precursor to their creations. They found that further enlightenment and new knowledge was gained through the use of the tools while performing their work. As they became more familiar with the new range of behaviors that became possible with the new tools, they became aware of improvements that would lead to further capability and understanding.

The theories of the Organismic Period accepted the construction and use of new knowledge to be of perpetual concern to humans striving to *design* internalized (e.g., planning, creativity, imagination, decision-making, and adapting) behaviors, as well as manifest behaviors. By focusing on ongoing collective processes, the Self-Redesign Era brought about organizational designs that outmoded those companies that retained Tool Implementation Era philosophies. The Self-Redesign Era assumed and capitalized upon a tremendous amount of knowledge that was available among all organizational members.

The Cognition and Social Learning Eras were heavily knowledge-based. Cognition theories were founded on internal information handling processes, while Social Learning theories focused on the subject's capacity for capturing and processing environmental information and knowledge. These theories focused on using subject peers as sources of information. Each of these views utilizes the role of technology in influencing subject behavior. In particular, information technology has influenced social learning studies in at least three ways. First, information networks connected massive global enterprises, enabling larger gatherings of workers with which to socialize. Second, information technology has improved the breadth of human interaction by connecting disparate users via networking (e.g., local area networks, the Internet, data warehousing, etc.). Third, powerful information processing terminals placed on the desktops of workers has made individuals behave in effectively more intelligent ways.

Techniques

A technique is a particular style or method used to perform work. Techniques first require a degree of expertness, upon which a decision is made regarding a particular method for accomplishing something. Techniques are the most complex category of technology, because they require an understanding about each of the other technology types: task, tool and knowledge.

Learning organizational behavior models, like Templeton and Snyder's (1999) Technology Control Model, treat collective cognition as the most important technology that can be adopted by any organization. The reason is that learning models subscribe to no particular organizational form in terms of its selection and configuration of technology (tasks, tools, knowledge, and techniques). Some entities have adopted different techniques of learning, or ways of using its learning skills.

A THEORY OF LEARNING MATURITY

Learning maturity is applicable when subjects use external structures (i.e., technologies) in new and novel ways to perform behaviors that were previously unattainable. For example, when a computer programmer edits code, he or she is performing behavioral outcomes that are not achievable without use of the applicable technology (a computer and the necessary software). Such behaviors could not be adequately explained by previous notions of learning (such as introspection, cognition, or social learning) because behavioral outcomes were perceived to be a function of natural intelligence and not dependent on technological variation (i.e., complexity, scarcity, and ease of learning). Three perspectives are essential to understanding the many concepts and relationships embodied in the proposed theory of learning maturity: description of the theory, the path to learning maturity, and the elements of learning maturity capability. These three sections ensue.

Learning Maturity Described

It is important to see learning maturity in its nomological network of related concepts. Previous conceptualizations of intelligence omit technological competencies altogether (see Figure 2). Adding learning maturity, a capability (such as cognition) that can impact behavioral outcomes (such as demonstrated intelligence) to the model greatly increases the implications for intelligence (Figure 3). For the purposes of discussion, an explanation of the following *effective intelligence equation* is necessary:

$$EI = NI + TI(f_{LM})$$

where:
EI = effective intelligence
NI = natural intelligence
TI = technological intelligence (which is a function of learning maturity)

Figure 2: Prominent Notion of the Determinants of Intelligence

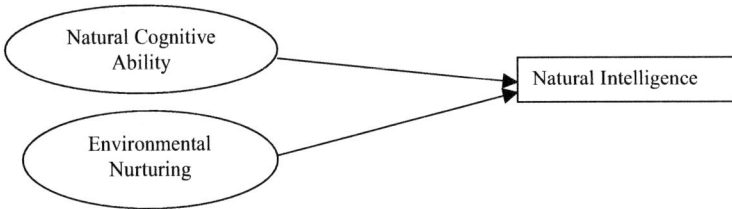

Figure 3: Proposed Model of Effective Intelligence

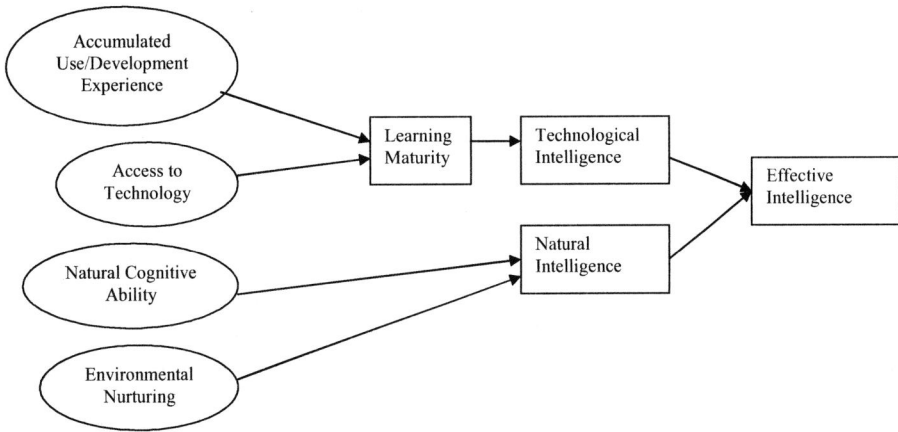

The effective intelligence equation indicates two distinct domains of intelligence: the natural and technological. In the natural domain, intelligence remains independent of technological interactions. The technological domain is the primary contribution of this chapter. It shows that effective intelligence can be augmented by the accessibility and the use of technology. That is, humans have the potential to behave more effectively intelligent with than without technology. It also shows that intelligence in the technological domain is a function of learning maturity (and accordingly subject to future research). Although the learning maturity concept is also distinct from natural intelligence, it has a direct effect on intelligence in the technological domain.

Figure 4 illustrates how the equation can be applied in greater detail. The Y axis indicates levels of intellectual competence, which is divided into three capabilities: effective intellectual potential, learning maturity, and the prominently accepted concept of intelligence quotient (IQ). Effective intellectual

Figure 4: The Effect of Technologically Mediated Learning Trials on Intellectual Outcomes

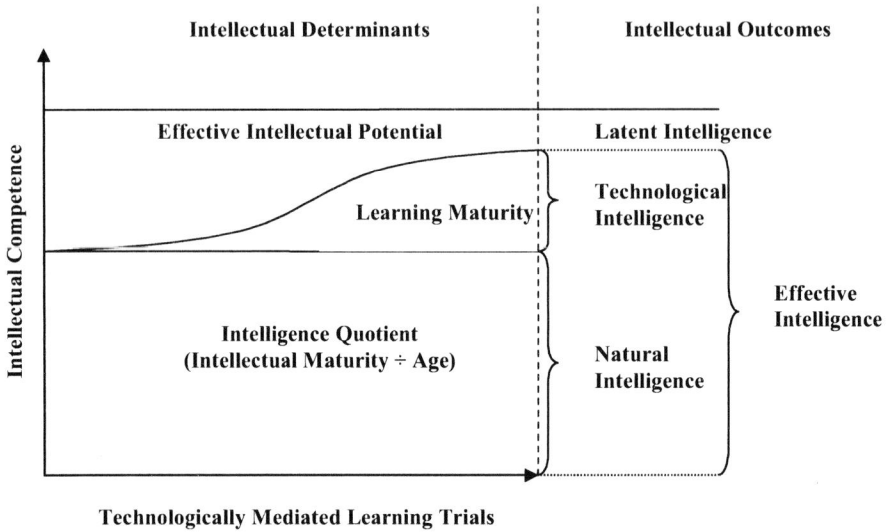

potential is the actor's capacity for intelligence, including natural and technology-dependent behaviors. Learning maturity is the actor's capability for performing behaviors dependent upon interactions with technology. Intelligence quotient is the traditional use of the term, indicating natural and nurtured intelligence.

The X axis represents the extent to which the actor has experienced technologically mediated learning trials, which is divided into two perspectives: determinants (stimuli or contexts) and outcomes (observable behavior). Each intellectual determinant has a counterpart in the outcomes perspective of intelligence: latent, technological, and natural. Latent intelligence is the difference between one's capacity for effective intelligence (effective intellectual potential) and manifested effective intelligence, which is dependent upon technological and natural intelligence. The figure shows that as an actor experiences technologically mediated learning trials (and those trials subsequently vary in complexity), learning maturity is developed. Technological intelligence is then substantiated as a part of effective intelligence.

Effective intelligence is the observed ability of an actor to demonstrate a wide range of intelligent outcomes, including those affected by natural and technical competencies. *Natural intelligence* is limited to the ability to react competently in task-oriented (simple) situations and is not affected by the influence of technology. *Technological intelligence* is the ability of an actor to use and develop technology for intended purposes. Shown as a cause-effect model in Figure 3, a significant feature of the model is that TI is a function of LM (the structure of such will require additional research not provided here). The significance of learning maturity is that it is a important way to maximize *effective intelligence* in the full range of situated actions. Learning maturity enables actors to incorporate more complex technological forms in the confrontation of problem-solving situations. This model de-emphasizes the traditional focus on natural intelligence. It says that observed worker performance (measured in EI units) can be "nurtured" with technology.

Thus, learning maturity is one of the requisites for achieving intended behavioral outcomes and explains one's ability to perform in a range of problem-solving situations that are longer in term and more complex and ambiguous. It fills a void in the tradition of learning theory because previous conceptualizations ignore the fact that humans and organizations distinguish between technologies when confronted with problem situations. Discerning between technologies is crucial in modern, adaptive organizations as management grapples with decisions regarding future interaction (development and use) with technology.

The previous section explains that as learning thought has moved from mechanistic to organismic periods, we notice an increasing interest in explaining entity interactions with more complex technologies. It articulates a *technology complexity hierarchy* whereby different technologies have different complexities among other attributes. For instance, within the mechanistic-organizational period, learning theory began to be influenced by societal fascinations with the mechanical precision and workings of clocks in the 19th century, and advanced towards explaining the use of large, highly automated production machines in the Industrial Revolution. The period began with a concern for simple *tasks*, and ended with the newfound consideration of *tools*. Later, the more complex *techniques* for working and living created a need for more updated models for explaining behavior. For instance, increased support of individuals by intelligent terminals, increased telecommunications networking, and consequentially, the sharing and dissemination of knowledge, brought about the organismic-organizational era. These examples show a shift in interest from simple to complex knowledge artifacts and an ensuing *maturation* of the field. This notion extends prior conceptualizations about learning organizations purposing to simply accumulate its knowledge base.

The theory has implications for understanding the role of user versus developer in technology interactions. Using the example of learning research, the knowledge developer (researcher) takes on learning burdens (complexity, ambiguity, unstructuredness, and technology) and transfers a product (published research) to a less-consumed user (reader). Likewise, in the field of systems development, the goal is to transfer complexities associated with situated action (i.e., organizational decision-making) from the user to the developer, who we assume has greater learning maturity.

Reaching Learning Maturity

The learning theory eras and periods previously described indicate the evolutionary path of *deutero* learners (in the case, these are both organization scientists and the learning research community). Deutero learning is the act of learning how to learn, a crucial determinant of an actor's ability to reach maximum learning maturity. All processes and sub-processes of learning, however they manifest themselves, are subject to modification via deutero learning. These processes commonly include incremental and radical change and the reframing of mental models. Deutero learning is a key assumption to the learning maturity theory. An actor can only aspire to reach advanced levels of intelligence if it can control its level of intellectual process quality. Reaching learning maturity requires traversing an arduous path, as indicated by the publication process itself. Conveniently, lessons about evolving from immature to mature learners are embodied in practically all human endeavors. The following two sections describe key aspects of reaching learning maturity.

Evolving from Mechanistic- to Organismic-Individual Learning

Table 2 depicts the three factors and 16 criteria that differentiate the two periods of thought, and consequentially, the learning maturity of learning entities. The three factors that differentiate mechanistic and organismic learners are: epistemological focus, subject characteristics, and information processing style. This table serves as a guide for further reading in this section, and as a theoretic mechanism for developing measures that differentiate between mechanistic and organismic learners.

Despite its contribution to learning theory, mechanistic theories and modes of learning fall prey to two theoretic deficiencies. First, mechanistic theories imply an ignorance of confounding variables. For instance, the operant conditioning approach to learning was deficient because it did not consider the following important classifications of variables: (1) biological predispositions, (2) social, and (3) cognitive (Worchel & Shebilske, 1992). Biological predispositions involve considerations for the differences in the physical makeup of subjects. Social variables related to how the subject learns from other subjects in social settings, a common occurrence in human subjects.

Second, hypothesis testing of mechanistic theories was too strict for practical use (in interactions with complex technologies in particular). S-R learning models denied that consciousness is a relevant factor in determining human behavior, and empirical propositions that used the theory suggested that conditioning was simple, unconscious, and automatic. In short, S-R has been criticized because it explains only reactionary, blind, or automatic adjustments and does not explain the creation of new knowledge (Miller, 1996). Concerning hypothesis testing, the mechanistic S-R viewpoint was found to be severely limited. This was due to strict cause-effect relationships, which were often

Table 2:   Factors and Criteria that Differentiate Between Mechanistic and Organismic-Individual Learning

Factor	Criteria	Mechanistic	Organismic
Epistemological Focus	Technological Influence	Tasks and tools	Knowledge and techniques
	Nature of Testing	Confirmatory	Eternally exploratory
	Variable Relationships	Strict cause-effect	Loose association
	Variables Considered	Externally observed stimuli and responses	Subject thinking, feeling, & intentions
	Variable Predisposition	Behavioral outcomes & results:	Causes of behavioral outcomes and results:
		˄ Achievement of desired consequences	˄ Entity inputs
		˄ Identifiable and measurable behavior	˄ Processes
		˄ Account for what subjects are doing	˄ Precursors and contexts
	Contributions	˄ Learning is a continuous, repetitive process	˄ Confounding variables (biological, social, & cognitive, etc.)
		˄ Learning can be observed	˄ Internalized mental processes (perceptions, memory, attitudes, decision-making, etc.)
		˄ Environment influences behavior	˄ Precursors to behavior (planning, creativity, imagination, decision-making, adapting, etc.)
Subject Characteristics	Role of Environmental Variables	Determinant	Partially explanatory
	Role of Subject	Unconscious	Self determining & developing
	Subject Understanding	Parsed (considers outward behavior only)	Holistic
	Source of Information	Environment	Environment, social peers, and internalized phenomena (knowledge, beliefs, standards, experience, goals, etc.)
Information Processing Style	Behavioral Causes	Environment only	Environment & internalized phenomena
	Means for control	Externally controlled reinforcement	Self-reinforcement
	Adaptation Processes	Conditioning (classical & operant)	Cognition and information processing models
	Adaptation Mode	Responsive, reactionary	Interactive
	Adaptation Complexity	Simple, Unconscious & Automatic	First filters through consciousness
	Outcomes	Behavior	Behavior & behavioral consequences

found to be invalid in empirical analyses. Mental processes and states often confounded tests of the S-R relationship, causing problems with proposed conjectures. This problem was alleviated by successful separation of the subject's intention to behave from the subject's actual behavior.

Evolving from Mechanistic- to Organismic-Organizational Learning

Although it made momentous philosophical contributions to societies relative to the Pre-Learning Period, the mechanistic-organizational era was not suited for adaptation to more complex technologies. Table 3 serves as the integrative reference for describing factors and criteria that differentiate mechanistic and organismic learning organizations.

Although organizations were eventually recognized as learning entities by the conclusion of the mechanistic OL period, it was supplanted due to serious faults in its assumptions. Mechanistic OL had three primary faults: (1) it was too incrementalist for modern rates of technological proliferation, (2) it ignored the intellectual capital and knowledge of the organization and its members, and (3) it focused too heavily upon outcomes.

The Tool Adoption Era also had serious faults. First, it assumed that organizations could sustain themselves over time by remaining highly incrementalist, mechanistic, simplistic, and reactionary. The common theme among all deficiencies with the mechanistic era was that performance was measured by focusing on effects and outcomes and not on causes and preconditions. Historically, top management primarily focused on decreasing visible costs while increasing productivity counts, an effectively short-term strategy. This period is well documented in Edward Deming's (1986) condemnation of "VNO" (visible numbers only), a shortsighted managerial philosophy that overemphasizes organizational results (i.e., earnings per share, profit, market share, etc.). The eradication of this problem is the focus of the *process change* and *quality* and *knowledge management* movements that persist today. These movements brought about the *Organismic Period* of organizational learning.

In sum, mechanistic theories are flawed because they are extremely simplistic in nature: they account for what subjects are doing, not what they are thinking, feeling, or intend to do. The inclusion of cognition and information-handling processes soon supplanted conditioning. The *Organismic Period* built on the Mechanistic Period of learning by contributing an important set of variables that are internalized by subjects.

Four Learning Maturity Capabilities

It is commonly held that learning results in an accumulation of knowledge in organizational memory. Another key outcome of learning is the actor's capability improvements. This section builds on that understanding by describing how some learning behaviors are better suited for learning complex technologies.

Table 3: Factors and Criteria that Differentiate Between Mechanistic- and Organismic-Organizational Learning

Factor	Criteria	Mechanistic	Organismic
	Managerial ideal	Reward and punish based on results	Eliminate behaviors and structures that counter *learning*; Design effective *knowledge* structures; *Educate* about organizational disciplines
Epistemological Focus	Variable predisposition	Focus on outcomes	Focus on collective intellectual processes and states
	Dependent variables	'VNO' measures: costs, aggregate productivity, profit, units produced, etc.	Quality measures: effectiveness, customer and worker satisfaction, learning ability, competence, etc.
	Independent variables	'VNO', demography, & environment	Technique, skill, knowledge, strategic positioning, etc.
	Structural setting	Hierarchical	Designed for incremental and radical change
Subject	Control mechanisms	Policy, structure, hierarchy	Motivation from coaching, support, & feedback
Characteristics	IT assimilation approach	Piecemeal & ad hoc	Fits OL processing paradigm
	Cultural rigidity	Formal	Informal
	Source of competency	Functional areas	Learning processes (i.e., DLL, SLL, & deutero)
	Knowledge acquisition mechanism	Top management directorate	Learning-facilitating organizational designs
Information	Adaptation complexity	Simplistic; reactionary	Complex; deutero learning
Processing	Goal of decision-making	Discrete conclusions	Solutions on continuous scale
Style	Decision-making style	Logical, concrete reasoning	Intuition; inclusive of sustaining relationships and context
	Emphasis on knowledge during decision-making	Based on minimal competence	Heavy reliance upon investigation of process
	Attitude towards risk	Fear of failure	Risk taking yields new knowledge

Thus, learning maturity is the capacity each entity has for learning in situations where learning is contextually delimited. Among the attributes of learning situations are complexity, ambiguity, structure, and technology. Mature learners operate well in a wider range of situations relative to immature learners. In this vein, it is strongly related to intelligence, environmental adaptability, and the attainment of all beneficial consequences attributed to learning (Templeton & Snyder, 2000). However, learning maturity includes considerations of technological use and development. Technology attributes include ease of use and development, relative advantage, accessibility, compatibility, and others, which in turn affect the learning maturity needed on behalf of the user-actor.

Based on the aforementioned observed history of thought on learning, there are four capabilities of learning maturity. First, mature learners are competent at *continuous change*, which involves continuous writing to organizational memory. In the review of learning literature above, for both levels of analysis, there are three distinct periods found in the long tradition of learning research: pre-learning, mechanistic, and organismic. Within these periods, long traditions of purposeful incremental adaptation ensued within the field of inquiry.

Second, competence in *discontinuous change* is a natural consequence of being and one important element of learning maturity. It is important for actors to anticipate and plan and design for periods of abrupt change. This is supported by several major specific contributions to learning theory emphasized in the history.

Third, mature learners competently *redefine the organizational memory structure* since organizations change priorities due to environmental change. In the learning history, it was shown that the technology variable has consistently had a discrete, yet major impact on developments in learning paradigms at the individual and organizational levels. As technology becomes more complex, difficult to learn, and scarce, markets and environments pertaining to a given technology become more turbulent, causing a need for greater learning (and learning maturity).

Fourth, *structuration* is an element of learning maturity capability. In the case history described, many of the structures created, articulated, and studied in the field were done so because of the natural demands of its participants. Members of organizations demand structure, and organizations need structure for future learning to occur. Mature learning organizations strive to create structures that fit existing worldviews and purpose to enable self design and control. For instance, the current research proposes a theory of learning maturity, based on an entity's capacity for learning complex technologies. This research contributes factors, each composed of multiple criteria that differentiate between low (mechanistic) and high (organismic) learning maturity. The theory extends decades of cumulative research on how organizations and individuals interact with (use and develop) technology by focusing on the issue

of capability. Thus, the process of structuration continues as a crucial consequence of the existence of the field of learning theory.

SUMMARY AND CONCLUSION

The case learning history, provided in the long tradition of research on
individual and organizational learning, provided several important elements in the
discussion of learning maturity. The two major periods found in the cumulative
traditions of both levels of analysis are *mechanistic* and *organismic*. From a
broad standpoint, this evolution was necessitated because of incompleteness in
prior theoretical conceptualizations. One primary inhibitor in the continued
development of the field (towards measurement and determinism) is a more
complete treatment of technology. The recurring influence of (a broad definition
of) technology on learning theory is observable. As technologies have grown
more complex over time, learning paradigms at the individual and organizational
levels have adapted in order to fit the technological environment. This phenomenon occurs as a result of the difficulty in learning more advanced, complex
technologies, which contributes to a greater environmental turbulence and,
consequently, a greater need for learning. Four technology categories were
presented, based on increasing complexity, and decreasing ease of learning.
These categories were used to explain changes in learning theory, and to suggest
an explanation for why humans and organizations strive to learn technologies that
are growing more complex.

The chapter presented a theory of learning maturity whereby there are two
beneficial consequences of its development. First, this research offers new
explanations for influencing the progression of learning theory, based on
observations made about the cumulative tradition of research on the subject at
two levels of analysis: individual and organizational. The theory shows how
learning theory will continue to advance, based upon the increased complexities
of technologies with which entities interact. Although the relationship between
technology and theoretic development is more discrete at the human level of
analysis, the influence appears to apply towards understanding the future of
learning for both subject levels. Second, for the first time, the theory leads to
important new propositions about modern learning theory. Founded upon
assumptions about technological complexity, the theory explains why entities
interact with situations where learning is most difficult. The theory espouses the
belief that entities seek to learn complex technologies, because they wish to
exploit situations of scarcity in the face of environmental uncertainty about
acquisition and use.

It is proposed here that mechanistic and organismic learning exists in all
consciously adapting entities to some extent. Three primary factors distinguish
between mechanistic and organismic learners: epistemological focus, subject

characteristics, and information processing style. These factors were used to develop 16 specific criteria that are unique to individual and organizational subjects. The taxonomies include criteria for differentiating between learning mature and immature subjects. Additionally, four capabilities of mature learners was derived from the study. First, from the case discussion, it is clear from the review of the development of learning theory that the field experiences periods of incremental adjustment. Second, migration between the periods and eras of learning discourse indicates that the field also experiences disruptive periods. Third, the collective memory of the field is always being redefined through theoretical developments such as learning maturity. Finally, the process of structuration is evident in the consistent inclusion of additional theorems, frameworks, terms, and ideas generated in the field. Learning theories have been consistently supplanted generally to provide new theoretical structures. For instance, the mechanistic theories were supplanted because: (1) they tended to ignore confounding issues, (2) assumptions about cause-effect were too strict, (3) had little regard for environmental interaction, (4) were too incrementalist, (5) ignored intellectual capital and processes, and (6) focused too heavily upon outcomes.

This chapter uncovers several avenues for further research. The taxonomy can be used in future research to develop empirical measures of learning maturity in organizations and their members. The theory should be applied to varying situations involving requisites for mature learning, including classrooms, high-technology labor markets, and learning organizations. The theory can help explain why some individuals and organizations seek knowledge about complex technologies and some do not. It can also explain the scarcity of knowledge in high-demand fields that require information systems' development and use.

ACKNOWLEDGMENTS

The author greatly appreciates Craig Knight for his consultation on this research.

REFERENCES

Argyris, C. & Schon, D. A. (1978). *Organizational Learning: A Theory of Action Perspective*. Reading, MA: Addison-Wesley.

Bandura, A. (1977). *Social Learning Theory*. Englewood Cliffs, NJ: Prentice-Hall.

Bandura, A. (1982). Self-efficacy mechanism in human agency. *American Psychologist*, 18, 122-147.

Bowditch, J. L. & Buono, A. F. (1989). *A Primer on Organizational Behavior* (2nd ed.). New York: John Wiley & Sons.

Cyert, R. M. & March, J. G. (1963). *A Behavioral Theory of the Firm.* Englewood Cliffs, NJ: Prentice Hall.

Deming, W. E. (1986). *Out of the Crisis.* Cambridge, MA: MIT Press.

Dodgson, M. (1993). Organizational learning: A review of some literatures. *Organization Studies,* 14(3), 375-394.

Drucker, P. F. (1989). *The New Realities.* New York: Harper and Row.

Fayol, H. (1949). *General and Industrial Management* (C. Storrs, Trans.). London: Pitman.

Hammer, M. & Champy, J. (1993). *Reengineering the Corporation.* New York: Harper Collins.

Huber, G. P. (1991). Organizational learning: The contributing processes and the literatures. *Organization Science,* 2(1), 88-115.

Kiernan, J. M. (1993). The new strategic architecture: Learning to compete in the twenty-first century. *Academy of Management Executive,* 7(1), 7-21.

Kleiner, A. & Roth, G. (1997). How to make experience your company's best teacher. *Harvard Business Review,* 75(5), 172-178.

Kuhn, T. S. (1962). *The Structure of Scientific Revolutions.* Chicago, IL: University of Chicago Press.

Lee, A. (1970). *Systems Analysis Frameworks.* New York: John Wiley and Sons.

Lippitt, R., Watson, J., & Westley, B. (1958). *The Dynamics of Planned Change.* New York: Harcourt, Brace.

Luthans, F. (1995). *Organizational Behavior* (7th ed.). New York: McGraw-Hill.

Luthans, F. & Kreitner, R. (1975). *Organizational Behavior Modification.* Glenview: Scott Foresman.

Marshall, G. (1994). *The Concise Oxford Dictionary of Sociology.* Oxford: Oxford University.

Martin, P. Y. & Turner, B. A. (1986). Grounded Theory and organizational research. *The Journal of Applied Behavioral Science,* 22(2), 141-157.

McGregor, D. (1960). *The Human Side of Enterprise.* New York: McGraw-Hill.

Miller, D. (1996). A preliminary typology of organizational learning: Synthesizing the literature. *Journal of Management,* 22(3), 485-505.

Orlikowski, W. (1992). The duality of technology: Rethinking the concept of technology in organizations. *Organization Science,* 3(3), 398-427.

Pavlov, I. P. (1927). *Conditioned Reflexes.* New York: Oxford University Press.

Pucik, V. (1988). Strategic alliances with the Japanese: Implications for human resource management. In F. Contractor & P. Lorange (Eds.), *Cooperative Strategies in International Business.* Lexington, MA: Lexington Books.

Schein, E. H. (1996). Culture: The missing concept in organization studies. *Administrative Science Quarterly,* 41(2), 229-240.

Shani, A. B. & Lau, J. B. (1996). *Behavior in Organizations: An Experiential Approach* (6ᵗʰ ed.). Chicago, IL: Irwin.

Skinner, B. F. (1938). *The Behavior of Organisms.* Englewood Cliffs, NJ: Prentice-Hall.

Smith, A. (1776). *An Inquiry into the Nature and Causes of the Wealth of Nations.* Printed for W. Strahan and T. Cadell. London.

Taylor, F. W. (1911). *The Principles of Scientific Management.* New York: Harper Brothers.

Templeton, G. & Snyder, C. (1999). A model of organizational learning based on control. *International Journal of Technology Management*, 18(5-8), 705-719.

Templeton, G. F. & Snyder, C. A. (2000). Precursors, contexts, and consequences of organizational learning. *International Journal of Technology Management*, 20(5/6/7/8), 765-781.

Templeton, G. F., Lewis, B. R. & Snyder, C. A. (2002). Development of a measure for the organizational learning construct. *Journal of Management Information Systems*, 19(2), 175-218.

Thorndike, E. L. (1911). *Animal Intelligence.* New York: MacMillan.

Uzumeri, M. V. & Nembhard, D. A. (1998). A population of learners: A new way to measure organizational learning. *Journal of Operations Management*, 16(5), 515-528.

Waterworth, C. J. (2000). Relearning the learning curve: A review of the derivation and applications of learning-curve theory. *Project Management Journal*, 31(1), 24-31.

Watson, J. B. (1913). Psychology as the behaviorist views it. *Psychological Review*, 20, 158-177.

Watson, J. B. (1924). *Behaviorism.* Chicago, IL: University of Chicago Press.

Weber, M. (1995). Bureaucracy. In S. A. Theodoulou & M. A. Cahn (Eds.), *Public Policy: The Essential Readings.* Englewood Cliffs, NJ: Prentice Hall.

Worchel, S. & Shebilske, W. (1992). *Psychology: Principles and Applications* (4th ed.), Englewood Cliffs, NJ: Prentice Hall.

Wright, T. P. (1936). Factors affecting the cost of airplanes. *Journal of the Aeronautical Sciences*, 3(4).

ENDNOTES

[1]   Throughout this chapter, the term "entity" will be consistently addressed. It is a general term, referring to both individuals and organizations, the two primary enactors of learning discussed in this chapter.

[2]   Throughout this chapter, I use the four-component (tasks, techniques, knowledge, and tools) taxonomy observed in the literature by Orlikowski (1992) to define the term "technology."

[3]   An historical review and analysis of learning curve theory can be found in Waterworth (2000).

[4]   Templeton and Snyder's (1999) *Technology Control Model (TCM)*, explains a great deal about how organizations learn. The TCM decomposes OL into seven salient learning processes (operations, knowledge acquisition, decision-making, incremental change, radical change, ideals, and standards) and two learning modes (SLL and DLL).

[5]   Orlikowski's (1992) "duality of technology" theory suggests that learning entities have been both enabled and constrained by technological progress.

Chapter XIII

An Investigation to an Enabling Role of Knowledge Management Between Learning Organization and Organizational Learning

Juin-Cherng Lu
Ming Chuan University, Taiwan

Chia-Wen Tsai
Ming Chuan University, Taiwan

ABSTRACT

This chapter is an exploratory investigation of the relationship and interaction between the learning organization and organizational learning in terms of an enabling role *of knowledge management. In the severe and dynamic business environment, organizations should respond quickly to their rivals and environment by transforming into a learning organization. A learning organization could provoke innovation and learning through its structure, task and process redesigns, and evermore adapt gradually toward the eventual goal of organizational learning. Therefore, the dynamic process between the learning organization and organizational learning is an important issue of current knowledge management and practice — that is, the enabling role of knowledge management could enhance the interaction between learning organization and organizational learning. Furthermore, the authors will explore the relationship and interaction between the learning organization and organizational learning in terms of knowledge management processes in business. Two cases, TSMC and Winbond, the semiconductor and high-tech firms in Taiwan, will be studied to illustrate the findings and insights for the study and the chapter.*

INTRODUCTION

Today a "Third Industrial Revolution" is under way; knowledge will replace land and a firm's resources as important asset (Thurow, 1999). Even Drucker (1993) argues that in the new economy, knowledge is not just another resource alongside the traditional factors of production — labor, capital and land — but is the only meaningful resource today. Tangible assets will be decreased or consumed because of use, but intangible assets — knowledge, information and technology will grow through sharing and application. In many industries, firms could sustain their competitive advantage if their abilities for learning and evolution are faster than their competitors. Thus, organizations should learn to survive in the fast-changing and intensely competitive environment, continually redesigning themselves into learning organizations (Daft, 1998).

Knowledge is a limitless resource in the knowledge-based economy, therefore, organizations should learn, store, transfer and apply knowledge to add value or gain competitive advantage (Sveiby, 1997). Knowledge management refers to identifying and leveraging the collective knowledge within the organization to help in competing (von Krogh, 1998). But in a severe and dynamic environment, organizations should respond quickly to their rivals and their environment by transforming into a learning organization, an organic and flexible company, to foster knowledge flow and sharing among the departments and task groups. A learning organization could provoke innovation and learning through its structure, task and process redesigns, and adapt gradually toward the eventual goal of organizational learning. Therefore, the dynamic process between the learning organization and organizational learning is an important issue of current knowledge management and practice — that is, an enabling role of knowledge management could change the interaction between the learning organization and organizational learning. But what is and how does knowledge management play this enabling role? The research question can be depicted as shown in Figure 1.

This study will try to find the relationship and interaction between the learning organization and organizational learning in terms of an enabling role of knowledge management. We hope to provide some new insights for firms as they translate their organizations into learning organizations and implement knowledge management practices to provoke organizational learning.

Figure 1: The Dynamic Process and Interaction Between OL and LO

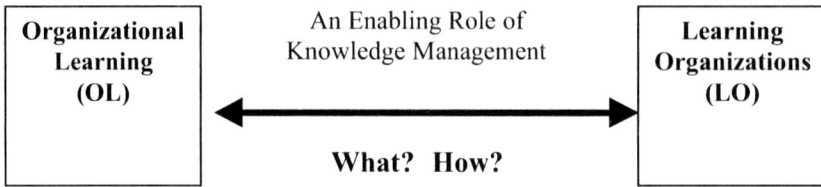

| Organizational Learning (OL) | An Enabling Role of Knowledge Management ◄──────► What? How? | Learning Organizations (LO) |

LEARNING ORGANIZATION

Learning organizations can be described as places where people continually expand their capacities to create the results they truly desire, where expansive and new patterns of thinking are nurtured, where collective aspiration is set free, and where people are continually learning how to learn together (Senge, 1990). It also can be defined as one in which everyone is engaged in identifying and solving problems, enabling the organization to continuously experiment, change, and improve, thus increasing its capacity to grow, learn, and achieve its purpose (Daft & Marcic, 1998). Most definitions focus on the importance of acquiring, improving, and transferring knowledge, facilitating individual and collective learning, integrating and modifying behaviors and practices of the organization as a result of the learning (Appelbaum & Reichart, 1998; Ellinger, Ellinger, Yang, & Howton, 2002).

Learning organizations are also generally described as being market-oriented; having an entrepreneurial culture as well as a flexible, organic structure; and having facilitative leadership (Lundberg, 1995; Luthans, Rubach, & Marsnik, 1995; Slater & Narver, 1995; Watkins & Marsick, 1996). When the environment is complicated and dynamic, organizations need to create, validate and apply new knowledge into their products, processes and services for eventual value-adding (Bhatt, 2001). Learning organizations take action, reflect and adjust course as they seek to enhance the speed and effectiveness by which they learn how to change (Rowden, 2001).

A learning organization could facilitate the learning of all of its members and continuously transform itself (Hawkins, 1991; Pedler, Boydell, & Burgoyne, 1988). It also improves its knowledge and understanding of the environment over time by facilitating and making use of the learning of individual members (Galer & Kees, 1992). After all, Garvin (1993) argued that a learning organization is an organization skilled in creating, acquiring and transferring knowledge, and modifying its behavior to reflect new knowledge and insights.

ORGANIZATIONAL LEARNING

Nevis, DiBella and Gould (1995) defined organizational learning as the capacity or processes within an organization to maintain or improve performance based on experience. Organizational learning occurs when workers act as learning agents for the organization, responding to changes from the internal and external environments by detecting and correcting errors and embedding the results of their inquiries in private images and shared maps of the organization. Organizational learning is at the heart of continuous improvement today. While companies learn, the crucial and key point is to learn fast enough to sustain the competitive advantage (De Geus, 1988). How effectively an organization learns can dictate whether it will improve, and how fast, or if it is destined to lose ground to competitors who can and do learn (Lynn, 1998). The abilities to continuously learn, adapt and improve on its capabilities are all key elements to gain competitive advantage.

Continuous learning is essential for surviving in dynamic and competitive environments, but the key to gain competitive advantage is the method and speed of learning (De Geus, 1988; Garvin, 1993; Nonaka, 1991; Popper & Lipshitz, 2000; Senge, 1990; Lennon & Wollin, 2001). Argyris and Schon (1978) proposed three processes of organizational learning: (1) Single-loop learning: individuals respond to errors by modifying strategies and assumptions within constant organizational norms, (2) Double-loop learning: the response to detected error takes the form of joint inquiry into organizational norms themselves, so as to resolve their inconsistency and make the new norms more effectively realizable, (3) Deutero-learning: workers learn about previous contexts for learning, and reflect on and inquire into previous contexts for learning. They also reflect on and inquire into previous episodes of organizational learning or failure to learn. They discover what they did that facilitated or inhibited learning and then they invent new strategies for learning.

Kanevsk and Housel (1999) argued that corporate success largely rests on the ability to translate learning from these changes into knowledge that will result in new or modified products. Learning is a critical element ensuring that a corporation makes the necessary adjustments to the new market by continuing to produce valuable products. Hence, the organization must track the effectiveness with which corporations change learning into knowledge that is valuable to customers. A "Learning-Knowledge-Value Spiral" illustrates the process of transforming learning into value (Kanevsk & Housel, 1999), as shown in Figure 2. Any company has to understand that learning from the market must be translated into knowledge that can be applied to its production processes, resulting in changes to its product or service. This "learning to knowledge to new value" cycle must spiral upwards if any company is to flourish, not to mention to survive at all.

Figure 2: A Learning-Knowledge-Value Spiral

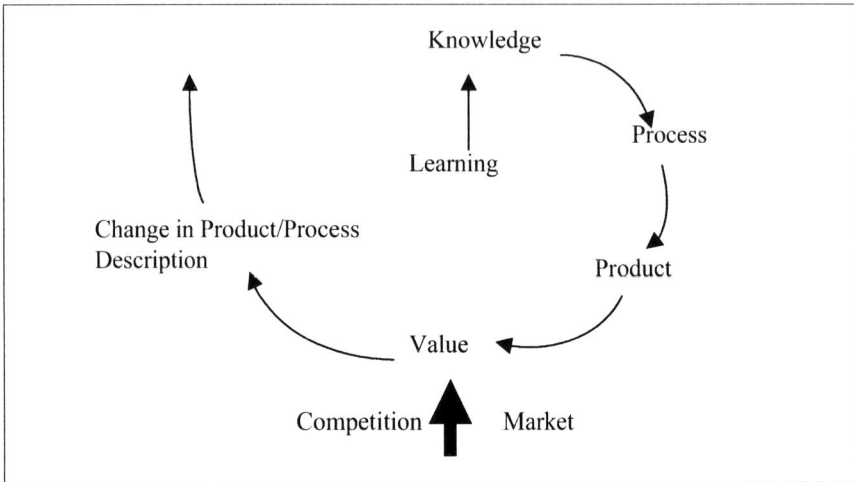

Source: Kanevsk and Housel (1999)

An organization can't create knowledge on its own without the initiative of the individual and the interaction that takes place within the group. But, having an insight or a hunch that is highly personal is of little value to the company unless the individual can convert it into explicit knowledge to be shared with others in the company (Nonaka & Takeuchi, 1995). In terms of the process of activity, organizational learning is the social process from individual, group, to the whole organization — that is, organizational learning begins with the individual to affect the groups or departments, and then extends to the organization (Dodgson, 1993). It is not organizational learning if it can't shape any force to affect the organization (Lu, 1996).

But what's the relationship between the learning organization and organizational learning? Organizational learning means activities or processes of learning in organizations, while a learning organization is an ideal form of organization that successfully practices all of these activities (Örtenblad, 2001). Popper and Lipshitz (2000) pointed out that learning organizations are organizations that have embedded institutionalized learning mechanisms into a learning culture. Marquardt (1996) notes that learning organizations focus on the "what" — the characteristics, principles, and systems of an organization that produces and learns collectively, while organizational learning refers to the "how" — the proficiencies and processes of knowledge development. Organizational learning is a concept used to describe certain types of activity that take place in an organization, and the learning organization refers to a particular type of organization in and of itself (Tsang, 1997; DiBella, 1995; Elkjaer, 1999; Finger & Bürgin Brand, 1999; Lundberg, 1995). DeBella and Nevis (1997) argued that a learning organization is a systems-level concept; it has been characterized as having the capability to adapt to changes in its environment and to respond to lessons of experience by altering organizational behavior. In contrast, organizational learning is a term used to describe certain types of activities or processes that may occur at any one of several levels of analysis or as part of an organizational change process. Thus it's something that takes place in all organizations, whereas the learning organization is a particular type or form of organization in and of itself. In summary, learning organizations focus on learning at the organization level, but an organization will learn when the organizational knowledge is out of date, incorrect, or insufficient, and then feedback the learning to the organization. Therefore, we could demonstrate that there exists an interactive relationship between the learning organization and organizational learning.

KNOWLEDGE MANAGEMENT AS AN ENABLING ROLE

Knowledge management is concerned with systematic, effective management and utilization of an organization's knowledge resources (Demarest, 1997). It consists of the creation, storage, arrangement, retrieval and distribution of an organization's knowledge (Demarest, 1997; Saffady, 2000). Alavi and Leidner (2001) classified the processes of knowledge management into four steps: knowledge creation, knowledge storage/retrieval, knowledge transfer and knowledge application, representing a detailed process view of organizational knowledge management with a focus on the role of Information Technology. This systematic framework is shown as Figure 3.

Knowledge Creation

Organizational knowledge creation involves developing new content or replacing existing content within the organization's tacit and explicit knowledge

Figure 3: Four Processes of Knowledge Management

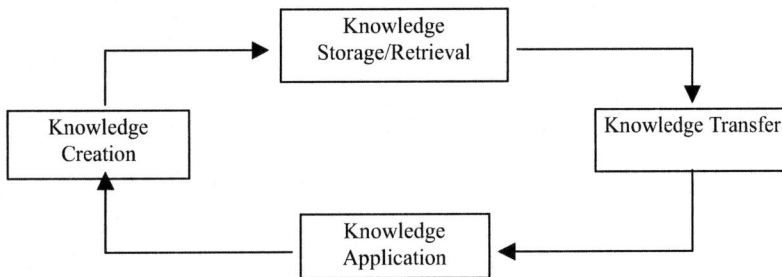

Modified from Alavi and Leidner (2001)

(Pentland, 1995). In today's rapidly changing environment, organizations have to focus on the creation of knowledge to prevent existing knowledge from obsolescing quickly. When organizations innovate, they do not simply process information from the outside in, but solve existing problems and adapt to the dynamic environment. They actually create new knowledge and information, from the inside out, in order to redefine both problems and solutions and, in the process, to recreate their environment (Nonaka & Takeuchi, 1995). New knowledge is a necessary raw material for innovation and the creation of knowledge, both are closely tied to new products and services (Hauschild, Licht, & Stein, 2001). When a firm starts to develop new products or services, or when organizational knowledge is antiquated or insufficient, a firm could innovate and create new knowledge by organizational learning activities to face the challenges.

Knowledge Storage/Retrieval

While new knowledge is developed by individuals, organizations play a critical role in articulating and amplifying that knowledge (Nonaka, 1994). The storage, organization, and retrieval of organizational knowledge are referred to as organizational memory (Stein & Zwass, 1995; Malhotra, 2000). Organizational memory includes knowledge residing in various component forms, including structured information stored in electronic databases, written documentation, expert systems, documented organizational procedures and processes and tacit knowledge acquired by individuals and networks of individuals (Tan, Teo, Tan, & Wei, 1999).

The individual's knowledge is not equal to the organizational knowledge. The organizational knowledge is of company-level and it should be identified or shared by the members and correlated to a knowledge system (Lu, 1996). Hence, to translate to a learning organization that is full of knowledge, there should be a mechanism and system to store the knowledge for the further application. The strategy for knowledge management should reflect the firm's competitive strategy: how it creates value for customers, how that value supports a business model, and how the organization's people deliver on the value. Two strategies are being used for storing knowledge (Hansen, Nohria, & Tierney, 1999):
1.   Codification: Provide high-quality, reliable, and fast information-systems implementation by reusing codified knowledge;
2.   Personalization: Provide creative, analytically rigorous advice on high-level strategic problems by channeling individual expertise.

Knowledge Transfer

The distribution and transfer of knowledge is an important process in knowledge management (Alavi & Leidner, 2001; Huber, 1991). Knowledge should be shared and generalized within the organization. In addition, generalization occurs not only when single ideas are moved, but also when the entire process of moving ideas becomes institutionalized within an organization (Yeung, Ulrich, Nason, & von Glinow, 1999). The institutional process embedded in a firm and the capability of generalizing ideas consistently are important elements to meet the real goal of knowledge management.

Organizations should provide several ways and mechanisms to transfer and distribute knowledge to ensure unrestricted transferring. For example, knowledge that is more or less explicit can be embedded in procedures or represented in documents and databases and then transferred accurately. But, transfer of tacit knowledge generally requires extensive personal contacts (Davenport & Prusak, 1998). Hung (2001) found that two approaches facilitate the efficiency of knowledge transfer among employees:

1. Systematic mechanism: refers to the centralized management that stores the knowledge in the institutional systems built upon information and network technology and disseminating the knowledge through the network.
2. Socialized mechanism: refers to an extensive notion, including many heterogenous ways of social interaction, such as the learning community, virtual community, yellow page (of specialists), institutional community, knowledge intermediary within a company, and a speech or conference outside a company.

Knowledge Application

Knowledge application means making knowledge more active and relevant for firms in creating value, since organizational knowledge needs to be employed into a company's products, processes and services (Bhatt, 2001; Demarest, 1997). The source of competitive advantage resides in the application of the knowledge rather than in the knowledge itself (Alavi & Leidner, 2001). Using knowledge more powerfully than your competitors is a key to battling it out in the global information era (Prokesch, 1997). Employees use all available resources, including the corporate knowledge base, to improve their chances of reaching the goals of the organization (Hauschild et al., 2001). Learning from the experience of others and reusing materials that have been effective elsewhere improves the quality and speed of problem solving (Cross & Baird, 2000). Knowledge should be really used to create value for the company and when it is applied, the company can judge the validity and suitability. Knowledge application is essential when the organization transforms into a learning organization and helps the organization to retain correct and valuable knowledge.

RESEARCH METHOD
Case Selection and Data Collection

This case study is applied to illustrate how high-tech firms implement knowledge management practices to transform themselves into learning organizations. The case selection is very important in this study and should be guided by principles (Yin, 1994). Kofman and Senge (1995) suggested that a learning organization should be grounded in three foundations: a culture based on transcendent human values of love, wonder, humility and compassion; a set of practices for generative conversation and coordinated action; and finally, a capacity to see and work with the flow of life as a system. Two cases, Taiwan Semiconductor Manufacturing Corporation (TSMC) and Winbond, have been selected, because of their reputation for their knowledge management practices, to illustrate the different enabling roles of knowledge management in the interaction between learning organizations and organizational learning. TSMC is the world's largest and most successful dedicated independent semiconductor foundry. Winbond is the largest integrated circuit (IC) supplier in Taiwan's IC industry. In addition, the Chief Knowledge Officer (CKO) of the firms promises to provide case interviews. Also, case data collection from multiple evidence resources, company profiles and internal documents is to control the construct validity of the study, and the chain of evidence is found to keep track of the processes of implementing knowledge management in TSMC and Winbond. Besides, data and content from the firm's web site and knowledge portal is collected and analyzed systematically.

Case Illustration: TSMC and Winbond

TSMC: Company Overview

TSMC, founded in 1987 and located in the Hsin-Chu Science-Based Industrial Park of Taiwan, is listed on the New York Stock Exchange (TSM). As the first "pure play" foundry company, TSMC has experienced strong growth by being a true partner with its customers by designing and manufacturing IC products for them. The evolution of advanced IC technology over the past decade has been so rapid that it has changed the ways that companies do business. Demands for faster time-to-market and design cycle have increased, as well as demands for higher speed and product quality. These are some reasons companies around the world turn to TSMC as their manufacturing partner. TSMC puts more resources into its manufacturing facilities and capacity than nearly anyone else. It continues to be the trusted source for a global collection of innovative and savvy businesses, large and small, who appreciate their steadily increasing manufacturing capacity and consistent volume production levels. TSMC enhances its ability to serve its customers by operating, expanding and developing many new facilities as we enter into the new decade:

*   Nine 8-inch wafer Fabs in full operation (Fabs 3, 4, 5, 6, 7A, 7B, 8A, 8B, plus WaferTech).
*   One 8-inch wafer Fab facility through our TSMC affiliate-Vanguard International Semiconductor Corporation.

- Ground-breaking for the company's two initial 12-inch wafer fabs took place in late 1999 in Hsin-Chu Science-based Park and Tainan Science-based Industrial Park.
- A joint venture with Philips Semiconductor and with Singapore's EDB Investments (SSMC) will also bring increased capacity in the coming years.

TSMC: Knowledge Management Practices

1. Knowledge Creation: TSMC maintains a stable relationship with their customers, has extended their production, innovated their service in eFoundry via the Internet, owns the most advanced process technologies and leads the market. One of the main reasons for its growth is the investment in the innovation of production technologies and the development of value innovation ability that enables TSMC to be the leader. To be more competitive, TSMC has concentrated its attention on the modification and the coordination of various technologies to decrease production costs, reduce its defect rate, cut down the product cycle time, and improve productivity (Hung, 2001). TSMC is not only devoted to technical innovation but also to the innovation of customer service. Morris Chang, the TSMC chairman, announced that TSMC is a customer-oriented service business and he stressed the importance of service innovation. In July 2000, TSMC proposed the idea of eFoundry that allows their customers to be served via the Internet. The vision of eFoundry is to offer the best services for customers; that they can gain benefits from eFoundry without paying a lot for establishment and management. TSMC offers customers a highly integrated supply chain management system with reliability, security, speed and transparency through strategic use of Information Technology. This innovative strategy has enabled TSMC to maintain its superior position and more competitive edge. TSMC continues to boost its learning capabilities and create new knowledge, such that its organizational learning occurs not necessarily because of the shortage of knowledge, but out of the desire to maintain its superior market position. As we found, knowledge creation plays a key role as TSMC engages in organizational learning.

2. Knowledge Storage/Retrieval: Dr. Tsai, the President and Chief Operating Officer, drives the knowledge management activities in TSMC and founded eight technical boards that are categorized according to the processes in the semiconductor industry. The workers have to join relevant technical boards to share information and knowledge. The manager of IC Design, Dr. Kao, indicates that TSMC should translate the records of the best machines, equipment and technical processes into know-how that can be shared, and then transfer that knowledge to the new foundry. He said that, "The best knowledge of building foundries in the world was filed in our technical board." Any employee in any foundry can share best techniques and

knowledge with others on the technical board. The technical board checks and reviews records in which the experience of work will be encoded, stored and shared. As the evidence shows, TSMC pays much attention to knowledge storage and retrieval.

3.   Knowledge Transfer: TSMC promotes two approaches for knowledge transfer (Hung, 2001): (a) Sharing: The experiences of engineers are codified and stored in the knowledge system. As the production process can be scientifically measured, it's easy to translate processes into explicit knowledge and to accumulate it. Besides the technical knowledge, information about decision-making is also stored in the Documentation Center after review by the managers. Then, that information can be shared and referred to by the relevant workers. (b) Collaboration: TSMC builds communities among the departments to help the knowledge demander track the knowledge provider and ask for support. This is a social mechanism in which all workers can seek support from those experienced workers through the TSMC Yellow Pages. The effect of knowledge transfer in such a dynamic sharing mechanism is better than the static knowledge system. Through the combination of an active knowledge network and static knowledge system, working knowledge is shared continuously. Sharing and collaboration improve the knowledge transfer in TSMC and help to create more new knowledge. It also enables the positive cycle of knowledge creation, storage and transfer.

4.   Knowledge Application: TSMC's employees are urged to apply knowledge to their work and benefit from doing so. Owing to efficient knowledge management, TSMC grew rapidly in the past 12 years and there are five new factories still in the process of construction. Moreover, factories in Singapore and Boston are now in the planning stage. As for process technology, TSMC developed 0.18 micron logic, copper process technology and the embedded process technology applied in sys-on-a-chip. TSMC provides support to the process technology and design of semiconductor to satisfy customers' needs. The primary process technology is 0.35 micron, but it will increase that technology from 0.25 micron to the advanced 0.18 micron at the same time that it goes into mass production. Now, TMSC has also started to test 0.15 micron and plans 0.13 micron process technology for mass production on its schedule. The advanced process technologies significantly cut down the production costs, so that TSMC has made more profit and gains competitive advantage in the world.

The ability of continuous improvement, learning and innovation leads to high efficiency in integrating and coordinating the varied process technologies, and reduces the production cost, while achieving high product quality, low defect rate and short cycle time. The main reason for TSMC superiority is its concentration on technological evolution and innovation of new knowledge and process technology. In addition, TSMC provides the standard circuit component-base and intellectual property (IP) for customers to strengthen their design service abilities.

Winbond: Company Overview

Winbond Electronics Corporation, established in 1987 in the Hsinchu Science-based Industrial Park, Taiwan, is the largest brand name IC supplier in search of excellence in process technology, worldwide marketing networks and wafer processing. After 14 years of growth and accumulation of bountiful assets in products and technologies, Winbond has started to design, develop and market its own products under its brand name and aims at a broad range of product lines to meet the demands of the information industry and satisfy customers' needs. The products include PC and peripheral ICs, micro-based consumer ICs, Network Access ICs, Memory ICs, etc. Winbond, on the average, invests more than 10% of annual revenues into R&D and has built on its extensive technical knowledge and technological experiences. For the past few years, Winbond investment in R&D has yielded substantial growth in technology and helped it to forge strategic alliances, combining R&D with leading global companies. R&D centers have been set up in China and the United States, both tasked with aggressively absorbing new market trends. Winbond's depth in design IP, combined with skilled production capability, allows the company to effectively leverage its efforts to a number of growing markets.

Winbond: Knowledge Management Practices

1. Knowledge Creation: Since 1991, Winbond has been honored by receiving the R&D Investment Award from the Hsinchu Science-Based Park. The company has a long history of knowledge management and patent production worldwide — already surpassing 1,000 patents. In 1998, the company made the top 300 American Patents list. In 1999, Winbond became the winner of the Gold Medal of National Invention by the Bureau of IP, the Ministry of Economic Affairs. Winbond has been named "Outstanding Electronics Component Supplier" for two years in a row and was also selected as the best performing manufacturing company in Taiwan. Dr. Tauso, the manager of knowledge management, implied that the company does emphasize the storage, transfer and application of knowledge rather than the creation of knowledge. But it does not mean that Winbond ignores the importance of knowledge creation. In fact, Winbond is checking and counting its intangible assets first and foremost. As the knowledge is refined, shared and applied, if the knowledge is incorrect, out of date, or not suitable for use, it might force the company to engage in another wave of organizational learning based on the knowledge creation.

2.   Knowledge Storage/Retrieval: With the speedy change in the electronics industry, Winbond tends to collect and check the knowledge, then store it in Winbond's knowledge bank after the investigation and refinement by the technical board. To make the knowledge more accessible to workers, Winbond uploads it to the Intranet, so that workers may obtain the knowledge and experience online easily. As the invention of IC is highly specialized in varied fields of knowledge, the invention of new products design needs clear standard interfaces and technical definitions within the IC framework. Hence, it's easy to transfer an individual's knowledge to codified knowledge, and accumulate it systematically. This crucial knowledge is standardized and stored in Winbond's knowledge systems for those who would request it.

The knowledge systems comprise patents databases, learning materials and technical information, etc. Technical information is subdivided into debug/design reports, IP code and IP Map. Furthermore, to prevent knowledge from being stolen, there is a security mechanism. Some IP and debug/design contents are designed to be online training courses to reduce the training time for newcomers. Most patent information is classified into company patent and market patent information provided for administrators and executives to reference when making decisions. The evidence shows that Winbond pays much attention to knowledge storage/retrieval.

3.   Knowledge Transfer: Winbond's technical information and learning materials are explicit knowledge for workers to obtain knowledge and peers' experience through the Intranet immediately. Moreover, senior engineers' experiences can be also transferred to the new employees through IP Map or Yellow Pages, when they are vague about the knowledge or going to check it out. The knowledge department plays the role of mediating for workers to search for the knowledge source. As to knowledge that is unclear or value undefined, Winbond provides an online forum to facilitate sharing that implicit knowledge. This online forum is divided into two kinds — public and nonpublic with some confidential issues reserved for qualified members only. The main purpose of the Knowledge Management Center is to increase the volume and value of organizational knowledge and to spread knowledge throughout the firm. As the knowledge management practices in Winbond imply, it plays a significant role in knowledge storage/ retrieval and knowledge transfer.

4.   Knowledge Application: Winbond set up the Knowledge Management Center to advance product technology and improve the performance of service innovation on its core competence by applying the knowledge. But during transformation to a learning organization, Winbond emphasizes more of the practice of knowledge application to gain competitive advantage in the IC battle. According to the statistics in the Knowledge Management

Center, most engineers encountered similar problems in their work before, but now engineers need not waste time in solving the same problems or recommitting the same errors due to the functions of the center, which has reduced their products' defect rate to 2~3% and cut the cycle time down to 75%. The evidence implies that Winbond takes advantage of organizational knowledge to improve the quality of products, lower defect rate and decrease cycle time of production, and utilizes organizational knowledge to lead the firm.

Case Reasoning and Discussion

TSMC's technology innovation is the wellspring of its growth and is vital to all sectors from strategic planning to management of technology and production. TSMC regards employees and shareholders as important constituents and its goal is to provide better salary and benefit packages for employees. TSMC has implemented an open-style management system designed to keep all lines of communication free in the working environment, and employees are instructed to treat each other sincerely, honestly and cooperatively.

Winbond's human resource is an important asset for company to go from strengths to high quality. It provides suitable working conditions, munificent salaries and bonuses for its employees. In addition, Winbond provides 1,200 training programs and more than 20 Web-based training courses for employees to pursue further upgrades and learning. The continuous-learning culture in Winbond has been established and, furthermore, it also set up many channels (like IP Map, Expert Yellow Pages) for workers to solve their problems or seek help based on the Knowledge Portal.

TSMC and Winbond, famous high-tech companies in the world, put knowledge management into practice and the way they learn, providing many consultations and references due to making efforts to transform into learning organizations. Such dynamic interaction between the learning organization and organizational learning is an important issue for the academic and in practice. This study would provide practical implications and insights for business and research.

Insights from Case Study

With the stiff global competition, high-tech companies face the challenge of shorter product life cycles, the rapid depreciation of tangible assets and the transience of employees. It is essential for firms to put knowledge management into practice positively and actively. Based on the literature and cases studies of TSMC and Winbond, the authors offer the following *insights* for managers or readers seeking to develop the enabling role of knowledge management in their companies. Table 1 shows the *comparison* of the case studies in terms of an enabling role of knowledge management and the organization.

Table 1: The Comparison of Case Studies: TSMC vs. Winbond

Item comparison	TSMC	Winbond
Industry	"pure" foundry company	IC design and manufacturing
Enabling role of KM (Knowledge Management)	Focus more on knowledge creation, comparatively (on knowledge innovation)	Focus more on knowledge storage/retrieval, comparatively (on knowledge checking)
Organizational type toward KM	Foster the organizational learning aggressively	Foster move toward a learning organization gradually
KM Mechanism	8 Technical boards; Sharing and Collaboration	KM department and KM Center / IP code and IP map
The KM Agent	The President (Dr. Tsai)	The KM Manager (Dr. Tauso)
KM Strategy	Facilitate faster design cycle, time-to-market and the high quality of product/service	Facilitate checking and counting the intangible asset of IC know-ledge by refinements
Key success factor (KSF)	Technology innovation based on knowledge innovation	Knowledge refinements based on knowledge storage/retrieval
Competitive Advantage via KM practices	Toward customer-oriented service business via the eFoundry with advanced process technologies	Low defect rate and short cycle time to cut down IC product cost. Reduce training cost and keep experience value-added

Insight 1. There exists empirically an interactive and recurring relationship between the learning organization and organizational learning. The former is an organization that fills with knowledge and embeds an institutionalized learning mechanism into the learning culture. This type of organization will continue learning to create new knowledge to gain or sustain its competitive advantage. The learning results and accumulated knowledge will modify the organization itself. This feedback continuously transforms the learning organization.

Insight 2. When organizations transform to learning organizations, the processes of knowledge storage/retrieval, transfer and application play more important roles in the knowledge management process because knowledge must be stored in the organization, and then transferred to people who need to apply that knowledge in productivity. Gradually, as learning organizations continue learning, knowledge creation becomes more important than other factors in the process of knowledge management. This is an interaction between organizational learning, with emphasis on knowledge creation, and the learning organization, with emphasis on knowledge storage/retrieval, transfer and application, in terms of an enabling role of knowledge management.

Insight 3. The strategies for knowledge management and practices differ because of different implementation stages or the nature of the company. For example, Winbond doesn't focus mainly on creating knowledge but on checking and reviewing the existent intangible assets; while TSMC does make much effort to create more technology knowledge in order to safeguard its leading advantage in the world.

Knowledge management for firms should refer to the source of competitive advantage or "dynamic capabilities," emphasizing the dynamic character of the environment and capabilities of appropriately adapting, integrating and reconfiguring internal and external organizational skills, resources and competencies. This study suggests that the competitive advantage of firms lies in their managerial and organizational processes, where processes include the routines and patterns of current practice, learning, the endowments of technology and intellectual property. As the cases show, TSMC and Winbond's timely response and rapid development of product innovation, coupled with the enabling role of knowledge management to effectively coordinate and redeploy internal and external competences of knowledge-based innovation, requires careful analysis of various kinds of knowledge. The results indicate there is an interactive relationship between the learning organization and organizational learning. Organizational learning emphasizes mainly knowledge creation, but the learning organization mainly emphasizes knowledge storage/retrieval, transfer and application, in terms of the enabling role of knowledge management. Therefore, firms should transform themselves into learning organizations to foster organizational learning by implementing knowledge management practices in order to gain or sustain a competitive advantage in the knowledge-based economy.

CONCLUSION AND SUGGESTION

This chapter depicts the relationship and interaction between the learning organization and organizational learning in terms of the enabling role of knowledge management in business, However, the result of this case study is difficult to infer from two cases and the generalization of the findings is limited to these contexts (Yin, 1994). But two cases, TSMC and Winbond, are studied to suggest that the enabling role of knowledge management plays the *dynamic relationship* between the two constructs — the learning organization and organizational learning. Future research may apply the quantitative methods to study the solid relationships between the learning organization and knowledge management, and organizational learning and knowledge management, respectively.

The *practical implication* of the chapter would be helpful to certain high-tech industries. For example, an enabling role of knowledge management could provoke the emphases on the importance of knowledge creation for the turbulent environment; otherwise, on the importance of knowledge storage/retrieval, transfer and application for the static environment. Firms would define their organizational status and starting point to foster implementation of knowledge management practice based on their goals. Therefore, the interchange transformation of organizational learning and the learning organization should be dynamic adaptation systematically.

REFERENCES

Alavi, M. & Leidner, D. E. (2001). Review: Knowledge management and knowledge management systems: Conceptual foundations and research issues. *MIS Quarterly*, 25(1), 107-136.

Appelbaum, S. H. & Reichart, W. (1998). How to measure an organization's learning ability: The facilitating factors – Part II. *Journal of Workplace Learning*, 10(1), 15-28.

Argyris, C. & Schon, D. (1978). *Organizational Learning: A Theory of Action Perspective*. Addison-Wesley Publishing.

Bhatt, G. D. (2001). Knowledge management in organizations: Examining the interaction between technologies, techniques, and people. *Journal of Knowledge Management,* 5(1), 68-75.

Cross, R. & Baird, L. (2000, Spring). Technology is not enough: Improving performance by building organizational memory. *Sloan Management Review*, 41(3), 69-78.

Daft, R. & Marcic, D. (1998). *Understanding Management.* Ft. Worth, TX: Dryden Press.

Daft, R. L. (1998). *Organization Theory and Design.* South-Western College Press.

Davenport, T. H. & Prusak, L. (1998). *Working Knowledge: How Organizations Manage What They Know.* Harvard Business School Press.

De Geus, A. P. (1988, March/April). Planning as Learning. *Harvard Business Review*, 66, 70-74.

DeBella, A. J. & Nevis, E. C. (1997). *How Organizations Learn.* Jossey-Bass Publishers.

Demarest, M. (1997). Understanding Knowledge Management. *Long Range Planning*, 30(3), 374-384.

DiBella, A. J (1995). Developing learning organizations: A matter of perspective. *Academy of Management: Best Papers Proceedings*, 287-290.

Dodgson, M. (1993). Organizational learning: A review of some literatures. *Organization Studies*, 375-394.

Drucker, P. F. (1993). *Post-Capitalist Society.* Oxford: Butterworth Heinemann.

Elkjaer, B. (1999). In search of a social learning theory. In M. Easterby-Smith, J. Burgoyne & L. Araujo (Eds.), *Organizational Learning and the*

Learning Organization: Developments in Theory and Practice (pp. 75-91). London: Sage.

Ellinger, A. D., Ellinger A. E., Yang, B., & Howton, S. W. (2002). The relationship between the learning organization concept and firms' financial performance: An empirical assessment. *Human Resource Development Quarterly*, 13(1), 5-21.

Finger, M. & Bürgin Brand, S. (1999). The concept of the learning organization applied to the transformation of the public sector: Conceptual contributions for theory development. In M. Easterby-Smith, J. Burgoyne & L. Araujo (Eds.), *Organizational Learning and the Learning Organization: Developments in Theory and Practice* (pp. 130-156). London: Sage.

Galer, G. & Kees, H. (1992). The learning organization: How planners create organization learning. *Marketing Intelligence and Planning*, 5-12.

Garvin, D. A. (1993). Building a learning organization. *Harvard Business Review*, 78-91.

Hansen, M. T., Nohria, N., & Tierney, T. (1999, March/April). What's your strategy for managing knowledge? *Harvard Business Review*, 106-116.

Hauschild, S., Licht, T., & Stein, W. (2001). Creating a knowledge culture. *The McKinsey Quarterly*, 1, 74-81.

Hawkins, P. (1991). The spiritual dimension of the learning organization. *Management Education and Development*, 22(3), 172-187.

Huber, G. (1991). Organizational learning: The contributing processes and the literatures. *Organization Science*, 2(1), 88-115.

Hung, K. Y. (2001). *Knowledge Management Mechanisms and Enterprise's Innovation Ability: An Exploratory Study to Build a Positive Research Model.* Unpublished doctoral dissertation, Graduate Institute of Business Administration, National Taiwan University.

Kanevsky, V. & Housel, T. (1999). The learning-knowledge-value cycle. In G. von Krogh, J. Roos & D. Kleine (Eds.), *Knowing in Firms* (pp. 269-284). Corwin Press.

Kofman, K. & Senge, P. M. (1993). Communities of commitment: The heart of learning organizations. *Organizational Dynamics*, 22(2), 5-24.

Lennon, A. & Wollin, A. (2001). Learning organizations: Empirically investigating metaphors. *Journal of Intellectual Capital*, 2(4), 410-422.

Lu, W. S. (1996). *A Theoretical Inquiry into Organizational Learning.* Unpublished doctoral dissertation, Graduate Institute of Public Administration National Chengchi University, Taiwan.

Lundberg, C. C. (1995). Learning in and by organizations: Three conceptual issues. *International Journal of Organizational Analysis*, 3(1), 10-23.

Luthans, F., Rubach, M. J., & Marsnik, P. (1995). Going beyond total quality: The characteristics, techniques and measures of learning organizations. *International Journal of Organizational Analysis*, 3(1), 24-44.

Lynn, G. (1998). New product team learning: Developing and profiting from your knowledge capital. *California Management Review*, 40(4), 15-26.

Malhotra, Y. (2000). Knowledge management & new organization forms: A framework for business model innovation. *Information Resources Management Journal*, 13(1), 5-14.

Marquardt, M. J. (1996). *Building the Learning Organization: A Systems Approach to Quantum Improvement and Global Success.* New York: McGraw-Hill.

Nevis, E. C., DiBella, A. J., & Gould, J. M. (1995, Winter). Understanding organizations as learning systems. *Sloan Management Review*, 73-85.

Nonaka, I. (1991). The knowledge-creating company. *Harvard Business Review*, 69(9), 96-104.

Nonaka, I. (1994). A dynamic theory of organizational knowledge creation. *Organization Science*, 5(1), 14-37.

Nonaka, I. & Takeuchi, H. (1995). *The Knowledge-Creating Company.* Oxford University Press.

Örtenblad, A. (2001). On differences between organizational learning and learning organization. *The Learning Organization*, 8(3), 125-133.

Pedler, M., Boydell, T., & Burgoyne, J. (1988). *Learning Company Project Report.* Train Lund, Sweden.

Pentland, B. T. (1995). Information Systems and Organizational Learning: The Social Epistemology of Organizational Knowledge Systems. *Account, Management and Information Technologies*, 1-21.

Popper, M. & Lipshitz, R. (2000). Organizational learning: Mechanisms, culture, and feasibility. *Management Learning*, 31(2), 181-196.

Prokesch, S. E. (1997, September/October). Unleashing the power of learning: An interview with British Petroleum's John Browne. *Harvard Business Review*, 5-19.

Rowden, R. W. (2001). The learning organization and strategic change. *SAM Advanced Management Journal*, 11-24.

Saffady, W. (2000). Knowledge management: An overview. *Information Management Journal*, 34(3), 4-8.

Senge, P. M. (1990). *The Fifth Discipline: The Art and Practice of the Learning Organization.* New York: Doubleday.

Slater, S. F. & Narver, J. C. (1995). Market orientation and the learning organization. *Journal of Marketing*, 59, 63-74.

Stein, E. W. & Zwass, V. (1995). Actualizing organizational memory with information systems. *Information Systems Research*, 6(2), 85-117.

Sveiby, K. E. (1997). *The New Organizational Wealth: Managing & Measuring Knowledge-Based Assets.* Berrett-Koehler.

Tan, S. S., Teo, H. H., Tan, B. C., & Wei, K. K. (1999). Developing a preliminary framework for knowledge management in organizations. In *Proceedings of the Fourth Americas Conference on Information Systems*, Baltimore, MD (pp. 629-631).

Thurow, L. C. (1999). *Building Wealth: The New Rules for Individuals, Companies, and Action in a Knowledge Based Economic*. Harper Business Press.

Tsang, E. W. K. (1997). Organizational learning and the learning organization: A dichotomy between descriptive and prescriptive research. *Human Relations*, 50(1), 73-89.

von Krogh, G. (1998). Care in knowledge creation. *California Management Review*, 40(3), 133-153.

Watkins, K. E. & Marsick, V. J. (1996). *In Action: Creating the learning organization*. Alexandria, VA: American Society for Training and Development.

Yeung, A. K., Ulrich D. O., Nason, S. W., & von Ginow, M. A. (1999). *Organizational Learning Capability*. New York: Oxford University Press.

Yin, R. K. (1994). *Case Study Research Design and Methods* (2nd edition). Thousand Oaks, CA: Sage.

SECTION V:

FUTURE ORGANIZATIONS

Chapter XIV

21st Century Organizations and the Basis for Achieving Optimal Cross-Functional Integration in New Product Development

J. Daniel Sherman
University of Alabama in Huntsville, USA

ABSTRACT

The theoretical basis for achieving optimal levels of cross-functional integration in new product development and the management of large scale engineering projects is developed in this chapter. Sources of environmental uncertainty and their effects on integration requirements are identified based on the literature. Structural modes of integration are discussed and presented in a theoretical framework based on degree of integration required, progressive combined information processing capacity, and cost.

INTRODUCTION

In any complex, new product development project or large-scale engineering project, the effective integration of diverse inputs from cross-functional groups is of critical importance to meeting schedule and budget requirements and is often critical to the success of the new product or system. In the case of incremental innovations, smaller scale projects, or larger projects where integration is not complex, the organization can utilize small, dedicated teams with lower cross-functional integration requirements. However, with larger scale projects with interdependent subsystems and coordination required across functional areas and across organizations (i.e., contractors or suppliers), the issues of integration become more crucial.

BASIS FOR INTEGRATION REQUIREMENTS

Integration requirements can be partially understood through an analysis of technological and environmental uncertainty (Thompson, 1967; Lawrence & Lorsch, 1967) or through the analysis of the information processing requirements of the new product development effort (Galbraith, 1973; Moenaert & Souder, 1990b). With greater levels of uncertainty associated with a new technology or project, greater amounts of information must be processed between decision makers during development (Moenaert & Souder, 1996). If the technology and the market are well understood, then planning will be less uncertain. However, if these are not well understood, then information must be acquired during the development effort, which may necessitate ongoing changes in priorities, schedules, resource allocations, staffing requirements, etc. Therefore, a greater amount of information must be processed among decision makers during product development (Galbraith, 1973, 1977).

Uncertainty can be conceptualized as the difference between the amount of information required to complete a task and the amount of information previously possessed by the organization (Souder, Sherman, & Davies-Cooper, 1998). With generally increased levels of uncertainty, integration is affected because planning and decision-making are subject to ongoing modification. This increases information processing demands across the organization. This has implications for both management information systems design and organizational design.

Specific sources of uncertainty include customer uncertainty, competitive uncertainty, resource uncertainty, and technological uncertainty. Customer or consumer uncertainty refers to unrealized user requirements (Moenaert & Souder, 1990a, 1990b). Competitive uncertainty is a function of the absence of information regarding the activities of competitors (Clark, 1985; Duncan, 1972; Souder & Sherman, 1993). Technological uncertainty refers to the lack of

Figure 1: Sources of Uncertainty

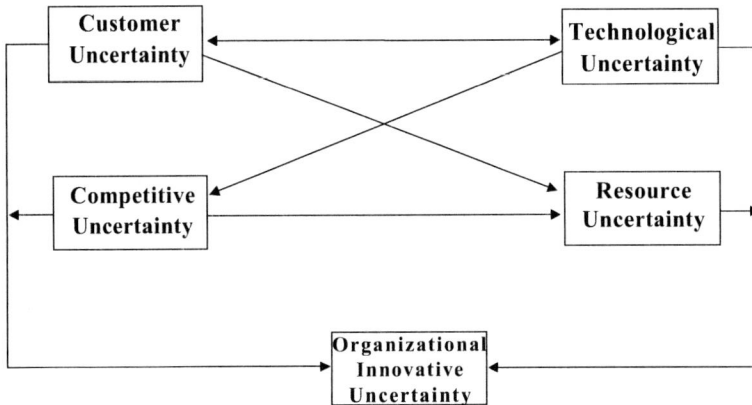

Source: Moenaert and Souder (1990b)

knowledge regarding the solution of technical problems (Moenaert & Souder, 1990b). Resource uncertainty refers to the absence of information regarding financial, technical or human resources needed to successfully develop the new product (Cooper, 1986; Rubenstein, Chakrabarti, O'Keefe, Souder, & Young, 1976). In this category, human resource uncertainty refers to incomplete information regarding staffing requirements to complete the project and, in some cases, uncertainty regarding manufacturing capabilities. Financial resource uncertainty is the level of uncertainty regarding costs of development. Finally, technical resource uncertainty is uncertainty regarding laboratory equipment or pilot plant facilities required (Moenaert & Souder, 1990a, 1990b).

Figure 1, based on Moenaert and Souder (1990b), illustrates how these four major sources of uncertainty combine to influence the general level of uncertainty the organization faces in new product innovation. It is implicit that customer uncertainty and technological uncertainty are usually positively related. With higher customer and technological uncertainty there is also generally greater uncertainty regarding the competitive environment. These three factors jointly affect the organization's resource uncertainty (Milliken, 1987; Moenaert & Souder, 1990a, 1990b). The arrows in Figure 1 illustrate these relationships among the various sources of uncertainty. As the combined level of uncertainty increases, the requirements for integration within R&D, and integration with other organizational units (e.g., marketing, manufacturing, purchasing, etc.) increase (Souder & Sherman, 1993). When contractors or suppliers are involved, integration demands increase across these supply chains.

ORGANIZATIONAL STRUCTURE
AND INTEGRATION

Standardized Processes, Organizational Hierarchy, and Informal Direct Contact

In order to achieve integration across functional departments or groups, the most basic mechanism is the design of standardized processes. This often entails the design of a wide range of management information systems making full use of information systems technology. As exceptional cases, problems or the need for management decisions are encountered, the hierarchy itself is the next basic mode of integration. Under conditions that are characterized by low uncertainty and are highly routine, standardized processes and the organizational hierarchy may be the primary modes of cross-functional integration (Souder & Sherman, 1993). However, with even moderate exceptions and problems requiring decisions in lateral information processing, overreliance on hierarchical coordination becomes inefficient. Hence, the third most basic mode of integration that cuts across lines of authority is the informal direct contact between managers. This usually takes the form of telephone interaction, e-mail interactions, or meetings. If a decision is limited in scope, the solution can be developed that incorporates the expertise of personnel in the respective departments or work units. As noted by Galbraith (1973), from an information processing perspective, informal direct contact with decentralized decision making prevents upward referral and overload of the organizational hierarchy. Of course, higher levels of management may be involved in approving the decision or actually involved in the process if the magnitude of the problem requires higher level involvement. However, for those design decisions or technical problems which are limited in scope, informal direct contact between the relevant technical managers with formalized approval is the third most fundamental form of integration.

Liaison Coordinating Positions

Based on the work of Galbraith (1973, 1977), the next progressive level of integration requires the creation of liaison positions. When the volume of communication or information flow between two groups becomes significantly high, the liaison role can be used to serve as a point of contact and to coordinate activity. Such positions are particularly useful in cross-functional (intraorganizational) interfaces, such as the ones that exist between government laboratories and project offices or between R&D and marketing divisions (Sherman & Souder, 1996). They may also be necessary in cross-organizational coordination, such as the interface between a government laboratory and a contractor or between a firm and a supplier. The creation of these integrating roles bypasses the lines of communication involved in the upward referral of requests for information or technical assistance which may result in selective filtering, time delays in response, or simply the failure to initiate needed communication (Souder & Chakrabarti, 1978).

Temporary Cross-Functional Teams

The next progressive level of integration involves the temporary cross-functional team or task force (Galbraith, 1973). Liaison positions work well for coordination between two units or functional organizations. However, when a technical problem or decision arises that requires inputs from several units or functions, a temporary cross-functional team is needed. Such teams may be composed of representative managers or technical specialists from the relevant functional groups, departments or divisions. Some team members may be assigned temporarily, but on a full-time basis. Others will be assigned on a part-time temporary basis. Personnel assignment decisions would naturally be a function of the task requirements. Teams of this nature should be differentiated from permanent cross-functional teams in that these are temporary groups that exist only until the technical problem is solved or design decision reached.

Permanent Cross-Functional Teams

The next progressive mode of integration extends the temporary cross-functional team to the permanent (or semipermanent) cross-functional team. Some individuals may be assigned on a full-time basis. Again, these assignment decisions are a function of the task requirements. The use of cross-functional teams should be differentiated from a project organization in that personnel typically continue to report to their functional managers in their respective functional units.

Current developments in the use of teams and concurrent engineering are indicative of the recognition of inadequacies of cross-functional integration in the past. Over utilization of functional structures has resulted in patterns of sequential new product development processes. This is sometimes referred to as a "throwing over the wall" characterization of the movement of design data. Current applications in re-engineering organizational structures and processes are a response in many industries and many organizations to the fundamental problem of poor integration in the past. The movement away from sequential design and development processes to concurrent processes using cross-functional teams is a correction which reduces product development cycle times and improves coordination in product development. This movement away from sequential to concurrent coordination is facilitated by the use of computer-aided design and the use of networked workstations. In some cases the use of networked workstations may cross organizational boundaries to include contractor or supplier-integrated design databases.

Integrative Project Manager Positions

A central issue and a primary problem in the coordination of the activities of the cross-functional teams is that of leadership. With limited numbers of teams the problems of leadership and coordination can be managed by the relevant functional managers and by the personnel on the teams. In some cases leadership responsibility can be centered in the department where the work (or technical problem) primarily exists. Clearly autonomous (or self- managing) work team principles can be used with teams of this nature. This may solve the intra-group coordination problems, but coordination with other functional units and other cross-functional teams may be problematic. In any case, this issue inevitably leads to the next progressive form of integration. As noted by Galbraith (1973, 1977), this is the creation of the role of the manager with integrative responsibility. At this stage of integration, such managers serve in integrating roles that cut across departments or, in some cases, across organizations.

With the creation of the integrative project manager role, with responsibility for coordinating cross-functionally, we have by definition created a matrix organization. Prior to this stage of integration, coordination was achieved by functional managers and by the teams themselves. With the creation of the integrative project manager position and the matrix structure, the capacity for integration is ostensibly at a higher level (cf, Galbraith, 1973, 1977).

Three Matrix Structures

Three basic types of matrix structures exist. These are the functional matrix, the balanced matrix, and the project matrix (Gobeli & Larson, 1987). In the functional matrix system a project manager with limited authority is designated to coordinate the project across different functional areas. Here functional managers retain primary responsibility and authority for their specific segments of the project. Some personnel may be assigned from the functional areas to the project manager on either a full-time or part-time basis. However, much of the work is conducted in the functional areas with cross-functional team members working with the project manager to coordinate with the functional managers. In the functional matrix the project manager operates primarily on the basis of expert power and referent power. However, the project manager will have some limited, formal authority based on the fact that he or she will typically report to a general manager. A major problem with this system is that the limited, formal authority severely restricts the ability of this individual to coordinate efforts across departments. The common solution to this problem is to give the project manager greater budget authority.

Increasing the budget authority of the project manager leads to the second type of matrix organization. This is the balanced matrix. Here the project manager is assigned to oversee the project and shares the responsibility and authority for completing the project with the functional managers (Gobeli & Larson, 1987). Project and functional managers jointly approve a wide range of decisions relevant to project completion.

The third form of matrix is the project matrix. In this form the authority of the project manger is increased further (Gobeli & Larson, 1987). He or she now assumes primary responsibility for completing the project. The role of functional managers is to assign personnel as needed and to provide technical expertise. With the high level of budget authority assigned to the project manager, full or partial time is acquired from necessary personnel drawn from the functional organizations.

It is important to note that each of these three types of matrix structures has equal information processing capacity in terms of integration. In other words, as modes of integration they are approximately equivalent as organizational systems for processing the flow of information in product development. Therefore, the decision regarding which should be utilized is a function of the overall portions of personnel needed in functional versus project tasks, the determination of where authority should be concentrated based on strategic priorities, organizational size, the nature of the product development project, and other criteria.

Starting Points for the Graduated Sequence of Modes of Integration

Thus far, this discussion has begun with the assumption of a functional structure and added successive graduating modes of integration. Each additional mode includes and builds upon the preceding modes. It is important to observe that rather than beginning with a functional structure, the organization could also begin with a project structure and then follow the same logical sequence to achieve necessary coordination among project offices. This would include, in graduating sequence: the implementation of standardized processes (utilizing information systems technology), hierarchical coordination, direct contact among managers, the creation of formal liaison positions, the use of temporary teams crossing project or supporting departments, the implementation of semipermanent teams, and the use of a matrix structure. The decision whether to begin with a functional structure or a project structure and then add successive modes of integration should be based on the initial assessment of task interdependency based on the seminal work of Thompson (1967).

Achieving Optimal Cross-Functional Integration

Based on these observations, it should be concluded that the decision regarding the mode of integration and consequent organizational structure cannot be made solely on the basis of a single criteria. Rather, the issue of cost effectiveness must be considered and this should result in a decision based on optimization (Nadler & Tushman, 1997). With each successive mode of integration, personnel (man/hours) costs and administrative overhead costs increase. This means that one should only utilize the modes of integration that are necessary and not exceed these modes unless the integration requirements are justified and it is cost effective to implement. In this sense, instituting the appropriate modes of integration and the appropriate levels of each is always a problem of optimization. Insufficient utilization of the appropriate modes of integration based on the level of environmental uncertainty is suboptimal. In contrast, utilization of higher level modes of integration when they are not required, based on the level of environmental uncertainty, is also suboptimal. For example, a matrix organization should only be used if the integration needs require this level of integration. If more basic modes of integration are significantly more cost-effective and the greater integration capability cannot justify the additional cost, then a matrix should not be utilized. This would be, by definition, suboptimal. Figure 2 illustrates the relationships between each successive mode of integration, combined information processing capacity, and costs.

The logic of progressive modes of integration is not contained to the individual firm. It can be extended, at least in part, from intra-organizational cross-functional integration, to interorganizational strategic alliances, supply chain integration, and network structures. Strategic alliances and network structures allow firms to bring resources and core competencies together on a

Figure 2: Modes of Integration, Information Processing Capacity and Cost

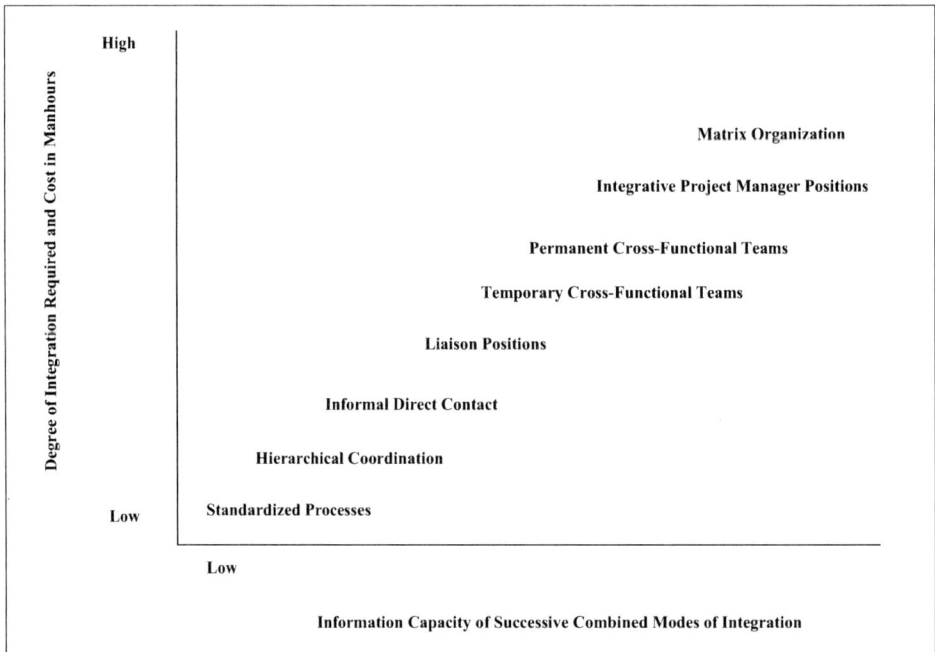

long-term basis in order to find new ways to reduce costs, to increase product quality, and to develop new innovative products. Network structures are simply a series of strategic alliances with suppliers, distributors, or other firms within the industry.

Similar to intra-organizational cross-functional integration, interfaces between organizations may include standardized processes making full use of information systems technology to coordinate routine transactions or electronically transfer design or manufacturing data during product development. Direct contact among managers from the respective coordinating organizations, the use of liaisons, and temporary or semipermanent interorganizational teams are then employed based on the integration requirements.

ILLUSTRATION OF EFFECTIVE INTEGRATION: THE BOEING 777

The development of the Boeing 777 aircraft effectively illustrates the general principles presented in this chapter. This example is presented as a model for 21st century product development based on several criteria. First, Boeing utilized the modes of integration described in this chapter for both cross-functional integration and interorganizational or supply chain integration in the development of the 777 aircraft. Secondly, Boeing made full use of information systems technology in the development of the 777. This marriage of IT and the effective use of structural modes of integration resulted in reduced schedule, effective cost control, and exceptional technical performance.

In designing the 777 Boeing utilized approximately 240 teams known as design-build teams. These teams included cross-functional representation from the pertinent engineering design functions, manufacturing, operations, and finance. In addition, the teams also included representation from customer support, the customer (airlines), and relevant suppliers (Condit, 1994). The design-build teams were organized around specific components, systems, or subsystems of the aircraft, rather than around functional specializations. Boeing's use of customer representation and input on the design-build teams was unprecedented in commercial aircraft development.

Commercial airlines that participated in the project included American, Delta, United, British Airways, Cathay Pacific, Quantas, Japan Airlines, and All Nippon Airways (Woolsey, 1991). Based on inputs from the customer airlines, approximately 1,200 design modifications were implemented. Many of these customer requirements were in the critical area of aircraft maintainability. Traditional approaches to customer input (i.e., use of the second mode of integration, hierarchical coordination) would have taken the form of correspondence and meetings at an upper management level. In contrast, by having actual airline maintenance personnel participate on the teams, improvements resulted that would otherwise be imperceptible to design engineers and airline management (Condit, 1994). Some examples included redesigning the avionics bay so maintenance engineers could physically maneuver, moving light positions to improve night visibility for maintenance crews, enlarging push buttons on exterior access panels so that maintenance crews working in cold climates would not need to remove gloves, and improved interior design flexibility (Proctor, 1994).

Suppliers were also included on the design-build teams. This included 545 suppliers with 58 of the suppliers headquartered in 12 different countries. Integration was facilitated with the use of the three dimensional CATIA computer-aided design software and the networking of over 2,000 workstations. This allowed suppliers to have real-time interactive interface with the design data (Proctor, 1994). The 777 was the first commercial aircraft ever to be 100 percent digitally designed. Traditional methods using blueprints, large mockups and models were eliminated completely. The simultaneous supplier and manufacturing inputs facilitated concurrent engineering. CATIA pre-assembly checks allowed engineers to visualize components and to query the system to identify interferences or misalignments requiring engineering change orders. CATIA was also utilized to identify gaps, confirm tolerances, and analyze stresses on parts and systems. This combination of information technology and use of optimal modes of integration allowed tool designers to obtain updated design data to facilitate the timely development of tooling (O'Lone, 1992).

In the development of the 777, Boeing utilized the same graduated sequence of modes of integration outlined in Figure 2. This included the use of standardized processes of coordination, the use of the organizational hierarchy, informal direct contact among managers in the form of telephone, e-mail, and meetings, the use of liaison coordinating positions, and the use of temporary cross-functional/cross-organizational teams (i.e., design-build teams). By combining these organizational modes of integration with the networking of workstations among Boeing engineering functions, manufacturing, and suppliers, a number of improvements over past aircraft development projects were realized. There was a reduction in engineering change orders by more than 50 percent compared to the Boeing 767, the predecessor to the 777 (Proctor, 1994). Because the design-build teams effectively incorporated customer requirements and manufacturing requirements into the design, the 777 development was highly cost-effective. This program represented a significant contrast to the classical, sequential approach where the product moves from design to engineering to manufacturing, and then finally to the customer.

CONCLUSION

In this chapter the theoretical basis for cross-functional integration requirements and a theoretical model based on the earlier work of Galbraith (1973, 1977) for determining optimal modes of integration have been further developed. The importance of achieving optimal levels of cross-functional integration is extremely important in complex organizations involved in product development and functioning in dynamic environments. In new product development or in the management of large-scale engineering projects, the effective integration of diverse inputs from multiple functional specializations is crucial to the success of the new product or system. In a highly competitive environment, issues related to product development cycle time and the cost-effectiveness of the modes of integration utilized are of considerable importance. Failure to employ the appropriate modes of integration can result in reduced levels of product quality, the launching of new products that do not fully meet customer requirements, and longer cycle times in development due to overreliance on sequential processes or engineering redesign necessitated by defective cross-functional integration (Sherman, Souder, & Jenssen, 2000).

Based on the cost-effectiveness criteria, it is suggested that organizations should always favor the use of the least complex successive modes of integration that have the capability to achieve the required levels of integration in a particular situation (Nadler & Tushman, 1997). However, just as matrix structures were overutilized in many industries 20 to 30 years ago, the current conventional wisdom favors the use of project structures and cross-functional teams as a monolithic solution to the problem of integration. This chapter has shown that the indiscriminate use of overly powerful modes of integration result in lower cost-effectiveness. Being cognizant that each mode implicitly includes each preceding mode of integration, one should employ only the level that is necessary.

Furthermore, in dynamic market environments the challenge is not to create a highly integrated steady-state efficient organization, but rather a highly responsive, environmentally adaptive organization (Nadler & Tushman, 1997). Under these conditions the modes of integration should be employed flexibly in response to emerging market opportunities and in response to the changing internal requirements for integration as each particular new product innovation moves through the development cycle.

While these issues are of significant importance to technical managers, suboptimal cross-functional integration or non-cost-effective integration continues to be problematic in many firms and in many industries. The theoretical development presented in this chapter represents one further step in providing guidance to technical managers on decisions regarding structural modes of integration.

REFERENCES

Clark, K. (1985). The interaction of design hierarchies and market concepts in technological evolution. *Research Policy,* 14, 235-251.

Condit, P. M. (1994). Focusing on the customer: How Boeing does it. *Research-Technology Management*, 37(1), 33-37.

Cooper, R. (1986). *Winning at New Products.* Reading, MA: Addison-Wesley.

Duncan, R. (1972). Characteristics of organizational environments and perceived environmental uncertainty. *Administrative Science Quarterly*, 17, 313-327.

Galbraith, J. R. (1973). *Designing Complex Organizations.* Reading, MA: Addison-Wesley.

Galbraith, J. R. (1977). *Organization Design.* Reading, MA: Addison-Wesley.

Gobeli, D. H. & Larson, E. W. (1987). Relative effectiveness of different project structures. *Project Management Journal*, 18(2), 81-85.

Lawrence, P. R. & Lorsch, J. (1967). Differentiation and integration in complex organizations. *Administrative Science Quarterly,* 12, 1-47.

Milliken, F. (1987). Three types of perceived uncertainty about the environment: State, effect, and response uncertainty. *Academy of Management Review,* 12, 133-143.

Moenaert, R. & Souder, W. E. (1990a). An information transfer model for integrating marketing and R&D personnel in new product development projects. *Journal of Product Innovation Management,* 7, 91-107.

Moenaert, R. & Souder, W. E. (1990b). An analysis of the use of extrafunctional information by R&D and marketing personnel. *Journal of Product Innovation Management,* 7, 213-229.

Moenaert, R. & Souder, W. E. (1996). Context and antecedents of information utility at the R&D/marketing interface. *Management Science*, 42(11), 1592-1610.

Nadler, D. A. & Tushman, M. L. (1997). *Competing by Design: The Power of Organizational Architecture.* Oxford University Press.

O'Lone, R. G. (1992, October). Final Assembly of 777 nears. *Aviation Week and Space Technology,* (12), 48-50.

Proctor, P. (1994, April). Boeing rolls out 777 to tentative market. *Aviation Week and Space Technology*, (11), 36-51.

Rubenstein, A., Chakrabarti, A., O'Keefe, R., Souder, W., & Young, H. (1976). Factors influencing innovation success at the project level. *Research Management,* 19, 15-20.

Sherman, J. D. & Souder, W. E. (1996). Factors influencing effective integration in technical organizations. In G. H. Gaynor (Ed.), *Handbook of Technology Management.* New York: McGraw-Hill.

Sherman, J. D., Souder, W. E., & Jenssen, S. A. (2000). Differential effects of the primary forms of cross functional integration on product development cycle time. *Journal of Product Innovation Management*, 17(4), 257-267.

Souder, W. E. & Chakrabarti, A. (1978). The R&D/marketing interface: Results from an empirical study of innovation projects. *IEEE Transactions on Engineering Management,* 4, 88-93.

Souder, W. E. & Sherman, J. D. (1993). Organizational design and organizational development solutions to the problem of R&D/marketing integration. In R. Woodman & W. Pasmore (Eds.), *Research in Organizational Change and Development* (Volume 7). Greenwich, CT: JAI Press.

Souder, W. E., Sherman, J.D. & Davies-Cooper, R. (1998). Environmental uncertainty, organizational integration and new product development effectiveness: A test of contingency theory. *Journal of Product Innovation Management*, 15, 520-533.

Thompson, J. D. (1967). *Organizations in Action.* New York: McGraw-Hill.

Woolsey, J. P. (1991, April). 777: A program of new concepts. *Air Transport World*, 60-64

Chapter XV

Fractal Approach to Managing Intelligent Enterprises

Kwangyeol Ryu
Pohang University of Science and Technology, Korea

Mooyoung Jung
Pohang University of Science and Technology, Korea

ABSTRACT

This chapter introduces a fractal-based approach to managing intelligent enterprises. Faced with intense competition in the growing global market, fundamental changes are mandatory in business models, management approaches, and technology resources. In this chapter, therefore, several strategic issues for managing intelligent enterprises are discussed in a comprehensive manner, including: (1) fractal models of an intelligent enterprise with new hierarchies and structures for future organizations, (2) strategic supply chain models of e-biz companies based on fractal architectures, and (3) Fractal Manufacturing System (FrMS) as a type of a future manufacturing system. The authors hope that understanding the proposed methodologies and approaches based on the fractal concept will not only facilitate the realization of fractal-based systems, but also give readers an insight into the requirements of future organizations.

INTRODUCTION

To facilitate effective and efficient Information and Communication Technologies (ICTs) in enterprises, an organization can autonomously change itself to take advantage of the changes in the environment. Globalization of enterprises brings complicated structures and relationships not only to persons in a group of an enterprise but also to groups in the enterprise. Complex structure, however, prohibits members of an organization from communicating opinions with each other. It finally seems to decrease the ability to accurately make ventures on rapidly emerging markets and technologies. Therefore, an intelligent enterprise must be autonomous, adaptable, flexible, and applicable to any situation in a comprehensive and consistent manner to cope with variously growing customer requirements. Overcoming spatial limitations, a spontaneous structural rearrangement of an organization is a prerequisite for survival in turbulent electronic market places.

A fundamental goal of any enterprise is to maximize the profit or minimize the cost. However, this truism alone cannot play the role of a locomotive for a successful enterprise. Corporate culture and relations with business customers are also important factors for managing enterprises. Now more than ever before, enterprises constantly persevere in their efforts to defend themselves against competition. They also try to maintain the innovative potentials needed for survival through the revolutionary change of their organizational matters, such as reconfiguration of the structure and Workflow Management (WfM) of the enterprise. Research on Supply Chain Management (SCM) continues for managing enterprises in the Internet era as the term *e*-SCM implies. These are, however, nothing more than one of several new strategic methods that are being used nowadays to increase the profitability of a business model. To achieve the highest goal of an enterprise, various technologies are needed for managing an enterprise.

In this chapter, several strategic issues for managing intelligent enterprises are discussed in a comprehensive manner. As a challenging theoretical framework of the intelligent enterprise of the 21st century, fractal-based approaches are fully discussed throughout this chapter. Intelligent enterprises can apply the characteristics of a fractal to identify, define, and explore the subject matters closely related to their businesses. First, new hierarchies and structures for future organizations are suggested by considering the methods for making profits through understanding and solving organizational problems. Then the definition and modeling of a fractal-based system are followed by methodologies of applying fractal models to an intelligent enterprise. Also discussed is a Workflow Management System (WfMS) for fractal-based systems. We propose supply chains and strategic models based on fractal architectures, focusing on numerical models for solving SCM problems in e-biz companies. Finally, we propose a Fractal Manufacturing System (FrMS) as a type of future manufacturing system.

BACKGROUND

Future Organizations

Future organizations must have a well-organized structure both inside and outside of the enterprise. The requirement of today's customers becomes diversified and specialized. To cope with dynamically changing trends of customers, an organization can make special groups to perform collaborative works at any time. Co-works between different departments in organizations are proved to make more efficient solutions. However, most of the organizations still stick to keeping traditional hierarchy, such as a pyramidal structure as illustrated in Figure 1(a). Management functions and value-creation functions are separated in such a structure. Central commands for performing processes are delivered in a top-down manner, and feedbacks are delivered in the opposite direction.

With such hierarchy, we cannot get out of fundamental shortcomings that usually come from the structure of the organization. The vertically-linked relationships might prohibit persons in lower levels of the organization from doing active and spontaneous thinking. The hierarchy makes a latent barrier interrupting organic interactions and communications between departments. Also, the organization with a hierarchy frequently makes decisions on aims of a department level in a narrow-minded view without a comprehensive understanding of the organization's goal, directions, and its circumstances. Therefore, we need new hierarchies and structures that can encourage all the members in the organization in order to make better performance and quality services to the customers with the structural flexibility. Future organizations should be composed of multi-functional entities as shown in Figure 1(b). To cope with the dynamically changing environment, the role of each entity and the structure of an organization can be continuously and autonomously reconfigured. Differences between hierarchical organizations and fractal-based organizations based on dynamic structure are summarized in Table 1.

The characteristics of future organizations include autonomy, increased professionalism, higher personal mobility within the organization, a high degree

Figure 1: Organizational Structures

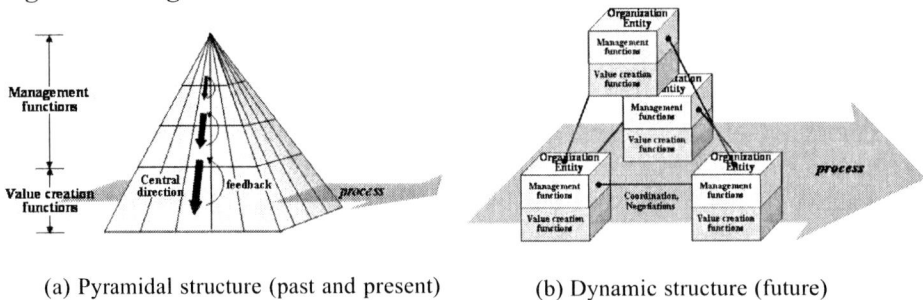

(a) Pyramidal structure (past and present)   (b) Dynamic structure (future)

Table 1: Differences Between Hierarchical Organizations and Fractal-Based Organizations

	Hierarchical Organization	Fractal-based Organization
Structure	Hierarchically structured once only, at a specific point in time	Subject to a constant process of change (dynamically restructured)
Entity relationships	Administrative higher unit and passive lower units	Coordinative higher fractal and active lower fractals
Task processing	Perform tasks according to specified objectives	Perform tasks through goal-formation process
Unit function	Each unit has its own functions according to its position and role	Every fractal has same functions but its roles can be dynamically changed
Adaptability	Suitable for a stable environment	Suitable for a turbulent environment
Flexibility	Inflexible	Flexible

of differentiation, a lower level of formality, more specialization, and so on (Stanton, 1979). However, the tone of the organization's image has drastically changed in the last few years. Organizations are becoming more and more global and virtual. Spatial limitations are negligible. Instead, virtual integration of the distributed organization becomes an important issue. Competencies for future organizations will be based on new principles like interdependency, flexibility, tolerance to the dynamically changing environment, and partnership instead of the past principles such as ownership, stability, and controllability. For example, Somerville and Mroz (Hesselbein et al., 1998) propose seven competencies for future organization; higher purpose, responsible leadership, multidisciplinary teaming, organic partnerships, knowledge networking, global search, and embracing change.

To accurately understand the future organization, we need first to understand the purposes and structure of the organization. Many models have been introduced for future organizations. Specifically, several models for future organizations are introduced in the book whose title is *The Organization of the Future* (Hesselbein et al., 1998). Hesselbein proposes "circular organizations" which have more flexible and dynamic structure compared to the past hierarchical pyramid-shaped organization. In this organization, ability of the members is considered more important than their position or rank in the organization so that all members can achieve and advance by demonstrating their originality. To maintain effective partnerships, a leader of an organization must consider three essential facts: managing for the mission, managing for innovation, and managing for diversity. Galbraith proposes "reconfigurable organizations" for future organizations (Hesselbein et al., 1998). The competitiveness of an organization cannot be maintained for a long time compared to the past. This originates from the disappearance of sustainability of competitive advantage in the fluctuating market. To keep the organization competitive, we need a reconfigurable organization. Reconfigurable organization can be facilitated by activating the role of cross-functional teams. Furthermore, the innovations for accounting, human resource management, and information system should be conducted to make organizations reconfigurable. Ashkenas proposes "boundaryless organizations" which can speed up decision-making processes and the spread of ideas and knowledge (Hesselbein et al., 1998). Boundaryless organizations can overcome inner boundaries such as hierarchical boundaries, functional boundaries between departments, and outer boundaries, including boundaries to the suppliers or customers.

The ideal organization of the future, however, can comprehensively integrate the above-mentioned characteristics. Especially, structural flexibility is the core power of future organizations. It is defined as the ability to change and reconfigure organizational structure quickly, depending on the situation of the organization's environment. Structural flexibility helps organizations adapt to changes in their competitive environments, allowing them to maintain a responsive posture. It enhances internal communications, cooperation and coordination between teams, task forces, and lateral information processing, all of which are necessary to accommodate changes in strategy, technology, and product (Daft, 1994; Hayes & Jaikumar, 1988). Organizations can be endowed with structural flexibility by employing the inherent characteristics of a fractal.

A Fractal and Fractal-Based Future Organizations

A fractal is generally defined as "an independently acting corporate entity whose goal and performance can be precisely described" (Warnecke, 1993). The term "fractal" was coined to describe organisms and structures in nature, which arrive at multiple and complex solutions by using a small number of self-imitating elements. Fractals communicate directly with their counterpart fractals following an efficient communication scheme. Fractals can be distributed without the restriction of space. They select relevant methods to achieve their goal by performing tasks with many beneficial characteristics. Essential features of fractals are summarized as follows (Warnecke, 1993):

- Fractals are self-similar and provide services;
- Fractals proceed self-organization in two ways;
   - *operative way:* procedures are optimally organized with suitable methods.
   - *tactical and strategic way:* fractals determine, formulate, and try to achieve their goals dynamically and autonomously. Fractals also regenerate, restructure, and evaporate themselves.
- Fractals are goal-oriented; the goal system composed of the coherent combination of individual goals is free from contradictions while attaining the objective of achieving corporate goals.

- For the characteristic of dynamics, fractals should be networked through efficient information and communication systems though they are spatially distributed.

Fractal-based organizations are composed of self-similar entities, referred to as fractals. Decisions are made through cooperation and negotiations with associates that each have an equal responsibility. The role of each fractal changes, depending on the circumscribing status of the dynamic and turbulent environment. The structure of fractal-based organizations can be regarded as a hybrid type of structure. However, fractal-based organizations can change their structure, operational policy, and even strategy dynamically and flexibly in order to perform specific missions. The general concept of fractal-based organizations and expectations hopefully derived from using such organizations are illustrated in Figure 2.

Figure 2: General Concept of Fractal-Based Organization and Future Expectations

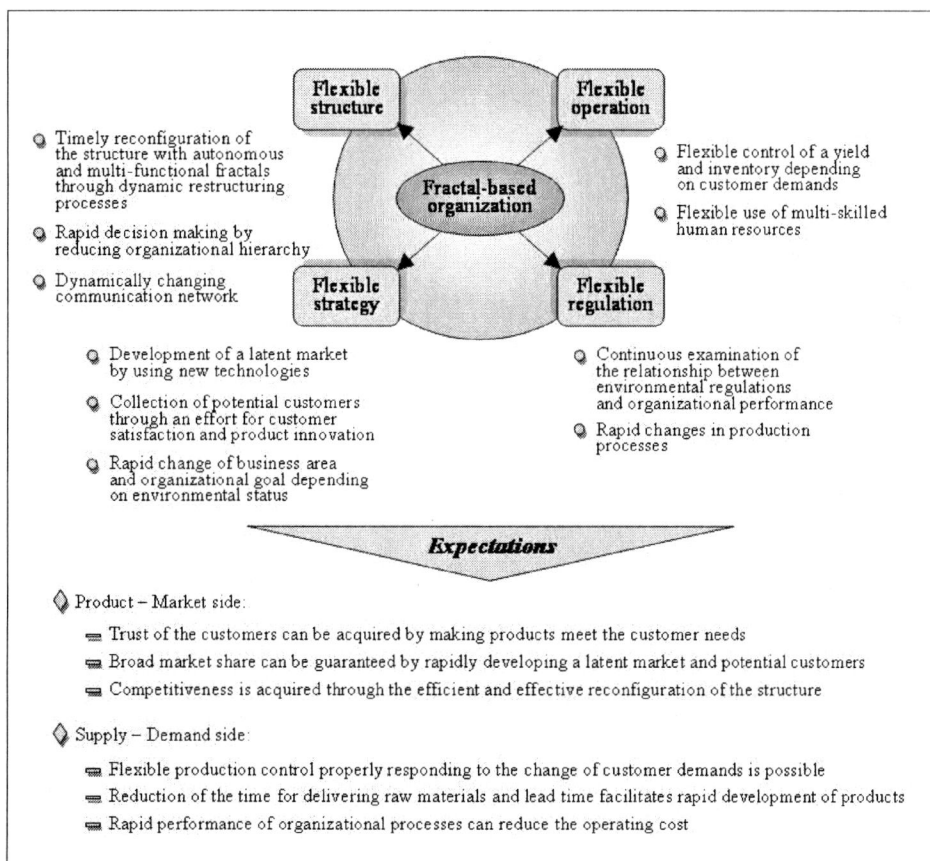

FRACTAL-BASED ENTERPRISE MANAGEMENT SYSTEM

The fractal will be the central structuring element of the intelligent enterprise in the near future. Future organizations will have an extremely complex structure and management system. Therefore, it becomes more difficult to precisely understand the workflow of the organization. However, we can capture all information about processes performed in the organization through the repeated application of a very simple set of rules of self-similar structures.

Characteristics of Fractal-Based Systems

Fractals have several special features that can be used to manage intelligent enterprises. In Warnecke's (1993) book, *Fractal Company*, a structural feature of an organization is referred to as self-similarity. Functions, actions, and workflows of fractals can be defined, captured and controlled regardless of the fractal size. Therefore, we can organize the fractal structure from individuals to the whole enterprise in the same manner as self-similarity. The conceptual structure of a fractal-based organization is illustrated in Figure 3 by using the IDEF0 format. The structure in the figure seems to be similar to a hybrid type that combines benefits of hierarchical and heterarchical structure. However, the difference between a fractal structure and a normal hybrid type is that the fractal structure can be autonomously restructured at any time if the organization needs to change it. In other words, the total number and composition of fractals can be changed depending on the situation of circumstances.

Figure 3: Conceptual Structure of the Fractal-Based Organization

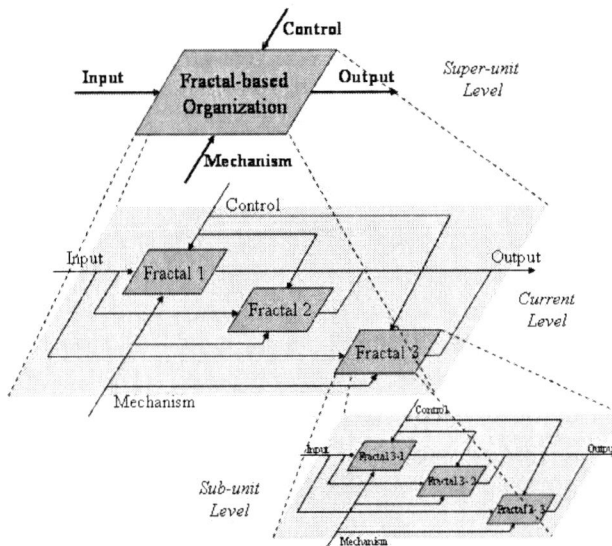

Fractal-specific characteristics include self-similarity, self-organization, self-optimization, goal-orientation, dynamics and vitality (Warnecke, 1993). Embodiment and implementation of these characteristics into the intelligent enterprise give such advantages as flexibility, co-operability, and adaptability.

Self-Similarity

The characteristic of self-similarity not only refers to the structural characteristics of organizational design, but also circumscribes the manner of performing a job (service), as well as the formulation and pursuit of goals (Warnecke, 1993). To achieve goals in an organization, there can be a variety of possible solutions to individual problems. This can make fractals with identical goals, even though input and output variables have quite different internal structures. Fractals are called "self-similar" if they can make the same outputs with the same inputs regardless of their internal structure, as illustrated in Figure 4. The characteristic of self-similarity makes it easy to understand organizational structure so that we can efficiently organize, reconfigure, control, and manage enterprises.

Self-Organization

Self-organization affects both the theoretical and operational methods. Theoretical self-organization method, referred to as self-optimization, is a method of applying suitable methods to fractals for: (1) controlling processes and workflows, and (2) optimizing the composition of fractals in the system. For example, if the workloads of fractals are not balanced, the performance of the entire system decreases. Among various numerical optimization techniques, fractals select the most suitable method and use it to find an optimal configuration. The operational self-organization method, referred to as the dynamic restructuring process (DRP), is a method of reorganizing fractals in the system by reconfiguring fractals' network connections. Figure 5 illustrates the DRP. After informing the necessity of the DRP by a self-optimization module, fractals (fractal A and B) first change physical network connections between them, and then reorganize their structure to more stable structures (new fractal A, B and C).

Figure 4: Self-Similar Fractals with Different Internal Structures (after Warnecke, 1993)

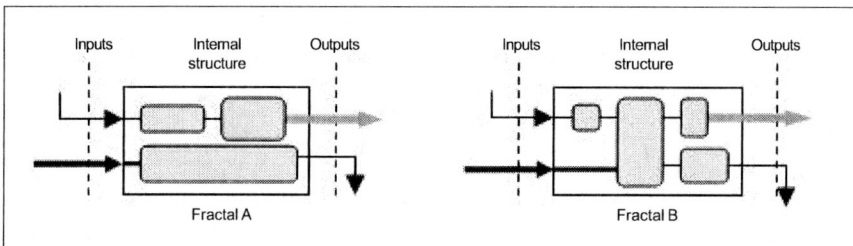

Figure 5: Dynamic Restructuring Process (DRP)

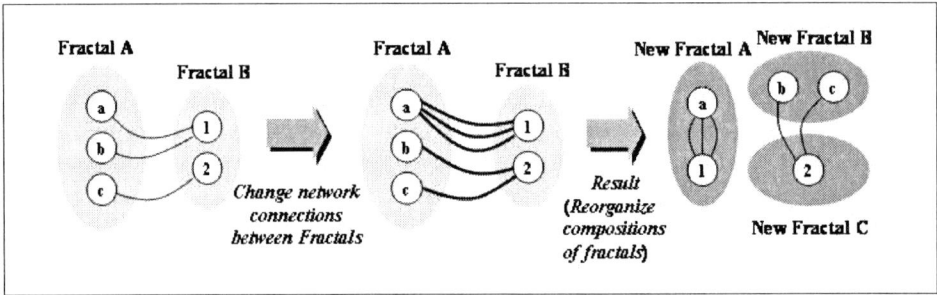

Goal-Orientation

Every fractal has an individual goal. Fractals perform a goal-formation process to generate their own goal by coordinating processes with the participating fractals and by modifying the goal as necessary (Warnecke, 1993). To coherently achieve their goals, goal consistency supported by an inheritance mechanism should be maintained. Warnecke (1993) pointed out that the goal-formation process is a reliable method for revealing any conflicts between competing goals. The fractals must continue to develop their goal autonomously in order to harmonize the system by resolving conflicts. The organizational goal can be achieved in an iterative fashion by developing the individual goals of each fractal and its feedback (see Figure 6).

Figure 6: Goal-Formation Process of a Fractal-Based Organization

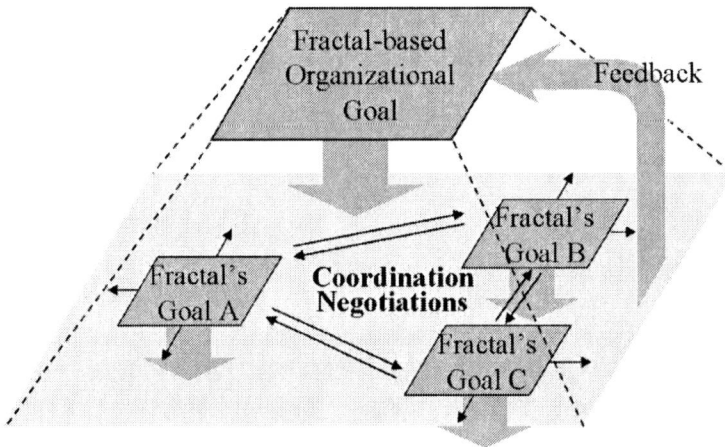

Dynamics and Vitality

Cooperation and coordination between self-organizing fractals are characterized by a high individual dynamics and an ability to adapt to the dynamically changing environment. Also, a fractal must have the decisive characteristic of vitality, which is drawn from the field of biology or medicine (Warnecke, 1993). This term is used to describe the behavioral characteristic of a fractal from its birth to death. During its living period, it serves the organization involved through iteratively correcting its relations and goals, cooperating and negotiating with others. To find the best lifecycle of fractals is regarded as an important issue for strategic operations of the fractals.

Fractal Architecture

Every fractal in an organization has the same functional modules including an observer, an analyzer, a resolver, an organizer, and a reporter as illustrated in Figure 7 (Ryu et al., 2000). Self-similar fractals deal with their jobs by cooperating and negotiating with other fractals according to their goal. All information and messages including workflows is conveyed from the reporters to the observers between fractals not only on different levels but also on the same level to perform a certain process in a customer-specific value chain. If a fractal exists on the lowest level, sensory signals must be captured directly from the environment, and action commands must be sent to the environment to achieve

Figure 7: Functional Modules and Their Relationships in a Fractal

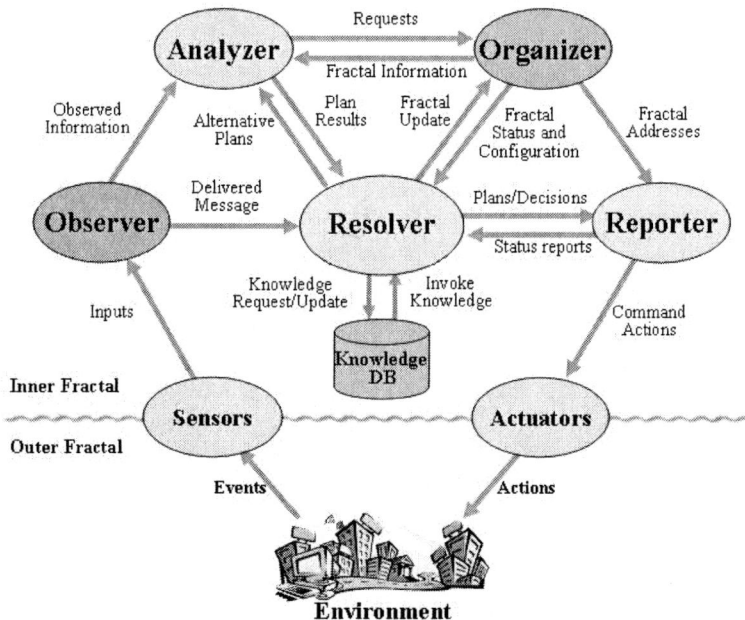

suitable actions. The rest of the communication messages between fractals, except the bottom-level fractals, are transferred via observers and reporters directly.

An observer monitors messages and information from outer fractals, and transmits composite information to correspondent modules. Based on the observed information by the observer and on the alternative plans made by a resolver, an analyzer first evaluates alternative job profiles with status information, then rates dispatching rules, and simulates analyzed job profiles in real-time. The analyzer finally reports the results to the resolver so that the resolver can use the results in making decisions. A resolver plays the most important role in a fractal, generating job profiles, goal-formation processes, and decision-making processes. An organizer manages the fractal status and fractal addresses, particularly for the dynamic restructuring process (DRP). The organizer may use numerical optimization techniques to find an optimal configuration while reconfiguring fractals. A reporter reports on information and the results of all processes in a fractal to the requesters. These functions of each module can be modeled by using IDEF0 modeling technique as illustrated in Figure 8.

Figure 8: The Function Model of a Fractal Using IDEF0

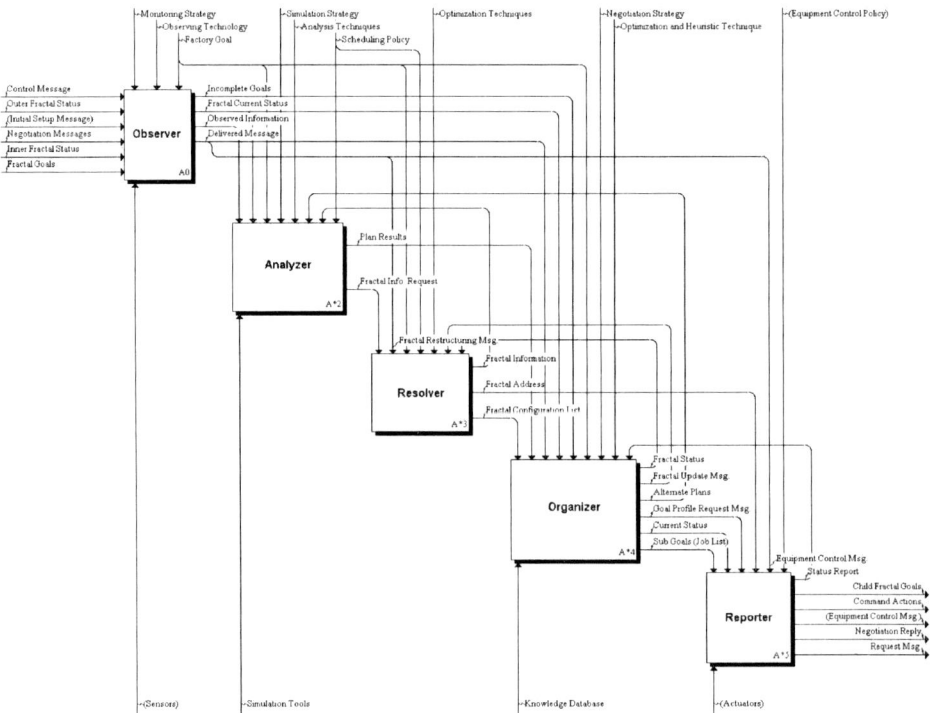

Workflow Management in Fractal-Based Organizations

Numerous products dealing with the workflow of varying functionalities have been released in the last few years. Efforts on standardizing workflow concepts and interfaces are in progress under the auspices of the Workflow Management Coalition (WfMC) and the Object Management Group (OMG). Even though there are many definitions of workflow and workflow management system (WfMS), WfMC defines workflow and WfMS as follows (Hollingsworth, 1995):

* *Workflow:* the computerized facilitation or automation of a business process, in whole or in part.
* *Workflow management system:* a system that completely defines, manages, and executes "workflows" through the execution of software whose order of execution is driven by a computer representation of the workflow logic.

Workflow Management System (WfMS) architectures have evolved from supporting mostly single workgroup-type environments to provide enterprise-wide functionality. With such enhancements as EDI (Electronic Data Interchange) on the Internet and the emerging XML (eXtended Markup Language), a single workflow is allowed to span widely spread objects, processing tasks across the networks. Users have demanded better tools to help them in using WfMSs effectively. With the automated WfMS: (1) work does not get misplaced

Figure 9: Information Flow Between Fractals

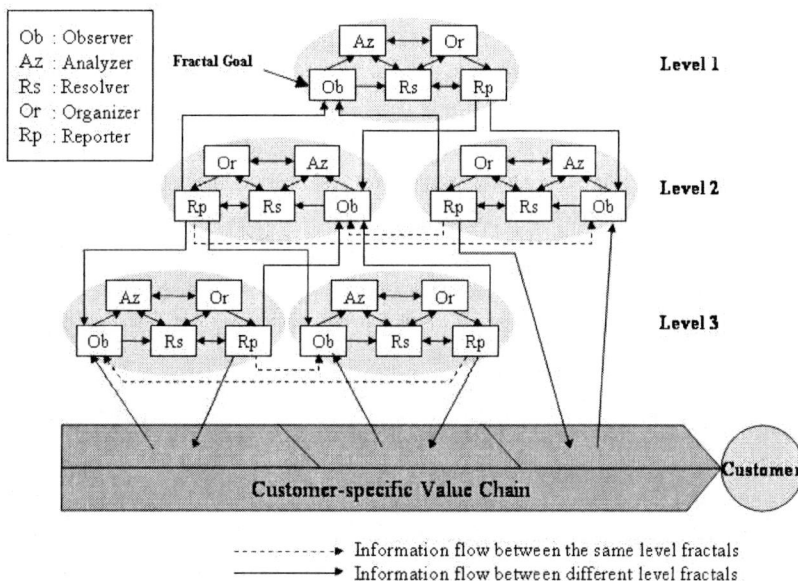

Figure 10: Components and Interactions of a Workflow Management System

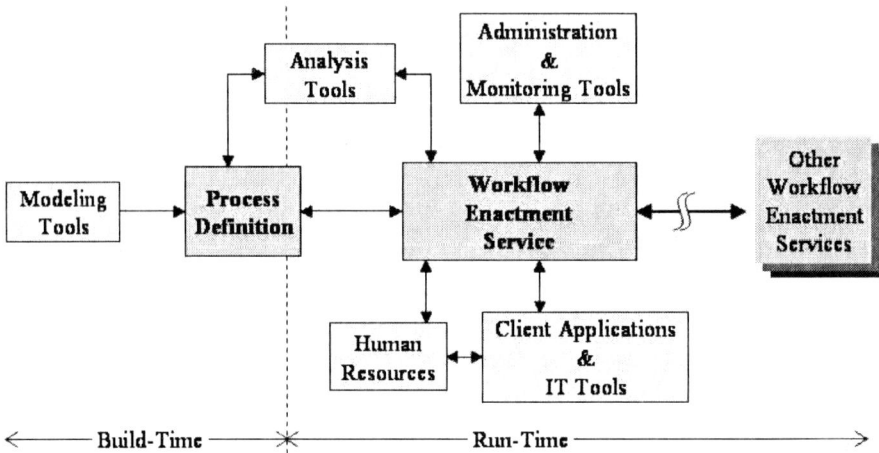

or stalled, (2) the managers can focus on staff and business issues, (3) the procedures are formally documented and followed exactly, (4) the best resource (person or machine) is assigned to handle each case, and the most important cases are assigned first, and (5) concurrent work processing, so-called parallel processing, is far more practical than in a traditional and manual workflow (Plesums, 2002).

In fractal-based organizations, all information and processes flow through observers and reporters, the gateway of a fractal. Fractals communicate with fractals at the same level and with vertically linked fractals as illustrated in Figure 9. Cooperation for WfM is executed by resolvers using workflow engines.

The WfMC is the main organization involved in workflow management standardization efforts (http://www.wfmc.org/). The workflow standards exist at three levels (the reference model, the abstract specifications, and the bindings). WfMC defined a reference model, which has identified five interfaces to the workflow engine for a WfMS architecture. The interfaces/APIs are: (1) Process definition, (2) Client interfaces, (3) Invoked applications, (4) External workflow services, and (5) Administration and monitoring (Plesums, 2002). Each step of the workflow is executed for a specific case independent of the other cases.

As depicted in Figure 10, a WfMS is composed of two main components: the workflow model (process definition) and the workflow execution module (workflow enactment service) (Ellis & Keddara, 1993). The former is used to define business processes using modeling tools during build-time. Defined processes can be modified after they are analyzed. The workflow enactment service is defined as a software service that may consist of one or more workflow engines in order to create, manage and execute workflow instances (Hollingsworth, 1995). It provides a run-time environment, in which process instantiation and activation occurs, utilizing one or more WfM engines belonging to the resolver of a fractal. The workflow enactment service uses administration and monitoring tools, analysis tools, and client application and IT tools to manage the execution and sequencing of the various tasks of the workflow process.

The resolver in a fractal may have one or more workflow engines to manage workflows of a system. The resolver can communicate or negotiate with other fractals in order to deal with ad hoc, or collaborative, workflow (Voorhoeve & Aalst, 1997) according to process definition, which is modeled in build-time. Ad hoc workflow covers cases derived from a predefined or template process and allows that the template be modified to meet some specific requirements for each case. If necessary, the resolver sends the feedback to the managers, enabling them to modify the process definition. In fractal-based organizations, the WfMS can exist separately from other systems such as production management system and supply chain management system. However, two main components, the workflow model and the workflow execution module, have to be inside of a fractal to perform tasks, because the highest-level fractal eventually means the organization itself.

WfMSs may be implemented in a variety of ways by using various ICTs. Although there are many WfMSs proposed to date, all WFMSs show certain common characteristics that workflows are controlled and managed by several functions defined with workflow models. For more efficient management of workflows, we need an insight for penetrating the process flows by fully understanding the whole structure and characteristics of an organization. To do so, it is necessary to comprehensively study supply chain management (SCM), which provides various types of modeling techniques for representing organizational relations.

STRATEGIC SUPPLY CHAIN MODEL FOR FUTURE ORGANIZATIONS

Many researchers have studied ways to optimize supply chains so that business organizations, manufacturers, and suppliers can maximize their profit. Even though such efforts related to SCM have already led to ample research and contributions to the economy, the diverse target areas vary according to their purposes, including logistics (Alvarado & Kotzab, 2001; Korpela et al., 2001a), transportation (Vidal & Goetschalckx, 2001), and manufacturing (Dong & Chen, 2001; Jeong et al., 2002; Li & O'Brien, 2001). The growing awareness of the critical impact of SCM on a company's competitiveness and strategic advantage has made supply chain an essential strategic issue, and it has received a high degree of emphasis in every industrial area (Clinton & Calantone, 1997; O'Laughlin & Copacino, 1994). The relationships between manufacturers and their suppliers have been mainly considered in SCM. Involvement of the supplier in developing products, cost and quality of delivered materials, and risks of supply disruptions are some of the major factors considered in the relationship (De Toni & Nassimbeni, 1999).

Recently, the areas concerned in SCM are shifting from a manufacturer-oriented viewpoint to a customer-oriented viewpoint (Korpela et al., 2001b). Especially, the customer has become the most important member of the supply chain of e-biz companies, which have greatly proliferated in the last decade because of the spread of network-related facilities and the World Wide Web. The high degree of uncertainty of customer demand to e-biz companies makes it difficult to deal with customer requirements. This problem, along with the high market share of e-biz companies, makes research in this area indispensable. Therefore, this section will illustrate the fractal-based framework of SCM to cope with difficulties in supply chains of e-biz companies by applying the fractal concept. Thus, it is necessary to focus on e-biz companies to fully understand SCM of today and of future organizations.

The type of e-biz companies that are the focus of this section is B2C (Business to Customer), which sells goods or provides services to customers via Web pages. As illustrated in Figure 11, an e-biz company gets orders from customers and distributes them to several manufacturers, i.e., it intermediates

Figure 11: Supply Chain Network in an E-Biz Company

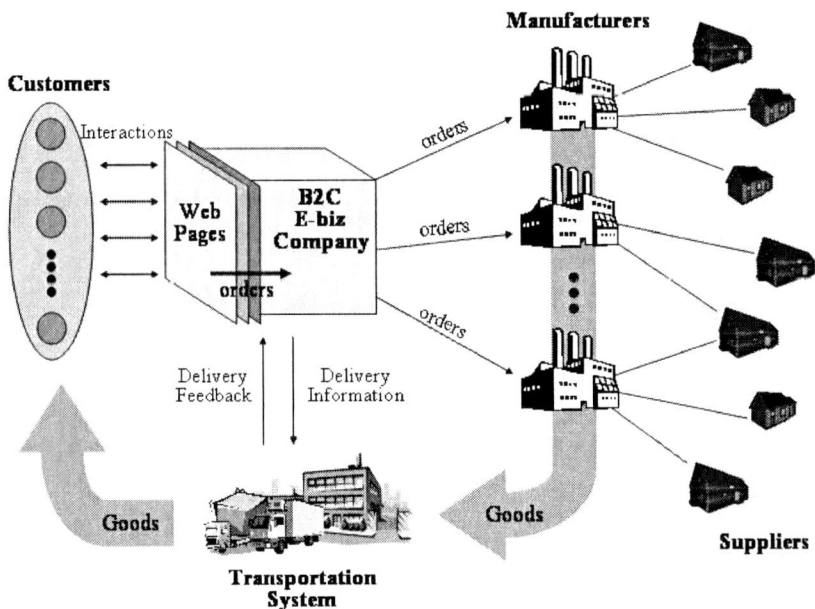

between customers and manufacturers. Usually, an e-biz company functioning as a B2C interacts with a few designated transportation systems with which they have a contract. We assume that there is one transportation system concerned. This section proposes a fractal-based framework so that we can apply the fractal concept to SCM for managing e-biz companies.

Fractal-Based SCM (*f*SCM) Framework

*f*SC headed by an e-biz company includes customers, manufacturers, suppliers, and a transportation system. Consistent with the fractal concept, each member of the supply chain becomes a fractal, and any combination of every member can be another fractal. *f*SCM itself can even be modeled as a fractal (*e-biz_fractal* in Figure 12). Assume that there are four departments in an e-biz company as illustrated in Figure 12. Three of them (I1 to I3) deal with customers' orders categorized into items, and the other (I4) interacts with a designated transportation system. This company interacts with three manufacturers (M1 to M3) supported by multiple suppliers (S1 to S7). In this case, each department of the company and each manufacturer can be considered as a fractal (*fr_e*1 to *fr_e*4, and *fr_m*1 to *fr_m*3, respectively). The supply chain of the e-biz company (*e-biz_fractal*) can be decomposed into several fractals including *fr_*1 to *fr_*4 as illustrated in Figure 12.

The *f*SCM framework can give us several advantages for solving the problems of SCM such as the following:

* *Understanding and managing a complicated system becomes easy:* the system that was developed under the *f*SCM framework can be easily

Figure 12: Composition of Fractals in a Fractal-Based Supply Chain

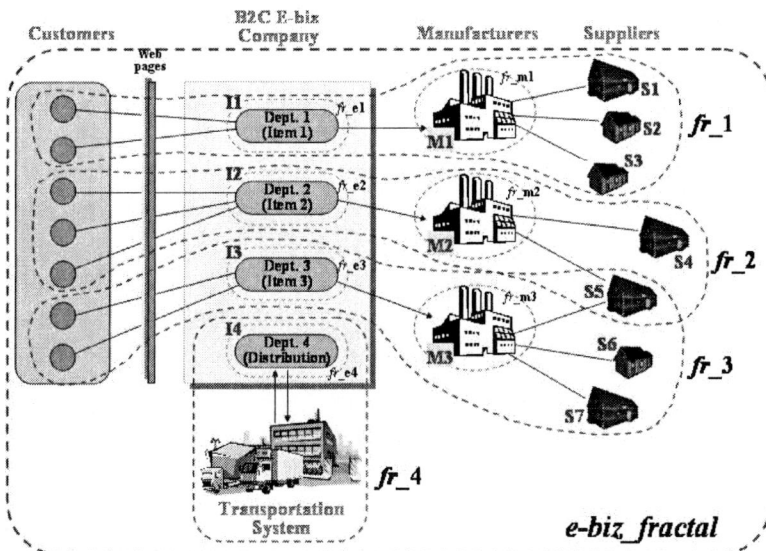

understood and managed because similar functional modules are iteratively applied to a system with various fractal levels, and communications can also be actively performed between members in supply chains.

- *Fractal-specific characteristics can be adapted in a system:* a system developed under the fractal concept already has several designated characteristics of fractals including self-similarity, self-organization (self-optimization and dynamic restructuring process), goal-formation, and so on. Self-organization facilitates the generation of rules for optimizing the goal and structure of fractals while performing goal-formation processes. Rules for optimizations are to be customized depending on the position of the fractals such as their level (e.g., top, intermediate, and bottom level) and whom they represent (e.g., customers, an e-biz company, manufacturers, etc.). With characteristics of fractals, updates and reorganization of fractal models become easier.

- *Local optimization reduces computational loads and time:* the optimization of the system under *f*SCM is performed through local optimization rather than global optimization. The fractal-based framework distributes calculation loads, reduces calculation time, and encourages rapid responses of the system by decomposing the SCM model into several fractal models. A large SCM problem can be divided into smaller ones so that the problems can be solved in an easier, faster, and more accurate manner.

- *Flexible management of supply chains is possible:* if there are supply chain models in a system for a specific member of supply chains, such models can be merged into a fractal model as a part of it. For example, if a company has used a model to minimize the production cost while producing goods, and if the company intends to optimize whole processes as well as manufacturing process now, then the old model can be incorporated into a new model while the consistency of goals is maintained. The allowance of model integration makes it possible to manage supply chains with higher flexibility.

Functional Modules in *f*SCM

The five functional modules in a fractal perform assigned jobs to achieve their goals through negotiations and cooperation between each other. Especially, the role of an analyzer and a resolver is more crucial than others because they perform operations required to make decisions in *f*SCM.

Analyzer

An analyzer performs profit analysis of the fractal based on its status and cost information. The analyzer first gathers transaction records from the database, and periodically checks the position within the target area by analyzing their cost and profit status. In order to analyze the status of *f*SCM, fractals use

Figure 13: Functional Model of an Analyzer

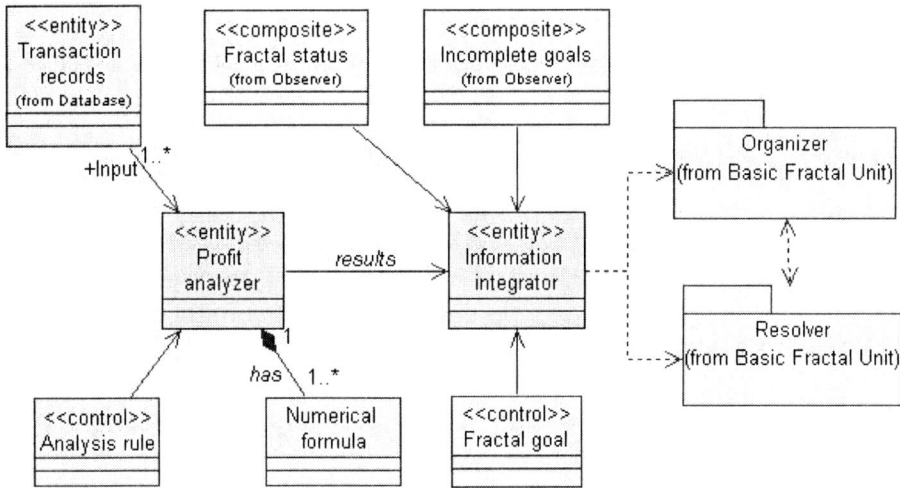

numerical formula. Then the analyzer integrates information so that it can help the resolver to make decisions. Finally, the analyzer reports the results to the resolver to facilitate optimization processes. These functions can be represented by using the class diagram of UML (Unified Modeling Language) as illustrated in Figure 13.

Resolver

Based on the current status information and results from the analyzer, the resolver employs a variety of numerical optimization or heuristic techniques to make the optimal goal for the fractal during the goal-formation processes. In *f*SCM, the mixed integer programming (MIP) technique is used. Negotiations, cooperation, and coordination processes among fractals are initiated by the resolver, if needed. The resolver is given an ability to allow the fractal to have an insight for making future strategies. For example, the resolver of the top-level fractal, which represents the e-biz company, supports decision makers or executives to make company's goals and strategies with useful information. Figure 14 illustrates the functions of the resolver.

Conceptual Modeling of fSCM

The analyzers perform profit analysis of the fractal. Typical of the characteristics of an e-biz company, it normally does not produce but instead purchases final products and delivers them to customers as a shopping agent does. If a fractal contains *n* sub-fractals, the profit of the fractal (p_f) can be optimized as follows:

Figure 14: Functional Model of a Resolver

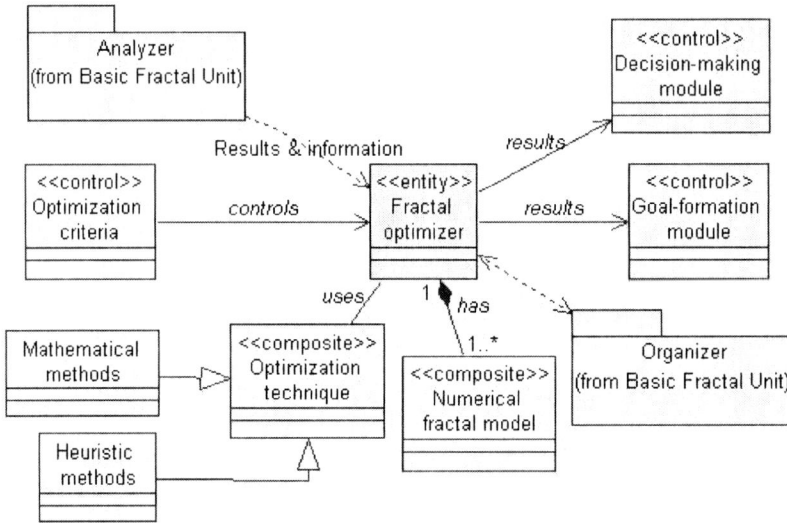

$$p_f = \sum_{i=1}^{n} p_i - C^f \tag{1}$$

where:
p_i = profit of sub-fractal i (i = 1, ..., n)
C^f = additional fixed cost for the fractal f

The profit of sub-fractals can be calculated in a similar manner until the calculation of the profit of all fractals is finished. Additional fixed cost is to be customized depending on the situation of a fractal. The results of the analysis will be used to optimize the goal of each fractal by a resolver. The optimization process is first performed locally at each sub-fractal, and then the supervisory fractal integrates them. The goal of the fractal (g_f) can be optimized as follows:

$$g_f - g_1 \oplus g_2 \oplus \cdots \oplus g_n \oplus F_f \tag{2}$$

where:
g_i = goal of the sub-fractal i (i = 1, ..., n)
F_f = numerical expression for additional factors of fractal f

The sign '$\oplus$' means the integration of models. Depending on the goal of a fractal, the model can be maximized or minimized during optimization processes. However, the consistency of goals should be maintained. For example, once the fractal decides to maximize its goal, then other goals also should be maximized. Integration of numerical models can be applied iteratively to any level of fractals in a manner similar to Equation (1). The complicated and integrated numerical models of the top-level fractal can be built from the simple model of the bottom-level fractals by adapting simple models iteratively. The results of adaptation at each level are used not only to control intra-fractal processes but also to give information to upper-level fractals. The e-biz company reflects the results of the fractals at lower levels and returns feedback to them.

After optimizations are achieved in each fractal (for example, from *fr*_1 to *fr*_4 in Figure 12), the results are sent to the upper-level fractal, i.e., *e-biz_fractal*. The analyzer of the *e-biz_fractal* merges the scattered results into a new one with fixed costs. The resolver uses other decision variables for choosing proper advertisement agencies. However, the numerical model of the *e-biz_fractal* is not a perfect model because the consideration of advertisement agencies is an example of possible factors that are handled only in the company-level fractal. Each e-biz company functioning as a B2C must determine a frequency at which to perform optimization, e.g., daily, weekly, monthly, and so on. However, the company may perform this process elastically depending on the environment.

Numerical Example

We have developed a numerical model based on the proposed *f*SCM framework. After gathering the required information from web sites of an e-biz company, we optimized the model to obtain useful information and results. The objective function is to minimize the total cost of the company, and the goal consistency of fractals is kept during the optimization process. Although detailed descriptions on numerical models are omitted in this chapter, Figure 15 illustrates the result of the optimization process for *fr*_1 as an example.

Figure 15: The Result of the Optimization Process (fr_1)

Min.
Objective function value = 21435

1) Decision Variables: Products in Department 1

	r1	r2	r3	r4	r5	r6	r7	r8	r9	r10
x_J	1	1	1	0	1	1	1	1	1	1
k1(y_r1)	300	0	0	0	0	0	0	100	0	0
k2(y_r2)	0	230	0	0	0	0	0	0	0	0
k3(y_r3)	0	0	300	0	0	125	0	0	0	0
k4(y_r4)	0	0	0	0	600	0	245	0	0	0
k5(y_r5)	0	0	0	0	0	0	0	0	850	0
k6(y_r6)	0	0	0	0	0	0	0	0	0	150

2) Demands

	r1	r2	r3	r4	r5	r6	r7	r8	r9	r10
d_J	300	230	300	40	600	125	245	100	850	150
v_J	7	12	4	6	13	6	13	15	17	5
d_J * x_J	300	230	300	0	600	125	245	100	850	150
Const. 4	=<=	=<=	=<=	=<=	=<=	=<=	=<=	=<=	=<=	=<=
Sum of y_rk	300	230	300	0	600	125	245	100	850	150

3) Refunds

	r1	r2	r3	r4	r5	r6	r7	r8	r9	r10
# of refund	10	11	2	5	4	1	12	0	7	2
Unit cost for refund	6	10	3	5	3	4	8	12	2	4
r_J	60	110	6	25	12	4	96	0	14	8
r_J * x_J	60	110	6	0	12	4	96	0	14	8
Const. 5	<=	<=	<=	<=	<=	<=	<=	<=	<=	<=
Gamma r	90	115	45	10	90	25	102	60	85	30

4) Capa([y_rk])

	r1	r2	r3	r4	r5	r6	r7	r8	r9	r10
k1	300	400	0	0	0	0	0	100	0	0
k2	200	250	0	0	0	0	0	150	0	0
k3	500	200	350	50	800	200	0	0	0	0
k4	0	0	400	30	650	300	250	0	0	0
k5	0	0	0	0	0	350	300	200	900	150
k6	0	0	0	0	0	0	0	250	700	200

Const. 6

	r1	r2	r3	r4	r5	r6	r7	r8	r9	r10
k1	=<=	<=	=<=	=<=	=<=	=<=	=<=	<=	=<=	=<=
k2	<=	<=	=<=	=<=	=<=	=<=	=<=	<=	=<=	=<=
k3	<=	<=	<=	<=	<=	<=	<=	=<=	=<=	=<=
k4	=<=	=<=	<=	<=	<=	<=	<=	=<=	=<=	=<=
k5	=<=	=<=	=<=	=<=	=<=	=<=	<=	=<=	<=	<=
k6	=<=	=<=	=<=	=<=	=<=	=<=	=<=	<=	<=	=<=

5) Brand

	r1	r2	r3	r4	r5	r6	r7	r8	r9	r10
Sum of	1	1	1	0	1	1	1	1	1	1
Sign(y_rk)	=<=	=<=	=<=	<=	=<=	=<=	=<=	=<=	=<=	=<=
	1	1	1	1	1	1	1	1	1	1

6) c_rk

	r1	r2	r3	r4	r5	r6	r7	r8	r9	r10
k1	6	11	0	0	0	0	0	12	0	0
k2	6	10	0	0	0	0	0	13	0	0
k3	7	10	3	5	4	0	0	0	0	0
k4	0	0	5	5	3	5	8	0	0	0
k5	0	0	0	0	0	5	9	14	2	5
k6	0	0	0	0	0	0	0	13	3	4

INTELLIGENT
MANUFACTURING ENTERPRISES

To meet dynamically changing customer requirements is also difficult in manufacturing domains because existing control systems are not flexible enough to handle changes in the circumscribing environment. The manufacturing system of the future must be flexible, highly reconfigurable, and easily adaptable to the dynamic environment. Furthermore, it has to be an intelligent, autonomous, and distributed system composed of independent functional modules. As the model of future manufacturing systems, a bionic or biological manufacturing system (BMS) (Okino, 1993; Ueda, 1992), a holonic manufacturing system (HMS) (Brussel et al., 1998; Seidel et al., 1994), and a fractal manufacturing system (FrMS) (Ryu et al., 2000; Ryu et al., 2001; Ryu & Jung, 2002; Tirpak et al., 1992; Warnecke, 1993) have been proposed in the distributed manufacturing system (DMS) paradigm.

Distributed Manufacturing System (DMS)

The BMS considers manufacturing systems as biological organs, and the equipment or components in the system as cells from a biological viewpoint. The BMS aims to deal with non-pre-deterministic changes in manufacturing environments based on biologically-inspired ideas such as self-growth, self-organization, adaptation, and evolution (Ueda et al., 1997). The modelon concept is applied to model the cells, the organs, or the living beings in BMS. Each modelon has a static set of properties and behaviors. Cells change their own conditions by the

Figure 16: Structural Similarity Between Biology and Manufacturing

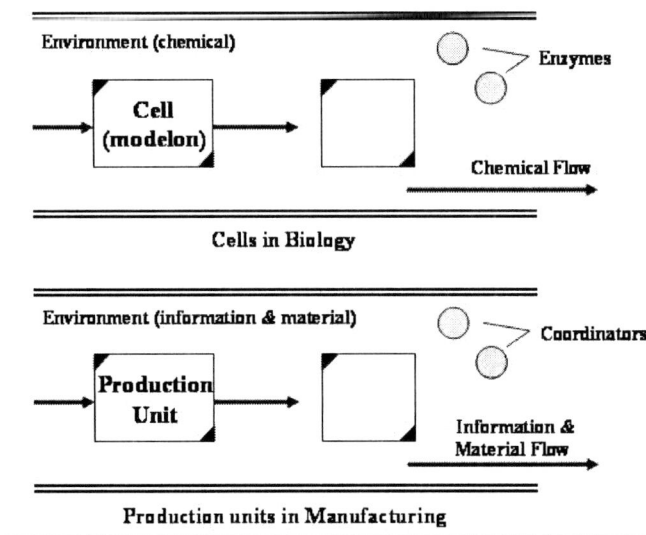

exchange of information with the internal and external environment. They can be combined with other modelons in a hierarchical structure, forming distinct entities as well as designated modelons. These properties correspond closely with autonomously operating manufacturing entities as illustrated in Figure 16 (Tharumarajah et al., 1996). The notion of DNA inheritance is translated into a manufacturing context by the properties and behaviors of modelons.

HMS is a well-known approach to developing distributed manufacturing systems. Koesler (1967) first coined the term, holon, meaning simultaneously a whole and a part of the whole, and his work provides a useful background to HMS research. Holons in HMS consist of several basic holons including a resource, product, and order holon. They can also be made up of other holons, possessing both self-assertive and integrative tendencies. The HMS consortium under the intelligent manufacturing system program developed more specific and detailed definitions for terminologies such as holon, holarchy, and holonic system (Seidel et al., 1994). A holarchy is defined as a hierarchy or self-regulating holons which function (a) as autonomous wholes in supra-ordination to their parts, (b) as dependent parts in subordination to controls on higher levels, and (c) in coordination with their local environment (Tharumarajah et al., 1996). Figure 17 illustrates basic holons of an HMS and their relations (Brussel et al., 1999).

The FrMS is a new manufacturing concept evolved from the "fractal factory" introduced by Warnecke (1993). The general definition of a fractal provides a starting point for understanding the basic concept of the FrMS. One weakness of that definition, however, is that it only concerns with theoretical issues of manufacturing systems. In other words, it does not regard the implementation of fractals. Therefore, we provide a modified definition of a fractal as follows:

• A fractal is a self-similar mobile agent whose goal can be achieved for itself through cooperation, coordination, and negotiations with others, and it can

Figure 17: Basic Holons and Their Relations

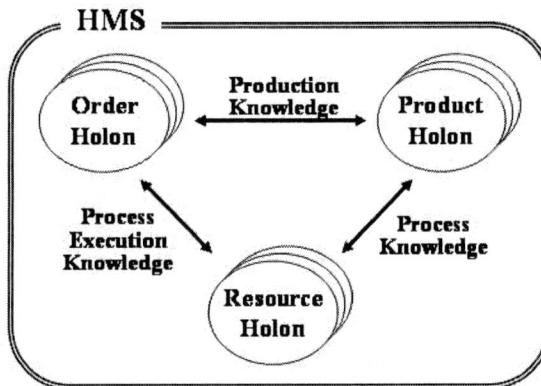

reorganize the system to a more efficient and effective one through a
dynamic restructuring process.
- The FrMS is a highly flexible system developed and operated under the
fractal architecture.

A fractal has not only fractal-specific characteristics including self-similarity, self-organization, self-optimization, goal-orientation, and dynamics, but also
has characteristics of an agent such as autonomy, mobility, intelligence, cooperation, and adaptability, because it is a set of agents. Automatic reconfiguration of
a system through a dynamic restructuring process (DRP) is the most distinctive
characteristic of the FrMS. The scope of the reconfiguration does not include
reconfigurable hardware (http://ercrms.engin.umich.edu/research/research.html)
and layout design. Rather, it focuses on the structure of software components
that can be reorganized with software manipulations. Fractals make complex
decisions on the user's behalf under their own control. The reconfiguration or
restructuring considers both dynamic clustering of the agents and construction/
destruction/cloning of agents, which affect the number of agents in the system.
The function of a fractal is not specifically designated at the time of its first
installation in the FrMS. The reconfiguration also includes situations where the
agents' enrollments are changed, meaning that the agents are assigned a new
goal and new jobs, but their composition does not change. In view of consisting
modules, a fractal can be called a basic fractal unit (BFU). Several researchers
have tried to adapt the fractal concept to manufacturing systems to facilitate
integration of systems with higher performance and flexibility (Ryu et al., 2000;
Ryu et al., 2001; Tirpak et al., 1992; Warnecke, 1993).

The basic concept of the BMS and the HMS resembles that of the FrMS in
view of the underlying principles of designing highly flexible and dynamic
manufacturing systems. However, the three concepts differ in their structural
and functional aspects. For detailed comparisons, refer to the research of
Tharumarajah et al. (1996) and Sousa et al. (1999). The basic unit of FrMS,
HMS, and BMS is an autonomous and dynamic entity, namely fractal (or referred
to as BFU — basic fractal unit), holon, and cell (or Modelon), respectively. Each
unit is predefined at the beginning stage. The functions of a fractal, a holon, and
a modelon are also initially predefined. However, the point of time at which to
define the functions of basic units is explicitly different. In BMS, the functions
of each modelon defined at the time of designing can be divided into several sub
functions or merged into bigger functions during the operating time. However,
the boundary of functions is maintained throughout the system lifetime, i.e., new
functions are not defined during the system operation. In HMS, the functions of
each holon are predefined based on the functional decomposition of a system at
the time of designing. For example, some basic holons are defined and named by
their functions such as the product holon (dealing with the information about

product), the resource holon (managing resource information), and the order holon (managing orders). When the system needs enhanced functions, several holons are freely defined and used in the system such as a planning holon or a scheduling holon. The functions of these holons are not changed during the whole system lifetime. However, the functions of each fractal in the FrMS can be dynamically changed at any time according to the individual goal and the system goal. The fractal, which deals with equipment at a certain period of time in the lowest level, can manage strategic information to achieve its goal. The fractal structure is very flexible and can be dynamically reorganized because of the re-definability of functions of each fractal.

Formal modeling of agents and fractal-specific characteristics provide a foundation for the development of the FrMS. However, various difficulties have, to date, prevented a fractal-based system from being embodied such as lack of computing powers, insufficient researches on methodology and technology focusing on the implementation of fractal-based systems, inefficient negotiation schemes for agents, etc. This section, therefore, proposes the FrMS as a next generation manufacturing system, discussing the characteristics of the system and the methodology for developing the FrMS. The topics discussed are the definition of agents constructing a fractal, the modeling of fractal-specific characteristics, a novel negotiation scheme for efficient communications among agents, and a prototype of agents.

Figure 18: Reorganization of the System Using a Dynamic Restructuring Process in the FrMS

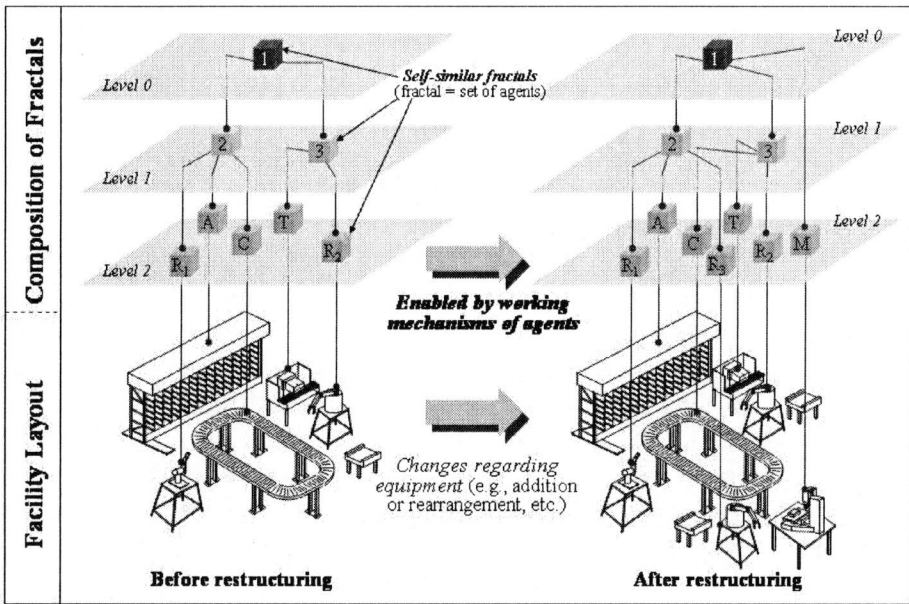

Agent-Based FrMS

Figure 18 depicts an overview of the FrMS. Every controller at every level in the system has a self-similar functional structure composed of an observer, an analyzer, a resolver, an organizer, and a reporter. After the initial setup of a system, the configuration of the system can be reorganized in response to disturbances such as breakdowns, unexpected variations in processing times, and failed operations. The system will also need to be reconfigured when the set of parts to be produced in the system changes due to a change in customer needs. In these cases, fractals in the FrMS autonomously and dynamically change their structure, taking appropriate actions of agents. Figure 18 shows two facility layouts and the corresponding compositions of fractals before and after the restructuring process. When a machine (M) and a robot (R3) are added to the system, fractals reorganize themselves with the mechanism of dynamic restructuring process (DRP) in a way that the system continues to work with the greatest efficiency.

Agents in FrMS

Agent technology has been widely used for various applications including information filtering and gathering (Chen & Sycara, 1998), knowledge management (Baek et al., 1999), supply chain management (Kaihara, 2001), manufacturing architecture, and system and design (Fisher, 1999; Khoo et al., 2001; Maturana & Norrie, 1996). While the features and characteristics of an agent vary depending on the application, some common features found across different applications are as follows:

- *Autonomy:* capability of moving and acting for itself in order to achieve goals;
- *Mobility:* migrating capability of its location from one place to other places, (an agent with mobility is called a mobile agent, usually known as a software agent);
- *Intelligence:* capability of learning and solving problems;
- *Cooperativeness:* capability of helping others if requested;
- *Adaptability:* capability of being effectively used at various domains;
- *Reliability:* capability of dealing with unknown situations (disturbances) and continuing actions if committed.

The mobility of agents is a useful feature in a distributed and dynamic system. A mobile agent is not bound to the system where it begins execution. It can travel freely among the controllers in a network and transport itself from one system in a network to another. The following are some advantages of the use of mobile agents in a system (Lange & Oshims, 1998): (1) it reduces the network load, (2) it overcomes network latency, (3) it encapsulates protocols, (4) it is executed asynchronously and autonomously, (5) it adapts dynamically to the environment, (6) it is naturally heterogeneous, and (7) it is robust and fault-tolerant.

The types and functions of agents that implement functional modules of an FrMS have been briefly described, and their initial development has been published in the earlier literature (Ryu et al., 2001). The names, types, and functions of agents in the FrMS are described as follows. The terms "-M" and "-S" written after the abbreviated name of each agent represent mobile agents and software agents respectively.

1. *Agents for an Observer*
- **Network Monitoring Agent (NMA-S):** NMA monitors messages from other fractals through TCP/IP. It receives messages from the upper/same/lower-level fractals, such as requests for negotiations, negotiation replies, job orders, status information, etc. The NMA delivers those messages to the resolver or the analyzer.
- **Equipment Monitoring Agent (EMA-S):** EMA monitors messages directly coming from equipment through a serial communication protocol such as RS232/422. Information on the status of equipment, including signals indicating the start and completion of jobs, are detected by the EMA. However, the fractal need not directly control equipment if it is not included in a bottom level.
2. *Agents for an Analyzer*
- **Schedule Evaluation Agent (SEA-S):** SEA evaluates job profiles generated by the resolver. It helps the resolver to select the best job profile with respect to the current situation of the fractal.
- **Dispatching-rule Rating Agent (DRA-S):** DRA chooses the best dispatching rule for achieving its goals among several rules, such as shortest processing time (SPT), earliest due date (EDD), etc.
- **Real-time Simulation Agent (RSA-S):** RSA performs real-time simulations in the on-line state with the results of the analyzed job profiles and the best dispatching rule. The RSA reports the results of simulations to the resolver.
3. *Agents for a Resolver*
- **Schedule Generation Agent (SGA-M):** SGA generates operational commands or alternative job profiles for achieving the fractal's goals. After evaluation and analysis of alternatives in the analyzer, the SGA selects the best job profile. It must have mobility in order to use SEA, DRA, and RSA in the analyzer.
- **Goal Formation Agent (GFA-S):** GFA modifies incomplete goals delivered from the upper-level fractal, and tries to make the goals complete by

considering the current situation of the fractal. GFA divides the goal of the fractal into several sub-goals, and sends them to the sub-fractals.

- **Task Governing Agent (TGA-S):** TGA generates tasks from the best job profile and its goals. It also performs tasks after arriving at the target fractal. When it finishes performing tasks, it sends acknowledgment to its sender.
- **Negotiation Agent (NEA-M):** NEA moves to other fractals to deliver negotiation messages or to gather negotiation replies created by participating agents. It filters out unreasonable replies by a pre-evaluation process and brings the rest back to the resolver.
- **Knowledge Database Agent (KDA-M):** KDA invokes knowledge data from the knowledge database to make decisions. It accumulates new knowledge or updates the existing knowledge.
- **Decision-Making Agent (DMA-S):** DMA performs several operations during the decision-making processes. A DMA creates NEAs to negotiate with other fractals and KDAs to use the knowledge database. After making decisions, the DMA generates several TGAs. Further, the DMA provides a context to agents for negotiation.

4. *Agents for an Organizer*
- **Fractal Status Manager (FSM-S):** FSM collects and manages the information on the status of fractals that is used for analyzing job profiles in the analyzer. It also makes negotiation replies to the status requests from other fractals.
- **Fractal Address Manager (FAM-S):** FAM manages information about the addresses of fractals in lower levels and at the same level. A fractal address is the fractal's physical address on the network, such as an IP address. The reporter uses a fractal's address to confirm the destination of tasks and messages.
- **Restructuring Agent (REA-M):** REA performs several operations related to dynamic restructuring processes, such as BFU generation, BFU deletion, and the evaluation of the fractal's performance. The performance of a fractal is its utilization, e.g., total number of processed jobs or the portion of processing time within total time, etc. If the REA decides that a fractal needs to be restructured, it gathers information about fractal and network addresses, and fractal status. It moves to the DMA and lets it generate a series of jobs for a restructuring process. The cloning mechanism is used to create a new BFU. After creation, the REA tells the FAM to update the addresses of other fractals.

5. *Agents for a Reporter*
- **Network Command Agent (NCA-M):** All tasks or messages are delivered to other fractals by the NCA. NCA gets the network address of

the destination from the FAM and notifies the TGAs and NEAs of it before starting to migrate to other places to comply with the traveling list.

- **Equipment Command Agent (ECA-S):** When ECA gets tasks for controlling equipment from a TGA, it specifies or divides the tasks into several commands that can be accepted and performed by the equipment. Then, it sends the machine commands to the equipment. Like the EMA, the ECA is not needed for a fractal at the bottom level.

6. *Miscellaneous Agents*

- **System Agent (STA-S):** STA manages device hardware and basic operating systems of physical controllers. It maintains the specifications of controllers so that REA can find the proper specification for a new controller, which has to be set up as a fractal among available candidates during dynamic restructuring processes. It can also help to copy agents by doing preparation work such as making directories or installing device drivers by giving notice to an installer about software for equipment.

- **Network Agent (NTA-S):** NTA manages the network addresses of the unassigned controllers in the system. If the system needs more controllers during the restructuring process, the REA confirms the information about the unassigned controllers from the NTA before cloning agents. When a fractal changes the information about the unassigned controllers, it must notify other fractals so that they can update their information.

UML Models For Fractal-Specific Characteristics

Characteristics that differentiate an FrMS from other manufacturing systems include: (1) self-similarity, (2) self-organization, and (3) goal-orientation. Specifically, the dynamic restructuring process (DRP), which is a part of self-organization, is the most distinctive characteristic.

Self-Similarity

To achieve goals in a manufacturing system, there can be various possible solutions with respect to the individual problems. Even if there may exist several components with the same goal in the system, conditions or situations may be different because of the dynamically changing status in the manufacturing shop floor. Self-similar structure of each fractal can be affirmatively used to develop control software for manufacturing resource in the design phase because control modules or agents can be generated from the common structures. Therefore, a fractal designed at one level can be applied to other levels in the FrMS because of the self-similarity of fractals.

Self-Organization

The dynamic restructuring process (DRP), one of the most important operational self-optimization methods, supports the reorganization of network connections between fractals so that the FrMS can be optimized and adapted to a dynamically changing environment. The DRP continuously changes the structure of the whole system depending on the fractals' goals and external environmental conditions. For example, it is supposed that an unexpected event causes a controller to malfunction, or the type of parts that have to be produced in a system changes. In that case, controllers need to be changed or reorganized. The FrMS can perform these tasks automatically and dynamically with little intervention from human operators by using the DRP.

The REA (Restructuring Agent) in an organizer leads the DRP. Figure 19 illustrates the activities of the DRP using the UML activity diagram. If the REA decides to perform the DRP based on the results of periodic evaluations of a fractal's performance, it first makes a new structure of fractals by employing a resource optimizer. The REA also employs the DMA (Decision-Making Agent) if it needs to negotiate with other fractals. The REA sends a request for the address information to an NTA (Network Agent). It also sends a request for the specification for a new controller to the FSM (Fractal Status Manager) if the system needs more controllers. Then, the REA sends a request to the FAM to get the addresses of fractals associated with the DRP. The REA creates a restructuring message, and informs the DMA of the DRP to make it generate the series of jobs for restructuring the fractals. The task executor in each of the TGAs (Task Governing Agents) conducts DRP-related jobs. Finally, the REA informs the FAM that fractal address information must be updated before finishing the DRP.

Goal-Orientation

The FrMS continues to develop goals autonomously in order to operate and harmonize the system by resolving conflicts. Basically, efficient production may be a usual goal. Such goals, however, change to other goals. But, in accordance with the surrounding environment, this goal may be changed to completing production at the earliest possible time or minimizing defects. The change of the goal at the highest level gives rise to the changes of the goal in sub-fractals. At the bottom level, if a fractal controls a machining center, shortening the processing time or the optimization of tool paths may be exemplary goals. From the goal of the top-level fractal, i.e., factory goal, the goals of lower-level fractals are generated and pruned by the goal-formation process.

The system should allow fractals to negotiate their goals with other fractals at any time, since it is very hard to anticipate which situations will require negotiation. For negotiations between agents, the contract net protocol (CNP) is still widely used, which was proposed by Smith (1980). This approach is an opportunistic system for allocating tasks. It defines a protocol that specifies the interchange between agents when an agent request bids and awards contracts to other counterpart agents. However, the CNP is somewhat expensive in terms

Figure 19: Activity Diagram for Dynamic Restructuring Process

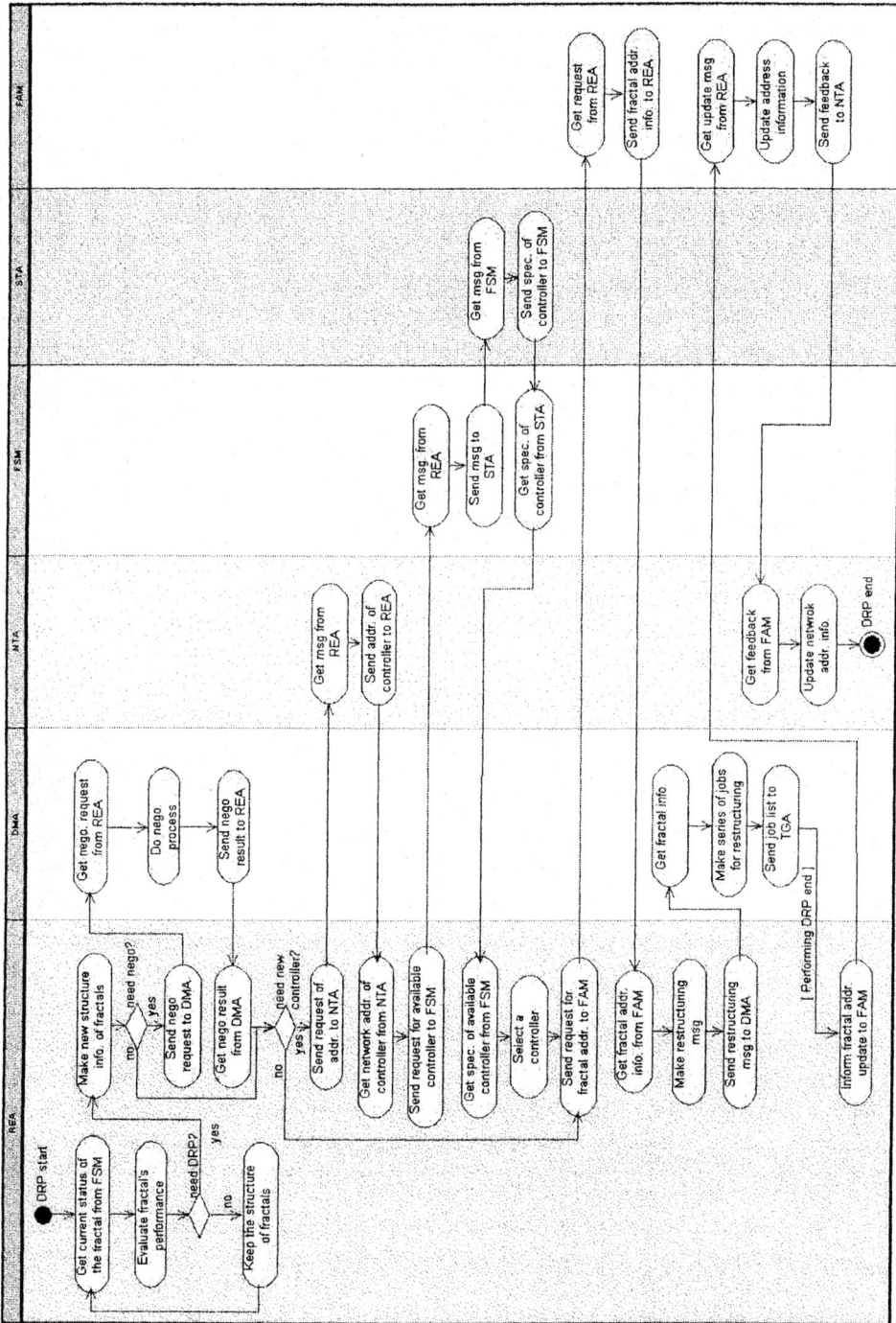

Figure 20: MANPro-Based Negotiation in the FrMS

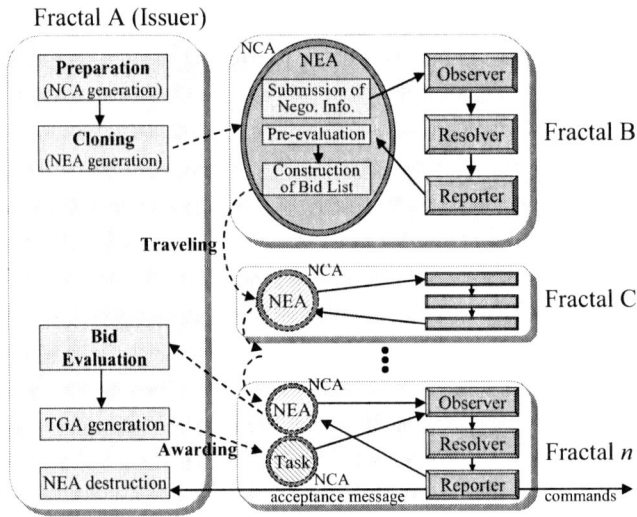

of network bandwidth when many loads are needed during communications. To efficiently load off in a system operated by mobile agents, a mobile agent-based negotiation process (MANPro) was proposed (Shin et al., 2001). The negotiation in the MANPro has four phases: (1) preparation, (2) cloning, (3) traveling and evaluation, and (4) awarding. Figure 20 illustrates the MANPro-based negotiation process in the FrMS. When a fractal needs to negotiate with others, the DMA (Decision-Making Agent) determines a route for the agent's traveling and creates an NCA (Network Command Agent) during the preparation phase. Then, the DMA creates an NEA (Negotiation Agent) during the cloning phase, which contains information about a negotiation, pre-evaluation methods, and conflict-resolution methods. After being moved to the reporter, the NEA is encrypted to the NCA and then starts the navigation according to its traveling list in order to gather negotiation replies from others. During a traveling and evaluation phase, the NEA pre-evaluates negotiation replies from other fractals. If the reply does not meet the pre-evaluation requirements, it is dropped. Otherwise, the NEA adds the pre-evaluation result to the *reply_list*. After making a complete *reply_list*, the NEA goes back to the DMA and reports the results necessary for the decision-making. If DMA determines an awardee (fractal), then it generates TGAs (Task Governing Agents) and sends them to the awardee after they are encrypted by NCAs. When the fractal receives tasks from the issuer, it sends back an acceptance message so that the issuer can destruct the NEA that was used for the negotiation.

Prototype Agents (DMA and NEA)

Before developing all 18 agents of a fractal, a DMA (Decision-Making Agent) and an NEA (Negotiation Agent) have first been developed as a prototype implementation. The major focus of this development was the implementation of the functions of MANPro. Each agent has been designed with UML and developed with Aglets™ (Lange & Oshims, 1998, http://www.trl.ibm.com/aglets/index_e.htm). Aglets™ is the Java™-based agent development tool developed by IBM Japan. Environments are provided on the host computers by specialized servers, which understand the Agent Transfer Protocol (ATP) and provide security and other services. The most important reason to use a Java™-based language is to facilitate platform-independent systems. Furthermore, Aglets™ is an open source program so that programmers can customize their own programming environments while they develop agents. Figure 21 illustrates the procedure for creating DMA (Decision-Making Agent) and NEA (Negotiation Agent) from Tahiti, an agent server. The "create" button displays the list of registered agents to the users. When a user chooses DMA from the list, a DMA is created as illustrated in Figure 21. The "Make NEA" button belonging to the DMA is used to create an NEA.

Figure 22 illustrates the negotiations between the DMA and the NEA on the basis of the MANPro protocol. As shown in the current address field of each DMA, each DMA is expected to be on a different (distributed) server. As shown in the figure, four prototype agents have been tested on the same machine (POSCIM) with different port numbers (e.g., 4434, 4444, 4445, 4446) for the ease of presentation. Similarly, the same system has been successfully tested on distributed machines.

Figure 21: The Procedure for Making DMA and NEA from Tahiti

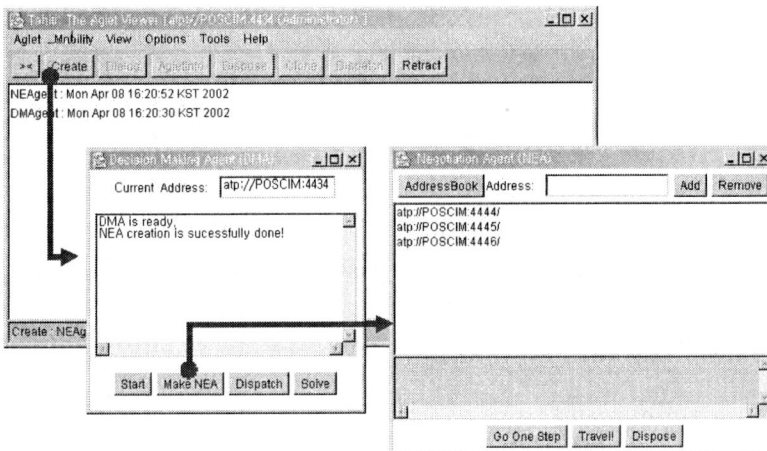

Figure 22: Negotiations Between NEA and DMAs

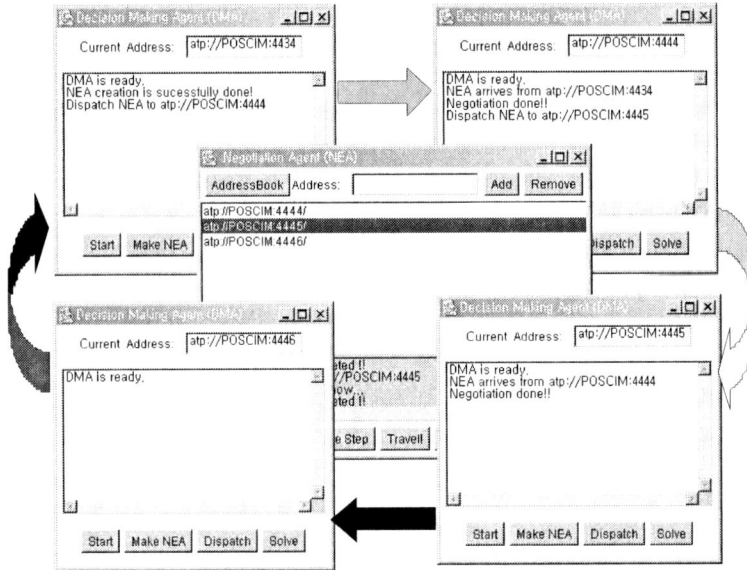

The current status display of the agents in Figure 22 shows that an NEA has been created by a DMA (port: 4434), and that it is currently traveling according to its traveling list. The status display also says that the NEA has just finished negotiating with a DMA (port: 4445), and that the NEA is about to physically move to another DMA (port: 4446). After finishing negotiations with all the other DMAs, the NEA will be returned to the original place (DMA, port: 4434) and will submit the final report to the DMA. The time taken for the NEA to travel these DMAs is less than a second, but will vary depending on the functions of the NEA. The execution time in a MANPro-based negotiation may be arguable by other researchers. However, owing to the rapid increase of computing power, the execution time will be significantly reduced and, therefore, it will not be a major burden in the near future.

CONCLUSION

In this chapter, we specified a fractal-based framework following three perspectives: (a) fractal-based enterprise management system, (b) strategic supply chain model for future organizations, and (c) intelligent manufacturing enterprises.

Fractals are autonomous, flexible, and self-similar. In order to survive in a competitively and dynamically changing market environment, future organizations must have a powerful weapon, namely the fractal. The fractal is the simplest but most powerful concept. It will be adapted almost everywhere in the near future. It will increasingly be recognized as a factor not only influencing organizational structure but also will become a significant competitive factor. We can embody it in the structure of future organizations including e-biz enterprises, supply chain networks, manufacturing systems, and many other areas.

Like many other approaches we know, however, the fractal-based framework is not a magic bullet for future organizations. It, too, has its demerits or deficiencies. For example, since the fractal-based system follows the environment of distributed systems, it is difficult to globally optimize the system, and it is hard to control just as the distributed systems are in general. It is not yet able to guarantee the safety of the whole system during the operation. Adaptation of the fractal concept can also bring about other deficiencies. However, they have not been proved yet one way or the other since the research on fractal-based system is still in an elementary stage. Waste of the system resources might be another possible deficiency. Self-similar fractals should have the same functional modules within themselves. Although, according to the function of a fractal, some modules might be temporarily unnecessary, they have to be maintained throughout the system life-time. If those modules are removed, then we will be able to prevent the waste of system resources. Workloads burdening the network and the system also can decrease. However, they still have a potential use sometime in the future when the function of the fractal might change. The elimination of such modules may take superfluous time to download required functional modules into the fractal again. This problem, however, is likely to be ignored soon owing to the rapid enhancement of hardware technologies.

From understanding to the implementation of organizations or systems, we can comprehensively develop and manage the organization or the system by using the fractal concept in a coherent manner. For the wide spread of a fractal-based system in the future, we must first grasp the characteristics of a fractal in each field, then implement and customize the system by using core technologies specialized in each field. Flexibility is regarded as a matter of survival, not as an option. To cope with the dynamically changing environment, the organization also has to continuously and autonomously change itself. This may be possible by using the concept and the useful features of a fractal.

ACKNOWLEDGMENTS

This research was supported in part by grant No. 2001-1-31500-005-1 from the Basic Research Program of the Korea Science & Engineering Foundation and the BK 21 Project in 2002. The authors would like to express their gratitude for the support.

REFERENCES

Alvarado, U. Y. & Kotzab, H. (2001). Supply chain management: The integration of logistics in marketing. *Industrial Marketing Management*, 30(2), 183-198.

Baek, S., Liebowitz, J., Prasad, S., & Granger, M. (1999). Intelligent agents for knowledge management — toward intelligent Web-based collaboration within virtual teams. *Knowledge Management Handbook*, CRC Press.

Brussel, H. V., Wyns, J., Valckenaers, P., Bongaerts, L., & Peeters, P. (1998). Reference architecture for holonic manufacturing systems: PROSA. *Computers in Industry*, 37(3), 255-274.

Chen, L. & Sycara, K. (1998). Webmate: A personal agent for browsing and searching. Paper presented at *The 2nd International Conference on Autonomous Agents and Multi Agent Systems (Agents '98),* Minneapolis/St. Paul, MN (pp. 132-139).

Clinton, S. R. & Calantone, R. J. (1997). Logistics strategy: Does it travel well? *Logistics Information Management*, 10(5), 224-234.

Daft, R. L. (1994). *Management*. Fort Worth, TX: The Dryden Press.

De Toni, A. & Nassimbeni, G. (1999). Buyer-supplier operational practices, sourcing policies and plant performances: Results of an empirical research. *International Journal of Production Research*, 37, 567-619.

Dong, M. & Chen, F. F. (2001). Process modeling and analysis of manufacturing supply chain networks using object-oriented Petri nets. *Robotics and Computer-Integrated Manufacturing*, 17(1/2), 121-129.

Ellis, C. A. & Keddara, K. (1993). *Dynamic change within workflow systems* [Technical Report]. University of Colorado.

Fisher, K. (1999). Agent-based design of holonic manufacturing system. *Robotics and Autonomous Systems*, 27, 3-13.

Hayes, R. H. & Jaikumar, R. (1988, September/October). Manufacturing's crisis: New technologies, obsolete organizations. *Harvard Business Review*, 77-85.

Hesselbein, F., Beckhard, R., & Goldsmith, M. (1998). *The Organization of the Future*. San Francisco, CA: Jossey-Bass.

Hollingsworth, D. (1995). *The Workflow Management Coalition Specification* (Document No. TC00-1003). The Workflow Reference Model (Issue 1.1 ed., p. 6). UK: The Workflow Management Coalition.

IBM Japan. Aglets homepage. Retrieved from the World Wide Web: http://www.trl.ibm.com/aglets/index_e.htm.

Jeong, B., Jung, H., & Park, N. (2002). A computerized causal forecasting system using genetic algorithms in supply chain management. *Journal of Systems and Software*, 60(3), 223-237.

Kaihara, T. (2001). Supply chain management with market economics. *International Journal of Production Economics*, 73, 5-14.

Khoo, L. P., Lee, S. G., & Yin, X. F. (2001). Agent-based multiple shop floor manufacturing scheduler. *International Journal of Production Research*, 39(14), 3023-3040.

Koestler, A. (1967). *The Ghost in the Machine*. London: Arcana Books.

Korpela, J., Lehmusvaara, A., & Tuominen, M. (2001a). An analytic approach to supply chain development. *International Journal of Production Economics*, 71(1-3), 145-155.

Korpela, J., Lehmusvaara, A., & Tuominen, M. (2001b). Customer service based design of the supply chain. *International Journal of Production Economics*, 69, 193-204.

Lange, D. B. & Oshims, M. (1998). *Programming and Developing Java™ Mobile Agents with Aglets™*. Addison-Wesley.

Li, D. & O'Brien C. (2001). A quantitative analysis of relationships between product types and supply chain strategies. *International Journal of Production Economics*, 73(1), 29-39.

Maturana, F. P. & Norrie, D. H. (1996). Multi-agent mediator architecture for distributed manufacturing. *Journal of Intelligent Manufacturing*, 7, 257-270.

O'Laughlin, K. A. & Copacino, W. C. (1994). Logistics Strategy. In J. F. Robeson (Ed.), *The Logistics Handbook*. New York: The Free Press.

Okino, N. (1993). Bionic manufacturing systems. Paper presented at the *CIRP Seminar on Flexible Manufacturing Systems Past-Present-Future*, Bled, Slovenia (pp. 73-95).

Plesums, C. (2002). Introduction to Workflow. In L. Fisher (Ed.), *The Workflow Handbook 2002*. The Workflow Management Coalition.

Ryu, K. & Jung, M. (2002). Dynamic modeling of fractal-specific characteristics in fractal manufacturing system. Paper presented at *The 35th CIRP International Seminar on Manufacturing Systems*, Seoul, Korea (May 13-15, pp. 444-450).

Ryu, K., Shin, M., & Jung, M. (2001). A methodology for implementing agent-based controllers in the Fractal Manufacturing System. Paper presented at the *Fifth Conference on Engineering Design & Automation,* Las Vegas, Nevada, USA (August 5-8, pp. 91-96).

Ryu, K., Shin, M., Kim, K., & Jung, M. (2000). Intelligent control architecture for Fractal Manufacturing System. Paper presented at the *Third Asia-Pacific Conference on Industrial Engineering and Management Systems*, Hong Kong (December 20-22, pp. 594-598).

Seidel, D., Hopf, M., Prado, J. M., Garcia-Herreros, E., Strasser, T. D., & Christensen, J. H. (1994). HMS–Strategies. *The Report of HMS Consortium*.

Shin, M., Ryu, K., & Jung, M. (2001). A Novel Negotiation Protocol for Agent-based Control Architecture. Paper presented at the *Fifth Conference on*

Engineering Design & Automation, Las Vegas, Nevada (August 5-8, pp. 700-705).

Smith, R. G. (1980). The contract net protocol: High-level communication and control in a distributed problem solver. *IEEE Trans. on Computers*, 29(12), 1104-1113.

Sousa, P., Silva, N., Heikkila, T., Kollingbaum, M., & Valckenaers, P. (1999, September). Aspects of co-operation in distributed manufacturing systems. Paper presented at the *Second International Workshop on Intelligent Manufacturing Systems (IMS-Europe'99),* Leuven, Belgium (pp. 695-717).

Stanton, R. R. (1979). Future Organizations: A model of structural response to organizational environment.

About the Authors

Jatinder N. D. Gupta is currently Eminent Scholar of Management of Technology, Professor of Management Information Systems, Industrial and Systems Engineering and Engineering Management, and Chairperson of the Department of Accounting and Information Systems at the University of Alabama in Huntsville, Alabama, USA. Most recently, he was Professor of Management, Information and Communication Sciences, and Industry and Technology at Ball State University, Muncie, Indiana. He holds a Ph.D. in Industrial Engineering (with specialization in Production Management and Information Systems) from Texas Tech University. Co-author of a textbook in Operations Research, Dr. Gupta serves on the editorial boards of several national and international journals. Recipient of the Outstanding Faculty and Outstanding Researcher awards from Ball State University, he has published numerous papers in such journals as *Journal of Management Information Systems*, *International Journal of Information Management*, *Operations Research*, *INFORMS Journal of Computing, Annals of Operations Research*, and *Mathematics of Operations Research*. More recently, he served as a Co-editor of several special issues including the *Neural Networks in Business* of *Computers and Operations Research* and books that included *Decision Making Support Systems: Achievements and Challenges for the New Decade* published by Idea Group Publishing. His current research interests include e-Commerce, Supply Chain Management, Information and Decision Technologies, Scheduling, Planning and Control, Organizational Learning and Effectiveness, Systems Education, Knowledge Management, and Enterprise Integration. Dr. Gupta has held elected and appointed positions in several academic and professional societies including the Association for Information Systems, Production and Operations Management Society (POMS), the Decision Sciences Institute (DSI), and the Information Resources Management Association (IRMA).

Sushil K. Sharma is currently Assistant Professor in the Department of Information Systems & Operations Management, at Ball State University, Muncie, Indiana, USA. He received his Ph.D. in Information Systems from Pune University in India. Prior to joining Ball State, Dr. Sharma held the Associate Professor position at the Indian Institute of Management, Lucknow (India) and Visiting Research Associate Professor position at the Department of Management Science, University of Waterloo, Canada. Co-author of two textbooks *(Programming in C,* and *Understanding Unix)*, Dr. Sharma's research contributions have appeared in many peer-reviewed national and international journals, conferences and seminar proceedings. He has extensive experience in providing consulting services to several government and private organizations including World Bank funded projects in the areas of Information Systems, e-Commerce, and Knowledge Management. Dr. Sharma's primary teaching and research interests are in e-Commerce, Networking Environments, Network Security, ERP Systems, Database Management Systems, and Knowledge Management.

*   *   *

Bernardo Bátiz-Lazo is a Lecturer in Management, Open University Business School (UK). Dr. Bátiz was awarded his Ph.D. in Business Administration at Manchester, Business School, University of Manchester. Prior to university life, he worked as Trader and Research Analyst in capital and derivatives markets in both the U.S. and Mexico. Since 1991, he has been active in teaching and researching Financial Markets and Financial institutions. He lectures regularly on Comparative Financial Markets, and the Strategic Management of Banking Organizations to graduates and specialists in the UK, Germany, Portugal, Spain, and Sweden. He has been an external advisor for blue chip companies such as Banco Comercial del Perú, Bank of Cyprus, IBM, BBC, and the Jefferson Smurfit Group.

Murat Baygeldi is a Ph.D. student in Information Systems at the London School of Economics. He has studied Business Administration in Germany and England. He has more than 15 years experience working for international companies. His research interests are in e-Business, and Evaluation of Productivity, and have published articles related to e-Business. He was recently a Research Assistant with the national UK e-Business project, focusing on the Organizational and Management Issues.

Lisa J. Burnell is an Assistant Professor in the Computer Science Department at Texas Christian University, USA. Her previous experience is in the Aerospace and Transportation industries. Dr. Burnell has a Ph.D. and master's in Computer Science, and a B.A. in Mathematics, all from The University of Texas, Arlington. Her research interests are Probabilistic Reasoning, Decision-Theoretic Inference, and Software Engineering Methodologies.

John R. Durrett is an Assistant Professor of Information Systems at Texas Tech University, USA. He received his Ph.D. from the University of Texas at Austin in Information Systems, his M.B.A. and B.A. from West Texas A&M. His research and teaching interests are Distributed Systems Design, eLearning, and Network Security.

Hamada H. Ghenniwa is an Assistant Professor at the Department of Electrical and Computer Engineering, the University of Western Ontario, Canada. Dr. Ghenniwa's main research expertise includes Computational Intelligence with a specific focus on Intelligent Agents, Cooperation and Coordination Theory as well as their application to Cooperative Distributed Systems, such as Electronic Business and Commerce, Enterprise Integration, Healthcare, Real-Time Systems and Manufacturing. He is the head of Cooperative Distributed Systems Engineering group in Bell-Centre for Information Engineering at the University of Western Ontario. He has authored and co-authored more than 60 papers in refereed journals and conference proceedings as well as technical and industrial project reports. Dr. Ghenniwa is currently leading research and industrial projects concerned with Integration in Distributed Information Systems, Business-to-Business e-Commerce, and Multi-Agent Systems for Manufacturing Control.

Jorge F. S. Gomes is currently Assistant Professor at the Superior Institute of Applied Psychology, Lisbon, Portugal, where he teaches undergraduate and post-graduate courses on Organizational Behavior and Research Methods, and has recently been appointed director of the Masters in Organizational Behavior, and the *Journal Comportamento Organizacional e Gestão*. He is also Senior Researcher at the University of Twente in The Netherlands, where he conducts research on New Product Development and Product Innovation. Together with other universities in Europe, he has established a Network on Organization of Innovation in 2002. Dr. Gomes is also consultant in Human Resources Management and Innovation Management in Portugal. He received a Ph.D. in Business Administration from Manchester Business School, UK. His research interests include the Management of Innovation and Knowledge, and the Structuring of Project Teams. He has published in the *International Journal of Management Review, Comportamento Organizacional e Gestão, Technovation,* and

Creativity and Innovation Management, and at the present moment has several forthcoming manuscripts in other international journals and books.

Jeffrey Hsu is an Assistant Professor of Information Systems at the Silberman College of Business Administration, Fairleigh Dickinson University, USA. He holds a Ph.D. in Management Information Systems from Rutgers University, three master's degrees, and several professional certifications. He is the author of six books, including numerous papers and articles, and has professional experience in the IT industry. His current research interests include Human-Computer Interaction, e-Commerce, Groupware, Distance Learning, CRM, and Data Mining.

Michael N. Huhns is a Professor of Computer Science and Engineering, and Director of the Center for Information Technology at the University of South Carolina, USA. Prior to this, he managed several research projects at MCC in Austin, Texas, and was an Adjunct Professor in Computer Sciences at the University of Texas. He received the B.S. degree from the University of Michigan, and the M.S. and Ph.D. degrees in Electrical Engineering from the University of Southern California. He is the author of more than 180 technical papers in Machine Intelligence, and an editor of three books on Multiagent Systems. He is also an editor for seven international journals. His research interests are in the areas of Cooperative Information Systems, Multiagent Systems, and Enterprise Integration.

Mooyoung Jung is a Professor of Industrial Engineering at Pohang University of Science & Technology (POSTECH) in Korea. Since receiving his Ph.D. in 1984 from Kansas State University, Dr. Jung has published more than 130 technical papers in the fields of CIM, Intelligent Manufacturing, and Agile Manufacturing. He is currently an Associate Editor of the *International Journal of Engineering Design and Automation*, and an editorial board member of the *International Journal of Industrial Engineering*, and the *International Journal of Computers & Industrial Engineering*. His current research includes Web Services Technology, Distributed Manufacturing Systems, and Bio-informatics.

Dohoon Kim is currently an Assistant Professor at the College of Business Administration in Kyung Hee University, Seoul, Korea. He received his Ph.D. and M.S. in Operations Research and Information Systems Management from Korea Advanced Institute of Science and Technology, after majoring in International Economics and Statistics in Seoul National University for Sc.B. Previously, he worked for Interlink Co., Seoul as Technology Analyst, and a Fulbright

Fellow researcher at the University of Pennsylvania. His current research focus is on IT Outsourcing and Agent-Based Network Service Management.

Juin-Cherng Lu is the Chairman of Department of Information Management, Ming Chuan University, Taipei, Taiwan. Dr. Lu studies Knowledge Management, Electronic Commerce and Business, and Management Information Systems. He also is a consultant to Taiwan's small-and-medium businesses for helping Organizational Transformation, and New Business Models Design. His research focus is the Transformation of Internet-Based Business Models, and Strategic Planning and Implementation of Knowledge Management System (Knowledge Portal).

Ross A. Lumley is Assistant Professor of Information Systems in the School of Business and Public Management at George Washington University, USA. He is also the Director of the Capital Markets Laboratory in the School of Business and Public Management. He holds a B.S. degree from the University of California, Berkeley, and an M.S. and Ph.D. from the University of Texas, Dallas. Dr. Lumley's research interests include Electronic Financial Commerce Systems, Knowledge Management Systems, and Multi-Agent Systems.

Maria Manuel Mendes is a Senior Consultant, Deloitte & Touche - Quality Firm, SA (Portugal). Maria worked for her degree in Computer Science and Business Management at the Instituto Superior de Ciências do Trabalho e da Empresa (ISCTE), while being involved in the Technology and Computer Support Centre of ISCTE. As a key member of ISCTE's Telecommunications and Internet Research Department, she developed several research projects around eCommerce and eLearning as well as being responsible for the development of HTML and Internet Training Applications for External Organizations. Maria then joined the Business Consulting division of Arthur Andersen (now Deloitte and Touche) in Lisbon. Her responsibilities in the Human Capital division have included Change Management projects in the Portuguese market. Other responsibilities included projects dealing with Organizational Design, Re-Engineering, ERPs, Business Processes Analysis, eLearning Strategy and Implementation, Change Enablement, etc. She is also an Internal Facilitator for training courses for national and international audiences, as well as being the main liaison person in charge of all research and development for the e-Learning practice at the Lisbon office.

Karen Neville holds both an M.S. in Management Information Systems and a B.S. in Business Information Systems from University College Cork, Ireland, where she is employed as a College Lecturer. She is currently registered as a Ph.D. student, under the supervision of Professor Philip Powell, at the University of Bath, UK. Her publications, to date, include papers focusing on ICT initiatives, e-Learning, and Educational Systems that have been published in some of the top information systems conferences and journals. The focus of her research has now expanded to incorporate the areas of Knowledge Management and Security.

Mark Nissen is Associate Professor of Information Systems and Management at the Naval Postgraduate School, and a Young Investigator. His research focuses on the study of Knowledge and Systems for Innovation, and he approaches technology, work and organizations as an integrated design problem. Dr. Nissen's publications span the Information Systems, Project Management and related fields, and he received the Menneken Faculty Award for Excellence in Scientific Research, the top research award available to faculty at the Naval Postgraduate School. Before his Information Systems doctoral work at the University of Southern California, he acquired more than a dozen years' management experience in the aerospace and electronics industries, and he spent a few years as a direct-commissioned officer in the Naval Reserve.

Philip Powell is Professor of Information Management and Director of the Center for Information Management at the University of Bath, UK. He was formerly, Professor of Information Systems, University of London, and Director of the Information Systems Research Unit at Warwick Business School. Prior to becoming an academic he worked in insurance, accounting, and computing. He is the author of four books on Information Systems and Financial Modeling including *Management Accounting: A Model Building Approach, Information Systems: A Management Perspective,* and *Developing Decision Support Systems for Health Care Management.* He has published numerous book chapters and his work has appeared in over seventy international journals, and more than 100 conferences. He is Managing Editor of the *Information Systems Journal*, Book Reviews Editor of the *Journal of Strategic Information Systems*, and on a number of other editorial boards. He is President of the UK Academy for Information Systems. He serves on the Alliance for IS Skills steering group.

John W. Priest is a Professor of Industrial and Manufacturing Engineering at the University of Texas at Arlington, USA. Dr. Priest is author or coauthor of more than 130 technical articles, predominately on the Product Development Process, Design for Manufacturing, and Technical Risk Management. Between 1978 and 1999 he has worked on government task forces to improve the product development process including Decision Support Systems and Knowledge Management. Prior to joining academia, Dr. Priest worked full time for Rockwell International Communications (now Alcatel), Texas Instruments, and General Motors.

Bonnie Rubenstein Montano is an Assistant Professor of Management Information Systems at the McDonough School of Business, Georgetown University, USA. Her current research is in the areas of Intelligent Decision Support, Knowledge Management, and Organizational Learning. She has completed funded research for the U.S. Social Security Administration, the Health Care Financing Administration, and the Naval Postgraduate School. She has published in such journals as *Decision Support Systems, IEEE Journal of Evolutionary Computation, European Journal of Operational Research,* and *ASCE Journal of Urban Planning and Development*

Kwangyeol Ryu is a Ph.D. candidate in the Department of Industrial Engineering at Pohang University of Science & Technology (POSTECH) in Korea. He received his B.S. and M.S. degrees in Industrial Engineering from POSTECH in 1997 and 1999, respectively. His research interests include: Mobile Agent Systems, Distributed and Dynamic Control of Automated Manufacturing System focusing on the Fractal Manufacturing System (FrMS), and Integration of Supply Chains based on the Fractal Concept.

J. Daniel Sherman received a B.S. degree from the University of Iowa, an M.A. degree from Yale University, and a Ph.D. in Organizational Theory/ Organizational Behavior from the University of Alabama. In 1989-1990, he was a visiting scholar at the Stanford Center for Organization Research at Stanford University. He currently serves as the Associate Dean of the College of Administrative Science at the University of Alabama in Huntsville, USA. He is the author of more than 50 research publications including publications in *The Journal of Product Innovation Management, Academy of Management Journal, Journal of Management, Personnel Psychology, Psychological Bulletin,* and *IEEE Transactions on Engineering Management.*

Steve Smithson is a Senior Lecturer in Information Systems at the London School of Economics with a Ph.D. in Information Systems from the same institution. He was Editor of the *European Journal of Information Systems* from its inception in 1991 until the end of December 1999. His research interests lie in Information Systems Management, the Evaluation of Information Systems, and Developments in e-Business. He has published numerous journal articles and conference papers, as well as four books. He was recently involved with a national UK e-Business project, focusing on the Organizational and Management Issues of e-Business.

Gary F. Templeton is an Assistant Professor of MIS in the College of Business and Industry at Mississippi State University, USA. He has previously taught MIS courses at Athens State University, Syracuse University, Auburn University, and the University of Alabama in Huntsville. He has a B.S. degree in Business Administration (Finance major), M.B.A., M.S. in MIS, and a Ph.D. in MIS. He has published in the *Journal of MIS*, *Communications of the ACM*, and *the International Journal of Technology Management*. He was awarded the NASA Faculty Fellow for the summers of 2002 and 2003.

Chia-Wen Tsai is a Writer and Lecturer at National Open University, Business Innovation and Incubation Center of Ming Chuan University, and Kuang Wu Institute of Technology in Taiwan. He studied Electronic Commerce, Knowledge Management, Organizational Learning, and Service Management in Ming Chuan University. He is interested in the Change of Environment and Competition Caused by Technology. His research focus is the Transformation and Organizational Change of Business Models in the Internet-Based and Knowledge-Based Age.

Nilmini Wickramasinghe is an Assistant Professor in the Computer and Information Science Department at the James J. Nance College of Business Administration at Cleveland State University, Ohio, USA. Earlier, she was a Senior Lecturer in Business Information Systems at the University of Melbourne, Australia. She holds a Ph.D. in Management Information Systems from Case Western Reserve University. She is currently researching and published in the areas of Management of Technology, Health Care, as well as IS issues especially as they relate to Knowledge Work and e-Business.

Index

A

Actor Network Theory (ANT) 109
actors 116
application service providers (ASP) 128
ASP business models 128
ASP industry 128
auction market session 64

B

balanced matrix 304
behaviorism 253
black boxes 116
Boeing 777 307
business process re-engineering (BPR) 5
business-centric knowledge-oriented architecture 48
business-rules systems (BRS) 211
business-specific service agents 62

C

case-based reasoning (CBR) 210
change agents 250
Chicago Board of Trade (CBOT) 113
classical conditioning 254

Cognition Era 255
cognitive learning theories 255
collaborative applications 40
commodity market service 63
communication systems layer 36
communities of practice (CoPs) 17
competitive advantage 186
concept mapping 10
conceptual indexing 11
conditioning 253
content management software 40
Contingency Theory 205
cooperative distributed system 47
cross-functional integration 299

D

data marts 39
data warehouse 39
distributed manufacturing system (DMS) 332
dynamic and complex domains (DCD) 204

E

e-biz companies 312
e-business era 32

e-business value chain 130
e-commerce 32
economic development 29
economy model 52
electronic communication networks
   (ECNs) 85
electronic data interchange (EDI) 47
electronic documents 89
electronic exchanges 84
electronic information dissemination 89
electronic market 109
electronic trading systems 114
eMarketplace 47
Emergent Learning Era 257
end-user application layer 41
enterprise data source layer 38
enterprise information portals (EIPs) 41
enterprise intelligence 128
enterprise model 51
enterprise resource planning (ERP) 47
eProcurement model 49
eShop model 49
Eurex 110
expert systems 209
explicit knowledge 4, 169

F

financial markets 80
FIXML 93
fractal approach 312
fractal architecture 321
fractal manufacturing system (FrMS)
   312
fractal-based systems 318
fractals 316
fraud detection 13
functional matrix 304

G

global manufacturing 194
goal-orientation 320
Grounded Theory development 250
groupware 90

I

Industry Evolution 128
informal direct contact 302
information and communication technologies (ICTs) 313
information dissemination 88
information modeling 11
information sharing 11
information society 249
information technology 187
information technology assessment 29
integration agents 67
integrative project manager positions
   304
intelligent agents 81, 98
intelligent enterprises 32, 312
intelligent manufacturing enterprises
   331
Internet 80
Internet Age 80
IT outsourcing 128

K

knowledge application 153, 285
knowledge base (KB) 153, 170
knowledge base support environment
   169
knowledge creation 153, 283
knowledge flows 185
knowledge hierarchy 187
knowledge management (KM) 1, 29,
   96, 150, 186, 278
knowledge management life cycle 188
knowledge management systems 203
knowledge repository layer 39
knowledge sharing 11, 231
knowledge sharing and dissemination
   153
knowledge storage 284
knowledge storage and retrieval 153
knowledge transfer 284
knowledge-based organization 2, 186
knowledge-based systems (KBS) 187,
   209
knowledge-flow dynamics 192

Knowledge-Flow Theory 188
knowledge retrieval 284

L

law of effect 254
learning culture 20
learning histories 249
learning maturity 249
learning networks 171
learning organizations 250, 278
liaison coordinating positions 302

M

management processes 20
market service agents 63
markup languages 89
master teaching 252
Mechanistic-Individual Learning Period
    253
Mechanistic-Organizational Learning
    Period 257
middleware layer 40
modes of integration 305
multi-agent systems (MAS) 100

N

new product development (NPD) 150,
    299
New York Stock Exchange (NYSE) 83
NewLearning Project 154
NYSE Trading Floor 83

O

object management group (OMG) 323
operant conditioning 254
Organismic-Individual Learning Period
    255
organizational hierarchy 302
organizational knowledge management
    230
organizational learning 5, 19, 278
organizational memory 23

P

permanent cross-functional teams 303
portfolio management 101
Portuguese higher education 149
Pre-learning Period 252, 256
project matrix 304

R

real world simulations 169
reinforcement process 253
RIXML 92

S

self-control 256
self-efficacy 256
self-organization 319
self-similarity 319
semantic networks 10
service level agreement (SLA) 128
seven knowledge layers 3
Social Learning Era 255
social learning theories 255
software agents 47
standardized processes 302
stimuli 253
stock trading 102
straight-through-processing (STP) 94
strategic transfer 16
student mentoring system 177
supply chain management (SCM) 313
supply chain model 325
supply-chain 47
supply-chain Integration 53
SWIFT 93
symbolism 256
system development 150

T

T+1 processing 95
tacit knowledge 4, 169
temporary cross-functional teams 303
Third Industrial Revolution 279
Tool Implementation Era 257
total quality management (TQM) 5

traditional classroom 170
traditional training 171
TSMC 287

U

user interface agents 62

V

value chain 128
vicarious learning 256
virtual advisor 220
virtual communities 230
virtual library 178

W

Web services 212
Web-based access system 41
Web-based learning systems 173
wide-area communications network
    (WAN) 113
Winbond 289
wireless networks 95
workflow management (WfM) 313
workflow management coalition (WfMC)
    322

X

XML 91

Y

Yin-Yang model 35

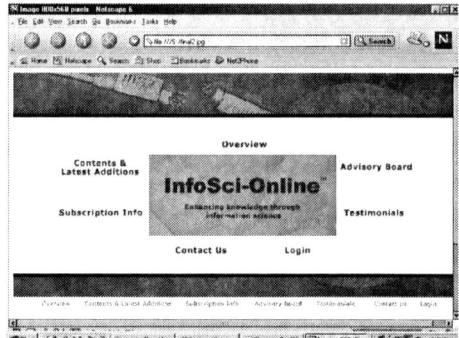